Easy Grammar: Grade 5

Wanda C. Phillips

Easy Grammar Systems
Post Office Box 25970
Scottsdale, Arizona 85255

www.easygrammar.com

© 2006

TABLE OF CONTENTS

NOUNS

PLEASE READ!

Please teach prepositions, verbs, nouns, adjectives, adverbs, and pronouns **in** the **order** presented in this text. Concepts are introduced, reintroduced, and built upon throughout this text to help create *mastery learning*. Feel free to teach capitalization, punctuation, and other concepts whenever you choose.

> (For example, some teachers like to teach the capitalization unit while their students are memorizing the list of prepositions and doing the activities that help them to learn their prepositions. They, then, teach the preposition unit and proceed on, taking time at some point to teach the punctuation unit. The key is that they teach the parts of speech sequentially.)

TO THE TEACHER pages are **very important**. Please read the entire note. You will be given additional information or tips and strategies for effective teaching. Also, please refer to the answer key (on the opposite page from each worksheet) before discussing a lesson. Advice and important notes often appear there.

As in all good teaching, **glean** what you will and use what is appropriate for your students' needs *and* your style of teaching.

I recommend that students use **highlighters** to mark rules. Be sure to tell students exactly what you want them to highlight. (Otherwise, some tend to mark everything!) Also, ascertain that students stay with you in the discussions and marking process. If students jump ahead, they lose valuable learning.

Throughout this text, I will refer to using **white-boards** for both the introduction and review of a lesson. These are extremely valuable; students will love writing your examples as well as their own on white-boards. (You will find a multitude of uses for white-boards in English *and* in other subjects.) Visit www.easygrammar.com for ordering information. (I'm not sure why students find it so appealing to write on white-boards rather than regular paper. However, I've seen *eager responses* every year I used them!)

PLEASE, PLEASE, PLEASE...

Be enthusiastic in your teaching of English. Let's help students to become excited about learning to use grammar as a tool for speaking and writing properly.

A student workbook entitled **Easy Grammar Grade 5 Student Workbook** is available. This workbook does not include an answer key or strategies for effective teaching. In addition, tests are not included.

Easy Grammar Grade 5 Student Test Booklet is now available; this contains a pre-assessment test, all unit tests and cumulative tests, and a post-assessment test.

Correlation pages for **Easy Grammar: Grade 5** and **Easy Grammar Grade 5 Student Workbook** have been placed throughout this textbook. Also, a correlation of teacher edition pages and workbook pages has been placed at the back of this text.

Why Should I Use *Easy Grammar: Grade 5*?

EASY TO TEACH ~ EASY TO LEARN ~ EASY TO REMEMBER

Easy Grammar: Grade 5 uses a unique approach. Students memorize and learn prepositions first. Next, they learn about a prepositional phrase. In a scaffolding approach, *Easy Grammar* teaches students how to recognize and then delete prepositional phrases from any sentence. Let me assure you that *Easy Grammar* is as the name implies: *EASY—YET THOROUGH!*

1. In a step-by-step manner (scaffolding), students learn to identify prepositional phrases and to delete them from a sentence.

2. After a prepositional phrase is crossed out, the student no longer needs to be concerned with it. **The subject and verb won't be in a prepositional phrase.** * This makes it very easy to determine subject and verb of a sentence.

    In the following sentence, students who do not use this approach may respond that the subject is *Eric* or *Mika.*

    A game between Eric and Mika is in progress.

    The prepositional approach eliminates the guessing. Prepositional phrases are crossed out. Therefore, the subject and verb of a sentence are readily determined.

    A <u>game</u> ~~between Eric and Mika~~ <u>is</u> ~~in progress~~.

3. In using this process, students are actively engaged in learning. They *love* the "hands-on" process, and using it helps them to be successful!

4. This approach is used periodically throughout the text in order for students to understand other concepts such as direct objects, subject/verb agreement, etc. In addition, strategies for effective teaching are presented throughout.

*99% of the time

♥♥♥♥♥♥♥♥♥♥♥♥♥♥♥♥♥♥♥♥♥♥♥♥♥♥♥♥♥♥♥♥♥♥♥

Another important difference of **Easy Grammar** texts is that concepts are

introduced and reviewed throughout the school year. In addition,

reviews and cumulative reviews are provided along the way to help

insure **mastery learning**. This signifies that students fully understand a

concept and are able to use it appropriately when the need arises.

♥♥♥♥♥♥♥♥♥♥♥♥♥♥♥♥♥♥♥♥♥♥♥♥♥♥♥♥♥♥♥♥♥♥♥

IMPORTANT QUESTIONS:

Q. Are workbooks available?

♥ **Easy Grammar Workbook 5** saves time and cost of copying. Students
have the advantage of having all of the concepts in their own book. This
makes references to former work as well as organizational skills easier.

Q. Should I use **Daily Grams: Guided Review Aiding Mastery Skills –
Grade 5** along with this text?

♥ Yes! In fact, you will find the first ten lessons of **Daily Grams: Grade 5** in
the last section of this text. Try them with your students. Copy each **Daily
Grams** lesson (day) for your students to do at the beginning of each class. It
should take only about 10 minutes for students to complete it *and* for you to
discuss it with them. **Daily Grams: Grade 5** is especially effective for
reinforcing capitalization and punctuation usage, grammar usage, sentence
combining for improved writing skills, and various other concepts. (Go to
www.easygrammar.com for **Daily Grams: Grade 5** "Scope and Sequence.")

Q. Does this text have a writing section?

♥ Yes! A section regarding writing sentences begins after the pronoun unit.
Students will learn to write sentences containing appositives, sentences using
semicolons, and compound sentences.

TO THE TEACHER: <u>**Assessment Information**</u>

EXTREMELY IMPORTANT

An assessment test is provided on the next six pages. (Answers are on pages *692-696*).

1. Please have students take this assessment before beginning any lessons. Although it appears lengthy, many white spaces have been created for visual ease. This assessment should not take students long to complete. For the pre-assessment, you may want to tell students to leave an answer blank if they don't know. (This usually places students in a more relaxed mode.)

2. Score the assessment and review it for information regarding the level of each student's understanding.

(I recommend that you do not share the pre-assessment results with students. If the score is low, a student may feel deflated before he begins this easy ~ yet thorough ~ approach to grammar and usage. Students' scores on last year's standardized tests may be reviewed to determine areas of strengths and weaknesses, also.)

3. After scoring the assessment, please store it somewhere to be retrieved **after** the student completes it as a post assessment at the end of the year. After you have scored the post assessment, share both the pre and post results with students so that they can see their increase in understanding. This is a positive gesture in that students can **internalize success** and can see results of their year-long work. (You may want to schedule an *individual conference* with each student to discuss their pre and post assessment results.

SCORING: I have provided one method of scoring in the answer key that follows

this assessment. You will note that I place more points in usage than I do on such items as identification of nouns or sentence types. You may disagree. Please feel free to determine which areas you consider most important and to create your own scoring rubric. However, be sure that you use the same method of scoring for **both** the pre and post assessments.

Note: Deletion of prepositional phrases has only been suggested (not graded). By learning how the process works, students will use them as a tool when completing the assessment.

TO THE TEACHER: Information Regarding Student Test Booklet

The student test booklet begins with a pre-assessment and ends with an identical post-assessment. The pre-assessment is found on pages 1 – 5; the post-assessment appears on pages 33 – 37.

The test booklet has been designed with teachers in mind. Tests are arranged so that students can remove each test without affecting other tests in the booklet. Obviously, the test booklet can be used in a multitude of ways. Use it in the manner that works best for you and your students.

Test Booklet Pages Correlated with Teacher Edition Answer Key Pages:

	BOOKLET PAGES	TEACHER ED. PAGES
Grade 5 PRE-ASSESSMENT	1-6	692-696
Preposition Test	7	46
Verb Test	9-11	162, 164, 166
Cumulative Test (End of Verb Unit)	13	178
Noun Test	15-16	262, 264
Cumulative Test (End of Noun Unit)	17-19	284 , 286, 288
Adjective Test	21	338
Cumulative Test (End of Adjective Unit)	23-26	354, 356, 358, 360
Adverb Test	27	424
Cumulative Test (End of Adverb Unit)	29-32	440, 442, 444, 446
Pronoun Test	33	490
Cumulative Test (End of Pronoun Unit)	35-40	506, 508, 510, 512, 514, 516
Capitalization Test	41	576
Punctuation Test	43	642
Grade 5 POST-ASSESSMENT	45-50	692-696

Name_____   **Assessment Test**

Date_____   **Pre-Post**

A. Sentence Types:
Directions: Write the sentence type on the line.

1. _____   You're right!

2. _____   My dog has fleas.

3. _____   Stand in this line.

4. _____   May I have a pear?

B. Sentences, Fragments, and Run-Ons:
Directions: Write **S** if the words form a sentence. Write **F** if the words
form a fragment. Write **R-O** if the words form a run-on.

1. ____   I want a teddy bear my sister wants a stuffed pig.

2. ____   Your juice by the side of the bed warm.

3. ____   Catches the bus each morning at 7 o'clock to go to school early.

4. ____   Do you know today's date?

C. Friendly Letters:
Directions: Label the parts of this friendly letter:

_____   **5 North Drive**
                                 South Beach, OR   97366
                                 June 22, 20—

Dear Terri,   _____

**What are you doing this summer? Did you join a basketball
team? Have you gone hiking in the hills near your ranch? Are you
and your family coming to Oregon again this summer?** _____

                                 Always, _____
                                 Bo   _____

D. Capitalization:
Directions: Write a capital letter above any word that should be capitalized.

1. bo travels on interstate 65 to diamond caverns near nolin lake state park.

2. "our women's club visited temple sinai on dole street," said dr. jo ming.

3. do mom and i need to buy german chocolate at mayday foods?

4. dear jane,

   did your aunt jenny study english or history at phoenix college
   during the summer she spent in the west?
   your friend,
jose

5. have you visited cliff house at point lobos near the golden gate bridge?

E. Punctuation:
Directions: Insert needed punctuation.

1. Hannah was the meeting held on Mon Sept 12 2005 asked Ty

2. Tate said quietly I dont want Johns two toned rusted bike

3. Has Mr Dee your neighbor moved to 2 N Dale Ln Culver City CA 90232

4. Yikes We have to leave at 4 00 and take the following straws ice and twenty two cups

5. Yes he read the book entitled Call of the Wild but he hasn't had the opportunity to read The Raven a poem by E A Poe

F. Subjects and Verbs:
Directions: Underline the subject once and the verb or verb phrase twice.
Note: Crossing out prepositional phrases will help you.

1. After the snowstorm, many small children began to play in the snow.

2. One of the pilots stood and greeted passengers at the airport.

3. The doctor and his patient will talk about a pimple under his arm.

4. Stand by the man with the briefcase for a quick snapshot.

G. Contractions:
Directions: Write the contraction.

1. she is - _____
2. has not - _____
3. I would - _____

4. I shall - _____
5. cannot - _____
6. will not - _____

7. who is - _____
8. is not - _____
9. I have - _____

H. You're/Your, It's/Its, and They're/Their/There:
Directions: Circle the correct word.

1. (There, Their, They're) playing soccer this afternoon.

2. (You're, Your) usually on time.

3. When (its, it's) sunny, they eat (there, their, they're) lunch outside.

I. Subject-Verb Agreement:
Directions: Underline the subject once. Underline the verb that agrees twice.

1. Chan and his brother (listen, listens) to country music.

2. Her job for social services (seem, seems) like a good one.

3. One of the girls (sleep, sleeps) late.

J. Irregular Verbs:
Directions: Underline the subject once and the correct verb phrase twice.

1. Peter should have (ran, run) in the first race.

2. Was ice (froze, frozen) on the park's pond?

3. She must have (came, come) alone.

4. Two ladies have (laid, lain) by the pool for an hour.

5. They may have (went, gone) earlier.

6. Some horses had (drunk, drank) their water.

K. Tenses:
  Directions: Underline the subject once and the verb or verb phrase twice. Write the tense in the blank.

1. _____ Will you join our team?

2. _____ Water lapped into the canoe.

3. _____ My brothers like to drive to Tulsa.

L. Common and Proper Nouns:
  Directions: Place a ✓ if the noun is common.

1. ____ DOG   2. ____ POODLE   3. ____ FIFI

M. Singular and Plural Nouns:
  Directions: Write the correct spelling of each plural noun.

1. wax - _____   5. bluejay - _____

2. miss - _____   6. torch - _____

3. goose - _____   7. fun - _____

4. puff - _____   8. knife - _____

N. Possessive Nouns:
  Directions: Write the possessive in each blank.

1. dogs owned by his neighbor - _____

2. a closet used by guests - _____

3. tools shared by more than one craftsman - _____

O. Identifying Nouns:
  Directions: Circle any nouns.

1. My idea is to take this shovel, a sleeping bag, two tents, and some strong rope.

P. Usage and Knowledge:

1. Write a conjunction: _____

2. Write the antecedent: A crow flapped its wings. _____

3. Write an interjection: _____

4. Write a regular verb: _____

5. Write a linking verb: _____

6. What is the predicate adjective of this sentence? After the first washing, my new blue sweater became fuzzy. _____

7. Write an abstract noun: _____

8. Is the verb action, linking, or neither? The soup <u>tastes</u> spicy. _____

9. Circle the correct answer: I can't see (nobody, anybody) from here.

10. Circle the correct answer: Jacob painted the shed (hisself, himself).

11. Circle the correct answer: Don't walk so (slow, slowly).

12. Circle the correct answer: You played (good, well).

13. Circle the correct answer: I don't feel (good, well).

Q. Identifying Adjectives:
   Directions: Circle any adjective.

1. Several tourists visited two old German hotels near a steep, forested region.

R. Degrees of Adjectives:
   Directions: Circle the correct answer.

1. That city is (larger, largest) in the state.

2. Jacy becomes (more energetic, most energetic) after exercising.

3. Of the triplets, Faith is (more sensitive, most sensitive).

S. Adverbs:
   Directions: Circle any adverbs.

1. Bo is not usually very late, but he was today.

2. We are going downtown afterwards.

T. Degrees of Adverbs:
   Directions: Circle the correct answer.

1. Marco climbed (higher, highest) on his fifth try.

2. Of the two birds, the ostrich runs (more swiftly, most swiftly).

3. She hit the ball (farther, farthest) of the entire team.

U. Pronouns:
   Directions: Circle the correct answer.

1. (Me and Roy, Roy and I, Roy and me) looked at a magazine.

2. Do you want to go with Emma and (I, me)?

3. We should send (they, them) some maps.

4. The winner was (she, her).

5. Our friends and (we, us) will visit Austin next year.

6. From (who, whom) did you receive your package?

7. Each of the students must take (his, their) turn.

V. Nouns and Pronouns Used as Subjects, Direct Objects, Objects of the Preposition, and Predicate Nominatives:
   Directions: Look at the boldfaced word. Write **S.** for subject, **D.O.** for direct object, **O.P.** for object of the preposition, and **P.N.** for predicate nominative.

1. ____ Joe sliced an **apple**.   3. ____ After swimming, **we** eat a snack.

2. ____ One of the **boys** laughed.   4. ____ She in the black dress is my **sister**.

x

PREPOSITIONS

By definition, a preposition is a "relational or function word...that connects a lexical word, usually a noun or pronoun, or a syntactic construction to another element of the sentence, as to a verb, to a noun, or to an adjective..."

-Webster's New World Dictionary

The definition is difficult. You may merely wish to explain that a preposition begins a prepositional phrase. A prepositional phrase adds exactness, details, and/or clarity to our language.

Examples: The boy looked.

The boy ***in the baseball suit*** looked ***into the closet for a bat***.

Two women walked.

After the gentle rainfall, two women ***with their collies*** walked ***through a meadow of bright yellow daisies***.

ALPHABETICAL LIST OF COMMONLY USED PREPOSITIONS

A

about

above

across

after

against

along

amid

among

around

at

atop

B

before

behind

below

beneath

beside

between

beyond

but (meaning except)

by

C

concerning

D

down

during

E

except

F

for

from

I

in

inside

into

L

like

N

near

O

of

off

on

onto

out

outside

over

P

past

R

regarding

S

since

T

through

throughout

to

toward

U

under

underneath

until

up

upon

W

with

within

without

Note: When correcting this page with students, you may wish to have each student write his/her chosen preposition on a white-board*. (Write the three choices on the chalkboard. Tally results.) It's interesting for students to see which preposition has been chosen most often. You are also reinforcing the learning of the various prepositions.

A **preposition** begins a prepositional phrase. A **phrase** is a group of words. A prepositional phrase ends with a noun (something you can usually see) or pronoun (Examples: *me, him, her, us, them, you, it,* and *whom*).

Examples: The tricycle **in the backyard** is rusted.
The soccer player ran **toward me**.

Directions: Choose a preposition. Write it in the blank. Circle the prepositional phrase.

PREPOSITIONAL PHRASES HAVE BEEN ITALICIZED.

1.   She fell _____***over***_____ *some sharp rocks*.

  a. among

  b. over

  c. by

2.   A child crawled _____***under***_____ *the table*.

  a. under

  b. around

  c. onto

3.   A skunk sat _____***beside***_____ *a tree*.

  a. beside

  b. under

  c. behind

4.   Nicky ran _____***with***_____ *her teammate*.

  a. beside

  b. with

  c. behind

2

*See the last page for ordering these boards.

Name_____

Date_____

A **preposition** begins a prepositional phrase. A **phrase** is a group of words. A prepositional phrase ends with a noun (something you can usually see) or pronoun (Examples: *me, him, her, us, them, you, it,* and *whom*).

Examples: The tricycle **in the backyard** is rusted.

The soccer player ran **toward me**.

⧫⧫⧫⧫⧫⧫⧫⧫⧫⧫⧫⧫⧫⧫⧫⧫⧫⧫⧫⧫⧫⧫⧫⧫⧫⧫⧫⧫⧫⧫⧫⧫⧫⧫⧫⧫

Directions: Choose a preposition. Write it in the blank. Circle the prepositional phrase.

1. She fell _____ some sharp rocks.

       a. among

       b. over

       c. by

2. A child crawled _____ the table.

       a. under

       b. around

       c. onto

3. A skunk sat _____ a tree.

       a. beside

       b. under

       c. behind

4. Nicky ran _____ her teammate.

       a. beside

       b. with

       c. behind

WORKBOOK PAGE 3

Prepositional Phrases

Note: When correcting this page with students, you may wish to have each student write his or her chosen preposition on a white-board. (Write answers on the board. It's interesting for students to see which prepositions have been chosen. You are also reinforcing the learning of prepositions.)

A prepositional phrase begins with a preposition. A phrase is a group of words. Therefore, a prepositional phrase is a **group of words that begins with a preposition**.

Examples: **on** the boat
after the storm
from my dad
with his aunt
behind the shed

Note that the last word is something you can see (concrete noun). Some will end in a noun such as *love* that you can't see (abstract noun). A prepositional phrase may also end with *me, him, her, us, them, you, it,* or *whom*.

ANSWERS MAY VARY/REPRESENTATIVE ANSWERS:

Directions: Write a preposition (that makes sense) to complete each prepositional phrase. Do not reuse any preposition.

1. ____**before**____ school

2. ____**through**____ the forest

3. ____**beneath**____ our table

4. ____**along**____ a road

5. ____**from**____ his dad

6. ____**into**____ her car

7. ____**except**____ them

8. ____**without**____ your friend

9. ____**against**____ the building

10. ____**about**____ sports

11. ____**within**____ their house

12. ____**around**____ you

13. ____**outside**____ a cabin

14. ____**to**____ the barber

15. ____**for**____ us

16. ____**up**____ the hill

4

Name_____   **PREPOSITIONS**

Date_____   **Prepositional Phrases**

A prepositional phrase begins with a preposition. A phrase is a group of words. Therefore, a prepositional phrase is a **group of words that begins with a preposition**.

Examples: **on** the boat

after the storm

from my dad

with his aunt

behind the shed

Note that the last word is something you can see (concrete noun). Some will end in a noun such as *love* that you can't see (abstract noun). A prepositional phrase may also end with *me, him, her, us, them, you, it,* or *whom*.

ᔑᔑᔑᔑᔑᔑᔑᔑᔑᔑᔑᔑᔑᔑᔑᔑᔑᔑᔑᔑᔑᔑᔑᔑᔑᔑᔑᔑᔑᔑᔑᔑᔑᔑᔑᔑᔑ

Directions: Write a preposition (that makes sense) to complete each prepositional phrase. Do not reuse any preposition.

1. _____ school   9. _____ the building

2. _____ the forest   10. _____ sports

3. _____ our table   11. _____ their house

4. _____ a road   12. _____ you

5. _____ his dad   13. _____ a cabin

6. _____ her car   14. _____ the barber

7. _____ them   15. _____ us

8. _____ your friend   16. _____ the hill

PREPOSITIONS

Object of the Preposition

A word that ends a prepositional phrase may be a **pronoun**. A pronoun takes the place of a noun. Pronouns used frequently in prepositional phrases are *me, him, her, us, them, you, it,* and *whom*.

Examples: Kami received tulips **from her *brother***. (noun)
Kami received tulips **from *him***. (pronoun)

Other pronouns may be used. Some examples are *none, someone, anyone, somebody, anybody,* and *any*.

Example: Kami received tulips **from *someone***.

๛๛๛๛๛๛๛๛๛๛๛๛๛๛๛๛๛๛๛๛๛๛๛๛๛๛๛๛๛๛๛๛

Directions: In Part A, write a person's name in the blank.
In Part B, replace the name by writing an appropriate pronoun in the blank. Write the prepositional phrase in the next blank.

Example: A. The email was for __**Mary**__ and __**Nikko**__.
(my mother's name)   (my name)
B. The email was for __**us**__. __**for us**__

ANSWERS MAY VARY/REPRESENTATIVE ANSWERS:

1. I went with my best friend to the mall.

    A. I went **with** _____**Madison**_____ to a fair.
    (my best friend's name)
    B. I went **with** _____**her**_____ to a fair.   ____**with her**____

2. A clown walked toward a person.

    A. A clown walked **toward** _____**Micah**_____.
    (your name)
    B. A clown walked **toward** _____**me**_____.   ____**toward me**____

3. The message was from one person and a second person.

    A. The message was **from** _____**Sam**_____ and ____**Aren**____.
    (a friend)   (another friend)
    B. The message was **from** _____**them**_____.   ____**from them**____

A word that ends a prepositional phrase may be a **pronoun**. A pronoun takes the place of a noun. Pronouns used frequently in prepositional phrases are *me, him, her, us, them, you, it,* and *whom*.

> Examples: Kami received tulips **from her *brother***. (noun)
> Kami received tulips **from *him***.   (pronoun)

Other pronouns may be used. Some examples are *none, someone, anyone, somebody, anybody,* and *any*.

> Example: Kami received tulips **from *someone***.

༄༄༄༄༄༄༄༄༄༄༄༄༄༄༄༄༄༄༄༄༄༄༄༄༄༄༄༄༄༄༄༄༄༄

Directions: In Part A, write a person's name in the blank.
In Part B, replace the name by writing an appropriate pronoun in the blank. Write the prepositional phrase in the next blank.

> Example: A. The email was for ___**Mary**___ and ___**Nikko**___.
> (my mother's name)   (my name)
> B. The email was for ___**us**___. ___**for us**___

1. I went with my best friend to the mall.

    A. I went **with** _____ to a fair.
    (my best friend's name)
    B. I went **with** _____ to a fair.   _____

2. A clown walked toward a person.

    A. A clown walked **toward** _____.
    (your name)
    B. A clown walked **toward** _____.   _____

3. The message was from one person and a second person.

    A. The message was **from** _____ and _____.
    (a friend)   (another friend)
    B. The message was **from** _____.   _____

A word that ends a prepositional phrase may be a **noun** or **pronoun**. This word is called the **object of a preposition**. Usually, the object of a preposition is a noun.

> Example: Leah works **with *Dan***.   (*Dan* is a noun.)

The object of the preposition may be a pronoun.

> Example: Leah works **with *him***.   (*Him* is a pronoun.)

෯෯෯෯෯෯෯෯෯෯෯෯෯෯෯෯෯෯෯෯෯෯෯෯෯෯෯෯෯෯෯෯෯෯෯෯෯෯෯

Directions: Write an appropriate object of the preposition in each space. Do not use an answer more than once. Circle the prepositional phrase.

ANSWERS MAY VARY/REPRESENTATIVE ANSWERS:
**Note: Before discussing answers with the entire class, you may want to have
students compare answers with a partner. Encourage each to say his or her
entire prepositional phrase. This will help to reinforce the concept.**

1. Are you eating lunch **with** ___**me, us, Tama**___?

2. That woman **in the** ___**suit, audience, van**___ is my neighbor.

3. You must stay here **until**___**5 o'clock, noon, sundown**___.

4. Has Ted eaten at **that**___**deli, café, restaurant**___?

5. Part **of her** ___**hand, leg, face**___ was swollen.

6. My mother went to a movie **after**___**lunch, work, dark**___.

7. He stepped **among some** ___**bushes, rocks, chairs**___and picked up
    a small carton.

8. That truck **without a** ___**windshield, door, hood**___ looks odd.

9. They leaned **against a** ___**wall, tree, shed**___ and talked.

10. Laura sat **on an old** ___**log, chair, pillow**___ while talking on her
    cellular telephone.

8

A word that ends a prepositional phrase may be a **noun** or **pronoun**. This word is called the **object of a preposition**. Usually, the object of a preposition is a noun.

> Example: Leah works **with *Dan***.   (*Dan* is a noun.)

The object of the preposition may be a pronoun.

> Example: Leah works **with *him***.   (*Him* is a pronoun.)

❧❧❧❧❧❧❧❧❧❧❧❧❧❧❧❧❧❧❧❧❧❧❧❧❧❧❧❧❧❧❧❧❧❧❧❧

Directions: Write an appropriate object of the preposition in each space. Do not use an answer more than once. Circle the prepositional phrase.

1.   Are you eating lunch **with** _____?

2.   That woman **in the** _____ is my neighbor.

3.   You must stay here **until** _____.

4.   Has Ted eaten at **that** _____?

5.   Part **of her** _____ was swollen.

6.   My mother went to a movie **after** _____.

7.   He stepped **among some** _____ and picked up a small carton.

8.   That truck **without a** _____ looks odd.

9.   They leaned **against a** _____ and talked.

10.   Laura sat **on an old** _____ while talking on her cellular telephone.

DELETING PREPOSITIONAL PHRASES

To help make our language easy to understand, we will **delete (cross out) any prepositional phrases** in a sentence. After a prepositional phrase has been deleted, it cannot serve as subject* or verb of that sentence.

Example: In the middle of the storm, our lights dimmed for a few minutes.

First, we must delete (cross out) all prepositional phrases.

~~In the middle of the storm~~, our lights dimmed ~~for a few minutes~~.

When we delete a prepositional phrase, it's just like erasing it from the sentence.

...our lights dimmed...

Look at the remaining words. To determine the **SUBJECT** of the sentence, we simply ask *who* or *what* the sentence is talking "about." *Storm* cannot be the subject because we have deleted *storm* as part of a prepositional phrase.

What is being discussed? *Lights!* Thus, *lights* is the subject. We place one line under *lights* to show that it is the subject of the sentence.

...our lights dimmed...

After we know the subject, we ask what is (was) or what happens (happened). This is the **VERB** of the sentence. What happened to the lights? What did they do? They *dimmed*. Therefore, *dimmed* is the verb. Place a double line under the word to show that it is a verb.

...our lights dimmed...

In this sentence, *lights* is the subject and *dimmed* is the verb.

Crossing out prepositional phrases takes the guesswork out of determining subject and verb.

~~In the middle of the storm~~, our lights dimmed ~~for a few minutes~~.

*most of the time

11

WORKBOOK PAGE 6

Note: I recommend that you do this page <u>orally</u> with students. Be sure to point out the placement of the prepositional phrases in #9 and in #10.

Deleting (crossing out) any prepositional phrases helps to find the subject and the verb of a sentence.

> A **prepositional phrase** begins with a preposition and ends with a noun or pronoun. A pronoun is a word like ***me, him, her, us, them, you, it, whom,*** or ***someone***. A pronoun takes the place of a noun. A noun is something that you can usually see.

> Examples: A <u>branch</u> ~~of a tree~~ <u>fell</u> ~~during the blizzard~~.

> <u>Marla</u> <u>sends</u> stories ~~to me~~.

Directions: Delete (cross out) any prepositional phrases. Underline the subject once and the verb twice.

1. The <u>students</u> <u>gathered</u> ~~around a telescope~~.

2. <u>Roses</u> <u>bloom</u> ~~outside my window~~.

3. Several <u>children</u> <u>rolled</u> ~~down a hill~~.

4. <u>Joey</u> <u>lives</u> ~~behind us~~.

5. Your <u>umbrella</u> <u>is</u> ~~inside the car~~.

6. Their <u>ball</u> <u>rolled</u> ~~past several toddlers~~.

7. A gray <u>horse</u> <u>walked</u> ~~toward me~~.

8. <u>Devi</u> <u>crawled</u> ~~over a white picket fence~~.

9. ~~After practice~~, the <u>coach</u> <u>talked</u> ~~about the next game~~.

10. The <u>teen</u> <u>sat</u> ~~between his parents throughout the baseball game~~.

Deleting (crossing out) any prepositional phrases helps to find the subject and the verb of a sentence.

A **prepositional phrase** begins with a preposition and ends with a noun or pronoun. A pronoun is a word like ***me, him, her, us, them, you, it, whom,*** or ***someone***. A pronoun takes the place of a noun. A noun is something that you can usually see.

Examples: A branch ~~of a tree~~ fell ~~during the blizzard~~.

Marla sends stories ~~to me~~.

෴෴෴෴෴෴෴෴෴෴෴෴෴෴෴෴෴෴෴෴

Directions: Delete (cross out) any prepositional phrases. Underline the subject once and the verb twice.

1. The students gathered around a telescope.

2. Roses bloom outside my window.

3. Several children rolled down a hill.

4. Joey lives behind us.

5. Your umbrella is inside the car.

6. Their ball rolled past several toddlers.

7. A gray horse walked toward me.

8. Devi crawled over a white picket fence.

9. After practice, the coach talked about the next game.

10. The teen sat between his parents throughout the baseball game.

PREPOSITIONS

Prepositional Phrases

Note: I recommend that you do #1-9 orally with your students. Before determining the subject in #2, #3, and #4, point out that we are looking for one word that tells *who* or *what.* In #9, be sure to discuss why *magazines* can't be the subject.

I suggest that you ask students to do #10. Then, as a class, discuss answers. Do likewise for the remainder of the page.

Directions: Delete (cross out) any prepositional phrases. Underline the subject once and the verb twice.

Example: ~~At the end of each day~~, she jogs ~~for an hour~~.

1. This subway winds ~~through the city~~.

2. A well-dressed lady walked ~~into a hair salon~~.

3. One carpenter worked ~~above a doorway~~ ~~in the dining room~~.

4. ~~At recess~~, two boys played ~~under an oak~~.

5. Baskets ~~for dirty towels~~ are ~~below that open drawer~~.

6. The man ~~in the black tie~~ is ~~from Oklahoma~~.

7. ~~Before the track meet~~, they sat ~~near us~~ ~~on the grass~~.

8. A truck ~~with huge tires~~ backed ~~into a parking space~~.

9. A stack ~~of old magazines~~ lay ~~by the front door~~.

10. ~~After lunch~~, the ferry goes ~~across the large lake~~.

11. The mirror ~~above our long table~~ fell ~~without warning~~.

12. The story ~~about mountain goats~~ is ~~beside your notebook~~.

13. Everyone ~~but Jessi~~ looked ~~for the missing sneaker~~.

14. Mike placed a small box ~~along an attic wall~~ and ~~between two trunks~~.

15. ~~On every day~~ ~~except Sunday~~, those divers jump ~~off high cliffs~~.

Directions: Delete (cross out) any prepositional phrases. Underline the subject
once and the verb twice.

Example: ~~At the end of each day~~, <u>she</u> <u>jogs</u> ~~for an hour~~.

1.   This subway winds through the city.

2.   A well-dressed lady walked into a hair salon.

3.   One carpenter worked above a doorway in the dining room.

4.   At recess, two boys played under an oak.

5.   Baskets for dirty towels are below that open drawer.

6.   The man in the black tie is from Oklahoma.

7.   Before the track meet, they sat near us on the grass.

8.   A truck with huge tires backed into a parking space.

9.   A stack of old magazines lay by the front door.

10.   After lunch, the ferry goes across the large lake.

11.   The mirror above our long table fell without warning.

12.   The story about mountain goats is beside your notebook.

13.   Everyone but Jessi looked for the missing sneaker.

14.   Mike placed a small box along an attic wall and between two trunks.

15.   On every day except Sunday, those divers jump off high cliffs.

Name_____ **PREPOSITIONS**

WORKBOOK PAGE 8

Date_____ **Helping Verbs**

Note: Students will be asked to memorize the list of 23 helping verbs later. However, you may wish to show them now how easy helping verbs are to learn: Practice the three beginning with *d*. (I call them the 3 *d's*.) Be "jazzy"; set them to a rhythm. After you have said them together a few times, have students write the 3 *d's* on their white boards. Then, go to the 3 *h's*, the 3 *m's*, and the 3 *ould's*, using the same process. When you come to *shall, will,* and *can,* show students the correlating helping verb: shall – should, will – would, and can – could. Before you begin the last two columns, say the infinitive, *to be,* and guide them in saying the last eight on the list. If you do this consistently for a few weeks and periodically throughout the year, students should master helping (auxiliary) verbs easily. (In addition, you are building success!)

A **verb phrase** is made up of at least one helping verb and a main verb. The last word in a verb phrase is called the main verb.

Verbs that can serve as helping (auxiliary) verbs are:

do	has	may	should	shall	is	were
does	have	might	would	will	am	be
did	had	must	could	can	are	being
					was	been

Sometimes, one of these serves as a main verb.

Examples: She **has** fifty cents.   main verb

She **has found** a dime. (helping verb) **has** + found

If the sentence is interrogative (a question), the verb phrase may be split.   **Has** she **found** a dime?

🙞🙞🙞🙞🙞🙞🙞🙞🙞🙞🙞🙞🙞🙞🙞🙞🙞🙞🙞🙞🙞

Directions: Delete (cross out) any prepositional phrases. Underline the subject once and the verb or verb phrase twice. In the blank, write H if the italicized verb serves as a helping verb. Write M if the italicized verb serves as a main verb.

1. __**M**__   <u>Juan</u> *is* ~~in the first grade~~.

2. __**H**__   <u>Juan</u> *is* <u>going</u> ~~with us~~.

3. __**H**__   <u>We</u> *have* <u>spoken</u> ~~with our principal~~.

4. __**M**__   <u>We</u> *have* a note ~~from our mother~~.

5. __**M**__   <u>Grandpa</u> *does* laundry ~~in the morning~~.

6. __**H**__   *Does* your <u>dad</u> <u>drive</u> ~~to his office~~?

16

A **verb phrase** is made up of at least one helping verb and a main verb. The last word in a verb phrase is called the main verb.

Verbs that can serve as helping (auxiliary) verbs are:

do	**has**	**may**	**should**	**shall**	**is**	**were**
does	**have**	**might**	**would**	**will**	**am**	**be**
did	**had**	**must**	**could**	**can**	**are**	**being**
					was	**been**

Sometimes, one of these serves as a main verb.

      Examples: She **has** fifty cents.   main verb

                  She **has found** a dime.   (helping verb) **has** + found

If the sentence is interrogative (a question), the verb phrase may be split.

        Has she **found** a dime?

      ॐॐॐॐॐॐॐॐॐॐॐॐॐॐॐॐॐॐॐॐ

Directions: Delete (cross out) any prepositional phrases. Underline the subject once and the verb or verb phrase twice. In the blank, write <u>H</u> if the italicized verb serves as a helping verb. Write <u>M</u> if the italicized verb serves as a main verb.

1. _____ Juan *is* in the first grade.

2. _____ Juan *is* going with us.

3. _____ We *have* spoken with our principal.

4. _____ We *have* a note from our mother.

5. _____ Grandpa *does* laundry in the morning.

6. _____ *Does* your dad drive to his office?

HELPING (AUXILIARY) VERBS:

do	has	may	should	shall	is	were
does	have	might	would	will	am	be
did	had	must	could	can	are	being
					was	been

A verb phrase may consist of just **one** helping verb and a main verb.

     Example: ***Can*** you **drill** a hole in this piece of wood?

A verb phrase may consist of **two or more** helping verbs and a main verb.

     Examples: My watch ***was broken*** for two weeks.
                   He ***must have been riding*** the entire afternoon.

Not is never part of a verb phrase. When you see **not** or the contraction, **n't**, in a sentence, box it immediately. Never underline it as part of a verb phrase.

     Example: Jordan **did** | *not* | **make** his bed.

              ฅ฿ฅ฿ฅ฿ฅ฿ฅ฿ฅ฿ฅ฿ฅ฿ฅ฿ฅ฿ฅ฿ฅ฿ฅ฿ฅ฿ฅ฿ฅ฿ฅ฿

Directions: Delete (cross out) any prepositional phrases. Underline the subject
               once and the verb phrase twice.
***Not* or *n't* will be boldfaced.**

1. Mark is studying ~~for a test~~.

2. Joan has **not** hiked ~~up Camelback Mountain~~.

3. This urn must have been found ~~in Peru~~.

4. We could have driven ~~past our freeway exit~~.

5. Was your dog waiting ~~by the front door~~?

6. Her horse can be taken ~~to a nearby ranch~~.

7. Does**n't** your neighbor build race cars ~~in his garage~~?

18

HELPING (AUXILIARY) VERBS:

do	has	may	should	shall	is	were
does	have	might	would	will	am	be
did	had	must	could	can	are	being
					was	been

A verb phrase may consist of just **one** helping verb and a main verb.

Example: ___*Can*___ you **drill** a hole in this piece of wood?

A verb phrase may consist of **two or more** helping verbs and a main verb.

Examples: My watch ___*was broken*___ for two weeks.
He ___*must have been riding*___ the entire afternoon.

Not is never part of a verb phrase. When you see **not** or the contraction, **n't**, in a sentence, box it immediately. Never underline it as part of a verb phrase.

Example: Jordan **did** | *not* | **make** his bed.

ରେ

Directions: Delete (cross out) any prepositional phrases. Underline the subject once and the verb phrase twice.

1.   Mark is studying for a test.

2.   Joan has not hiked up Camelback Mountain.

3.   This urn must have been found in Peru.

4.   We could have driven past our freeway exit.

5.   Was your dog waiting by the front door?

6.   Her horse can be taken to a nearby ranch.

7.   Doesn't your neighbor build race cars in his garage?

Most of the time, a prepositional phrase ends with only one word. This is called the object of the preposition.

O.P.

Example: His sister was standing on her **head**.

Sometimes, a prepositional phrase will end with two or more words. This is called a compound object of the preposition.

O.P.   O.P.

Example: I am leaving with **Kim** and **Alex**.

O.P.   O.P.   O.P.

My father is going to **Austin**, **Fort Worth**, or **Dallas**.

෨෨෨෨෨෨෨෨෨෨෨෨෨෨෨෨෨෨෨෨෨෨෨෨

Directions: Delete any prepositional phrases. Underline the subject once and the verb/verb phrase twice. Label each object of the preposition – **O.P.**

Not and *n't* should be boxed; they are boldfaced here.

O.P.   O.P.
1.   Their <u>mother</u> <u>makes</u> a soup ~~with beef and dumplings~~.

O.P.   O.P.
2.   A stray <u>dog</u> <u>came</u> ~~toward Gena and me~~.

O.P.   O.P.
3.   <u>I</u> <u>left</u> ~~without my raincoat or umbrella~~.

O.P.   O.P.   O.P.
4.   <u>They</u> <u>will</u> **not** <u>stay</u> ~~at the new hotel~~ ~~until June or July~~.

O.P.   O.P.
5.   A <u>package</u> ~~from their aunt and uncle~~ <u>was delivered</u> today.

O.P.   O.P.   O.P.   O.P.
6.   That <u>movie</u> <u>was</u> ~~about men and women~~ ~~in our fight for freedom~~.

O.P.   O.P.   O.P.   O.P.
7.   The <u>bag</u> ~~of bagels, buns, and muffins~~ <u>remained</u> ~~inside the car~~.

O.P.   O.P.   O.P.
8.   An <u>article</u> ~~concerning sailboats and motorboats~~ <u>appears</u> ~~in this magazine~~.

O.P.   O.P.
9.   <u>We</u> <u>have</u>**n't** <u>seen</u> him ~~since Monday or Tuesday~~.

20

Most of the time, a prepositional phrase ends with only one word. This is called the object of the preposition.

O.P.

          Example: His sister was standing on her ***head***.

Sometimes, a prepositional phrase will end with two or more words. This is called a compound object of the preposition.

O.P.   O.P.

          Example: I am leaving with ***Kim*** and ***Alex***.

O.P.   O.P.   O.P.

          My father is going to ***Austin***, ***Fort Worth***, or ***Dallas***.

ৰ্চৰ্চৰ্চৰ্চৰ্চৰ্চৰ্চৰ্চৰ্চৰ্চৰ্চৰ্চৰ্চৰ্চৰ্চৰ্চৰ্চৰ্চ

Directions: Delete any prepositional phrases. Underline the subject once and
          the verb/verb phrase twice. Label each object of the preposition –
          O.P.

1.   Their mother makes a soup with beef and dumplings.

2.   A stray dog came toward Gena and me.

3.   I left without my raincoat or umbrella.

4.   They will not stay at the new hotel until June or July.

5.   A package from their aunt and uncle was delivered today.

6.   That movie was about men and women in our fight for freedom.

7.   The bag of bagels, buns, and muffins remained inside the car.

8.   An article concerning sailboats and motorboats appears in this magazine.

9.   We haven't seen him since Monday or Tuesday.

Note: Reteach changing a question into a statement before determining subject and verb. Number 12 is a question.

Sometimes, a sentence will be about two or more things or people. This is called a **compound subject**.

Continue to cross out prepositional phrases so that you can find the subject and verb.

Examples: <u>**Joan**</u> and <u>**I**</u> live ~~on Byrd Street~~.

A <u>**skateboard**</u> and a <u>**bike**</u> are ~~in the driveway~~.

🙞🙞🙞🙞🙞🙞🙞🙞🙞🙞🙞🙞🙞🙞🙞🙞🙞🙞

Directions: Delete (cross out) any prepositional phrases. Underline the subject once and the verb twice.

1.   <u>Eggs</u> and <u>milk</u> <u>are</u> ~~in the refrigerator~~.

2.   My <u>mom</u> and <u>dad</u> <u>departed</u> ~~from the Orlando airport~~.

3.   A <u>robin</u> and two <u>cardinals</u> <u>flew</u> ~~along the path~~.

4.   My <u>dog</u> and <u>cat</u> <u>run</u> ~~through the sprinklers~~.

5.   ~~For lunch~~, the <u>boys</u> and <u>girls</u> <u>ate</u> tacos.

6.   A <u>tape</u> and a <u>CD</u> <u>lay</u> ~~under his bed~~.

7.   <u>Bicycles</u>, <u>tricycles</u>, and <u>skates</u> <u>are</u> ~~on sale~~ ~~at that store~~.

8.   ~~During spring break~~, <u>Dan</u>, <u>Deka</u>, and <u>I</u> <u>flew</u> ~~to Arizona~~.

9.   <u>Miss Smith</u> and her <u>friend</u> <u>turned</u> their horses ~~toward a sloping trail~~.

10. ~~On Fridays~~, the <u>doctor</u> and his <u>staff</u> <u>leave</u> ~~at noon~~.

11. ~~After recess~~, the <u>teacher</u> and <u>children</u> <u>walked</u> ~~into their classroom~~.

12. <u>Are</u> <u>peanuts</u> and chocolate <u>chips</u> ~~in this dessert~~?

22

Sometimes, a sentence will be about two or more things or people. This is called a **compound subject**.

Continue to cross out prepositional phrases so that you can find the subject and verb.

Examples: **Joan** and **I** live ~~on Byrd Street~~.

A **skateboard** and a **bike** are ~~in the driveway~~.

જજજજજજજજજજજજજજજજજજજજજ

Directions: Delete (cross out) any prepositional phrases. Underline the subject once and the verb twice.

1. Eggs and milk are in the refrigerator.

2. My mom and dad departed from the Orlando airport.

3. A robin and two cardinals flew along the path.

4. My dog and cat run through the sprinklers.

5. For lunch, the boys and girls ate tacos.

6. A tape and a CD lay under his bed.

7. Bicycles, tricycles, and skates are on sale at that store.

8. During spring break, Dan, Deka, and I flew to Arizona.

9. Miss Smith and her friend turned their horses toward a sloping trail.

10. On Fridays, the doctor and his staff leave at noon.

11. After recess, the teacher and children walked into their classroom.

12. Are peanuts and chocolate chips in this dessert?

Sometimes, two or more things *happen* or *are* in a sentence. This is called a **compound verb**.

Examples: A <u>finch</u> **chirped** and **darted** ~~around its cage~~.

The <u>child</u> **has** four dimes but **needs** six ~~for cheese strips~~.

Continue to delete prepositional phrases so that you can find subject and verb.

ఌఌఌఌఌఌఌఌఌఌఌఌఌఌఌఌఌఌ

Directions: Delete (cross out) any prepositional phrases. Underline the subject once and the verb twice.

1.   A <u>wolf</u> <u>stood</u> ~~atop a snowy hill~~ and <u>howled</u>.

2.   Several <u>tourists</u> <u>stopped</u> ~~by the seals~~ and <u>watched</u> them.

3.   This <u>soup</u> <u>is</u> delicious and <u>fights</u> ~~against colds~~.

4.   <u>They</u> <u>jumped</u> ~~off their bikes~~ and <u>rushed</u> ~~down the riverbank~~.

5.   Kevin's <u>fish</u> <u>floats</u> ~~near the top of the tank~~ and <u>blows</u> bubbles.

6.   ~~Before the football game~~, <u>we</u> <u>ate</u> fish and <u>drank</u> lemonade.

7.   <u>Oil</u> ~~in the pan~~ <u>heated</u> rapidly and <u>smoked</u> ~~for a few minutes~~.

8.   <u>She</u> <u>swims</u> ~~on a team~~ and <u>competes</u> ~~throughout the state~~.

9.   Their <u>parents</u> <u>are</u> ~~in the flooring business~~ and <u>sell</u> marble tile.

10.   <u>He</u> <u>tossed</u> the newspaper ~~onto a front porch~~ and <u>drove</u> ~~to the next house~~.

11.   Our <u>horse</u> <u>lies</u> ~~on its side~~ ~~inside the barn~~ or <u>stands</u> ~~in the meadow~~.

12.   The main <u>speaker</u> <u>smiled</u> and <u>shook</u> my hand ~~during the reception~~.

Sometimes, two or more things *happen* or *are* in a sentence. This is called a **compound verb**.

> Examples: A <u>finch</u> **chirped** and **darted** ~~around its cage~~.
>
> The <u>child</u> **has** four dimes but **needs** six ~~for cheese strips~~.

Continue to delete prepositional phrases so that you can find subject and verb.

ৡৡৡৡৡৡৡৡৡৡৡৡৡৡৡৡৡৡৡৡৡ

Directions: Delete (cross out) any prepositional phrases. Underline the subject once and the verb twice.

1. A wolf stood atop a snowy hill and howled.

2. Several tourists stopped by the seals and watched them.

3. This soup is delicious and fights against colds.

4. They jumped off their bikes and rushed down the riverbank.

5. Kevin's fish floats near the top of the tank and blows bubbles.

6. Before the football game, we ate fish and drank lemonade.

7. Oil in the pan heated rapidly and smoked for a few minutes.

8. She swims on a team and competes throughout the state.

9. Their parents are in the flooring business and sell marble tile.

10. He tossed the newspaper onto a front porch and drove to the next house.

11. Our horse lies on its side inside the barn or stands in the meadow.

12. The main speaker smiled and shook my hand during the reception.

PREPOSITIONS

WORKBOOK PAGE 13

Date_____   **Imperative Sentence**

Note: **Teach this concept very carefully. Provide many examples before doing the exercise. You may wish to do most of the lesson orally. Sentence #6 has a compound verb. Sentence #7 has a verb phrase.**

An **imperative sentence** gives a command.

Continue to cross out prepositional phrases so that you can find the subject and verb.

>   Example: Take this to the dry cleaner.

Although the word, you, is not stated, it's understood that someone wants **YOU** to do something. It could have been expressed in this manner:

>   Example: You take this to the dry cleaner.

However, that isn't the way we talk. We usually omit the word, *YOU*.
To show this in written form, we write *you* at the beginning of the sentence, underline it, and place parentheses around it. **(You)**

>   Example: **(You)** Take this ~~to the dry cleaner~~.

ॐ ॐ ॐ ॐ ॐ ॐ ॐ ॐ ॐ ॐ ॐ ॐ ॐ ॐ ॐ ॐ ॐ ॐ ॐ

Directions: Delete (cross out) any prepositional phrases. Underline the subject once and the verb or verb phrase twice.

>   **Remember**: verb phrase = helping verb(s) + main verb

1. **(You)** Color ~~inside the lines~~.

2. **(You)** Sit ~~with me~~ ~~during lunch~~.

3. **(You)** Drop this coin ~~into that box~~.

4. **(You)** Put this box ~~underneath the table~~.

5. **(You)** Look ~~out the window~~.

6. **(You)** Add two eggs and beat ~~for two minutes~~.

7. **(You)** Do **not** go ~~without us~~.

26

An **imperative sentence** gives a command.

Continue to cross out prepositional phrases so that you can find the subject and verb.

>   Example: Take this to the dry cleaner.

Although the word, you, is not stated, it's understood that someone wants **YOU** to do something. It could have been expressed in this manner:

>   Example: You take this to the dry cleaner.

However, that isn't the way we talk. We usually omit the word, *YOU*.
To show this in written form, we write *you* at the beginning of the sentence, underline it, and place parentheses around it. **(You)**

>   Example: **(You)** <u>Take</u> this ~~to the dry cleaner~~.

క్రాక్రాక్రాక్రాక్రాక్రాక్రాక్రాక్రాక్రాక్రాక్రాక్రాక్రాక్రా

Directions: Delete (cross out) any prepositional phrases. Underline the subject once and the verb or verb phrase twice.

>   **Remember**: verb phrase = helping verb(s) + main verb

1. Color inside the lines.

2. Sit with me during lunch.

3. Drop this coin into that box.

4. Put this box underneath the table.

5. Look out the window.

6. Add two eggs and beat for two minutes.

7. Do not go without us.

Note: **You may want to do most of this lesson orally.** (For Your Information: In #1, *to see* *alpacas* is actually an infinitive phrase used as a direct object. Obviously, this is not a fifth grade concept.)
As you have already learned:

To + a noun	=	prepositional phrase	Let's race **to that tree**.
To + a pronoun	=	prepositional phrase	Will you go **with us**?

To + verb is called an **infinitive**. We do not delete an infinitive. We simply place parentheses **(   )** around it.

Examples of infinitives: to add   Micah <u>likes</u> **(to add)**.
to pitch   Joanie <u>wants</u> **(to pitch)** first.
to think   We <u>have decided</u> **(to think)** ~~about our project~~.

ᴥᴥᴥᴥᴥᴥᴥᴥᴥᴥᴥᴥᴥᴥᴥᴥᴥᴥᴥᴥᴥᴥ

Directions: Delete (cross out) any prepositional phrases. Underline the subject once and the verb or verb phrase twice. Place any infinitive in parentheses ( ).

1.   Those <u>children</u> <u>want</u> **(**to see**)** alpacas.

2.   Her <u>wish</u> <u>was</u> **(**to go**)** ~~to Africa~~.

3.   Jeb's <u>grandparents</u> <u>like</u> **(**to snowboard**)**.

4.   His <u>goal</u> <u>is</u> **(**to move**)** ~~near Miami~~.

5.   Your <u>store</u> <u>needs</u> **(**to be**)** ~~in this spot~~.

6.   Several <u>students</u> <u>decided</u> **(**to rush**)** ~~through the test~~.

7.   The <u>nurse</u> <u>needs</u> **(**to take**)** information ~~from his patient~~.

8.   One <u>teller</u> <u>chose</u> **(**to stay**)** ~~at the bank for lunch~~.

9.   <u>You</u> <u>don't have</u> **(**to run**)**.

10. <u>Tara</u> and <u>Mike</u> <u>might want</u> **(**to change**)** their website.

11. <u>Loni</u> <u>wants</u> **(**to make**)** flower arrangements ~~with her brother~~.

28

As you have already learned:

To + a noun   =   prepositional phrase   Let's race **to that tree**.
To + a pronoun   =   prepositional phrase   Will you go **with us**?

To + verb is called an **infinitive**. We do not delete an infinitive. We simply place parentheses **(   )** around it.

Examples of infinitives: to add   Micah <u>likes</u> **(**to add**)**.
                              to pitch   Joanie <u>wants</u> **(**to pitch**)** first.
                              to think   We <u>have decided</u> **(**to think**)** ~~about our project~~.

    ఉ✿ఉ✿ఉ✿ఉ✿ఉ✿ఉ✿ఉ✿ఉ✿ఉ✿ఉ✿ఉ✿ఉ✿ఉ✿ఉ✿ఉ✿ఉ✿ఉ✿ఉ✿ఉ✿

Directions: Delete (cross out) any prepositional phrases. Underline the subject once and the verb or verb phrase twice. Place any infinitive in parentheses (   ).

1. Those children want to see alpacas.

2. Her wish was to go to Africa.

3. Jeb's grandparents like to snowboard.

4. His goal is to move near Miami.

5. Your store needs to be in this spot.

6. Several students decided to rush through the test.

7. The nurse needs to take information from his patient.

8. One teller chose to stay at the bank for lunch.

9. You don't have to run.

10. Tara and Mike might want to change their website.

11. Loni wants to make flower arrangements with her brother.

PREPOSITION or ADVERB?

Lesson 1   (pages 32-33)

This concept is difficult. The initial lesson is presented in a simplistic manner. The adverb in this lesson is always the last word. The idea that a word can serve as two possible parts of speech can be confusing. Be sure to go over the lesson aloud with your students.

Lesson 2   (pages 34-35):

This lesson teaches that a word originally learned as a preposition can serve as an adverb *somewhere in the sentence other than the last word*. This lesson is more difficult than the preceding lesson. Introduce the following sentence before reading the lesson on those pages.

Place these two sentences on the board.

I fell down.

I fell down the steps.

Ask which word in both sentences is on the preposition list. ***Down!*** Then, ask students which sentence contains a prepositional phrase.

I fell down the steps.

Draw a line through the prepositional phrase.   **I fell ~~down the steps~~.**

Look at the first sentence.   **I fell down.**

Does it have any words after *down*? No! Then, *down*, in this sentence is not a preposition. It stands alone; it is an **adverb**. *Down* tells *where* I fell.

                                                                                              Adv.
Have students label *down* as ***Adv.***, the abbreviation for adverb.   **I fell down.**

IMPORTANT NOTE:

This concept is introduced in this text. (It was not part of *Easy Grammar: Grade 4*.) Mastery may not occur. The concept will be reintroduced in *Easy Grammar: Grade 6*.

Note: You may want to do this lesson orally. You may wish to have students write each short example (on white-boards) as you present the lesson. Have students underline the subject once and the verb twice. Point out that the second and third examples are imperative sentences; thus, the subject is (You) - *you understood*. Then, in teaching that the last word serves as an adverb, have students label *Adv.* above each. The more participation you include when you are teaching a lesson, the better chance you have for student understanding. (This is not true, however, if students choose to draw pictures instead.)

Sometimes, a word that usually serves as a preposition will stand alone. This word frequently ends a sentence. Such words as *in, on, off, inside, out, outside, over, through, near, around, by, up*, and *down* can serve as either a preposition (when it begins a phrase) or as an adverb (when it stands alone).

           Examples: We looked **up**.

                     Come **in**.

                     Jump **on**.

When a word that usually is a preposition stands alone, it serves as an adverb telling *where*.

           Examples: We looked **up**.   Where did we look?   **UP!**

                      Come **in**.   Where are we to come?   **IN!**

                      Jump **on**.   Where are we to jump?   **ON!**

         🙢🙢🙢🙢🙢🙢🙢🙢🙢🙢🙢🙢🙢🙢🙢🙢🙢🙢🙢🙢

Directions: Write a word that you learned on your list of prepositions in each blank. Label it **Adv.** to show that it serves as an adverb. Then, rewrite the word in the next blank and read that sentence.

               Adv.   **ANSWERS MAY VARY/REPRESENTATIVE ANSWERS:**

1. Hang _____**on**_____.   _**On**_____   tells where to hang.
                Adv.
2. They went _____**by**_____.   _**By**_____   tells where they went.
                Adv.
3. Stand _____**up**_____.   _**Up**_____   tells where to stand.
                Adv.
4. The dog ran _**around**___.   _**Around**_   tells where the dog ran.
                Adv.
5. You may come _**through**_.   _**Through**_   tells where you may come.
                Adv.
6. I jumped _____**off**_____.   _**Off**_____   tells where I jumped.
                Adv.
7. His cat sleeps _**inside**_.   _**Inside**_____   tells where his cat sleeps.

32

Sometimes, a word that usually serves as a preposition will stand alone. This word frequently ends a sentence. Such words as ***in, on, off, inside, out, outside, over, through, near, around, by, up,*** and ***down*** can serve as either a preposition (when it begins a phrase) or as an adverb (when it stands alone).

> Examples: We looked **up**.
>
> Come **in**.
>
> Jump **on**.

When a word that usually is a preposition stands alone, it serves as an adverb telling *where*.

> Examples: We looked **up**.   <u>Where</u> did we look?   ***UP!***
>
> Come **in**.   <u>Where</u> are we to come?   ***IN!***
>
> Jump **on**.   <u>Where</u> are we to jump?   ***ON!***

👏👏👏👏👏👏👏👏👏👏👏👏👏👏👏👏👏👏👏👏👏

Directions: Write a word that you learned on your list of prepositions in each blank. Label it **Adv.** to show that it serves as an adverb. Then, rewrite the word in the next blank and read that sentence.

1. Hang _____.   _____ tells where to hang.

2. They went _____.   _____ tells where they went.

3. Stand _____.   _____ tells where to stand.

4. The dog ran _____.   _____ tells where the dog ran.

5. You may come _____.   _____ tells where you may come.

6. I jumped _____.   _____ tells where I jumped.

7. His cat sleeps _____.   _____ tells where his cat sleeps.

Name_____   **PREPOSITIONS**

Date_____   **Preposition or Adverb?**

Note: You may want to do this lesson orally.

Do you remember what a **phrase** is? It's made up of more than one word. A **prepositional phrase** begins with a preposition and ends with a noun (or pronoun). It has to have more than one word.

                              prepositional phrase

        Example: She parks her car *outside her bedroom window*.

When a word that usually is a preposition stands alone, it cannot be part of a prepositional phrase. That word serves as an **adverb** (Adv.).

                              Adv.

        Example: The children rushed outside.

                     ***Where** did the children rush?* **OUTSIDE!**

Sometimes, a sentence will contain an adverb and no prepositional phrase.

                              Adv.

        Example: We walked **outside** (to talk).

                     ❧❧❧❧❧❧❧❧❧

Sometimes, a sentence will have an adverb and a prepositional phrase side by side. If you see two words that you learned as prepositions next to each other, both (usually) cannot serve as prepositions. One has to be an adverb.

                              Adv.

        Example: She walked **over** ~~to our table~~ and shook my hand.

                     ❧❧❧❧❧❧❧❧❧❧❧❧❧❧❧❧❧❧❧❧

Directions: Delete (cross out) any prepositional phrases. Underline the subject once and the verb twice. Label any adverb that tells *where* – **Adv.**

           Adv.
1. <u>Carl</u> <u><u>looked</u></u> up.

           Adv.
2. <u>Mom</u> <u><u>walked</u></u> over ~~to her neighbor's apartment~~.

                Adv.
3. The <u>mechanic</u> <u><u>stooped</u></u> down ~~by the car~~.

              Adv.
4. <u>Hannah</u> <u><u>stayed</u></u> inside ~~during the rain shower~~.

              Adv.
5. The <u>model</u> <u><u>stepped</u></u> out ~~onto the runway~~.

            Adv.
6. A <u>bunny</u> <u><u>snuggled</u></u> in ~~among some soft green bushes~~.

            Adv.
7. (<u>You</u>) <u><u>Come</u></u> by ~~for two hours~~.

34

Do you remember what a **phrase** is? It's made up of more than one word. A **prepositional phrase** begins with a preposition and ends with a noun (or pronoun). It has to have more than one word.

prepositional phrase

Example: She parks her car *outside her bedroom window*.

When a word that usually is a preposition stands alone, it cannot be part of a prepositional phrase. That word serves as an **adverb** (Adv.).

Adv.

Example: The children rushed outside.

Where did the children rush? *OUTSIDE!*

Sometimes, a sentence will contain an adverb and no prepositional phrase.

Adv.

Example: We walked **outside** (to talk).

ૐ ૐ ૐ ૐ ૐ ૐ ૐ ૐ

Sometimes, a sentence will have an adverb and a prepositional phrase side by side. If you see two words that we learned as prepositions next to each other, both (usually) cannot serve as prepositions. One has to be an adverb.

Adv.

Example: She walked **over** ~~to our table~~ and shook my hand.

ૐ ૐ ૐ ૐ ૐ ૐ ૐ ૐ ૐ ૐ ૐ ૐ ૐ ૐ ૐ ૐ ૐ ૐ

Directions: Delete (cross out) any prepositional phrases. Underline the subject once and the verb twice. Label any adverb that tells *where* – **Adv.**

1. Carl looked up.

2. Mom walked over to her neighbor's apartment.

3. The mechanic stooped down by the car.

4. Hannah stayed inside during the rain shower.

5. The model stepped out onto the runway.

6. A bunny snuggled in among some soft green bushes.

7. Come by for two hours.

Name_____

Preposition Review

Date_____

A. **List of Prepositions:**

     Directions: Write the prepositions by adding missing letters.

A's

1. a b o u t
2. a b o v e
3. a c r o s s
4. a f t e r
5. a g a i n s t
6. a l o n g
7. a m i d
8. a m o n g
9. a r o u n d
10. a t
11. a t o p

B's

12. b e f o _ r e
13. b e h i n d
14. b e l o w
15. b e n e a t h
16. b e s i d e
17. b e t w e e n

18. b e y o n d
19. b u t (meaning except)
20. b y

C's

21. c o n c e r n i n g

D's

22. d o w n
23. d u r i n g

E's

24. e x c e p t

F's

25. f o r
26. f r o m

I's

27. i n
28. i n s i d e
29. i n t o

L's

30. l i k e

N's

31. n e a r

O's

32. o f
33. o f f
34. o n
35. o n t o
36. o u t
37. o u t s i d e
38. o v e r

P's

39. p a s t

R's

40. r e g a r d i n g

S's

41. s i n c e

T's

42. t h r o u g h
43. t h r o u g h o u t

44. t o
45. t o w a r d

U's

46. u n d e r
47. u n d e r n e a t h
48. u n t i l
49. u p
50. u p o n

W's

51. w i t h
52. w i t h i n
53. w i t h o u t

36

Name_____   **Preposition Review**

Date_____

A. **List of Prepositions:**
Directions: Write the prepositions by adding missing letters.

A's

1. _ b _ _ t

2. _ b _ v _

3. _ c r _ _ s

4. _ f t _ r

5. _ g _ _ n _ t

6. _ l _ n g

7. _ m _ d

8. _ m _ n _

9. _ r _ _ n _

10. _ t

11. _ t _ p

B's

12. _ e f _ _ e

13. _ e h _ n _

14. _ _ l _ w

15. _ e n _ _ t h

16. _ e _ _ d _

17. _ e _ w _ _ n

18. _ e y _ _ d

19. _ _ t (meaning except)

20. _ y

C's

21. c _ n c _ r _ i _ g

D's

22. _ _ w n

23. _ u r _ n g

E's

24. _ x c _ p _

F's

25. _ _ r

26. _ r _ m

I's

27. _ n

28. _ n _ _ d _

29. _ n t _

L's

30. _ _ k _

N's

31. _ _ _ r

O's

32. _ f

33. _ _ f

34. _ n

35. _ n t _

36. _ _ t

37. _ _ t s _ d _

38. _ v _ r

P's

39. _ _ s t

R's

40. _ e _ _ r d _ n g

S's

41. _ _ n c _

T's

42. _ h _ _ _ g h

43. _ _ r _ u _ _ _ u t

44. _ o

45. _ o _ _ r d

U's

46. _ _ d _ r

47. _ n d _ r n _ a t h

48. _ _ t _ l

49. _ p

50. _ p _ n

W's

51. _ i _ h

52. _ _ t _ i _

53. _ _ t h _ _ t

37

Name_____   **Preposition Review**

WORKBOOK PAGE 18

Date_____

Note: In part D, #1, some students may underline *colorful* as part of the verb. *To colorful* is not a verb infinitive. Try conjugating to colorful: Today *he colorfuls,* yesterday *he colofuled,* and tomorrow *he will colorful.* Do this with students; obviously, this conjugation doesn't make sense. Therefore, *colorful* is not part of a verb but a describing word (adjective) that modifies *shirts.*

B. **Subject/Verb:**

   Directions: Cross out any prepositional phrases. Underline the subject once and the verb twice.

1. Rats ate the corn ~~in the barn~~.

2. A navy pilot nodded ~~toward the officer~~.

3. His tennis shoes were ~~under his backpack~~.

4. Are dogs ~~like a shepherd~~ ~~in great demand~~?

5. ~~During the meeting~~, a woman ~~from Kentucky~~ spoke ~~about pollution~~.

C. **Verb Phrases:**

   Directions: Cross out any prepositional phrases. Underline the subject once and the verb phrase twice.

1. She must have caught a fish ~~before noon~~.

2. Their family is boating ~~at a nearby lake~~.

3. Joy may want that hose ~~near her car~~.

4. Did the parade come ~~past your house~~?

D. **Compound Objects of the Preposition:**

   Directions: Cross out any prepositional phrases. Underline the subject once and the verb twice.

1. Your shirt ~~with stars and stripes~~ is colorful.

2. A package ~~for my mother and dad~~ arrived.

3. They eat snacks ~~during the morning or the afternoon~~.

4. Eric played tennis ~~against Rafe and me~~.

5. A visiting nurse sat ~~between the patient and her son~~.

38

Name_____   **Preposition Review**

Date_____

B. **Subject/Verb:**
   Directions: Cross out any prepositional phrases. Underline the subject
   once and the verb twice.

1. Rats ate the corn in the barn.

2. A navy pilot nodded toward the officer.

3. His tennis shoes were under his backpack.

4. Are dogs like a shepherd in great demand?

5. During the meeting, a woman from Kentucky spoke about pollution.

C. **Verb Phrases:**
   Directions: Cross out any prepositional phrases. Underline the subject
   once and the verb phrase twice.

1. She must have caught a fish before noon.

2. Their family is boating at a nearby lake.

3. Joy may want that hose near her car.

4. Did the parade come past your house?

D. **Compound Objects of the Preposition:**
   Directions: Cross out any prepositional phrases. Underline the subject
   once and the verb twice.

1. Your shirt with stars and stripes is colorful.

2. A package for my mother and dad arrived.

3. They eat snacks during the morning or the afternoon.

4. Eric played tennis against Rafe and me.

5. A visiting nurse sat between the patient and her son.

WORKBOOK PAGE 19

E. **Compound Subjects:**
  Directions: Cross out any prepositional phrases. Underline the subject once and the verb twice.

1. <u>Lanny</u> and <u>Nell</u> <u>live</u> ~~behind them~~.

2. A <u>man</u> and his <u>friend</u> <u>walked</u> ~~beyond the old cemetery~~.

3. Her alarm <u>clock</u> and <u>calendar</u> <u>are</u> ~~beside her bed~~.

4. ~~During their garage sale~~, <u>Carla</u> and her <u>friends</u> <u>talked</u> ~~about vacations~~.

5. Several <u>cards</u> and <u>envelopes</u> <u>were</u> ~~under unopened letters~~.

F. **Compound Verbs:**
  Directions: Cross out any prepositional phrases. Underline the subject once and the verb twice.

1. <u>He</u> <u>coughed</u> and <u>blew</u> his nose.

2. A <u>whale</u> <u>eats</u> and <u>swims</u> ~~at the same time~~.

3. <u>Jessi</u> <u>jumped</u> ~~on the diving board~~ and <u>fell</u> ~~toward the ladder~~.

4. <u>She</u> <u>stopped</u> ~~by a creek~~ and <u>waded</u> ~~in the water~~.

5. <u>Rachel</u> <u>stands</u> and <u>waits</u> 10 minutes ~~for the bus~~ every morning.

G. **Imperative Sentences:**
  Directions: Cross out any prepositional phrases. Underline the subject once and the verb twice.

1. (<u>You</u>) <u>Keep</u> this ~~in your notebook~~.

2. (<u>You</u>) <u>Walk</u> ~~to the right of the ladder~~.

3. (<u>You</u>) <u>Step</u> ~~over the puddle~~.

4. (<u>You</u>) <u>Wait</u> ~~outside the gym~~ ~~until the end of basketball practice~~.

E. **Compound Subjects:**

   Directions: Cross out any prepositional phrases. Underline the subject
               once and the verb twice.

1. Lanny and Nell live behind them.

2. A man and his friend walked beyond the old cemetery.

3. Her alarm clock and calendar are beside her bed.

4. During their garage sale, Carla and her friends talked about vacations.

5. Several cards and envelopes were under unopened letters.

F. **Compound Verbs:**

   Directions: Cross out any prepositional phrases. Underline the subject
               once and the verb twice.

1. He coughed and blew his nose.

2. A whale eats and swims at the same time.

3. Jessi jumped on the diving board and fell toward the ladder.

4. She stopped by a creek and waded in the water.

5. Rachel stands and waits 10 minutes for the bus every morning.

G. **Imperative Sentences:**

   Directions: Cross out any prepositional phrases. Underline the subject
               once and the verb twice.

1. Keep this in your notebook.

2. Walk to the right of the ladder.

3. Step over the puddle.

4. Wait outside the gym until the end of basketball practice.

Date_____

H. **Infinitives:**

   Directions: Cross out any prepositional phrases. Place parentheses around any infinitive. Underline the subject once and the verb twice.

1. They stood (to watch) the soccer game.

2. One artist began (to paint) a motorcycle.

3. Everyone ~~except Trina~~ likes (to lift) weights.

4. ~~Before breakfast~~, she sits (to exercise).

I. **Preposition or Adverb?:**

   Directions: Cross out any prepositional phrases. Underline the subject once and the verb twice. Write **A** if the boldfaced word serves as an adverb. Write **P** if the boldfaced word serves as a preposition that begins a prepositional phrase.

1. __**A**__   He fell **down**.

2. __**P**__   He fell ~~**down** the cellar steps~~.

3. __**A**__   Tara looked **up**.

4. __**A**__   Tara looked **up** ~~from her reading~~.

J. **Verb Phrases and *Not*:**

   Directions: Cross out any prepositional phrases. Box *not* or *n't*. Underline the subject once and the verb twice.

1. We could **not** row ~~across the lake after the storm~~.

2. Lynn has**n't** seen Tom ~~since Monday~~.

3. Flowers will **not** be planted ~~along this sidewalk~~.

4. Should**n't** you stand ~~against that wall for this game~~?

H. **Infinitives:**

Directions: Cross out any prepositional phrases. Place parentheses around any infinitive. Underline the subject once and the verb twice.

1. They stood to watch the soccer game.

2. One artist began to paint a motorcycle.

3. Everyone except Trina likes to lift weights.

4. Before breakfast, she sits to exercise.

I. **Preposition or Adverb?:**

Directions: Cross out any prepositional phrases. Underline the subject once and the verb twice. Write **A** if the boldfaced word serves as an adverb. Write **P** if the boldfaced word serves as a preposition that begins a prepositional phrase.

1. _____   He fell **down**.

2. _____   He fell **down** the cellar steps.

3. _____   Tara looked **up**.

4. _____   Tara looked **up** from her reading.

J. **Verb Phrases and *Not*:**

Directions: Cross out any prepositional phrases. Box *not* or *n't*.
Underline the subject once and the verb twice.

1. We could not row across the lake after the storm.

2. Lynn hasn't seen Tom since Monday.

3. Flowers will not be planted along this sidewalk.

4. Shouldn't you stand against that wall for this game?

WORKBOOK PAGE 21

Date_____

Note: Students have not been instructed to box *not* or *n't* or to place parentheses around an infinitive. You may wish to add these instructions.

K. **General Review:**

Directions: Cross out any prepositional phrases. Underline the subject once and the verb or verb phrase twice.

Example: Do you want (to step) out onto the patio?

***Not* and *n't* are boldfaced.**

1. A booklet regarding biking is on your bed.

2. I keep bleach on a shelf above my washing machine.

3. Everyone but my father slept inside our tent.

4. Tami and Dirk will **not** drive through a wild-animal park.

5. (You) Stay within the lines (to color).

6. We rushed out the door to the ice-cream truck.

7. During the party, one child danced atop a bench.

8. A visitor and her friends walked around the hotel before dinner.

9. A ski boat was placed upon a trailer and hauled to a lake.

10. The groomer asked questions concerning the dog's health.

11. The actor walked onto the stage with the director.

12. After the show, the singer stood amid several fans and signed autographs.

13. Has Mike placed his tennis racket beneath your chair?

14. From my seat near a large window, I could **not** see the speaker.

15. Each student between the ages of six and nine may enter the contest.

16. (You) Do**n't** wait until nighttime (to leave).

K. **General Review:**

Directions: Cross out any prepositional phrases. Underline the subject once and the verb or verb phrase twice.

Example: <u>Do</u> <u>you</u> <u>want</u> (to step) out ~~onto the patio~~?

1.   A booklet regarding biking is on your bed.

2.   I keep bleach on a shelf above my washing machine.

3.   Everyone but my father slept inside our tent.

4.   Tami and Dirk will not drive through a wild-animal park.

5.   Stay within the lines to color.

6.   We rushed out the door to the ice-cream truck.

7.   During the party, one child danced atop a bench.

8.   A visitor and her friends walked around the hotel before dinner.

9.   A ski boat was placed upon a trailer and hauled to a lake.

10.   The groomer asked questions concerning the dog's health.

11.   The actor walked onto the stage with the director.

12.   After the show, the singer stood amid several fans and signed autographs.

13.   Has Mike placed his tennis racket beneath your chair?

14.   From my seat near a large window, I could not see the speaker.

15.   Each student between the ages of six and nine may enter the contest.

16.   Don't wait until nighttime to leave.

Name_____   **Preposition Test**

Date_____

Total Points: 50

Directions: Cross out any prepositional phrases. Underline the subject
once and the verb twice.

1. My <u>brother</u> <u>lives</u> ~~near a cave in the desert~~.   (4 points)

2. A bowling <u>ball</u> <u>rolled</u> slowly ~~down the lane~~.   (3 points)

3. The <u>glass</u> ~~beside the sink~~ <u>contains</u> lemonade.   (3 points)

4. My <u>friend</u> <u>sat</u> ~~at a picnic table~~ ~~under an oak tree~~.   (4 points)

5. Their <u>aunt</u> and <u>uncle</u> <u>are</u> ~~from Denver or Dayton~~.   (3 points)

6. This <u>book</u> <u>is</u> an essay ~~concerning women~~ ~~during pioneer times~~.   (4 points)

7. ~~After the puppet show~~, <u>they</u> <u>went</u> ~~to a café for lunch~~.   (5 points)

8. A tall <u>lady</u> ~~without shoes~~ <u>nodded</u> and <u>walked</u> ~~past me~~.   (4 points)

9. <u>Everyone</u> ~~except their mother~~ <u>voted</u> ~~against the bill~~.   (4 points)

10. <u>He</u> always <u>stays</u> ~~with his friend~~ ~~until the end of summer~~.   (5 points)

11. (<u>You</u>) <u>Ask</u> your parents ~~about their childhood days~~.   (3 points)

12. ~~Throughout May~~, <u>they</u> <u>sit</u> ~~outside their classroom~~ (to read).   (4 points)

13. His <u>grandfather</u> <u>was</u> **not** ~~in the army~~ ~~before the Korean War~~.   (4 points)

46

Name_____   **Preposition Test**

Date_____

Directions: Cross out any prepositional phrases. Underline the subject
                once and the verb twice.

1. My brother lives near a cave in the desert.

2. A bowling ball rolled slowly down the lane.

3. The glass beside the sink contains lemonade.

4. My friend sat at a picnic table under an oak tree.

5. Their aunt and uncle are from Denver or Dayton.

6. This book is an essay concerning women during pioneer times.

7. After the puppet show, they went to a café for lunch.

8. A tall lady without shoes nodded and walked past me.

9. Everyone except their mother voted against the bill.

10. He always stays with his friend until the end of summer.

11. Ask your parents about their childhood days.

12. Throughout May, they sit outside their classroom to read.

13. His grandfather was not in the army before the Korean War.

Name_____ **Using Prepositional Phrases**

WORKBOOK PAGE 22

Date_____ **in Writing**

<u>Suggestion</u>: **Do this worksheet orally, sentence by sentence. Ask students to list as many possibilities as they can on their white-boards. Discuss how prepositional phrases change the meaning of each sentence.**

Good writing needs **details**. Prepositional phrases can be used as a tool to provide these.

Sometimes, the details will be near the end of a sentence.

A little boy walked **with his mother.**
through the woods.
to his friend's house.

Sometimes, the details will be used near the subject of the sentence.

A little boy **in a blue sailor hat** waved to me.
from Italy
under a table

૰૰૰૰૰૰૰૰૰૰૰૰૰૰૰૰૰૰૰૰

Directions: Write a prepositional phrase to add detail to each sentence. Do not use the same preposition more than once.

ANSWERS MAY VARY/REPRESENTATIVE ANSWERS:

1. Patty sat __**beside me, underneath a tree, with her dog**__.

2. A man stood __**between his friends, near a gas station, on a ladder**__.

3. That lady __**at the counter, in the red hat**__ is my neighbor.

4. We looked __**into a telescope, for a gift, through a hole**__.

5. My father likes to sing __**off key, in the shower, around the house**__.

6. The cabin __**in the woods, with a stone fireplace**__ is new.

7. A large truck sped __**toward us, across the road, past our car**__.

8. Those flowers __**by the front door, along that path**__ are pretty.

9. Place the newspaper __**under the porch bench, against this bag**__.

10. A teacher __**from Brazil, by the school entrance**__ spoke to us.

48

Good writing needs **details**. Prepositional phrases can be used as a tool to provide these.

Sometimes, the details will be near the end of a sentence.

A little boy walked **with his mother**.
through the woods.
to his friend's house.

Sometimes, the details will be used near the subject of the sentence.

A little boy **in a blue sailor hat** waved to me.
from Italy
under a table

🐦🐦🐦🐦🐦🐦🐦🐦🐦🐦🐦🐦🐦🐦🐦🐦🐦🐦🐦🐦🐦

Directions: Write a prepositional phrase to add detail to each sentence. Do not use the same preposition more than once.

1. Patty sat _____.

2. A man stood _____.

3. That lady _____ is my neighbor.

4. We looked _____.

5. My father likes to sing _____.

6. The cabin _____ is new.

7. A large truck sped _____.

8. Those flowers _____ are pretty.

9. Place the newspaper _____.

10. A teacher _____ spoke to us.

Note: This would be an ideal time to teach that a comma is placed between two descriptive adjectives unless one is a color.

Good writing uses **vivid details**. The reader should be able to picture descriptions.

Sometimes, we add describing words within a prepositional phrase. These provide vivid details.

His keys are lying **on a table**.

His keys are lying **on a <u>long, glass</u> table.**

Notice how details can change a sentence.

The woman **in an elegant, sequined dress** laughed.

The woman **in a dirty, frayed dress** laughed.

🐎🐎🐎🐎🐎🐎🐎🐎🐎🐎🐎🐎🐎🐎🐎🐎🐎🐎🐎

Directions: Rewrite each sentence, adding vivid details within each prepositional phrase. Make each sentence very different.

ANSWERS MAY VARY/REPRESENTATIVE ANSWERS:

1. They walked into a house.

> A.   ___**They walked into a spacious, expensive house.**___

> B.   ___**They walked into a small, comfortable house.**___

2. Two girls sat near a stream and talked.

> A.   ___**Two girls sat near a large, rushing stream and talked.**___

> B.   ___**Two girls sat near a quiet, rippling stream and talked.**___

3. A bunny hopped through the weeds.

> A.   ___**A bunny hopped through the tall, dry weeds.**___

> B.   ___**A bunny hopped through the yellow flowering weeds.**___

50

Using Prepositional Phrases

in Writing

Good writing uses **vivid details**. The reader should be able to picture descriptions.

Sometimes, we add describing words within a prepositional phrase. These provide vivid details.

> His keys are lying **on a table**.

> His keys are lying **on a long, glass table.**

Notice how details can change a sentence.

> The woman **in an elegant, sequined dress** laughed.

> The woman **in a dirty, frayed dress** laughed.

🐎🐎🐎🐎🐎🐎🐎🐎🐎🐎🐎🐎🐎🐎🐎🐎🐎🐎🐎🐎🐎

Directions: Rewrite each sentence, adding vivid details within each prepositional phrase. Make each sentence very different.

1. They walked into a house.

   A. _____

   B. _____

2. Two girls sat near a stream and talked.

   A. _____

   B. _____

3. A bunny hopped through the weeds.

   A. _____

   _____

   B. _____

   _____

TO THE TEACHER:

Notes and recommendations will continue to be presented throughout this text. When I offer these, I am not coming from an authoritarian perspective. I am simply sharing ideas. Glean what is applicable to your style of teaching and to your students' needs.

SUGGESTION:

After students have completed a worksheet individually, I sometimes ask them to stand. As students finish and stand, I pair them. Their task is **to compare answers**. If students disagree, their first reference is information provided in the text. If they still disagree, students may want to discuss the answer with you. After everyone has paired and finished, discuss answers orally.

a.   You may want to pair students who are strong in concepts with those who need help.

b.   Your classroom may become somewhat noisy. However, students can be trained to use "quiet" voices.

c.   Some students will finish earlier than others. This is where training students to always have a free-reading book is important. Students read until everyone is finished. (Obviously, if you have some students who take seemingly forever to complete worksheets on their own, some lateral thinking will be needed to solve this problem.)

d.   Students do need to be trained *how* to participate successfully in this activity. However, they love it. It's another strategy for fun, active learning.

VERBS

TEACHING *TO BE*:

Note: Before teaching *to be*, you will need to teach the concept of singular and plural. I recommend that you teach the material on these two pages in one lesson and do **no** worksheet(s).
Reteach the concept on the second day (with new examples and techniques). Then, proceed as usual.

❧Roam around the room, picking up an item such as a pencil. Teach that one (pencil) is **singular**. Pick up two pencils. Emphasize one pencil, two pencils. Two or more is **plural**. Think of creative ways to teach this concept. (Perhaps a student has two braids.) *Involve your students as much as possible when discussing examples.* Be sure to stress the terms, *singular* and *plural*.

❧Have students take out their white-boards. Have them list as many singular items as they can in 30 seconds. After time is called, ask them to tell a neighbor the plural form of each word written. (This tends to be somewhat noisy; you may have to model a "quiet" voice.)

After students understand singular and plural, they need to be taught about conjugating *to be*.

❧*Conjugate* means to give the various forms of a verb. Discuss that *to be* is an irregular verb and has its own pattern. We have to learn that pattern.

Additional Note: Be sure to discuss that *to + verb* is called an **infinitive**.
Throughout this unit, refer to **infinitives** so that students assimilate this term.

54

≈To teach about conjugating, introduce present and past time. (You are doing some pre-teaching of tenses.) Tense means time. Therefore, present tense means present time. We use *today* when discussing present tense.

To Be:

Present Tense: (Today)   I **am** here.

(Today)   Paul **is** here.
He **is** here.
Pam **is** here.
She **is** here.
Lunch **is** here.
It **is** here.

With **you** or with a **plural** subject, **are** is used.

(Today)   You **are** here.
(Today)   Many fans **are** here.

Past Tense:
Past tense means time that has already occurred. We use *yesterday* to make it easy. (However, it could have been a second ago.)

With a singular subject, **was** is used to form the past tense.

(Yesterday)   I **was** here.
(Yesterday)   Paul (He) **was** here.
Pam (She) **was** here.
Lunch (It) **was** here.

With *you* or with a plural subject, **were** is used.

(Yesterday)   You **were** here on time.
His friends **were** here.

Practice this concept orally, using white-boards and other activities.

A. **When using present time (today):**

> With the subject *I*, use ***am***.
> > I **am** funny.

> Singular means one. With most singular subjects, use ***is***.
> > Parker **is** funny.   She **is** funny.   It **is** funny.

> With the subject ***you***, use ***are***.
> > You **are** funny.

> Plural means more than one. With a plural subject, use ***are***.
> > Some jokes **are** funny.

B. **When using past time (yesterday):**

> With a singular subject, use ***was***.
> > I **was** funny.   Parker **was** funny.   She **was** funny.   It **was** funny.

> With ***you***, use ***were***.
> > You **were** funny.

> With a plural (more than one) subject, use ***were***.
> > Her jokes **were** funny.

ﮯﮯﮯﮯﮯﮯﮯﮯﮯﮯﮯﮯﮯﮯﮯﮯﮯﮯﮯﮯ

Directions: Write *is, am, are, was,* or *were* in the space provided.

1. Today, Char _____**is**_____ my best friend.

2. Last year, Mrs. Small _____**was**_____ my teacher.

3. The ripe berries _____**are/were**_____ on that bush.

4. I _____**am**_____ hungry now.

5. Yesterday, many horses _____**were**_____ in the corral.

6. At present, you _____**are**_____ the winner.

7. My parents _____**were**_____ in Santa Fe several years ago.

8. _____**Were**_____ you there last week?

56

VERBS

To Be

A. **When using present time (today):**

With the subject **I**, use ***am***.
   I **am** funny.

Singular means one. With most singular subjects, use ***is***.
   Parker **is** funny.   She **is** funny.   It **is** funny.

With the subject ***you***, use ***are***.
   You **are** funny.

Plural means more than one. With a plural subject, use ***are***.
   Some jokes **are** funny.

B. **When using past time (yesterday):**

With a singular subject, use ***was***.
   I **was** funny.   Parker **was** funny.   She **was** funny.   It **was** funny.

With ***you***, use ***were***.
   You **were** funny.

With a plural (more than one) subject, use ***were***.
   Her jokes **were** funny.

ৡৡৡৡৡৡৡৡৡৡৡৡৡৡৡৡৡৡৡৡৡৡ

Directions: Write *is, am, are, was,* or *were* in the space provided.

1. Today, Char _____ my best friend.

2. Last year, Mrs. Small _____ my teacher.

3. The ripe berries _____ on that bush.

4. I _____ hungry now.

5. Yesterday, many horses _____ in the corral.

6. At present, you _____ the winner.

7. My parents _____ in Santa Fe several years ago.

8. _____ you there last week?

The verb of a sentence expresses an action or makes a statement.
Verbs that simply state a fact are often called state-of-being verbs.

Examples: His mother **bought** several books.   (action)
Cooked pasta *is* in that pan.   (statement)

The verb, ***to be***, often makes a statement.
The parts of *to be* are <u>is</u>, <u>am</u>, <u>are</u>, <u>was</u>, <u>were</u>, <u>be</u>, <u>being</u>, and <u>been</u>.

(Today) I **am** hungry.   (Yesterday) I **was** hungry.
He **is** hungry.   You **were** hungry.
You **are** hungry.   We **were** hungry.
We **are** hungry.

സൗസൗസൗസൗസൗസൗസൗസൗസൗസൗസൗസൗ

Directions: In the space provided, write <u>**Yes**</u> if the boldfaced verb shows action.
Write <u>**No**</u> if the boldfaced verb does not show action.

1. __**Yes**__   The child **<u>rolled</u>** the ball to his parents.

2. __**No**__   Kami's dad **<u>is</u>** a mailman in their town.

3. __**Yes**__   Mrs. Luna **<u>fixes</u>** computers for a living.

4. __**No**__   Two cherries **<u>were</u>** on the dessert.

5. __**Yes**__   After a few minutes, a waitress **<u>brought</u>** our drinks.

6. __**Yes**__   Her friend **<u>pans</u>** for gold in the mountains.

7. __**Yes**__   That boy **<u>walks</u>** to football practice on Saturdays.

8. __**Yes**__   Grandma **<u>spoke</u>** with her doctor about a problem.

9. __**No**__   Spicy chicken wings **<u>are</u>** on the grill.

10. __**Yes**__   Kirk **<u>practices</u>** his flute every evening.

11. __**Yes**__   The gardener **<u>scattered</u>** mulch on the soil.

12. __**No**__   I **<u>am</u>** glad for you.

58

Name_____   **VERBS**

Date_____   **Action?**

The verb of a sentence expresses an action or makes a statement.
Verbs that simply state a fact are often called state-of-being verbs.

Examples: His mother **bought** several books.   (action)
            Cooked pasta *is* in that pan.   (statement)

The verb, ***to be***, often makes a statement.
The parts of *to be* are <u>is</u>, <u>am</u>, <u>are</u>, <u>was</u>, <u>were</u>, <u>be</u>, <u>being</u>, and <u>been</u>.

(Today)   I **am** hungry.   (Yesterday)   I **was** hungry.
          He **is** hungry.   You **were** hungry.
          You **are** hungry.   We **were** hungry.
          We **are** hungry.

ﾞﾞﾞﾞﾞﾞﾞﾞﾞﾞﾞﾞﾞﾞﾞﾞﾞﾞﾞﾞﾞﾞ

Directions: In the space provided, write **<u>Yes</u>** if the boldfaced verb shows action.
              Write **<u>No</u>** if the boldfaced verb does not show action.

1. _____   The child **<u>rolled</u>** the ball to his parents.

2. _____   Kami's dad **<u>is</u>** a mailman in their town.

3. _____   Mrs. Luna **<u>fixes</u>** computers for a living.

4. _____   Two cherries **<u>were</u>** on the dessert.

5. _____   After a few minutes, a waitress **<u>brought</u>** our drinks.

6. _____   Her friend **<u>pans</u>** for gold in the mountains.

7. _____   That boy **<u>walks</u>** to football practice on Saturdays.

8. _____   Grandma **<u>spoke</u>** with her doctor about a problem.

9. _____   Spicy chicken wings **<u>are</u>** on the grill.

10. _____   Kirk **<u>practices</u>** his flute every evening.

11. _____   The gardener **<u>scattered</u>** mulch on the soil.

12. _____   I **<u>am</u>** glad for you.

59

CONTRACTIONS

Suggestions for Mastery Learning:

1. Before introducing contractions, reproduce page 63. Give this to students as a **pretest**. Correct it by exchanging papers (unless you *want* to do it).

2. Have students **highlight** (or circle) the contractions written incorrectly. (Be sure to emphasize with students that their correction job is very important. We aren't taking a grade. The purpose of correcting is **to help** peers know which contractions they aren't writing properly.)

3. Return the corrected paper to the owner. Students now need to learn the highlighted (or circled) contractions.

4. **After** teaching contractions, give page 63 as a quiz.

5. Don't give up! Continue working with students individually. (Remember that your white boards can be used for individual work, too!)

Recommendations for Instruction:

    A. Make sure that students' apostrophes are slightly curved.

    B. Make sure that the apostrophe is placed exactly in the place of the omitted letter(s).

    C. Instruct students to write contractions in broken form so that mistakes are avoided.

        Example: *didn't*

Note that the space between the <u>n</u> and the <u>t</u>. In writing contractions in cursive, do not attach the <u>n</u> and <u>t</u>.

CONTRACTIONS

In forming a contraction, we draw together two words to make one word. We do this by dropping a letter or letters and inserting an apostrophe (') where the letter or letters have been left out.

A. Make sure that your apostrophe is slightly curved.

B. The apostrophe must be placed exactly where the letter or letters are missing.

C. Write contractions in broken form so that mistakes are avoided.

    didn't   Note the space between <u>n</u> and <u>t</u>. In cursive, do not attach the <u>n</u> and <u>t</u>.

CONTRACTION = VERB + WORD		CONTRACTION = WORD + VERB	
aren't	are + not	he's	he + is
can't	cannot	he'd	he + would
couldn't	could + not	here's	here + is
don't	do + not	I'd	I + would
doesn't	does + not	I'll	I + shall (will)
didn't	did + not	I'm	I + am
hasn't	has + not	it's	it + is
haven't	have + not	I've	I + have
hadn't	had + not	she'd	she + would
isn't	is + not	she's	she + is
mightn't	might + not	there's	there + is
mustn't	must + not	they'll	they + will
shouldn't	should + not	they're	they + are
wasn't	was + not	we're	we + are
weren't	were + not	we've	we + have
won't	will + not	what's	what + is
wouldn't	would + not	where's	where + is
		who's	who + is
		you'll	you + will
		you're	you + are

61

WORKBOOK PAGE 27

A **contraction** is a word made when two words are placed together and shortened.

રે રે રે રે રે રે રે રે રે રે રે રે રે રે રે રે રે રે

Directions: Write the contraction.

1. cannot - **can't**

2. he is - **he's**

3. have not - **haven't**

4. who is - **who's**

5. did not - **didn't**

6. will not - **won't**

7. we have - **we've**

8. we are - **we're**

9. I have - **I've**

10. what is - **what's**

11. he would - **he'd**

12. does not - **doesn't**

13. she would - **she'd**

14. was not - **wasn't**

15. I shall (will) - **I'll**

16. there is - **there's**

17. would not - **wouldn't**

18. they will - **they'll**

19. they are - **they're**

20. where is - **where's**

21. is not - **isn't**

22. should not - **shouldn't**

23. he will - **he'll**

24. I am - **I'm**

25. you will - **you'll**

26. had not - **hadn't**

27. you are - **you're**

28. were not - **weren't**

29. are not - **aren't**

30. she is - **she's**

31. has not - **hasn't**

32. it is - **it's**

33. you would - **you'd**

34. do not - **don't**

35. here is - **here's**

36. I would - **I'd**

A **contraction** is a word made when two words are placed together and shortened.

ởýởýởýởýởýởýởýởýởýởýởýởýởýởý

Directions: Write the contraction.

1. cannot - _____

2. he is - _____

3. have not - _____

4. who is - _____

5. did not - _____

6. will not - _____

7. we have - _____

8. we are - _____

9. I have - _____

10. what is - _____

11. he would - _____

12. does not - _____

13. she would - _____

14. was not - _____

15. I shall (will) - _____

16. there is - _____

17. would not - _____

18. they will - _____

19. they are - _____

20. where is - _____

21. is not - _____

22. should not - _____

23. he will - _____

24. I am - _____

25. you will - _____

26. had not - _____

27. you are - _____

28. were not - _____

29. are not - _____

30. she is - _____

31. has not - _____

32. it is - _____

33. you would - _____

34. do not - _____

35. here is - _____

36. I would - _____

A.   Directions: Write four contractions that begin with the pronoun I̲.

1.   __**I'll**__   2.   __**I'm**__   3.   __**I've**__   4.   __**I'd**__

B.   Directions: Write 17 contractions that end with n̲'̲t̲.

1.   __**aren't**__   10.   __**haven't**__

2.   __**can't**__   11.   __**mightn't**__

3.   __**couldn't**__   12.   __**mustn't**__

4.   __**don't**__   13.   __**shouldn't**__

5.   __**doesn't**__   14.   __**wasn't**__

6.   __**didn't**__   15.   __**weren't**__

7.   __**hasn't**__   16.   __**won't**__

8.   __**hadn't**__   17.   __**wouldn't**__

9.   __**isn't**__

C.   Directions: Write three contractions that begin with y̲o̲u̲.

1.   __**you'll**__   2.   __**you're**__   3.   __**you'd**__

D.   Directions: Write three contractions that begin with w̲h̲.

1.   __**what's**__   2.   __**where's**__   3.   __**who's**__

E.   Directions: Write two contractions that begin with w̲e̲.

1.   __**we're**__   2.   __**we've**__

F.   Directions: Write the following contractions.

1. he is - __**he's**__   2. there is - __**there's**__   3. she is - __**she's**__

A. Directions: Write four contractions that begin with the pronoun I.

1. _____   2. _____   3. _____   4. _____

B. Directions: Write 17 contractions that end with n't.

1. _____   10. _____

2. _____   11. _____

3. _____   12. _____

4. _____   13. _____

5. _____   14. _____

6. _____   15. _____

7. _____   16. _____

8. _____   17. _____

9. _____

C. Directions: Write three contractions that begin with you.

1. _____   2. _____   3. _____

D. Directions: Write three contractions that begin with wh.

1. _____   2. _____   3. _____

E. Directions: Write two contractions that begin with we.

1. _____   2. _____

F. Directions: Write the following contractions.

1. he is - _____   2. there is - _____   3. she is - _____

Directions: Write the contraction for the boldfaced words. Then, write an
             ending for each sentence.

Example: (**Where is**) _Where's_ _your brother____?

Contractions are in boldfaced print. Sentences will vary.

1. You (**are not**) _____aren't_____ _____a failure_____.

2. (**He is**) _____He's_____ _____my best friend_____.

3. Mike (**cannot**) _____can't_____ _____stand on his head_____.

4. (**I am**) _____I'm_____ _____going with you_____.

5. Next year, (**they will**) _____they'll_____ _____attend a rodeo_____.

6. I think that (**you are**) _____you're_____ _____a good skater_____.

7. Hank (**will not**) _____won't_____ _____be staying long_____.

8. (**What is**) _____What's_____ _____Florida's state bird_____?

9. (**Have not**) _____Haven't_____ _____you heard the news_____?

10. That car (**does not**) _____doesn't_____ _____have brakes_____.

11. (**Who is**) _____Who's_____ _____the man in a tuxedo_____?

12. (**I have**) _____I've_____ _____saved ten dollars_____.

13. Are you aware that (**it is**) _____it's_____ _____raining_____?

14. (**You will**) _____You'll_____ _____have to wait_____.

15. Those ideas (**were not**) _____weren't_____ _____suggested_____.

16. I (**should not**) _____shouldn't_____ _____stop trying_____.

17. (**They are**) _____They're_____ _____afraid of snakes_____.

Name_____   **VERBS**

Date_____   **Contractions**

Directions: Write the contraction for the boldfaced words. Then, write an
ending for each sentence.

Example: (**Where is**) _Where's_ _your brother_____?

1. You (**are not**) _____ _____.

2. (**He is**) _____ _____.

3. Mike (**cannot**) _____ _____.

4. (**I am**) _____ _____.

5. Next year, (**they will**) _____ _____.

6. I think that (**you are**) _____ _____.

7. Hank (**will not**) _____ _____.

8. (**What is**) _____ _____?

9. (**Have not**) _____ _____?

10. That car (**does not**) _____ _____.

11. (**Who is**) _____ _____?

12. (**I have**) _____ _____.

13. Are you aware that (**it is**) _____ _____?

14. (**You will**) _____ _____.

15. Those ideas (**were not**) _____ _____.

16. I (**should not**) _____ _____.

17. (**They are**) _____ _____.

67

Directions: Write the contraction for the boldfaced words. Then, write an
                       ending for each sentence.

1.   My neighbor (**could not**) _____**couldn't**_____ _____lift the heavy ladder__ .

2.   (**There is**) _____**There's**_____ _____mustard in the refrigerator_____ .

3.   The waiter (**did not**) _____**didn't**_____ _____bring extra napkins_____ .

4.   (**I shall**) _____**I'll**_____ _____give this to your sister_____ .

5.   During the holiday, (**they are**) _____**they're**_____ _____staying with me__ .

6.   (**Do not**) _____**Don't**_____ _____walk through the flooded street_____ .

7.   (**We are**) _____**We're**_____ _____playing hockey after school_____ .

8.   (**I would**) _____**I'd**_____ _____like to go to my friend's house_____ .

9.   (**Has not**) _____**Hasn't**_____ _____Deka finished her project_____ ?

10.   She (**was not**) _____**wasn't**_____ _____chosen for the play_____ .

11.   (**We have**) _____**We've**_____ _____made a card for Grandma_____ .

12.   (**Is not**) _____**Isn't**_____ _____a kangaroo a marsupial_____ ?

13.   The child (**would not**) _____**wouldn't**_____ _____sit still_____ .

14.   (**I would**) _____**I'd**_____ _____rather be outside_____ .

15.   My friends (**were not**) _____**weren't**_____ _____arriving until later_____ .

16.   (**Here is**) _____**Here's**_____ _____your ticket_____ .

17.   (**They will**) _____**They'll**_____ _____succeed_____ .

18.   My uncle (**had not**) _____**hadn't**_____ _____made reservations_____ .

68

Directions: Write the contraction for the boldfaced words. Then, write an
                      ending for each sentence.

1.   My neighbor (**could not**) _____ _____.

2.   (**There is**) _____ _____.

3.   The waiter (**did not**) _____ _____.

4.   (**I shall**) _____ _____.

5.   During the holiday, (**they are**) _____ _____.

6.   (**Do not**) _____ _____.

7.   (**We are**) _____ _____.

8.   (**I would**) _____ _____.

9.   (**Has not**) _____ _____?

10.   She (**was not**) _____ _____.

11.   (**We have**) _____ _____.

12.   (**Is not**) _____ _____?

13.   The child (**would not**) _____ _____.

14.   (**I would**) _____ _____.

15.   My friends (**were not**) _____ _____.

16.   (**Here is**) _____ _____.

17.   (**They will**) _____ _____.

18.   My uncle (**had not**) _____ _____.

You're/Your:

Have you ever received a note like this?   *Your a nice teacher.*

_(We always seem to have that one student who makes us aware that we need to reteach!)

> **You're = you + are**   You are a nice teacher. **You're** a nice teacher.
>
> *Your* **must possess or own something:**
>
> Your shoes are on the wrong feet.   **Your** what?   **Your** shoes!

Have students draw an arrow from *your* to the noun that *your* modifies.

Note: I recommend that you occasionally have students write a simple sentence such as "You're a good friend." You need to say the sentence; they need to write it on their white-boards. Note which students write the usage incorrectly. Provide additional instruction.

ఆఈ ఆఈ

It's/Its:

By teaching the simple idea of separating *it's* into *it is*, students are given another way to check their writing.

It's a beautiful day.   The bird caught **it's** foot in a twig. (Incorrect)
 It is a beautiful day.   The bird caught **it is** foot in a twig.
                              The bird caught **its** foot in a twig.   (Correct)

However, teach that *its* must have a *what* answer. Its what? Its foot!

Have students draw an arrow from *its* to the noun that *its* modifies.

Note: I recommend that you occasionally have students write a simple sentence such as "The cat licked its paws." You need to dictate the sentence and ask students to write it on their white-boards. Note which students write *its* incorrectly. Provide additional instruction.

ఆఈ ఆఈ

They're/Their/There:

Students need to understand that *they're* is a contraction for **they are**. Provide opportunities for students to create sentences using *they're* on white-boards.

Students need to comprehend that with *their*, they must be able to answer *what*.

> They burned their toast.   Their what?   Their toast!

Have students draw an arrow from *their* to what *their* modifies.

There is an adverb telling *where*. Often, *there* appears at the beginning of a sentence and does not seem to tell *where*. There is a storm coming. Find the subject and change the order of the words so that the sentence begins with the subject. A storm is coming there. Although this is a confusing use of *there*, students usually understand it.

70

You're / Your
It's / Its
They're / Their / There

A. **You're** is a contraction meaning you are. **Your** is a possessive pronoun. It will answer: your (what?). A quick way to check your choice in your writing is to say <u>you are</u> in the sentence.

    Examples: You're my buddy.
                  You are my buddy.   (correct)

                  Your sister called.
                  Your what?   *Your* sister!   (correct)

Could you use <u>you're sister called</u>? Try it. <u>You are sister called.</u> *Incorrect!*

B. **It's** is a contraction meaning it is. **Its** is a possessive pronoun; it will answer: its (what?).

    Examples: It's too hot.   (correct)
                  It is too hot.

                  The cat licked **its** kitten.   (correct)
                  Its what? *Its* kitten!

Could you use <u>it's kitten</u>? Try it. <u>The cat licked it is kitten.</u> *Incorrect!*

C. **They're** is a contraction meaning they are. **Their** is a possessive pronoun; it will answer: their (what?).

    Examples: They're ready.   (correct)
                  They are ready.

                  Their aunt is the owner of this store.
                  Their what? *Their* aunt!   (correct)

Could you use <u>they're aunt</u>? Try it. <u>They are aunt is the owner of this store.</u>
Incorrect!

There is an adverb that usually tells where.

    Example: I am going **there**.   Where?   There!   (correct)

There may begin a sentence.
    Example: **There** are three magazines for you.
Place the subject at the beginning of the sentence: Three magazines are **there** for you. You still use *there*. Do you see that *there* possibly tells *where*?

Name_____

WORKBOOK PAGE 32

Date_____

Contractions

and Confusing Words

Suggestion: Do this page orally. Walk students through the process of separating each contraction. In addition, if the answer is *its, your,* or *their,* make sure that students draw an arrow to the modified word.

Directions: Write the correct word. If the answer is ***its, your,*** or ***their,*** draw an arrow to the word it modifies (tells *what*).

MODIFIED WORDS ARE IN BOLDFACED ITALICS.

1. I'd like to play with (you're, your) _____**your**_____ *puppy*.

2. When (you're, your) _____**you're**_____ ready, please push this button.

3. (It's, Its) _____**It's**_____ raining again in the Northwest.

4. We went (they're, their, there) _____**there**_____ during spring break.

5. The train blew (it's, its) _____**its**_____ *whistle* several times.

6. (They're, Their, There) _____**Their**_____ *friends* live near a beach.

7. Do you know if (they're, their, there) _____**they're**_____ learning to ride horses?

8. When the bird hurt (it's, its) _____**its**_____ *wing*, Grandpa took care of it.

9. Van drank orange juice from (it's its) _____**its**_____ *container*.

10. I think (you're, your) _____**you're**_____ a very good sport.

11. Her boss and his wife invited her to (they're, their, there) _____**their**_____ *condo*.

12. The deli worker said, "(You're, Your) _____**Your**_____ *sandwich* is finished."

13. During autumn, (it's, it's) _____**it's**_____ fun to hike in the woods.

14. When (you're, your) _____**you're**_____ hungry, (they're, their, there)

    _____**there**_____ are snacks in the pantry.

15. "(They're, Their, There) _____**There**_____ must be a mistake!" she exclaimed.

72

Contractions

and Confusing Words

Directions: Write the correct word. If the answer is ***its, your***, or ***their***, draw
an arrow to the word it modifies (tells *what*).

1. I'd like to play with (you're, your) _____ puppy.

2. When (you're, your) _____ ready, please push this button.

3. (It's, Its) _____ raining again in the Northwest.

4. We went (they're, their, there) _____ during spring break.

5. The train blew (it's, its) _____ whistle several times.

6. (They're, Their, There) _____ friends live near a beach.

7. Do you know if (they're, their, there) _____ learning to ride
    horses?

8. When the bird hurt (it's, its) _____ wing, Grandpa took care of
    it.

9. Van drank orange juice from (it's, its) _____ container.

10. I think (you're, your) _____ a very good sport.

11. Her boss and his wife invited her to (they're, their, there) _____
    condo.

12. The deli worker said, "(You're, Your) _____ sandwich is
    finished."

13. During autumn, (it's, it's) _____ fun to hike in the woods.

14. When (you're, your) _____ hungry, (they're, their, there)

    _____ are snacks in the pantry.

15. "(They're, Their, There) _____ must be a mistake!" she
    exclaimed.

A. Directions: Write **it's** or **its** in the blank. If the answer is ***its***, draw an
                   arrow to the word it modifies (goes over to that word).

MODIFIED WORDS ARE IN BODLFACED ITALICS:

1. _____**It's**_____ a good idea to wear a jacket today.

2. "At the beginning of every day, _____**it's**_____ wise to write your goals,"
   the speaker said.

3. The car rolled down the street without _____**its**_____ ***driver***.

4. The toy was lying on the floor, and _____**its**_____ front ***wheels*** were
   missing.

5. When I cut a rose, _____**its**_____ ***leaves*** wilted.

B. Directions: Write **you're** or **your** in the blank. If the answer is ***your***, draw
                   an arrow to the word it modifies (goes over to that word).

1. Have you been told if _____**you're**___ a winner?

2. I wonder if _____**your**___ ***cousin*** joined the U. S. Army.

3. "_____**You're**___ not hurt," said the mother to the child.

4. _____**Your**___ ***friend*** hasn't ridden a subway yet.

C. Directions: Write **they're, their,** or **there** in the blank. If the answer is
                   their, draw an arrow to the word it modifies (goes over to that
                   word).

1. I believe that _____**they're**___ from Newberg, Oregon.

2. _____**Their**___ ***neighbor*** owns a boat _____**there**___ .

3. _____**There**___ have been no earthquakes in southern England.

4. Are you sure that _____**they're**___ visiting Key West?

5. Did a clerk ask for _____**their**___ ***money***?

74

A. Directions: Write **it's** or **its** in the blank. If the answer is **its**, draw an arrow to the word it modifies (goes over to that word).

1.   _____ a good idea to wear a jacket today.

2.   "At the beginning of every day, _____ wise to write your goals," the speaker said.

3.   The car rolled down the street without _____ driver.

4.   The toy was lying on the floor, and _____ front wheels were missing.

5.   When I cut a rose, _____ leaves wilted.

B. Directions: Write **you're** or **your** in the blank. If the answer is **your**, draw an arrow to the word it modifies (goes over to that word).

1.   Have you been told if _____ a winner?

2.   I wonder if _____ cousin joined the U. S. Army.

3.   "_____ not hurt," said the mother to the child.

4.   _____ friend hasn't ridden a subway yet.

C. Directions: Write **they're, their,** or **there** in the blank. If the answer is **their**, draw an arrow to the word it modifies (goes over to that word).

1.   I believe that _____ from Newberg, Oregon.

2.   _____ neighbor owns a boat _____.

3.   _____ have been no earthquakes in southern England.

4.   Are you sure that _____ visiting Key West?

5.   Did a clerk ask for _____ money?

TO THE TEACHER: Please read these two pages before teaching verb phrases.

VERBS

Be sure that students memorize and **learn** these 23 helping verbs:

do	has	may	can	could	is	were
does	have	might	shall	should	am	be
did	had	must	will	would	are	being
					was	been

Again, your white boards can serve as an additional teaching tool. Use them to practice the three helping verbs that begin with *d* (referred to as the 3 *d's - do, does, did*). Move then to the 3 *h's* (*has, have, had*), the 3 *m's* (*may, might, must*), and the 3 *"oulds"* (*could, would, should*). Show students that the helping verb that corresponds to *could* is *can*, to *should* is *shall*, and to *would* is *will*. Practice the *"oulds"* until students know them. Then, have students list the three helping verbs that match them: *could-can, should-shall, would-will*.

Learn the conjugation of *to be* together. Be sure to learn the helping verb list in segments. Also, practice **saying** them. Later in the day, if possible, practice by repeating the above sequence. Before leaving for the day, if possible, say or write them again, using a new strategy. (This is related to accelerated learning techniques.) I recommend that you practice these for two days before asking students to list them on a mastery quiz. (Students simply number a blank paper from 1-23 and write the auxiliary verbs.)

Note: A few years ago, I met a teacher who complained that her students couldn't determine verb phrases. I immediately asked, "Have you had your students *master* the 23 helping verbs?" Her response was negative. I shared how vital it is for students to memorize auxiliary verbs.

VERB PHRASES

Students have already been introduced to the concept of a *verb phrase*. Now we need to ascertain that students gain mastery of this concept. Although similar information has been duplicated in the student lessons, be sure to read the teaching strategies on the next page before doing the students' lesson with them.

76

A verb phrase is composed of one or more helping verbs plus a main verb. The **main verb** is the last part of a verb phrase.

Examples: You <u>may</u> **pick** these flowers.

Her <u>mom</u> <u>must have</u> **called** my mother.

verb phrase	=	helping verb(s)	+	main verb
may pick	=	may		pick
must have called	=	must have		called

A. Instruct students to continue to delete prepositional phrases. It makes finding a verb phrase easier.

B. Sometimes, a verb that can be a helping verb will stand alone in a sentence.

<u>Are</u> you my partner?   In this sentence, *are* is the only verb. There is no verb phrase.

<u>Are</u> <u>you</u> <u>going</u> ~~with us~~?   In this sentence, *are* is a helping verb; *are going* is the verb phrase.

C. If the sentence is interrogative, look for a helping verb **at or near the beginning** of the sentence. It may be helpful to restate the sentence in declarative form in order to determine the verb phrase more easily.

Example: <u>Have</u> you <u>seen</u> my sister?   You <u>have seen</u> my sister.

D. Teach students that **<u>not</u>** or **<u>n't</u>** is never part of a verb phrase. *Not* is an adverb. **Have students box <u>not</u> or <u>n't</u>**. This will keep them from underlining it as part of the verb phrase.

E. Sometimes, students will encounter a word that might look like it should be part of a verb phrase.

Example: She <u>is nice</u>.   (incorrect)
           She <u>is</u> nice.   (correct)

If this occurs, have students place *to* in front of a word they think is part of the verb phrase. This will form an infinitive: *to nice*. Then, to help students to determine if this can be part of a verb phrase, teach them to conjugate it by saying: *Today, I nice. Yesterday, I niced. Tomorrow, I shall nice.* Students usually laugh as they realize that the word is not part of the verb phrase.   77

AUXILIARY (HELPING) VERBS

You will need to learn these auxiliary (helping) verbs:

do	has	may	can	could	is	were
does	have	might	shall	should	am	be
did	had	must	will	would	are	being
					was	been

VERB PHRASE

A verb phrase is composed of one or more helping verbs plus a main verb.

The **main verb** is the last part of a verb phrase.

      Examples: They <u>were</u> **<u>talking</u>** loudly.

                The <u>doctor</u> <u>must have</u> **<u>left</u>** ~~for the day~~.

verb phrase	=	helping verb(s)	+	main verb
were talking	=	were		talking
must have left	=	must have		left

A. Continue to cross out prepositional phrases. They won't be part of a verb phrase.

B. Sometimes, a verb that can be a helping verb will stand alone in a sentence.

     <u>Are</u> those hamster yours?   In this sentence, <u>are</u> is the only verb. There is no verb phrase. *Are* is the main verb.

     <u>Are</u> <u>we</u> <u>staying</u> ~~until noon~~?   In this sentence, *are* is a helping verb; <u>are staying</u> is the verb phrase.

C. If the sentence is interrogative (asks a question), look for a helping verb **at or near the beginning** of the sentence. It may be helpful to restate the sentence in declarative (statement) form in order to determine the verb phrase more easily.

     Example: <u>Have</u> you <u>signed</u> your name?   You <u>have signed</u> your name.

D. **Not** or **n't** is never part of a verb phrase. *Not* is an adverb. **Box not or n't**. Do not underline it as part of a verb phrase.

     Example: The game <u>did</u> **| not |** <u>begin</u> ~~on time~~.

E. Sometimes, a word might look like it should be part of a verb phrase.

         Example: This apple <u>is bad</u>.   (incorrect)
                    This apple <u>is</u> bad.   (correct)

To test if a word can possibly be a verb, place *to* in front of the main verb: (to bad). Then, conjugate the verb by saying: "To bad: Today, I bad.
                                            Yesterday, I badded.
                                            Tomorrow, I shall bad."

To bad can't be conjugated; *bad* is not part of the verb phrase.

Name_____ **VERBS**

WORKBOOK PAGE 36

Date_____ **Verb Phrases**

Note: You may want to do this page orally and have students write the verb phrase (not just the main verb) on their white-boards. They need to practice double underlining the verb phrase. (You may want to see how many students' answers match the text answer.) Be sure that students box *not* or *n't.*

A verb phrase is made up of one or more helping verbs plus a main verb. The **main verb** is the last part of a verb phrase.

Directions: A helping verb appears in boldfaced print. Write an appropriate main verb and underline the verb phrase twice.

ANSWERS MAY VARY/REPRESENTATIVE ANSWERS: *Not* and *n't* have been boldfaced and italicized.

1. The vacuum cleaner **was** ___**lying**___ in the hallway.

2. Several children **had** ___**waved**___ at me.

3. She **may** ___**leave**___ in an hour.

4. You **should** ___**exercise**___ every day.

5. The baby **did** *not* ___**cry**___ for three hours.

6. **Does** Madison ___**attend**___ our school?

7. I **might** ___**ski**___ today.

B. Directions: Write an appropriate main verb and underline the verb phrase twice.

ANSWERS WILL VARY/REPRESENTATIVE ANSWERS: *Not* and *n't* have been boldfaced and italicized.

1. I **should have** ___**yelled**___ .

2. **Were** you ___**chosen**___ ?

3. The karate expert **is** ___**speaking**___ next.

4. Your short story **might be** ___**published**___ .

5. His brothers **do***n't* ___**skate**___ well.

6. Deka **may have been** ___**shopping**___ with her aunt.

7. That bush **has** *not* ___**bloomed**___ recently.

8. The bus **must have** ___**arrived**___ early.

80

A verb phrase is made up of one or more helping verbs plus a main

verb. The **main verb** is the last part of a verb phrase.

A. Directions: A helping verb appears in boldfaced print. Write an appropriate
main verb and underline the verb phrase twice.

1. The vacuum cleaner **was** _____ in the hallway.

2. Several children **had** _____ at me.

3. She **may** _____ in an hour.

4. You **should** _____ every day.

5. The baby **did** not _____ for three hours.

6. **Does** Madison _____ our school?

7. I **might** _____ today.

B. Directions: Write an appropriate main verb and underline the verb phrase
twice.

1. I should have _____.

2. Were you _____?

3. The karate expert is _____ next.

4. Your short story might be _____.

5. His brothers don't _____ well.

6. Deka may have been _____ with her aunt.

7. That bush has not _____ recently.

8. The bus must have _____ early.

81

WORKBOOK PAGE 37

A verb phrase is made up of one or more helping verbs plus a main verb. The **main verb** is the last part of a verb phrase.

Directions: Cross out any prepositional phrases. Underline the subject once and the verb phrase twice. Be sure to box *not* or *n't*.

Example: We <u>might be going</u> ~~to the beach~~ tomorrow.

1.   A police <u>officer</u> <u>may have stopped</u> a speeder.

2.   Two <u>workers</u> <u>were welding</u> two metal pieces.

3.   Jane's <u>father</u> <u>has won</u> a cooking award.

4.   <u>Do</u> <u>you</u> <u>eat</u> lunch ~~at a mall~~?

5.   Her <u>shirt</u> <u>had slipped</u> ~~from the ironing board~~.

6.   This <u>computer</u> <u>is</u> **not** <u>working</u>.

7.   <u>Does</u> <u>Toby</u> <u>live</u> ~~beside a church~~?

8.   One <u>designer</u> <u>has been working</u> ~~on a folding sofa~~.

9.   <u>Would</u> <u>you</u> ever <u>use</u> that screwdriver ~~without a handle~~?

10.   A <u>bulldozer</u> <u>can move</u> that mound ~~of dirt~~.

11.   <u>Plastic</u> <u>will be wrapped</u> ~~around a box~~.

12.   <u>I</u> <u>should</u> **not** <u>have told</u> anyone ~~about my idea~~.

13.   <u>Was</u>**n't** <u>Mary</u> <u>practicing</u> ~~for the relay~~ today?

14.   <u>Fireworks</u> <u>are being planned</u> ~~for the Fourth of July~~.

15.   <u>Shall</u> <u>I</u> <u>find</u> my guitar ~~for you~~?

16.   <u>Loni</u> <u>might have gone</u> ~~with her grandfather~~.

A verb phrase is made up of one or more helping verbs plus a main verb. The **main verb** is the last part of a verb phrase.

Directions: Cross out any prepositional phrases. Underline the subject once and the verb phrase twice. Be sure to box *not* or *n't*.

Example: We might be going to the beach tomorrow.

1.   A police officer may have stopped a speeder.

2.   Two workers were welding two metal pieces.

3.   Jane's father has won a cooking award.

4.   Do you eat lunch at a mall?

5.   Her shirt had slipped from the ironing board.

6.   This computer is not working.

7.   Does Toby live beside a church?

8.   One designer has been working on a folding sofa.

9.   Would you ever use a screwdriver without a handle?

10.   A bulldozer can move that mound of dirt.

11.   Plastic will be wrapped around a box.

12.   I should not have told anyone about my idea.

13.   Wasn't Mary practicing for the relay today?

14.   Fireworks are being planned for the Fourth of July.

15.   Shall I find my guitar for you?

16.   Loni might have gone with her grandfather.

Name_____   **VERBS**

Date_____   **Verb Phrases**

Directions: Cross out any prepositional phrases. Underline the subject once
and the verb phrase twice. Be sure to box *not* or *n't*.

Example: One ~~of the birds~~ is perched ~~on their brick wall~~.

1.   I am reading booklets about Canada.

2.   Pressure must be placed ~~on the bleeding arm~~.

3.   May I order an English muffin ~~without butter~~?

4.   Lance could **not** have walked there ~~in five minutes~~.

5.   Several walnut trees have been planted ~~near a stream~~ ~~within the city park~~.

6.   Did Erin move ~~from Santa Fe to Long Beach~~?

7.   Dad has shopped ~~at two stores~~ ~~for our groceries~~.

8.   Her father-in-law is driving a van ~~without a rear-view mirror~~.

9.   Marsha should have dropped these cards ~~into a nearby mailbox~~.

10. Are you frying or broiling the fish?

11. Lucy must have knitted Kim a scarf ~~for a birthday present~~.

12. Were**n't** your puppies born ~~on New Year's Eve~~?

13. A cow and its calf must have been taken ~~to another meadow~~.

14. A security guard would have checked all stores ~~in the mall~~.

15. Double-decker buses are running ~~through London's streets~~.

16. That guitar has been signed ~~by a famous musician~~.

17. (You) Call me ~~after your soccer game~~.

84

Directions: Cross out any prepositional phrases. Underline the subject once
                and the verb phrase twice. Be sure to box *not* or *n't*.

Example: One ~~of the birds~~ <u>is perched</u> ~~on their brick wall~~.

1.   I am reading booklets about Canada

2.   Pressure must be placed on the bleeding arm.

3.   May I order an English muffin without butter?

4.   Lance could not have walked there in five minutes.

5.   Several walnut trees have been planted near a stream within the city park.

6.   Did Erin move from Santa Fe to Long Beach?

7.   Dad has shopped at two stores for our groceries.

8.   Her father-in-law is driving a van without a rear-view mirror.

9.   Marsha should have dropped these cards into a nearby mailbox.

10.   Are you frying or broiling the fish?

11.   Lucy must have knitted Kim a scarf for a birthday present.

12.   Weren't your puppies born on New Year's Eve?

13.   A cow and its calf must have been taken to another meadow.

14.   A security guard would have checked all stores in the mall.

15.   Double-decker buses are running through London's streets.

16.   That guitar has been signed by a famous musician.

17.   Call me after your soccer game.

Name_____   **VERBS**

Date_____   **Regular and Irregular Verbs**

A regular verb adds <u>ed</u> to the past tense. You have learned that tense means time. Past tense refers to something that has already happened.

      Examples: to laugh   Mona laugh**ed** for several minutes.
                 to stir   Mona stir**red** pancake batter.

Important: Some regular verbs end in <u>e</u>. To form the past tense, drop the final <u>e</u> and add **ed**.

             Examples: to lik<u>**e**</u> - lik**ed**
                           to escap<u>**e**</u> - escap**ed**

An irregular verb does not add <u>ed</u> to the past tense. In fact, it usually changes form for both the past tense and part of a verb called the past participle. (Past participle is the form made by placing words like *has*, *have*, or *had* in front of a verb.)

   Examples: to know   Bo know**ed** the answer.   (Incorrect)
                              Bo **knew** the answer.   (Correct)

                              Bo has know**ed** her for a long time.   (Incorrect)
                              Bo has **known** her for a long time.   (Correct)

ନ୍ତନ୍ତନ୍ତନ୍ତନ୍ତନ୍ତନ୍ତନ୍ତନ୍ତନ୍ତନ୍ତନ୍ତନ୍ତନ୍ତନ୍ତ

Directions: Write the past tense (time) in the blank. Then, write **<u>R</u>** if the verb is regular and **<u>I</u>** if the verb is irregular.

          Example: to smile - ____**smiled**____   <u>R</u>

1. to pull - ____**pulled**____   <u>R</u>   8. to lock - ____**locked**____   <u>R</u>

2. to give - ____**gave**____   <u>I</u>   9. to hit - ____**hit**____   <u>I</u>

3. to ring - ____**rang**____   <u>I</u>   10. to find - ____**found**____   <u>I</u>

4. to believe - ____**believed**____   <u>R</u>   11. to erase - ____**erased**____   <u>R</u>

5. to break - ____**broke**____   <u>I</u>   12. to cut - ____**cut**____   <u>I</u>

6. to write - ____**wrote**____   <u>I</u>   13. to tap - ____**tapped**____   <u>R</u>

7. to search - ____**searched**____   <u>R</u>   14. to tape - ____**taped**____   <u>R</u>

A regular verb adds <u>ed</u> to the past tense. You have learned that tense means time. Past tense refers to something that has already happened.

     Examples: to laugh   Mona laugh**ed** for several minutes.
                  to stir   Mona stir**red** pancake batter.

Important: Some regular verbs end in <u>e</u>. To form the past tense, drop the final <u>e</u> and add **ed**.

           Examples: to lik**e** - lik**ed**
                         to escap**e** - escap**ed**

An irregular verb does not add <u>ed</u> to the past tense. In fact, it usually changes form for both the past tense and part of a verb called the past participle. (Past participle is the form made by placing words like *has*, *have*, or *had* in front of a verb.)

     Examples: to know   Bo know**ed** the answer.   (Incorrect)
                           Bo **knew** the answer.   (Correct)

                         Bo has know**ed** her for a long time.   (Incorrect)
                         Bo has **known** her for a long time.   (Correct)

ବ ବ ବ ବ ବ ବ ବ ବ ବ ବ ବ ବ ବ ବ ବ ବ ବ ବ ବ ବ

Directions: Write the past tense (time) in the blank. Then, write **R** if the verb is regular and **I** if the verb is irregular.

          Example: to smile - ____**smiled**____ __R__

1. to pull - _____ ____   8. to lock - _____ ____

2. to give - _____ ____   9. to hit - _____ ____

3. to ring - _____ ____   10. to find - _____ ____

4. to believe - _____ ____   11. to erase - _____ ____

5. to break - _____ ____   12. to cut - _____ ____

6. to write - _____ ____   13. to tap - _____ ____

7. to search - _____ ____   14. to tape - _____ ____

TO THE TEACHER:

IRREGULAR VERBS

A. Give the **pretest** on pages 90-91 **before** introducing the irregular verb list. Have students follow the directions and write the past participle form. This is extremely important. (Duplicate these pages later for a posttest.)

B. Correct pages 90-91 very carefully. If you have students correct each other's papers, you may wish to exchange again and do a recheck.

C. The corrected paper should be returned to the student. At this point, students need to have a list of irregular verbs. The list is in this teacher edition as well as in each student workbook. Students now need to highlight any irregular verbs they missed. This is necessary. (If students don't have highlighters, I recommend circling the incorrect irregular past participle.

D. The corrected paper becomes each student's individualized study list.

Please tell students that if they wrote these incorrectly, **they are probably saying them wrong as well**. The problem is that the incorrect usage may "sound" right to them. Convince students that this usage does not sound right to others. People do judge them on the use of their language. Be kind, but be emphatic. (I shared with my own students that a businessman purchased one of my *Easy Grammar* books because he did not receive a desired promotion. Upon asking for an explanation, the man was told by senior management that he used improper grammar, and this reflected poorly on the company.)

E. You need to provide activities that will help students master irregular verbs. Three such activities are suggested here:

1. **Verb Game** can be purchased. (See the last page for ordering.) Students are divided into two teams and are given cards that have various present, past, and past participle verbs on them. Students place these on their desks. When you say an infinitive, students on each team who have the present, the past, and the past participle of that irregular verb assemble in correct order in front of the classroom. (I suggest that you do not allow students to run.) The three team members who first assemble correctly and say the various verb forms earn a point. **This is a fun, active learning game.** Students usually love it!

88

2. This next venture is very "active." Student should enjoy it, and you may be amazed by their accelerated learning.

    a. You will need ample room; find a spacious area.

    b. Not all students will be participating in every "verb" activity; you may want to assign students who aren't involved with each verb to read independently. (They may be distracted, but, in this instance, don't worry about it.) **All students will need their highlighted list.**

    c. Tell students that you will announce each infinitive. Start with the second infinitive on the list (*to beat*).

    d. If students had the incorrect past participle of *to beat*, they need to join you.

    e. You will ask students who have come forward to say *have beaten* **21 times *while performing* a group action**.

        (I always tried to associate an appropriate action with the past participle. For example, with *have beaten*, we pretended to beat a rug – after I explained how my grandmother used to place her rugs over a clothes-line and hit them to shake out the dust.)

        (I also recommend moderate [such as a slow skip] to light [such as hand motions] while saying the correct past participle **21 times**. Always tell students that they may stop an activity but to continue to say the past participle form.

    f. When you have completed *have beaten*, proceed with the next past participle. Do likewise for **each** of the listed irregular verbs.

    Note: This activity will take a great deal of time; in fact, you may want to divide it into several sessions. However, students usually love it, and they tend to **master** irregular verbs easily.

3. **White-boards**** will be useful while practicing irregular verbs. A few suggested ideas are presented here:

    a. Say the infinitive to the entire class. Ask students to write *has*, *have*, or *had* plus the past participle on their white-boards. Intersperse this activity throughout the day.

    b. Have students work in pairs. Using their highlighted irregular verb list, have the pair practice the highlighted past participle form orally. Then, have one student say an infinitive while the partner writes *has*, *have*, or *had* plus the past participle on the white-board.

*See last page for ordering.

Name_____ **VERBS**

Date_____ **Pre/Post Quiz - Irregular Verbs**

A present participle is formed by adding <u>ing</u> *to a verb (example: to go =* <u>going</u>*). The past participle is formed by placing* <u>had</u> *in front of a verb (had* <u>gone</u>*).*

Directions: Write the past participle form for each verb.

<u>Infinitive</u>	<u>Present</u>	<u>Past</u>	<u>Present Participle</u>	<u>Past Participle</u>*
To be	is, am, are	was, were	being	1. **(had)**_____
To beat	beat(s)	beat	beating	2. **(had)**_____
To begin	begin(s)	began	beginning	3. **(had)**_____
To blow	blow(s)	blew	blowing	4. **(had)**_____
To break	break(s)	broke	breaking	5. **(had)**_____
To bring	bring(s)	brought	bringing	6. **(had)**_____
To burst	burst(s)	burst	bursting	7. **(had)**_____
To buy	buy(s)	bought	buying	8. **(had)**_____
To choose	choose(s)	chose	choosing	9. **(had)**_____
To come	come(s)	came	coming	10. **(had)**_____
To do	do, does	did	doing	11. **(had)**_____
To drink	drink(s)	drank	drinking	12. **(had)**_____
To drive	drive(s)	drove	driving	13. **(had)**_____
To eat	eat(s)	ate	eating	14. **(had)**_____
To fall	fall(s)	fell	falling	15. **(had)**_____
To find	find(s)	found	finding	16. **(had)**_____
To fly	fly, flies	flew	flying	17. **(had)**_____
To freeze	freeze(s)	froze	freezing	18. **(had)**_____
To give	give(s)	gave	giving	19. **(had)**_____
To go	go, goes	went	going	20. **(had)**_____
To grow	grow(s)	grew	growing	21. **(had)**_____
To have	have, has	had	having	22. **(had)**_____
To hang	hang(s)	hung**	hanging	23. **(had)**_____

****Uses a helping verb such as *has, have,* or *had.*

**Use the form of *to hang* when it means *to place an object.*

90

Infinitive	Present	Past	Present Participle	Past Participle*
To know	know(s)	knew	knowing	24. (had) _____
To lay	lay(s)	laid	laying	25. (had) _____
To leave	leave(s)	left	leaving	26. (had) _____
To lie**	lie(s)	lay	lying	27. (had) _____
To ride	ride(s)	rode	riding	28. (had) _____
To ring	ring(s)	rang	ringing	29. (had) _____
To rise	rise(s)	rose	rising	30. (had) _____
To run	run(s)	ran	running	31. (had) _____
To see	see(s)	saw	seeing	32. (had) _____
To set	set(s)	set	setting	33. (had) _____
To shake	shake(s)	shook	shaking	34. (had) _____
To sing	sing(s)	sang	singing	35. (had) _____
To sink	sink(s)	sank	sinking	36. (had) _____
To sit	sit(s)	sat	sitting	37. (had) _____
To speak	speak(s)	spoke	speaking	38. (had) _____
To spring	spring(s)	sprang	springing	39. (had) _____
To steal	steal(s)	stole	stealing	40. (had) _____
To swim	swim(s)	swam	swimming	41. (had) _____
To swear	swear(s)	swore	swearing	42. (had) _____
To take	take(s)	took	taking	43. (had) _____
To teach	teach(es)	taught	teaching	44. (had) _____
To throw	throw(s)	threw	throwing	45. (had) _____
To wear	wear(s)	wore	wearing	46. (had) _____
To write	write(s)	wrote	writing	47. (had) _____

*Uses a helping verb such as *has, have,* or *had*.
**meaning *to rest*

IRREGULAR VERBS

Infinitive	Present	Past	Present Participle	Past Participle*
To be	is, am, are	was, were	being	been
To beat	beat(s)	beat	beating	beaten
To begin	begin(s)	began	beginning	begun
To blow	blow(s)	blew	blowing	blown
To break	break(s)	broke	breaking	broken
To bring	bring(s)	brought	bringing	brought
To burst	burst(s)	burst	bursting	burst
To buy	buy(s)	bought	buying	bought
To choose	choose(s)	chose	choosing	chosen
To come	come(s)	came	coming	come
To do	do, does	did	doing	done
To drink	drink(s)	drank	drinking	drunk
To drive	drive(s)	drove	driving	driven
To eat	eat(s)	ate	eating	eaten
To fall	fall(s)	fell	falling	fallen
To find	find(s)	found	finding	found
To fly	fly, flies	flew	flying	flown
To freeze	freeze(s)	froze	freezing	frozen
To give	give(s)	gave	giving	given
To go	go, goes	went	going	gone
To grow	grow(s)	grew	growing	grown
To have	have, has	had	having	had
To hang	hang(s)	hung**	hanging	hung**

*Uses a helping verb such as *has*, *have*, or *had*. *A present participle is formed by adding* ing *to a verb (example: to go =* going*). The past participle is formed by placing* had *in front of a verb (had* gone*).*

**Use *hung* when referring to objects.

92

IRREGULAR VERBS

Infinitive	Present	Past	Present Participle	Past Participle*
To know	know(s)	knew	knowing	known
To lay	lay(s)	laid	laying	laid
To leave	leave(s)	left	leaving	left
To lie**	lie(s)	lay	lying	lain
To ride	ride(s)	rode	riding	ridden
To ring	ring(s)	rang	ringing	rung
To rise	rise(s)	rose	rising	risen
To run	run(s)	ran	running	run
To see	see(s)	saw	seeing	seen
To set	set(s)	set	setting	set
To shake	shake(s)	shook	shaking	shaken
To sing	sing(s)	sang	singing	sung
To sink	sink(s)	sank	sinking	sunk
To sit	sit(s)	sat	sitting	sat
To speak	speak(s)	spoke	speaking	spoken
To spring	spring(s)	sprang	springing	sprung
To steal	steal(s)	stole	stealing	stolen
To swim	swim(s)	swam	swimming	swum
To swear	swear(s)	swore	swearing	sworn
To take	take(s)	took	taking	taken
To teach	teach(es)	taught	teaching	taught
To throw	throw(s)	threw	throwing	thrown
To wear	wear(s)	wore	wearing	worn
To write	write(s)	wrote	writing	written

***Uses a helping verb such as *has, have,* or *had*.** (The tense that *to have* + *the past participle* forms is called the *perfect tense*. You will not learn the *perfect tense* this year.)
**meaning to rest
Note: There are other irregular verbs. Consult a dictionary if you are unsure.

Name_____ **VERBS**

Date_____ **Irregular Verbs**

Directions: Write the appropriate past participle. Then, underline the
verb phrase twice.

1. (to choose)   The homeowner had ____**chosen**____ wood flooring.

2. (to ride)   Nan and Van had ____**ridden**____ all morning.

3. (to leave)   Marco would have ____**left**____ a note.

4. (to eat)   Tugs must have ____**eaten**____ all his dog food.

5. (to wear)   Her back tire was ____**worn**____ down.

6. (to go)   They could have ____**gone**____ with their uncle.

7. (to begin)   Many swimmers had ____**begun**____ to shiver.

8. (to come)   Their guest might have ____**come**____ late.

9. (to speak)   Cross words must have been ____**spoken**____.

10. (to drive)   You should have ____**driven**____ faster.

11. (to see)   Has he ever ____**seen**____ a dragonfly?

12. (to fly)   I could **not** have ____**flown**____ on another flight.

13. (to drink)   The infant might have ____**drunk**____ her formula.

14. (to rise)   All of the bicycle racers had ____**risen**____ by
                   six o'clock.

15. (to throw)   Would your sister have ____**thrown**____ that?

16. (to fall)   By next week, all of the leaves will have ____**fallen**____.

17. (to find)   A hiker may have ____**found**____ a piece of old
                   pottery.

Name_____ **VERBS**

Date_____ **Irregular Verbs**

Directions: Write the appropriate past participle. Then, underline the
verb phrase twice.

1. (to choose) The homeowner had _____ wood flooring.

2. (to ride) Nan and Van had _____ all morning.

3. (to leave) Marco would have _____ a note.

4. (to eat) Tugs must have _____ all his dog food.

5. (to wear) Her back tire was _____ down.

6. (to go) They could have _____ with their uncle.

7. (to begin) Many swimmers had _____ to shiver.

8. (to come) Their guest might have _____ late.

9. (to speak) Cross words must have been _____.

10. (to drive) You should have _____ faster.

11. (to see) Has he ever _____ a dragonfly?

12. (to fly) I could not have _____ on another flight.

13. (to drink) The infant might have _____ her formula.

14. (to rise) All of the bicycle racers had _____ by
six o'clock.

15. (to throw) Would your sister have _____ that?

16. (to fall) By next week, all of the leaves will have _____.

17. (to find) A hiker may have _____ a piece of old
pottery.

Directions: Cross out any prepositional phrases. Underline the subject
                once and the verb phrase twice.

Example: The church <u>bells</u> <u>have</u> already (rang, <u>rung</u>).

1.   The <u>balloon</u> <u>had</u> (busted, <u>burst</u>) ~~from the heat~~.

2.   <u>Have</u> <u>you</u> (did, <u>done</u>) your homework?

3.   <u>Juice</u> <u>has been</u> (<u>frozen</u>, froze) ~~into popsicles~~.

4.   <u>I</u> <u>should have</u> (ran, <u>run</u>) ~~in the last race~~.

5.   His <u>wallet</u> <u>had been</u> (<u>stolen</u>, stole) yesterday.

6.   This <u>lamp</u> <u>may have been</u> (brung, <u>brought</u>) ~~to America by their grandmother~~.

7.   <u>Can</u> those <u>flowers</u> <u>be</u> (<u>grown</u>, grew) ~~in such a small pot~~?

8.   The <u>milkshakes</u> <u>had been</u> (shook, <u>shaken</u>) ~~in a blender~~.

9.   <u>He</u> <u>must have</u> (<u>written</u>, wrote) ~~for a free booklet~~.

10.   Several <u>songs</u> <u>were</u> (sang, <u>sung</u>) ~~before the program~~.

11.   <u>Could</u> <u>Mr. Frim</u> <u>have</u> (<u>taken</u>, took) the wrong train?

12.   <u>Has</u> your <u>family</u> ever (swam, <u>swum</u>) ~~in Bear Lake~~?

13.   This <u>package</u> <u>might have</u> (<u>come</u>, came) ~~without a zip code~~.

14.   <u>He</u> <u>would</u> **not** <u>have</u> (<u>known</u>, knew) ~~about this accident~~.

15.   Their <u>taxi</u> <u>had</u> (broke, <u>broken</u>) down ~~along a small canal~~.

16.   ~~By tomorrow~~, <u>she</u> <u>will have</u> (gave, <u>given</u>) her speech three times.

Directions: Cross out any prepositional phrases. Underline the subject
                      once and the verb phrase twice.

Example: The church <u>bells</u> <u>have</u> already (rang, <u>rung</u>).

1.   The balloon had (busted, burst) from the heat.

2.   Have you (did, done) your homework?

3.   Juice has been (frozen, froze) into popsicles.

4.   I should have (ran, run) in the last race.

5.   His wallet had been (stolen, stole) yesterday.

6.   This lamp may have been (brung, brought) to America by their
      grandmother.

7.   Can those flowers be (grown, grew) in such a small pot?

8.   The milkshakes had been (shook, shaken) in a blender.

9.   He must have (written, wrote) for a free booklet.

10.   Several songs were (sang, sung) before the program.

11.   Could Mr. Frim have (taken, took) the wrong train?

12.   Has your family ever (swam, swum) in Bear Lake?

13.   This package might have (come, came) without a zip code.

14.   He would not have (known, knew) about this accident.

15.   Their taxi had (broke, broken) down along a small canal.

16.   By tomorrow, she will have (gave, given) her speech three times.

TO THE TEACHER:
In order to teach *sit/set*, *rise/raise*, and *lie/lay* easily, students need to understand direct objects.

Definition: Direct objects occur after a verb and receive the action of the verb.
(The problem with the definition is that many students will be confused by it, **but do share it!**) Because direct objects receive the action of the verb, they are easier to teach through an activity and a series of steps than by definition.

Explaining a Direct Object:

Suggestion: Go to your door and open it. Then say, "I opened the door. What is the object I opened?" Students should readily see that the object you opened was a door.   (Now, you may want to have students open something—a book, a purse, a backpack and tell a neighbor the ***direct object***.) Continue to do other things like bouncing a ball. Use a variety of concrete examples. Let students *see* the direct object.

You may want to crumple a paper and throw it into a trash can. Say, "I threw a paper into the trash can." Write this sentence on the board and discuss markings.

D.O.

I threw a paper ~~into the trash can~~.

Explain that we will continue to delete prepositional phrases. What is the object I threw? Lead students to respond that you threw a paper. Therefore, *paper* is the direct object. **Also, remind students that a word in a prepositional phrase will not be a direct object.** This is important because without deleting the prepositional phrases, some students might say, "I threw the trash can."

Explain that a sentence containing a direct object must have an **action verb**. Review examples of action verbs. Be sure to emphasize that not all sentences with action verbs will have direct objects. Example: We screamed ~~in fun~~.

Recommendation:
Do page 101 orally with your students and allow that to be the day's lesson. (If you want to go to another topic, that's fine. However, stop teaching direct objects.)

On the second day, think of new examples to **reteach direct objects**. Using NEW examples, go through the same process you did on the previous day. Be sure to write a sentence that contains both a prepositional phrase and a direct object. In fact, you may want students to write a sentence containing a direct object on their **white-boards**. Ask students to exchange with a friend and let the friend delete any prepositional phrases, underline the subject once and the verb or verb phrase twice, and label the direct object. Students usually enjoy this. (Of course, if activities such as this lead to chaos with your particular group, you may want to have students do this activity individually.

98

On page 103, do numbers 1-5 orally with your students. If you feel they understand, let them continue. (You may want to allow students to compare answers with a neighbor. After everyone has finished, discuss each sentence as a class.)

<u>**SIT/SET**</u>, <u>**RISE/RAISE**</u>, and <u>**LIE/LAY**</u> **(See pages 104-105 for student pages.)** *Suggested active participation activities presented on this page may not be suitable for every class. Let your students and your behavioral expectations guide you.*

SIT/SET: A conjugation of both *to set* and *to sit* appears on page 104. (Students have not been formally introduced to tenses; therefore, take this part slowly.) **Be sure to discuss the forms!**

Explain that *to sit* does not require an object; it's something one can do alone. You sit on a chair. You can do that without help. *To set* means to place and requires a direct object. (Exceptions: The sun sets. Hens set.)

Have students sit on the floor (by their desks) as they say," I sit." Then, have them select an object from the desk and place it on the floor as they say, "I set _____ on the floor." Solicit answers (direct objects) from students. **Active participation enhances learning!**

Note: At this level, we are dealing with the active voice. In the passive voice, a direct object may not be used with *to set.* **For our purposes, active voice will be used. This is merely for your information**.

> Active Voice: I set the silver bank on the table.   (actively involved)
> Passive Voice: The silver bank had been set on the table.

RISE/RAISE: *To rise* is an irregular verb; *to raise* is a regular verb. **Teach the forms on page 104**. Discuss that some items can rise without help (the sun). Have students rise form their seats. Note than no one pulled them up; they did it on their own.

Explain to students that if they use *raise* in a sentence, they must have a direct object. Ask students to name "objects" that are raised. Possible responses include *hand, flag, chickens,* and *money.* Ask students to find an object in their desks and to hold it in the air. Take turns saying, "I raise (or *am raising*) _____." Discuss the various direct objects.

LIE/LAY: (*To lie* **in this text refers to a prone position, not to fibbing.**)
First, spend time discussing these two irregular verbs. Be sure that students understand both. These are very difficult, especially in that the past of *to lie* is the same word as the present of *to lay.* Have students think of *to lie* in terms of *to rest.*

Have students lie on the floor. Have them say, "I lie on the floor." Next, have them stand and say, "A minute ago, I **lay** on the floor." I **was lying** on the floor. I **had lain** there for a few seconds." **(You may wish to repeat this activity over a period of several days to help to ensure mastery. It's important that students <u>say</u> the correct forms.)**

Explain to students that *to lay* means *to place*. Therefore, there must be something to place (direct object). The words, <u>lays</u>, <u>laid</u>, and <u>laying</u> will require direct objects. If *lay* means *to place*, it will have a direct object.
Students will use their knowledge of prepositional phrases.

> Example: The child (lies, lays) by her dad.
> The <u>child</u> (<u>lies</u>, lays) ~~by her dad~~.

Students should know that this sentence can't possibly have a direct object. *By her dad* has been deleted. Hence, a child *lies* (*rests*). 99

Name_____ **VERBS**

Date_____ **Direct Objects**

Note: In Part A, if students use more than one word, make sure D.O. is placed over the object. For example, in #1, if a student writes _peach pie_, make sure that D.O. is placed above the word, _pie_.

A. Directions: Write a direct object for each sentence. Cross out any prepositional phrases. Underline the subject once and the verb twice.   Label the direct object – **D.O.**

ANSWERS MAY VARY/REPRESENTATIVE ANSWERS:

                                 D.O.
1. A <u>cook</u> <u>made</u> a _____**cheese souffle**_____ .

                         D.O.
2. <u>I</u> <u>dropped</u> my _____**fork**_____ ~~on the tile floor~~.

                       D.O.
3. <u>She</u> <u>loves</u> her _____**dog**_____ ~~with all her heart~~.

                           D.O.
4. <u>Jenny</u> <u>eats</u> _____**scrambled eggs**_____ ~~for breakfast~~.

                             D.O.
5. One <u>gardener</u> <u>picked</u> _____**peas**_____ ~~in her garden~~.

B. Directions: Cross out any prepositional phrases. Underline the subject once and the verb or verb phrase twice.   Label the direct object – **D.O.**

                        D.O.
1. Several scuba <u>divers</u> <u>checked</u> their gear.

                       D.O.
2. The <u>toddlers</u> <u>hugged</u> their puppy.

                      D.O.
3. The <u>camper</u> <u>placed</u> logs ~~by the fire~~.

                        D.O.
4. <u>We</u> <u>are sanding</u> a rusted chair.

                      D.O.
5. The <u>decorator</u> <u>hung</u> baskets ~~on the patio wall~~.

                        D.O.
6. One hotel <u>guest</u> <u>used</u> a private elevator.

                      D.O.
7. Usually, the <u>family</u> <u>lights</u> candles ~~during the evening~~.

                      D.O.
8. The post office <u>manager</u> <u>placed</u> a stamp ~~on an envelope~~.

                      D.O.
9. <u>Jody</u> <u>is carving</u> a wooden bowl.

                      D.O.
10. A <u>golfer</u> <u>carried</u> her clubs ~~to a golf cart~~.

                      D.O.
11. Three <u>workers</u> <u>washed</u> windows high ~~above the street~~.

100

A. Directions: Write a direct object for each sentence. Cross out any
                   prepositional phrases. Underline the subject once and the verb
                   twice.   Label the direct object – **D.O.**

1. A cook made a _____.

2. I dropped my _____ on the tile floor.

3. She loves her _____ with all her heart.

4. Jenny eats _____ for breakfast.

5. One gardener picked _____ in her garden.

B. Directions: Cross out any prepositional phrases. Underline the subject once
                   and the verb or verb phrase twice.   Label the direct object – **D.O.**

1.   Several scuba divers checked their gear.

2.   The toddlers hugged their puppy.

3.   The camper placed logs by the fire.

4.   We are sanding a rusted chair.

5.   The decorator hung baskets on the patio wall.

6.   One hotel guest used a private elevator.

7.   Usually, the family lights candles during the evening.

8.   The post office manager placed a stamp on an envelope.

9.   Jody is carving a wooden bowl.

10. A golfer carried her clubs to a golf cart.

11. Three workers washed windows high above the street.

Directions: Cross out any prepositional phrases. Underline the subject once
                   and the verb or verb phrase twice.   Label the direct object – **D.O.**

                                     D.O.
       Example: <u>Hannah</u> <u>leaned</u> her bat ~~against a tree~~.

               D.O.
1.   <u>Mark</u> <u>set</u> his car alarm.

                D.O.
2.   <u>Brittany</u> <u>played</u> a game ~~on the computer~~.

              D.O.
3.   An <u>actor</u> <u>wrote</u> a novel ~~about Hollywood~~.

                D.O.
4.   The <u>mother</u> <u>laid</u> the baby ~~in a cradle~~.

                D.O.
5.   Our <u>dog</u> <u>chased</u> a butterfly ~~across our lawn~~.

                  D.O.
6.   The car <u>dealer</u> <u>hid</u> the keys ~~under the seat~~.

               D.O.
7.   <u>Mary</u> <u>grooms</u> her horse ~~with great care~~.

                D.O.
8.   <u>You</u> <u>do</u> **not** <u>need</u> a partner ~~for this activity~~.

                 D.O.
9.   <u>They</u> <u>started</u> the softball game ~~without me~~.

                  D.O.
10.   <u>Has**n't**</u> <u>Charlie</u> <u>found</u> a summer job?

                D.O.
11.   <u>Mrs. Landis</u> <u>published</u> an article ~~regarding healthy food~~.

              D.O.
12.   Their <u>puppy</u> <u>must have chewed</u> a hole ~~near the corner of the sofa~~.

                  D.O.
13.   <u>Annie</u> and <u>Juan</u> <u>should</u> **not** <u>have taken</u> a vacation ~~to Phoenix in the
        summer~~.

                 D.O.
14.   ~~After a long lunch~~, the <u>storeowner</u> <u>lifted</u> bolts ~~of fabric onto racks~~.

              D.O.
15.   (<u>You</u>) <u>Place</u> this sign ~~across the street~~ and ~~beneath that pine tree~~.
102

Name_____   VERBS

Date_____   **Direct Objects**

Directions: Cross out any prepositional phrases.   Underline the subject once
              and the verb or verb phrase twice.   Label the direct object – **D.O.**

1.   Mark set his car alarm.

2.   Brittany played a game on the computer.

3.   An actor wrote a novel about Hollywood.

4.   The mother laid the baby in a cradle.

5.   Our dog chased a butterfly across our lawn.

6.   The car dealer hid the keys under the seat.

7.   Mary grooms her horse with great care.

8.   You do not need a partner for this activity.

9.   They started the softball game without me.

10.   Hasn't Charlie found a summer job?

11.   Mrs. Landis published an article regarding healthy food.

12.   Their puppy must have chewed a hole near the corner of the sofa.

13.   Annie and Juan should not have taken a vacation to Phoenix in the
      summer.

14.   After a long lunch, the storeowner lifted bolts of fabric onto racks.

15.   Place this sign across the street and beneath that pine tree.

Sit/Set
Rise/Raise
Lie/Lay

Sit/Set:

To sit means to rest.

To set means to place or put.

Infinitive	Present	Past	Present Participle	Past Participle
to sit	sit(s)	sat	sitting	(had) sat
to set	set(s)	set	setting	(had) set

Examples: He (sits, sets) near a window.

He (<u>sits</u>, sets) ~~near a window~~.

(There is no direct object. He "rests" near a window.)

To set requires a direct object.

She (sat, set) the timer.

D.O.

She (sat, <u>set</u>) the timer.

(When using *set*, label the direct object. What is the object she set?
Answer: timer)

Rise/Raise:

To rise means to go up without help.

To raise means to lift or go up (with help).

Infinitive	Present	Past	Present Participle	Past Participle
to rise	rise(s)	rose	rising	(had) risen
to raise	raise(s)	raised	raising	(had) raised

Examples: Smoke (rises, raises) in the air.

Smoke (<u>rises</u>, raises) ~~in the air~~.

Smoke goes up on its own. With *raises*, there must be a direct object. Because *in the air* has been deleted, the sentence can't contain a direct object.

To raise requires a direct object.

Mr. Clay (rose, raised) his hand.

                                      D.O.
<u>Mr. Clay</u> (rose, <u>raised</u>) his hand.

With *to raise*, a direct object is required. What did Mr. Clay raise? Answer: hand

Lie/Lay:

To lie means to rest.

To lay means to place.

Infinitive	Present	Past	Present Participle	Past Participle
to lie	lie(s)	lay	lying	(had) lain
to lay	lay(s)	laid	laying	(had) laid

To lie means <u>to rest</u>. Try inserting *rest* or *rests* when you are using *lie* in a sentence.

To lay means <u>to place</u>. **To lay needs a direct object**; there must be an object to place.

<u>Lays, laid, and laying will have a direct object. Lay will have a direct object if it means to place</u>.

Examples:

Ned (lies, lays) tile for a living.

                        D.O.
<u>Ned</u> (lies, <u>lays</u>) tile ~~for a living~~.

With <u>lays</u>, you must have a direct object.
What is the object Ned places? Answer: tile

Look at *laid* and *lain*:

He had (laid, lain) on a pool float.

<u>He</u> <u>had</u> (laid, <u>lain</u>) ~~on a pool float~~.

Lain refers to resting. (He had *rested* on a pool float.) Also, *on a pool float* has been deleted. Therefore, there is no direct object. To use *laid*, there must be a direct object in the sentence.

105

Note: Although the concept of compound direct objects is new, it should be easy to comprehend. It is recommended that this page be done orally with students.

Occasionally, there will be two or more direct objects in a sentence. This is called a compound direct object.

D.O.   D.O.

Example: Dad <u>spread</u> butter and jam <s>on our toast</s>.

A. Directions: Cross out any prepositional phrases. Underline the subject once and the verb twice.   Label any direct object – **D.O.**

D.O.   D.O.
1. <s>During the rehearsal dinner</s>, the <u>bride</u> <u>kissed</u> her mom and dad <s>on the cheek</s>.
     D.O.   D.O.
2. The <u>twins</u> <u>received</u> flowers and balloons <s>from their grandparents</s>.
     D.O.   D.O.
3. <u>Joel</u> <u>grabbed</u> an apple and a granola bar and <u>ran</u> <s>out the door</s>.

B. Directions: Cross out any prepositional phrases. Underline the subject once and the verb or verb phrase twice.   Label any direct object – **D.O.**

Remember: With *to lay* (*lays, laid, laying*), *to set,* and *to raise,* you must have a direct object. If the verb means *to place,* it must have a direct object.
               D.O.
1. A <u>detective</u> (sat, <u>set</u>) several papers <s>by his desk</s>.

2. Your <u>paintbrush</u> <u>is</u> (<u>lying</u>, laying) <s>by your pastel chalks</s>.
             D.O.
3. The <u>conductor</u> (rose, <u>raised</u>) his baton.
          D.O.
4. Their <u>dog</u> (lay, <u>laid</u>) his head <s>on my lap</s>.

5. <u>Tara</u> <u>had</u> (laid, <u>lain</u>) <s>under her beach umbrella for several hours</s>.
             D.O.   D.O.
6. Our <u>friend</u> (rises, <u>raises</u>) longhorn cattle and goats.

7. <s>During their morning walk</s>, <u>smoke</u> (<u>rose</u>, raised) <s>from many chimneys</s>.

8. (<u>You</u>) (<u>Sit</u>, Set) <s>along the low wall past the small wooden bridge</s>.

106

VERBS

Sit/Set, Rise/Raise
Lie/Lay

Occasionally, there will be two or more direct objects in a sentence. This is called a compound direct object.

             D.O.   **D.O.**

Example: Dad spread butter and jam on our toast.

A.   Directions: Cross out any prepositional phrases. Underline the subject once and the verb twice.   Label any direct object – **D.O.**

1.   During the rehearsal dinner, the bride kissed her mom and dad on the cheek.

2.   The twins received flowers and balloons from their grandparents.

3.   Joel grabbed an apple and a granola bar and ran out the door.

B.   Directions: Cross out any prepositional phrases. Underline the subject once and the verb or verb phrase twice.   Label any direct object – **D.O.**

Remember: With *to lay* (*lays, laid, laying*), *to set*, and *to raise*, you must have a direct object. If the verb means *to place*, it must have a direct object.

1.   A detective (sat, set) several papers by his desk.

2.   Your paintbrush is (lying, laying) by your pastel chalks.

3.   The conductor (rose, raised) his baton.

4.   Their dog (lay, laid) his head on my lap.

5.   Tara had (laid, lain) under her beach umbrella for several hours.

6.   Our friend (rises, raises) longhorn cattle and goats.

7.   During their morning walk, smoke (rose, raised) from many chimneys.

8.   (Sit, Set) along the low wall past the small wooden bridge.

VERBS

Date_____   **Sit/Set, Rise/Raise**
                                                Lie/Lay

Directions: Cross out any prepositional phrases. Underline the subject once
              and the verb twice.   Label any direct object – **D.O.**

Remember: **With *to lay (lays, laying, laid*), *to set*, and *to raise*, you must have
              a direct object.**

                                                        D.O.
          Example: I am (sitting, setting) your lunch ~~on the counter~~.

1.   A small snake (lay, laid) ~~under a porch swing~~.

2.   Steam (rose, raised) ~~from the kettle~~.

3.   Everyone ~~except Ronny~~ is (sitting, setting) ~~amid that clump of trees~~.
                           D.O.
4.   Lucy has been (lying, laying) brick ~~between her patio and shed~~.
                                   D.O.
5.   ~~Before his marriage~~, Mr. Lane (raised, rose) sheep ~~in Montana~~.

6.   He (sat, set) ~~across the aisle from me after art class~~.
                       D.O.
7.   The baby (lay, laid) his head ~~against his mother's arm~~.
                                 D.O.
8.   The waiters are (setting, sitting) the tables ~~within a small garden~~.

9.   Have you (laid, lain) ~~on a futon bed~~?

10. Her voice had (rose, risen) ~~to a high pitch~~.

11. Justin must have (set, sat) ~~beside his sister during church service~~.

12. My neighbor's dog (lies, lays) ~~outside her front door after breakfast~~.
                           D.O.
13. One gardener (raises, rises) orchids ~~in his greenhouse~~.
                           D.O.
14. That hotel maid (lies, lays) blankets ~~over the backs of chairs~~.
                         D.O.
15. A mechanic (sat, set) the car parts ~~on a bench by a window~~.

VERBS

Sit/Set, Rise/Raise
Lie/Lay

Directions: Cross out any prepositional phrases. Underline the subject once and the verb twice.   Label any direct object – **D.O.**

Remember: With *to lay* (*lays, laying, laid*), *to set*, and *to raise*, you must have a direct object.

                                                   D.O.

        Example: <u>I</u> <u><u>am</u></u> (sitting, <u>setting</u>) your lunch ~~on the counter~~.

1.   A small snake (lay, laid) under a porch swing.

2.   Steam (rose, raised) from the kettle.

3.   Everyone except Ronny is (sitting, setting) amid that clump of trees.

4.   Lucy has been (lying, laying) brick between her patio and shed.

5.   Before his marriage, Mr. Lane (raised, rose) sheep in Montana.

6.   He (sat, set) across the aisle from me after art class.

7.   The baby (lay, laid) his head against his mother's arm.

8.   The waiters are (setting, sitting) the tables within a small garden.

9.   Have you (laid, lain) on a futon bed?

10.   Her voice had (rose, risen) to a high pitch.

11.   Justin must have (set, sat) beside his sister during church service.

12.   My neighbor's dog (lies, lays) outside her front door after breakfast.

13.   One gardener (raises, rises) orchids in his greenhouse.

14.   That hotel maid (lies, lays) blankets over the backs of chairs.

15.   A mechanic (sat, set) the car parts on a bench by a window.

TENSES: Review the fact that **tense means time**.
Students will continue to delete prepositional phrases in sentences. This helps to determine subject and verb or verb phrase.

Present Tense:

Present tense means **present time**. Although present can mean at this moment, it is easier to use "today" as a point of reference for present tense. It's helpful for students to know that present tense never has a helping verb.

To form the present tense:

1. **If the subject is singular (one), add s to the verb** (**es** to some).

Examples:	to bark	That <u>dog</u> <u>bark**s**</u> too much.
	to relax	<u>Max</u> <u>relax**es**</u> ~~by reading~~.

2. **If the subject is you, I, or plural (more than one), simply remove the to from the infinitive.**

Example:	to search	**You** <u>search</u> too long ~~for lost items~~.
		I <u>search</u> ~~for old metal in the desert~~.
		They <u>search</u> ~~for 1950's furniture~~.

Past Tense:

Past tense indicates time that **has happened**. Although past can mean a second ago, it is easier to use the term, "yesterday." Teach students that past tense **never** has a helping verb.

1. **To form the past tense of a regular verb, add ed to the verb.**
    If the verb ends in **e**, drop the final **e** and add **ed**.

    to press - press**ed**   to blam<u>e</u> - blam**ed**

2. **To form the past tense of an irregular verb, change the verb to its appropriate form.**

    to drink - drank   to swim - swam

Future Tense:

Future tense indicates **time yet to happen**. *Shall* or *will* are added to the verb to form future tense; students must understand this. Future is any time yet to come; however, using "tomorrow" helps students to understand the tense.

Note: Although it has become acceptable to use *will* with any subject, encourage students to use *shall* with the pronoun, *I*. *Shall* may also be correctly used with the pronoun, *we*.

VERB TENSES
Tense means time.

Present Tense:

Present tense means **present time.** Although present can mean at this moment, it is easier to use "today" for present time. Present tense never has a helping verb.

To form the present tense, remove *to* from the infinitive: (infinitive = *to + verb*)

1. **If the subject is singular (one), add <u>s</u> to the verb (<u>es</u> to some).**

    Examples: to make   Their <u>cat</u> <u>make**s**</u> strange noises. (one animal)

    to turn   <u>He</u> <u>turn**s**</u> left ~~on Potter Street~~.   (one person)

2. **If the subject is <u>you</u>, <u>I</u>, or <u>plural</u> (more than one), simply remove the *to* from the infinitive.**

    Example: to drink   **You** <u>drink</u> water very slowly.

    I <u>drink</u> green tea.

    They <u>drink</u> bottled water.

Past Tense:

Past tense indicates time that **has happened**. Although past can mean a second ago, it is easier to use the term, "yesterday." Past tense never has a helping verb.

1. **To form the past tense of a regular verb, add <u>ed</u> to the verb.**
    If the verb ends in <u>e</u>, drop the final <u>e</u> and add <u>ed</u>.

    to start   A small boy <u>start**ed**</u> to play.

    to chang<u>e</u>   I <u>chang**ed**</u> a bandage ~~on my foot~~.

2. **To form the past tense of an irregular verb, change the verb to its appropriate form.**

    to teach   Her great uncle <u>taught</u> ~~in a one room school~~.

    to freeze   We froze a circle ~~of ice for the punch~~.

Future Tense:

Future tense indicates **time yet to happen**. There are two helping verbs that indicate future tense: ***shall*** and ***will***. Future may be any time yet to occur; however, to make it easier, we shall use "tomorrow" as a guide.

1. *Will* is most frequently used in forming the future tense.
2. *Shall* is used with the pronoun, *I.* (<u>I</u> <u>shall ask</u> my mother.)
    Shall may be used with *we*.

Directions: Write the present, past, and future tense of each verb.

1. **to smell**

    A. *present*   That old <u>cellar</u> _____**smells**_____ musty.

    B. *past*   The <u>kitchen</u> _____**smelled**_____ like bleach.

    C. *future*   <u>You</u> _____**will smell**_____ fresh after a shower.

2. **to blend**

    A. *present*   This <u>tile</u> _____**blends**_____ with the carpeting.

    B. *past*   <u>Peter</u> _____**blended**_____ a protein drink.

    C. *future*   <u>I</u> _____**shall blend**_____ some herbs for tea.

3. **to scrub**

    A. *present*   <u>Doctors</u> _____**scrub**_____ before surgery.

    B. *past*   <u>She</u> _____**scrubbed**_____ her toes with a loofa.

    C. *future*   A <u>janitor</u> _____**will scrub**_____ the mark from the floor.

4. **to do**

    A. *present*   <u>Dave</u> _____**does**_____ his dishes every night.

    B. *past*   A <u>friend</u> _____**did**_____ the actress's make-up.

    C. *future*   <u>She</u> _____**will do**_____ the data sheet tonight.

5. **to laugh**

    A. *present*   <u>Erica</u> _____**laughs**_____ frequently.

    B. *past*   <u>Mrs. Lambini</u> _____**laughed**_____ softly.

    C. *future*   Your <u>friend</u> _____**will laugh**_____ at your excuse.

Name_____   **VERBS**

Date_____   **Tenses**

Directions: Write the present, past, and future tense of each verb.

1. **to smell**

   A. *present*   That old <u>cellar</u> _____ musty.

   B. *past*   The <u>kitchen</u> _____ like bleach.

   C. *future*   <u>You</u> _____ fresh after a shower.

2. **to blend**

   A. *present*   This <u>tile</u> _____ with the carpeting.

   B. *past*   <u>Peter</u> _____ a protein drink.

   C. *future*   <u>I</u> _____ some herbs for tea.

3. **to scrub**

   A. *present*   <u>Doctors</u> _____ before surgery.

   B. *past*   <u>She</u> _____ her toes with a loofa.

   C. *future*   A <u>janitor</u> _____ the mark from the floor.

4. **to do**

   A. *present*   <u>Dave</u> _____ his dishes every night.

   B. *past*   A <u>friend</u> _____ the actress's make-up.

   C. *future*   <u>She</u> _____ the data sheet tonight.

5. **to laugh**

   A. *present*   <u>Erica</u> _____ frequently.

   B. *past*   <u>Mrs. Lambini</u> _____ softly.

   C. *future*   Your <u>friend</u> _____ at your excuse.

WORKBOOK PAGE 54

Present tense means now.

A.   Directions: Cross out any prepositional phrases. Underline the subject
                   once. Write the present tense of each verb.

1.   <u>Lani</u> (to spend) _____**spends**_____ summers ~~in Kansas~~.

2.   <u>I</u> (to want) _____**want**_____ a rabbit ~~with floppy ears~~.

3.   <u>You</u> (to eat) _____**eat**_____ too fast.

4.   Their two <u>spaniels</u> (to greet) _____**greet**_____ us ~~by the front door~~.

      ๛๛๛๛๛๛๛๛๛๛๛๛๛๛๛๛๛๛๛๛๛

Past tense means past time.

B.   Directions: Cross out any prepositional phrases. Underline the subject
                   once. Write the past tense of each verb.

1.   The <u>driver</u> (to listen) _____**listened**_____ ~~to the radio~~.

2.   Several wild <u>geese</u> (to fly) _____**flew**_____ ~~above our house~~.

3.   My <u>cousin</u> (to buy) _____**bought**_____ squash ~~at a farmer's market~~.

4.   The <u>host</u> (to reach) _____**reached**_____ ~~across the table~~.

      ๛๛๛๛๛๛๛๛๛๛๛๛๛๛๛๛๛๛๛๛๛

Future tense means time yet to occur.

C.   Directions: Cross out any prepositional phrases. Underline the subject
                   once. Write the future tense of each verb.

1.   A <u>doctor</u> (to examine) _____**will examine**_____ your rash.

2.   ~~After dinner~~, <u>I</u> (to send) _____**shall send***_____ you an email.

3.   ~~Before college~~, her <u>brother</u> (to work) _____**will work**_____ ~~with my dad~~.

*Shall is better; however, some accept will.

Present tense means now.

A. Directions: Cross out any prepositional phrases. Underline the subject once. Write the present tense of each verb.

1. Lani (to spend) _____ summers in Kansas.

2. I (to want) _____ a rabbit with floppy ears.

3. You (to eat) _____ too fast.

4. Their two spaniels (to greet) _____ us by the front door.

🐛🐛🐛🐛🐛🐛🐛🐛🐛🐛🐛🐛🐛🐛🐛🐛🐛🐛🐛🐛🐛

Past tense means past time.

B. Directions: Cross out any prepositional phrases. Underline the subject once. Write the past tense of each verb.

1. The driver (to listen) _____ to the radio.

2. Several wild geese (to fly) _____ above our house.

3. My cousin (to buy) _____ squash at a farmer's market.

4. The host (to reach) _____ across the table.

🐛🐛🐛🐛🐛🐛🐛🐛🐛🐛🐛🐛🐛🐛🐛🐛🐛🐛🐛🐛🐛

Future tense means time yet to occur.

C. Directions: Cross out any prepositional phrases. Underline the subject once. Write the future tense of each verb.

1. A doctor (to examine) _____ your rash.

2. After dinner, I (to send) _____ you an email.

3. Before college, her brother (to work) _____ with my dad.

WORKBOOK PAGE 55

VERBS

Tenses

Directions: Cross out any prepositional phrases. Underline the subject once
and the verb or verb phrase twice. Write *present*, *past*, or *future*
to show the verb tense.

to leave

1. _____**past**_____ Joe <u>left</u> ~~in a small blue truck~~.

2. _____**future**_____ <u>Everyone</u> ~~but Carlo~~ <u>will leave</u>.

3. _____**present**_____ <u>He</u> <u>leaves</u> his jacket ~~inside the front closet~~.

to place

1. _____**present**_____ <u>Mom</u> <u>places</u> our lunches ~~near the door~~.

2. _____**past**_____ <u>She</u> <u>placed</u> her drawings ~~beside an art book~~.

3. _____**future**_____ ~~For the wedding~~, a <u>florist</u> <u>will place</u> roses

~~throughout the chapel~~.

to punch

1. _____**past**_____ The <u>boxer</u> <u>punched</u> the bag hard.

2. _____**future**_____ <u>Will</u> <u>you</u> <u>punch</u> holes ~~at the top of this paper~~?

3. _____**present**_____ An <u>attendant</u> <u>punches</u> stars ~~in each ticket~~.

to drive

1. _____**future**_____ <u>Shannon</u> <u>will drive</u> Mrs. Hill ~~to the airport~~.

2. _____**past**_____ The <u>teenager</u> <u>drove</u> ~~through the parking lot~~.

3. _____**present**_____ <u>They</u> <u>drive</u> ~~under a narrow freeway bridge during
heavy traffic~~.

Directions: Cross out any prepositional phrases. Underline the subject once and the verb or verb phrase twice. Write *present*, *past*, or *future* to show the verb tense.

to leave

1. _____ Joe left in a small blue truck.

2. _____ Everyone but Carlo will leave.

3. _____ He leaves his jacket inside the front closet.

to place

1. _____ Mom places our lunches near the door.

2. _____ She placed her drawings beside an art book.

3. _____ For the wedding, a florist will place roses

                                                             throughout the chapel.

to punch

1. _____ The boxer punched the bag hard.

2. _____ Will you punch holes at the top of this paper?

3. _____ An attendant punches stars in each ticket.

to drive

1. _____ Shannon will drive Mrs. Hill to the airport.

2. _____ The teenager drove through the parking lot.

3. _____ They drive under a narrow freeway bridge during heavy traffic.

Name_____ **VERBS**

Date_____ **Tenses**

Directions: Write the correct tense.

1. _____**dumped**_____ We (past tense of *to dump*) water on our fire.

2. _____**veers**_____ This car (present tense of *to veer*) to the left.

3. _____**dripped**_____ Suds (past tense of *to drip*) down his finger.

4. _____**will record**_____ Their aunt (future tense of *to record*) a play for their family to watch later.

5. _____**hauls**_____ Trena (present tense of *to haul*) wood.

6. _____**waded**_____ Birds (past tense of *to wade*) in a lagoon.

7. _____**whisper**_____ They (present tense of *to whisper*) loudly.

8. _____**shall speak**_____ I (future of *to speak*) with the officer in charge.

9 _____**oozed**_____ Glue (past tense of *to ooze*) from the bottle without a cap.

10. _____**live**_____ Six wild parakeets (present tense of *to live*) in that tree.

11. _____**changes**_____ Grandma (present tense of *to change*) her oil.

12. _____**will thank**_____ You (future tense of *to thank*) us later.

13. _____**are**_____ My toes (present tense of *to be*) cold.

14. _____**went**_____ Carlotta (past tense of *to go*) to a car show after her track meet.

15. _____**will dissolve**_____ This gelatin (future tense of *to dissolve*) easily.

16. _____**grows**_____ Only one tomato (present tense of *to grow*) in her garden.

Directions: Write the correct tense.

1. _____   We (past tense of *to dump*) water on our fire.

2. _____   This car (present tense of *to veer*) to the left.

3. _____   Suds (past tense of *to drip*) down his finger.

4. _____   Their aunt (future tense of *to record*) a play for their family to watch later.

5. _____   Trena (present tense of *to haul*) wood.

6. _____   Birds (past tense of *to wade*) in a lagoon.

7. _____   They (present tense of *to whisper*) loudly.

8. _____   I (future of *to speak*) with the officer in charge.

9. _____   Glue (past tense of *to ooze*) from the bottle without a cap.

10. _____   Six wild parakeets (present tense of *to live*) in that tree.

11. _____   Grandma (present tense of *to change*) her oil.

12. _____   You (future tense of *to thank*) us later.

13. _____   My toes (present tense of *to be*) cold.

14. _____   Carlotta (past tense of *to go*) to a car show after her track meet.

15. _____   This gelatin (future tense of *to dissolve*) easily.

16. _____   Only one tomato (present tense of *to grow*) in her garden.

You need to learn the conjugation of *to be*: ***is, am, are, was, were, be,***
being, and ***been***.

Present Tense:

Singular:	**is**	That parking <u>meter</u> <u>is</u> new.
	am	<u>I</u> <u>am</u> a runner.
Plural:	**are**	These <u>pieces</u> of timber <u>are</u> from an old barn.

Past Tense:

Singular:	**was**	My <u>thumb</u> <u>was</u> in a bandage for two days.
Plural:	**were**	Seven <u>secretaries</u> <u>were</u> from an agency.

Future Tense: **be**   <u>I</u> <u>shall</u> <u>be</u> there soon.
                                        The <u>weather</u> <u>will</u> <u>be</u> good tomorrow.

The present participle of *to be* is *being*; the past participle of *to be* is *been*.
These are used with a helping verb or verbs to form more complex tenses.

        Examples: You <u>are being</u> very silly.
                        I <u>have been</u> to Dover twice.

Been can also be used as an auxiliary (helping) verb:

        Example: I <u>must have been doing</u> that wrong.

        ෨෨෨෨෨෨෨෨෨෨෨෨෨෨෨෨෨෨෨

Directions: Write the correct form of *to be* in the blank.

1.   Yesterday, I _____**was**_____ at an art museum in Seattle.

2.   You _____**are**_____ now at the intersection of Bill Road and Bo Street.

3.   I _____**am**_____ here now.

4.   _____**Is**_____ your team in the playoffs today?

5.   Marco and his brother _____**will be**_____ here next month.

6.   Last week, all of the writers _____**were**_____ in a meeting.

7.   They _____**are**_____ currently in the market for a new home.

120

You need to learn the conjugation of *to be*: ***is, am, are, was, were, be, being,*** and ***been***.

Present Tense:
Singular:	**is**	That parking <u>meter</u> <u>is</u> new.
	am	<u>I</u> <u>am</u> a runner.
Plural:	**are**	These <u>pieces</u> of timber <u>are</u> from an old barn.

Past Tense:
Singular:	**was**	My <u>thumb</u> <u>was</u> in a bandage for two days.
Plural:	**were**	Seven <u>secretaries</u> <u>were</u> from an agency.

Future Tense: **be**

<u>I</u> <u>shall be</u> there soon.
The <u>weather</u> <u>will be</u> good tomorrow.

The present participle of *to be* is *being*; the past participle of *to be* is *been*. These are used with a helping verb or verbs to form more complex tenses.

Examples: You <u>are being</u> very silly.
I <u>have been</u> to Dover twice.

Been can also be used as an auxiliary (helping) verb:

Example: I <u>must have been doing</u> that wrong.

ขงขงขงขงขงขงขงขงขงขงขงขงขงขง

Directions: Write the correct form of *to be* in the blank.

1. Yesterday, I _____ at an art museum in Seattle.

2. You _____ now at the intersection of Bill Road and Bo Street.

3. I _____ here now.

4. _____ your team in the playoffs today?

5. Marco and his brother _____ here next month.

6. Last week, all of the writers _____ in a meeting.

7. They _____ currently in the market for a new home.

TO THE TEACHER:

Students need to **review linking verbs** in order to understand proper usage of adverbs.

> He **feels** strange.

> He **acts** strangely.

> Both of these sentences are correct. Because *feels* is a linking verb in the first sentence, we place the adjective, *strange*, after it. *Acts*, however, is an action verb; it requires an adverb that tells *how*. Saying or writing *He acts strange* is wrong. *Strange* is an adjective; we need an adverb that tells *how* he acts. The adverb is *strangely.*

Be sure that your students memorize these linking verbs. Students who have mastered this list can focus more easily on concepts.

Linking Verbs:

to feel	to smell	to grow	to stay
to taste	to seem	to remain	to become
to look	to sound	to appear	to be (is, am, are, was, were, be, being, been)

After a linking verb, one uses an adjective, not an adverb.

> Example: She is sad.   (That is why we don't say: *She is sadly.*)

A problem arises because ***some*** of the linking verbs can be used also as action verbs.

> Example: I **look** tired.

Here, *look* is a linking verb. **Have students use the technique of replacing any possible linking verbs with a form of *to be*. If this can be done without changing the meaning of the sentence, the verb is usually linking.**

>   *am*
> Example: I **look** tired.

Look at this next sentence. Fortunately, most students can see that the verb, though on the linking verb list, is actually an action verb here.

Example: I **looked** for my missing sock.

If you use the technique of replacing the verb with an appropriate form of *to be*, it will be helpful and often humorous.

am
Example: I **looked** for my missing sock.

Students must understand that a linking verb must connect a subject

with an adjective that describes the subject (predicate adjective) **or a**

noun that means the same as the subject (predicate nominative). At this

point, the terms aren't as important as the concept. (Predicate nominatives will be taught in

the noun unit.)

Example: She **remained** in the garage.

Continue having students delete prepositional phrases from the sentence. The sentence above is an exception to using the replacement technique.

was
Example: She **remained** ~~in the garage~~.

You can say: *She was in the garage.* Therefore, students may believe that remained is used as a linking verb here. **It is not!**

In the garage is a prepositional phrase; we delete it from the sentence. Therefore, the only words remaining in the sentence are: *She remained.* Students need to understand that a linking verb must have a word (or words) that links back to the subject. Otherwise, it can't *link* the subject with anything. This is a difficult concept. Fortunately, it doesn't appear often.

Important Note: The following pages should help students see the difference between linking verbs and action verbs. First, be sure that your students have memorized their linking verbs. (It makes the process easier.) Then, encourage students to use the replacement technique. You are giving them a tool that can be used for proper usage throughout their lives.

Linking Verbs

Action verbs do just as the name states; they show action.

Linking verbs do not show action; they usually make a statement.

Linking Verbs:

to feel	to smell	to grow	to stay
to taste	to seem	to remain	to become
to look	to sound	to appear	to be (is, am, are, was, were, be, being, been)

Some verbs can be used as **either** a linking **verb or** an action verb. If you aren't sure, do this:

A.   First, see if the verb is on the list. If it isn't on the list, do **not** mark it as linking.

> Example: Chessa <u>shouted</u> to her friends.
>
> *Shouted* is not on the linking verb list.

B.   If the verb is on the list, try the technique of replacing it with a form of *to be*. (*Is, am, are, was,* or *were* usually works!) If this can be done *without changing the meaning of the sentence,* the verb is usually linking.

> Example: This pear <u>tastes</u> bitter.

To taste is on the list. Now, place a form of *to be* above *tastes*.

>   **is**
> Example: This pear <u>tastes</u> bitter.

Replacing *tastes* with *is* does not change the meaning of the sentence. Now, look to see if *tastes* links *pear* with *bitter*. We can say **bitter pear**. *Tastes* is a linking verb here.

Try this process with the next sentence:

Example: My dad always <u>tastes</u> his homemade soup.

To taste is on the list. Now, place a form of *to be* above *tastes*.

is
Example: My dad always <u>tastes</u> his homemade soup.
Replacing *tastes* with *is* definitely changes the meaning of the sentence. *Tastes* here shows action; it is **not** a linking verb.

This process should help you to determine if a verb is an action verb or a linking verb.

This is important because **after a linking verb**, you might use an adjective. This adjective will be a describing word.

He is a **slow** runner.   (adjective)
The runner is **slow**.   (adjective)

You add **ly** to *slow* to make it an adverb.

He runs **slowly**.   (adverb telling **how** he runs)

	Adjective	**Adverb**
Examples:	glad	gladly
	happy	happily
	certain	certainly
	legal	legally

Some adverbs that tell how do not add **ly**.

Examples:	fast	He is a **fast** runner.	(adjective)
		He runs **fast**.	(adverb)
	hard	I am a **hard** hitter.	(adjective)
		I hit the ball **hard**.	(adverb)

If you aren't sure if an adjective has a corresponding adverb form, use the **dictionary**.

Examples:	pretty	prettily
	ugly	ugily

However, for some words such as *silky* no adverb is given.

125

Name_____

WORKBOOK PAGE 60

Date_____

VERBS

Reviewing Linking Verbs

Directions: Write **L** in the space if the verb is on the linking verb list.

1. _____   to stop

2. __L__   to become

3. __L__   to sound

4. _____   to eat

5. __L__   to taste

6. __L__   to grow

7. _____   to go

8. __L__   to be

9. _____   to think

10. __L__   to feel

11. __L__   to seem

12. __L__   to stay

13. _____   to watch

14. __L__   to look

15. __L__   to appear

16. _____   to break

17. _____   to grab

18. __L__   to remain

126

Name_____   **VERBS**

Date_____   **Reviewing Linking**
                                                      Verbs

Directions: Write **L** in the space if the verb is on the linking verb list.

1. _____   to stop

2. _____   to become

3. _____   to sound

4. _____   to eat

5. _____   to taste

6. _____   to grow

7. _____   to go

8. _____   to be

9. _____   to think

10. _____   to feel

11. _____   to seem

12. _____   to stay

13. _____   to watch

14. _____   to look

15. _____   to appear

16. _____   to break

17. _____   to grab

18. _____   to remain

<u>**Note:**</u> **You may wish to require students to write a form of *to be* above each verb.**
Some verbs can be used **either** as a linking verb **or** as an action verb. If you
aren't sure, do the steps you practiced earlier:

    1.   Think about your list of linking verbs. Is the verb on that list?
        If it is not on the list, don't mark it as linking.

    2.   If the verb is on the linking verb list, write a form of *to be*
        above the verb. *Is, am, are, was,* or *were* usually works well.

    3.   Read the sentence, inserting the form of *to be*. If the meaning
        of the sentence is not changed, the verb usually is linking.

Examples: ____ We <u>listened</u> carefully. *Listened* is not on the list.
                  is
          L This shirt <u>feels</u> damp. *To feel* is on the list. Place a
                                       form of *to be* above it.
                    was
          ____ The baby <u>grew</u> rapidly.

To grow is on the list. Place a form of *to be* above it. **The baby was rapidly** makes no sense.
Grew in this sentence is an action verb.

     ॐॐॐॐॐॐॐॐॐॐॐॐॐॐॐॐॐॐ

Directions: Write **L** in the space if the verb is linking. <u>Suggestion:</u> Place a
               form of *to be* above each verb to help determine if the verb is linking.
                was
1. __**L**__ The crowd <u>remained</u> calm.
                are
2. __**L**__ Your answers <u>appear</u> correct.

3. _____ A bolt <u>lay</u> on the floor.   *To lie* is not on the linking verb list.
                were
4. __**L**__ The children <u>grew</u> restless.
                is
5. __**L**__ This fabric <u>looks</u> wrinkled.
                were
6. __**L**__ Your buzzers <u>sounded</u> loud.

7. _____ The gardener <u>smelled</u> the rose. *To smell* is on the linking verb list, but it is
                                             not used as a linking verb in this sentence.
                is
8. __**L**__ Her grandfather <u>seems</u> nice.

128

Some verbs can be used **either** as a linking verb **or** as an action verb. If you aren't sure, do the steps you practiced earlier:

1. Think about your list of linking verbs. Is the verb on that list? If it is not on the list, don't mark it as linking.

2. If the verb is on the linking verb list, write a form of *to be* above the verb. *Is, am, are, was,* or *were* usually works well.

3. Read the sentence, inserting the form of *to be*. If the meaning of the sentence is not changed, the verb usually is linking.

Examples: ____ We <u>listened</u> carefully.   *Listened* is not on the list.
                   is
              L This shirt <u>feels</u> damp.   *To feel* is on the list. Place a
                                                      form of *to be* above it.
                     was
              ____ The baby <u>grew</u> rapidly.

To grow is on the list. Place a form of *to be* above it. **The baby was rapidly** makes no sense.
Grew in this sentence is an action verb.

ৰ৾ৰ৾ৰ৾ৰ৾ৰ৾ৰ৾ৰ৾ৰ৾ৰ৾ৰ৾ৰ৾ৰ৾ৰ৾ৰ৾ৰ৾ৰ৾ৰ৾ৰ৾ৰ৾

Directions: Write **L** in the space if the verb is linking. <u>Suggestion</u>:   Place a form of *to be* above each verb to help determine if the verb is linking.

1. _____ The crowd <u>remained</u> calm.

2. _____ Your answers <u>appear</u> correct.

3. _____ A bolt <u>lay</u> on the floor.

4. _____ The children <u>grew</u> restless.

5. _____ This fabric <u>looks</u> wrinkled.

6. _____ Your buzzers <u>sounded</u> loud.

7. _____ The gardener <u>smelled</u> the rose.

8. _____ Her grandfather <u>seems</u> nice.

Name_____ **VERBS**

Date_____ **Reviewing Linking Verbs**

Directions: Delete prepositional phrases. Underline the subject once.
Write **L** in the space if the verb is linking.

Examples: _____ We <u>talked</u> together. *Talked* is not on the list.

is
__L__ She <u>seems</u> upset. *To seem* is on the list. Place a form of *to be* above it.

was
_____ A <u>clown</u> <u>appeared</u> suddenly.
To appear is on the list. Place a form of *to be* above it. **A clown was suddenly** makes no sense. *Appeared* in this sentence is not a linking verb.

was
1. __L__ The siren <u>sounded</u> shrill.
is
2. __L__ He <u>feels</u> slightly ill after a race.
is
3. __L__ Broccoli <u>tastes</u> good.
are
4. __L__ Our horses <u>seem</u> energetic today.
was
5. __L__ Their sister <u>appeared</u> nervous.

6. _____ Tate <u>tasted</u> the noodles.

7. _____ Leah <u>removed</u> the top of the paint can.
are
8. __L__ My eyes in that picture <u>look</u> odd.
was
9. __L__ A bellman <u>became</u> confused about the lady's luggage.
were
10. __L__ Those barbecued ribs <u>smelled</u> delicious.

11. __L__ I <u>am</u> very sleepy.

12. _____ Chase <u>washed</u> suds off his hands.
was
13. __L__ The weather <u>stayed</u> cold until April.

14. _____ During the dance, dessert <u>remained</u> ~~on the tables for two hours~~*.

130 *In deleting the prepositional phrases after the verb, there is nothing with which to link the verb.*

Name_____ **VERBS**

Date_____ **Reviewing Linking Verbs**

Directions: Delete any prepositional phrases. Underline the subject once.
Write **L** in the space if the verb is linking.

Examples: ____   We <u>talked</u> together.   *Talked* is not on the list.
                          is
                    L   <u>She</u> <u>seems</u> upset.   *To seem* is on the list. Place a
                                                                    form of *to be* above it.
                                    was
                    ____   A <u>clown</u> <u>appeared</u> suddenly.

To appear is on the list. Place a form of *to be* above it. ***A clown
was suddenly*** makes no sense. *Appeared* in this sentence is
not a linking verb.

1. _____   The siren <u>sounded</u> shrill.

2. _____   He <u>feels</u> slightly ill after a race.

3. _____   Broccoli <u>tastes</u> good.

4. _____   Our horses <u>seem</u> energetic today.

5. _____   Their sister <u>appeared</u> nervous.

6. _____   Tate <u>tasted</u> the noodles.

7. _____   Leah <u>removed</u> the top of the paint can.

8. _____   My eyes in that picture <u>look</u> odd.

9. _____   A bellman <u>became</u> confused about the lady's luggage.

10. _____   Those barbecued ribs <u>smelled</u> delicious.

11. _____   I <u>am</u> very sleepy.

12. _____   Chase <u>washed</u> suds off his hands.

13. _____   The weather <u>stayed</u> cold until April.

14. _____   During the dance, dessert <u>remained</u> on the table for two hours.

131

LINKING VERBS

Predicate Adjectives:

Do you remember that a linking verb actually joins or links the subject of the sentence with another word? Often, the word linked to the subject is an adjective, a describing word.

The <u>complete predicate</u> of a sentence **begins with the verb** and usually goes to the end of a sentence.

Example: Kami's stew **<u>tastes</u> salty**.

My cousin **<u>runs</u> fast in relay races**.

If the sentence is **interrogative** (a question), change the sentence to a statement before determining the complete predicate.

Example: Is this chicken spicy?

This chicken **<u>is</u> spicy**.   *Is spicy* is the complete predicate.

A **predicate adjective** (P.A.) is a describing word that happens **after the verb** and goes back to **describe the subject** of a sentence. Look at the last sentence.

P.A.
This <u>chicken</u> <u>is</u> spicy.

Spicy occurs after the verb (in the predicate). *Spicy* goes back to describe the subject, *chicken*. You can say, ***spicy chicken***. Spicy is called a predicate adjective. We label a predicate adjective with the letters, <u>P.A.</u>

<u>For a word to be a predicate adjective, it must:</u>
1. <u>Be in a sentence containing a **linking verb**</u>.
2. <u>Be in the **predicate** (after the verb)</u>.
3. **<u>Describe the subject</u>** of the sentence.

P.A.
Examples: Your <u>decorations</u> <u>look</u> good.   *good decorations*

P.A.
~~After playing in the mud~~, my <u>dogs</u> <u>were</u> dirty.   *dirty dogs*

132

Note that we shall continue to cross out prepositional phrases. *A predicate adjective won't be in a prepositional phrase.*

Be sure to follow the rules for finding a predicate adjective. <u>First, look to see if the verb is on your linking verb list</u>. Read the following sentence.

Before the prom, the young man gave a pink corsage to his date.

<u>Find the subject and the verb</u>. Start by deleting prepositional phrases.

~~Before the prom,~~ the young <u>man</u> <u>gave</u> a pink corsage ~~to his date~~.

Note that the verb is *gave*.

    a.   *Gave* is not on the linking verb list.

    b.   Therefore, *pink* can't possibly be a predicate adjective.

    c.   You can also see that *pink* describes *corsage*, not the *man*.

Compound Predicate Adjectives:

More than one predicate adjective may appear in a sentence.

                                                P.A.   P.A.

Examples: Your <u>hair</u> <u>seems</u> soft and shiny.   *soft hair*
                                                                   shiny hair

                                                P.A.   P.A.

             Chan's <u>fingers</u> <u>are</u> long and slender.   *long fingers*
                                                                slender fingers

ৡৡৡৡৡৡৡৡৡৡৡৡৡৡৡৡৡৡৡৡৡ

Remember: To check if the verb is linking, insert a form of to be for the verb. If you can do so and not change the meaning of the sentence, the verb generally will be a linking verb.

                                   was
His <u>decision</u> <u>remained</u> final.

Name_____   **LINKING VERBS**

Date_____   **Predicate Adjectives**

Note: In Part B, you may wish to have your students write the predicate adjective and the subject it modifies after the sentence. For example, #1 would state *correct directions.*

A.   Directions: Look at the verb in the sentence. Place an **X** in the blank of the sentence that has a linking verb.

Remember: Write *is, am, are, was,* or *were* above the verb to help you.

are
1.   **X**   You <u>look</u> relaxed.

____   My friend <u>looks</u> for caves.

2.   ____   Marla <u>tasted</u> her soup.

is
X   This frosting <u>tastes</u> sugary.

was
3.   **X**   I <u>grew</u> excited about that.

____   A cactus <u>will grow</u> there.

will be
4.   **X**   She <u>will remain</u> silent.

____   The captain <u>remained</u> on board.

ఴఴఴఴఴఴఴఴఴఴఴఴఴఴఴఴఴఴఴఴ

B.   Directions: Cross out any prepositional phrases. Underline the subject once and the verb or verb phrase twice. Label any predicate adjective – **P.A.**

                                 P.A.
1.   His <u>directions</u> <u>were</u> correct.

                                 P.A.
2.   These knife <u>blades</u> <u>seem</u> blunt.

                                 P.A.
3.   The garage <u>cabinets</u> <u>are</u> too wide.

                                 P.A.
4.   One <u>house</u> <s>on Willow Lane</s> <u>is</u> expensive.

                                 P.A.
5.   This <u>pasta</u> <u>tastes</u> very stale.

                                 P.A.
6.   Their <u>cellar</u> <u>smells</u> musty.

                                 P.A.
7.   <u>You</u> <u>appear</u> happy <s>about your decision</s>.

                                 P.A.
8.   <u>Many</u> <s>of the students</s> <u>remained</u> noisy <s>after the bell</s>.

                                 P.A.
9.   These floral coffee <u>cups</u> <u>will look</u> unusual <s>beside checked plates</s>.

                                 P.A.
10.   Their <u>grandparents</u> <u>become</u> energetic <s>after exercise class</s>.

                                 P.A.
11.   Her new <u>sunglasses</u> <u>are</u> plastic <s>with rhinestones</s>.

134

Name_____ **LINKING VERBS**

Date_____ **Predicate Adjectives**

A. Directions: Look at the verb in the sentence. Place an **X** in the blank of
                   the sentence that has a linking verb.

Remember: Write *is, am, are, was,* or *were* above the verb to help you.

1. ____   You <u>look</u> relaxed.   3. ____   I <u>grew</u> excited about that.

   ____   My friend <u>looks</u> for caves.   ____   A cactus <u>will grow</u> there.

2. ____   Marla <u>tasted</u> her soup.   4. ____   She <u>will remain</u> silent.

   ____   This frosting <u>tastes</u> sugary.   ____   The captain <u>remained</u> on
                                                    board.

෴෴෴෴෴෴෴෴෴෴෴෴෴෴෴෴෴෴෴෴෴෴

B. Directions: Cross out any prepositional phrases. Underline the subject
                   once and the verb or verb phrase twice. Label any predicate
                   adjective – **P.A.**

1. His directions were correct.

2. These knife blades seem blunt.

3. The garage cabinets are too wide.

4. One house on Willow Lane is expensive.

5. This pasta tastes very stale.

6. Their cellar smells musty.

7. You appear happy about your decision.

8. Many of the students remained noisy after the bell.

9. These floral coffee cups will look unusual beside checked plates.

10. Their grandparents become energetic after exercise class.

11. Her new sunglasses are plastic with rhinestones.

TO THE TEACHER:

Subject-Verb Agreement

Subject-verb agreement (singular) is explained on the following page. Although I have always considered this concept easy, I have spoken with eighth grade teachers who claim this is one of the most difficult concepts for their students. At this level, we must **emphasize** correct subject-verb agreement.

Subject-Verb Agreement

To understand this concept, you need to understand the difference between singular and plural.

Singular means one.   Example: That **dog** sneezes.   (one dog)

ঔ⤳ঔ⤳ঔ⤳ঔ⤳ঔ⤳ঔ⤳ঔ⤳ঔ⤳ঔ⤳ঔ⤳ঔ⤳ঔ⤳ঔ⤳ঔ⤳ঔ⤳ঔ⤳

If the subject of a sentence is singular (only one), the verb must be singular.

Most verbs simply add _s_ (or _es_) to the verb in present tense (present time).
Examples: My <u>gerbil</u> run**s**.   (one gerbil)

Mr. Lua teach**es** at a college.   (one man)

The pronouns, _I_ and _you_, will not add _s_.   I **like** carrots. You **like** carrots.

ঔ⤳ঔ⤳ঔ⤳ঔ⤳ঔ⤳ঔ⤳ঔ⤳ঔ⤳ঔ⤳ঔ⤳ঔ⤳ঔ⤳ঔ⤳ঔ⤳ঔ⤳ঔ⤳

English can be confusing. Some irregular verbs have their own patterns for forming the present tense. One that is used frequently is _to be:_
Examples: I **am** in training.

ঔ⤳Note that _am_ is used with _I_.)

One <u>woman</u> **is** in training.

ঔ⤳Note a singular form of _to be_: **is**.

You **are** the first to finish.

ঔ⤳Note that **are** is used with **you**.

<u>Manny</u> and <u>Dakota</u> **are** quiet.   They **are** quiet.

ঔ⤳Note that **are** is used with a plural subject.

Remember: **When using a singular subject, most verbs simply add <u>s</u> (or <u>es</u>) to the verb in the present tense (present time).**

Examples: A <u>firefly</u> glow**s**.

<u>He</u> watch**es** baseball on television.

However, the pronouns, *you* and *I,* will not add *s*.   <u>I</u> want a video. <u>You</u> want a video.

Remember: **Some irregular verbs have their own patterns for forming the present tense. One used frequently is *to be*.**

Examples: <u>I</u> **am** a nurse.
That football <u>player</u> **is** ~~in training~~.
<u>You</u> **are** angry.

ৡৡৡৡৡৡৡৡৡৡৡৡৡৡৡৡৡৡৡৡৡৡৡ

Directions: Delete prepositional phrases. Underline the subject once. Place two lines under the verb that agrees with the subject.

1.   A <u>panther</u> (run, **<u>runs</u>**) fast.

2.   <u>I</u> (**<u>swish</u>**, swishes) with mouthwash.

3.   The <u>child</u> ~~on the skates~~ (tie, **<u>ties</u>**) her shoestrings ~~by herself~~.

4.   <u>She</u> (wash, **<u>washes</u>**) her motorcycle ~~before each ride~~.

5.   <u>I</u> (**<u>am</u>**, is) the owner ~~of a new baby lamb~~.

6.   One <u>lady</u> ~~in the fabric store~~ (**<u>makes</u>**, make) pillows.

7.   This <u>daisy</u> ~~with orange petals~~ (close, **<u>closes</u>**) ~~at night~~.

8.   Their <u>dog</u> (wear, **<u>wears</u>**) a ribbon ~~atop her head~~.

9.   <u>You</u> (is, **<u>are</u>**) my best buddy.

10. One tennis <u>player</u> (**<u>wins</u>**, win) many trophies ~~for his team~~.

11. <u>Mindy</u> (fold, **<u>folds</u>**) clothes ~~at a laundry~~ ~~after school~~.

138

Name_____   **VERBS**

Date_____   **Subject-Verb Agreement**

Remember: **When using a singular subject, most verbs simply add s̲ (or e̲s̲) to the verb in the present tense (present time).**

        Examples: A firefly glow**s**.

                        H̲e̲ watch**es** baseball on television.

However, the pronouns, *you* and *I*, will not add s.   I̲ want a video. Y̲o̲u̲ want a video.

Remember: **Some irregular verbs have their own patterns for forming the present tense. One used frequently is *to be*.**

             Examples: I̲ **am** a nurse.
                            That football player̲ **is** ~~in training~~.
                            Y̲o̲u̲ **are** angry.

🙖🙖🙖🙖🙖🙖🙖🙖🙖🙖🙖🙖🙖🙖🙖🙖🙖🙖🙖🙖

Directions: Delete prepositional phrases. Underline the subject once. Place two lines under the verb that agrees with the subject.

1.   A panther (run, runs) fast.

2.   I (swish, swishes) with mouthwash.

3.   The child on the skates (tie, ties) her shoestrings by herself.

4.   She (wash, washes) her motorcycle before each ride.

5.   I (am, is) the owner of a new baby lamb.

6.   One lady in the fabric store (makes, make) pillows.

7.   This daisy with orange petals (close, closes) at night.

8.   Their dog (wear, wears) a ribbon atop her head.

9.   You (is, are) my best buddy.

10.   One tennis player (wins, win) many trophies for his team.

11.   Mindy (fold, folds) clothes at a laundry after school.

139

TO THE TEACHER:

Subject-Verb Agreement

In the following lesson, students will review singular subject – verb agreement and learn about subject – verb agreement with plural nouns. Students will be provided a follow-up worksheet using both singular and plural subjects, which will help them to understand this concept.

I am including the teaching of a compound subject using *or*. You may want to teach the concept. However, some students may become overwhelmed by the additional information if I place yet another concept in the next lesson.

If a compound subject (two or more) is joined by <u>or</u>, follow these rules:

- If the subject closer to the verb is singular, add <u>s</u> (or <u>es</u>) to most verbs.
    Example: His <u>sisters</u> or **Mark** <u>goes</u> sailing.

    If the closer subject used is singular with a form of *to be*, use <u>is</u> for present tense and <u>was</u> for past tense.
    Example: Two <u>balls</u> or a <u>bat</u> <u>is</u> in the bag.
    Two <u>balls</u> or a <u>bat</u> <u>was</u> in the bag.

- If the subject closer to the verb is plural, do not add <u>s</u> (or <u>es</u>) to the verb.
    Example: <u>Mark</u> or his **sisters** <u>go</u> sailing.

    With a form of *to be*, if the closer subject is plural, use <u>are</u> for present tense and <u>were</u> for past tense.
    Example: A bat or two <u>balls</u> <u>are</u> in the bag.
    A bat or two <u>balls</u> <u>were</u> in the bag.

Subject-Verb Agreement with Singular Subjects

This is material that you have learned; however, a review will enhance learning.

Present Tense (time):

If the subject of a sentence is singular (one), the verb must be singular.

Add **s** (or **es**) to most verbs.

> Example: That <u>dog</u> **sneezes**.   (one dog)

The pronouns, **I** and **you**, will **not add s**.

> Examples: <u>I</u> **pick** berries in the summer.   <u>You</u> **pick** berries in the summer.

Some irregular verbs such as *to be*, change forms. (With the pronoun, **you**, *are* is

used.)   Examples: <u>I</u> **am** an animal lover.

> This <u>wand</u> **is** made of metal. (one wand)
>
> <u>You</u> **are** smart!

ళ్ళళ్ళళ్ళళ్ళళ్ళళ్ళళ్ళళ్ళళ్ళళ్ళళ్ళళ్ళ

Subject-Verb Agreement with Plural Subjects

Present Tense (time):

If the subject of a sentence is plural (more than one), the verb must be plural.

Do **NOT** add **s** (or **es**).

> Examples: Those <u>dogs</u> **bark** constantly.   (more than one dog)
>
> Some <u>riders</u> **leave** the horse trail. (more than one rider)

Some irregular verbs such as *to be* change forms.

> Example: Several <u>seashells</u> **are** very pretty.

A **compound subject** joined by **and** requires that the verb **not** add the **s** (or **es**),

unless it is a special verb that follows its own pattern.

> Examples: <u>Beth</u> and <u>Tim</u> **go** to Aspen in the winter.
> compound subject
>
> After sundown, <u>Tess</u> and <u>I</u> **play** hide-and-seek.
> compound subject

141

When using a singular subject, most verbs simply add <u>s</u> (or <u>es</u>) to the verb in present tense (present time).

Example: My <u>sister</u> **uses** gel ~~on her hair~~.

<u>However, the pronouns, *I* and *you*, will not add *s*.</u>   I **use** gel.   You **use** gel.

Remember: Some irregular verbs have their own patterns for forming the present tense. One used frequently is *to be*:   <u>She</u> **is** a nurses' helper.

When using a plural subject, most verbs won't end in <u>s</u> (or <u>es</u>) in present tense.
Example: Some <u>teams</u> **win** often.

ॐॐॐॐॐॐॐॐॐॐॐॐॐॐॐॐॐॐ

Directions: Delete prepositional phrases. Underline the subject once. Place two lines under the verb that agrees with the subject.

1. Some fifth grade <u>students</u> (makes, **make**) beaded bracelets.

2. <u>Chessa</u> (mix, **mixes**) ice cream ~~with applesauce~~.

3. <u>He</u> and his <u>friends</u> (**sing**, sings) ~~without guitars~~.

4. That <u>photographer</u> (take, **takes**) pictures ~~after dark~~.

5. The <u>lady</u> ~~on stage~~ (model, **models**) ~~for a clothing store~~.

6.   My <u>uncle</u> (**butters**, butter) toast ~~on both sides~~.

7. <u>Jack</u> and <u>she</u> (is, **are**) advisors ~~to the president~~.

8. <u>Loni</u> (kiss, **kisses**) her new baby ~~under his toes~~.

9. Several <u>dogs</u> (<u>chase</u>, chases) balls ~~in the park~~ each Sunday.

10. That <u>gymnast</u> (perform, **performs**) ~~during half-time shows~~.

11. <u>Mom</u> and <u>Dad</u> (**play**, plays) soccer ~~on a parents' team~~.

12. <u>Tailors</u> ~~at that men's shop~~ (alters, **alter**) cuffs.

13. <u>One</u> ~~of the newswomen~~ (talk, **talks**) ~~about stocks~~.
142

VERBS

Subject-Verb Agreement

When using a singular subject, most verbs simply add s (or es) to the verb in present tense (present time).

Example: My <u>sister</u> **uses** gel ~~on her hair~~.

However, the pronoun, I, will not add s.   <u>I</u> **use** gel.   <u>You</u> **use** gel.

Remember: Some irregular verbs have their own patterns for forming the present tense. One used frequently is *to be*:   <u>She</u> **is** a nurses' helper.

When using a plural subject, most verbs won't end in s (or es) in present tense.

Example: Some <u>teams</u> **win** often.

ॐॐॐॐॐॐॐॐॐॐॐॐॐॐॐॐॐॐॐॐ

Directions: Delete prepositional phrases. Underline the subject once. Place two lines under the verb that agrees with the subject.

1.   Some fifth grade students (makes, make) beaded bracelets.

2.   Chessa (mix, mixes) ice cream with applesauce.

3.   He and his friends (sing, sings) without guitars.

4.   That photographer (take, takes) pictures after dark.

5.   The lady on stage (model, models) for a clothing store.

6.   My uncle (butters, butter) toast on both sides.

7.   Jack and she (is, are) advisors to the president.

8.   Loni (kiss, kisses) her new baby under his toes.

9.   Several dogs (chase, chases) balls in the park each Sunday.

10.   That gymnast (perform, performs) during half-time shows.

11.   Mom and Dad (play, plays) soccer on a parents' team.

12.   Tailors at that men's shop (alters, alter) cuffs.

13.   One of the newswomen (talk, talks) about stocks.

Name_____

VERBS

Date_____

Don't and Doesn't

Note: Students need to understand that they may actually use these words improperly due to familiarity. The problem is that improper usage *sounds* correct to them. Teach this very carefully. In choosing the correct word, it may be helpful to help students to separate each contraction into two words. I recommend that you do this worksheet orally with your students. Another worksheet ensues for student practive. However, I suggest that you wait until tomorrow to review and do the next lesson concerning *don't* and *doesn't*.

Some people have a problem with using doesn't and don't.

Use does (doesn't) with *he, she*, and other *singular* subjects.

        Examples: He doesn't like to play pool.
                       She doesn't want to stand on her head.
                       That giraffe doesn't have many spots.

Use do (don't) with the pronouns, *I* and *you*.   I don't chase bunnies.
                                         You don't seem to understand.

Use do (don't) with plural subjects.   Some athletes don't eat sweets.
                                    Peter and Leah don't carry their lunch.
                                    We don't need more straws.

🐎🐎🐎🐎🐎🐎🐎🐎🐎🐎🐎🐎🐎🐎🐎🐎🐎🐎🐎🐎

A.   Directions: Underline the subject once. Circle the correct word.
The correct word is boldfaced.

1. He (**doesn't**, don't) shop here.

2. Mom and my aunt (doesn't, **don't**) shop here.

3. My friends (doesn't, **don't**) bother me.

4. She (don't, **doesn't**) bother me.

🐎🐎🐎🐎🐎🐎🐎🐎🐎🐎🐎🐎

B.   Directions: Underline the subject once. Circle the correct word.
1. I (doesn't, **don't**) want any gravy.

2. We (doesn't, **don't**) gossip.

3. That seal (don't, **doesn't**) sleep often.

4. My one shoe (don't, **doesn't**) fit properly.

5. Your drink (**doesn't**, don't) look cold.

6. My doctor (don't, **doesn't**) take credit cards.

7. Marco and his sister (doesn't, **don't**) hike there.

Date_____

Some people have a problem with using <u>doesn't</u> and <u>don't</u>.

Use <u>does</u> (<u>doesn't</u>) with *he, she,* and other *singular* subjects.

Examples: <u>He</u> <u>does</u>n't like to play pool.
<u>She</u> <u>does</u>n't want to stand on her head.
That <u>giraffe</u> <u>does</u>n't have many spots.

Use <u>do</u> (<u>don't</u>) with the pronouns, *I* and *you*.   <u>I</u> <u>do</u>n't chase bunnies.
<u>You</u> <u>do</u>n't seem to understand.

Use <u>do</u> (<u>don't</u>) with plural subjects.   Some <u>athletes</u> <u>do</u>n't eat sweets.
<u>Peter</u> and <u>Leah</u> <u>do</u>n't carry their lunch.
<u>We</u> <u>do</u>n't need more straws.

∂∂∂∂∂∂∂∂∂∂∂∂∂∂∂∂∂∂∂∂∂

A.   Directions: Underline the subject once. Circle the correct word.

1.   He (doesn't, don't) shop here.

2.   Mom and my aunt (doesn't, don't) shop here.

3.   My friends (doesn't, don't) bother me.

4.   She (don't, doesn't) bother me.

∂∂∂∂∂∂∂∂∂∂∂

B.   Directions: Underline the subject once. Circle the correct word.

1.   I (doesn't, don't) want any gravy.

2.   We (doesn't, don't) gossip.

3.   That seal (don't, doesn't) sleep often.

4.   My one shoe (don't, doesn't) fit properly.

5.   Your drink (doesn't, don't) look cold.

6.   My doctor (don't, doesn't) take credit cards.

7.   Marco and his sister (doesn't, don't) hike there.

Name_____ **VERBS**

Don't and Doesn't

Date_____

Some people have a problem with using <u>doesn't</u> and <u>don't</u>.

Use <u>does</u> (<u>doesn't</u>) with *he, she*, and other *singular* subjects.
     Examples: He <u>does</u>n't dance.
                  She <u>does</u>n't whistle.
                  My grandpa <u>does</u>n't eat spinach.

Use <u>do</u> (<u>don't</u>) with the pronouns, *I* and *you*.   I <u>do</u>n't yell.
                                      You <u>do</u>n't have to reply.

Use <u>do</u> (<u>don't</u>) with plural subjects.   My <u>parents</u> <u>do</u>n't need help.
                             His <u>knees</u> and <u>ankles</u> <u>do</u>n't hurt today.
                             They <u>do</u>n't plant a garden.

A. Directions: Underline the subject once. Circle the correct word. (Be sure to cross out the prepositional phrase in number 12.)

The correct word is boldfaced.

1. That <u>crime</u> (**doesn't**, don't) occur often.

2. <u>I</u> (**don't**, doesn't) want this.

3. <u>He</u> (don't, **doesn't**) remember my name.

4. Her <u>cat</u> and <u>kittens</u> (**don't**, doesn't) go outside.

5. That <u>penguin</u> (don't, **doesn't**) waddle fast.

6. <u>We</u> (doesn't, **don't**) have a pool.

7. Your <u>idea</u> (don't, **doesn't**) sound silly.

8. (**Don't**, Doesn't) <u>clams</u> live long lives?

9. Brian's <u>father</u> (don't, **doesn't**) fish.

10. <u>She</u> usually (don't, **doesn't**) take a day off.

11. The <u>lifeguard</u> (**doesn't**, don't) talk often.

12. <u>One</u> ~~of their friends~~ (**doesn't**, don't) wash his own car.

146

Some people have a problem with using <u>doesn't</u> and <u>don't</u>.

Use <u>does</u> (<u>doesn't</u>) with *he*, *she*, and other *singular* subjects.
      Examples: <u>He</u> <u>doesn't</u> dance.
                  <u>She</u> <u>doesn't</u> whistle.
                  My grandpa <u>does</u>n't eat spinach.

Use <u>do</u> (<u>don't</u>) with the pronouns, *I* and *you*.   <u>I</u> <u>do</u>n't yell.
                                        <u>You</u> <u>do</u>n't have to reply.

Use <u>do</u> (<u>don't</u>) with plural subjects.   My <u>parents</u> <u>do</u>n't need help.
                                    His <u>knees</u> and <u>ankles</u> <u>do</u>n't hurt today.
                                    <u>They</u> <u>do</u>n't plant a garden.

೫-೫-೫-೫-೫-೫-೫-೫-೫-೫-೫-೫-೫-೫-೫-೫-೫-೫-೫-೫

A.   Directions: Underline the subject once. Circle the correct word. (Be sure to cross out the prepositional phrase in number 12.)

1.   That crime (doesn't, don't) occur often.

2.   I (don't, doesn't) want this.

3.   He (don't, doesn't) remember my name.

4.   Her cat and kittens (don't, doesn't) go outside.

5.   That penquin (don't, doesn't) waddle fast.

6.   We (doesn't, don't) have a pool.

7.   Your idea (don't, doesn't) sound silly.

8.   (Don't, Doesn't) clams live long lives?

9.   Brian's father (don't, doesn't) fish.

10.   She usually (don't, doesn't) take a day off.

11.   The lifeguard (doesn't, don't) talk often.

12.   One of their friends (doesn't, don't) wash his own car.

A transitive verb has a direct object.
Remember: A direct object occurs after the verb and receives the action of the verb.
                                          D.O.
          Example: I <u>threw</u> a ball.

A transitive verb has a direct object.   I <u>threw</u> a ball.   *Threw* is a transitive verb here.

It's easy to remember this by using the initials, **D.O.T**.   **D**irect **O**bject = **T**ransitive

If the sentence **does not contain a direct object**, the verb is *intransitive*.

🐚🐚🐚🐚🐚🐚🐚🐚🐚🐚🐚🐚🐚🐚🐚🐚🐚🐚🐚🐚

A. Directions: Underline the subject once and the verb or verb phrase twice.
                            Label the direct object.

	D.O.		D.O.
1.	<u>I</u> <u>spilled</u> my milk.	4.	<u>Rena</u> <u>shipped</u> a package.
	D.O.		D.O.
2.	His <u>mom</u> <u>makes</u> quilts.	5.	<u>Brad</u> <u>plays</u> the trombone.
	D.O.		D.O.
3.	<u>You</u> <u>told</u> the truth.	6.	A <u>waiter</u> <u>took</u> our order.

🐚🐚🐚🐚🐚🐚🐚🐚🐚🐚🐚🐚

B. Directions: Underline the subject once and the verb or verb phrase twice.
                            Label the direct object – **D.O.** If the sentence is transitive, write
                            T in the blank. If the sentence is intransitive, write **I** in the blank.

1. This light <u>bulb</u> no longer <u>works</u>.   _**I**_
                                          D.O.
2. A security <u>guard</u> <u>searched</u> my purse.   _**T**_
                                          D.O.
3. <u>Ms. Yazzie</u> <u>creates</u> beautiful Navajo rugs.   _**T**_
                                    D.O.
4. A <u>sailor</u> <u>checked</u> his email twice.   _**T**_

5. <u>They</u> <u>are</u> **not** <u>going</u> now.   _**I**_
                              D.O.
6. <u>Shawn</u> <u>starts</u> his computer early.   _**T**_

7. Their best <u>friend</u> <u>is</u> a social worker.   _**I**_
                                    D.O.
8.   A <u>salesperson</u> <u>handed</u> us free samples.   _**T**_

A transitive verb has a direct object.
Remember: A direct object occurs after the verb and receives the action of the verb.
                              D.O.
          Example: I <u>threw</u> a ball.

A transitive verb has a direct object.   I <u>threw</u> a ball.   *Threw* is a transitive verb here.

It's easy to remember this by using the initials, **D.O.T.**   **D**irect **O**bject = **T**ransitive

If the sentence **does not contain a direct object**, the verb is *intransitive*.

෯෯෯෯෯෯෯෯෯෯෯෯෯෯෯෯෯෯෯෯෯

A.   Directions: Underline the subject once and the verb or verb phrase twice.
                          Label the direct object.

1.   I spilled my milk.   4.   Rena shipped a package.

2.   His mom makes quilts.   5.   Brad plays the trombone.

3.   You told the truth.   6.   A waiter took our order.

෯෯෯෯෯෯෯෯෯෯෯෯෯

B.   Directions: Underline the subject once and the verb or verb phrase twice.
                          Label the direct object – **D.O.** If the sentence is transitive, write
                          T in the blank. If the sentence is intransitive, write **I** in the blank.

1.   This light bulb no longer works.   _____

2.   A security guard searched my purse.   _____

3.   Ms. Yazzie creates beautiful Navajo rugs.   _____

4.   A sailor checked his email twice.   _____

5.   They are not going now.   _____

6.   Shawn starts his computer early.   _____

7.   Their best friend is a social worker.   _____

8.   A salesperson handed us free samples.   _____

A.   **The Verb, *To Be*:**
   Directions: Fill in the blank with the correct form of the infinitive, *to be*.
1. Right now, I _____**am**_____ here.

2. You _____**are**_____ now correct.

3. He _____**is**_____ always funny.   **Technically, *was* can also be used.**

4. Yesterday, the children _____**were**_____ noisy.

5. Mr. Hanks _____**will be**_____ here tomorrow.
   ಸ಼ಸ಼ಸ಼ಸ಼ಸ಼ಸ಼ಸ಼ಸ಼ಸ಼ಸ಼ಸ಼ಸ಼

B.   **Contractions:**
   Directions: Write the contraction.

1. cannot - ____**can't**_____   6. they are - ____**they're**_____

2. he is - ____**he's**_____   7. where is - ____**where's**_____

3. have not - ____**haven't**_____   8. is not - ____**isn't**_____

4. who is - ____**who's**_____   9. should not - ____**shouldn't**_____

5. did not - ____**didn't**_____   10. he will - ____**he'll**_____
   ಸ಼ಸ಼ಸ಼ಸ಼ಸ಼ಸ಼ಸ಼ಸ಼ಸ಼ಸ಼ಸ಼ಸ಼

C.   **You're/Your, It's/Its, and They're/Their/There:**
   Directions: Circle the correct word.

1. The crafters placed (they're, **their**, there) carved ducks on display.

2. After you paint (you're, **your**) room, you may need a new bedspread.

3. The newly born colt stood on (it's, **its**) wobbly legs.

4. Do you know if (**they're**, their, there) ready for the outing?

5. I want a muffin if (**it's**, its) not moldy.

6. (They're, Their, **There**) may be an election soon.
150

Name_____   **VERBS**

Date_____   **Review**

A. **The Verb, *To Be*:**
    Directions: Fill in the blank with the correct form of the infinitive, *to be*.

1. Right now, I _____ here.

2. You _____ now correct.

3. He _____ always funny.

4. Yesterday, the children _____ noisy.

5. Mr. Hanks _____ here tomorrow.
    ೫ೀ೫ೀ೫ೀ೫ೀ೫ೀ೫ೀ೫ೀ೫ೀ೫ೀ೫ೀ೫ೀ

B. **Contractions:**
    Directions: Write the contraction.

1. cannot - _____   6. they are - _____

2. he is - _____   7. where is - _____

3. have not - _____   8. is not - _____

4. who is - _____   9. should not - _____

5. did not - _____   10. he will - _____
    ೫ೀ೫ೀ೫ೀ೫ೀ೫ೀ೫ೀ೫ೀ೫ೀ೫ೀ೫ೀ೫ೀ

C. **You're/Your, It's/Its, and They're/Their/There:**
    Directions: Circle the correct word.

1. The crafters placed (they're, their, there) carved ducks on display.

2. After you paint (you're, your) room, you may need a new bedspread.

3. The newly born colt stood on (it's, its) wobbly legs.

4. Do you know if (they're, their, there) ready for the outing?

5. I want a muffin if (it's, its) not moldy.

6. (They're, Their, There) may be an election soon.   151

D. **Auxiliary (Helping) Verbs:**

   Directions: Write the 23 helping verbs.

1. **do**	7. **may**	13. **could**	19. **was**
2. **does**	8. **might**	14. **should**	20. **were**
3. **did**	9. **must**	15. **would**	21. **be**
4. **has**	10. **can**	16. **is**	22. **being**
5. **have**	11. **shall**	17. **am**	23. **been**
6. **had**	12. **will**	18. **are**	

෧෧෧෧෧෧෧෧෧෧෧෧෧

E. **Irregular Verbs:**

   Directions: Underline the subject once and the correct verb phrase twice.

1. The <u>boy</u> <u>has</u> (chose, <u>chosen</u>) a striped wallpaper.

2. <u>They</u> <u>might have</u> (went, <u>gone</u>) early.

3. <u>Tim</u> <u>should have</u> (<u>driven</u>, drove) his pick-up truck.

4. Their <u>baby</u> <u>had</u> (<u>lain</u>, laid) quietly.

5. <u>I</u> <u>could have</u> (ran, <u>run</u>) farther.

෧෧෧෧෧෧෧෧෧෧෧෧෧

F. **Subjects, Verbs, and Direct Objects:**

   Directions: Cross out any prepositional phrases. Underline the subject
                subject once and the verb/verb phrase twice. Label any
                direct object – **D.O.**

1. A gum <u>wrapper</u> <u>is lying</u> ~~on the floor~~.
                              D.O.
2. <u>I</u> <u>should have written</u> my message.

3. ~~During a flood~~, those <u>deer</u> <u>must have moved</u> ~~to higher ground~~.
                              D.O.
4. <u>Could</u> <u>you</u> <u>have lost</u> your wallet ~~at the mall~~?

5. The <u>hammer</u> <u>was</u> **not** ~~with the other tools~~.

152

D. **Auxiliary (Helping) Verbs:**
     Directions: Write the 23 helping verbs.

1. d_____   7. m_____   13. c_____   19. w_____

2. d_____   8. m_____   14. s_____   20. w_____

3. d_____   9. m_____   15. w_____   21. b_____

4. h_____   10. c_____   16. i_____   22. b_____

5. h_____   11. s_____   17. a_____   23. b_____

6. h_____   12. w_____   18. a_____

🔀🔀🔀🔀🔀🔀🔀🔀🔀🔀🔀🔀

E. **Irregular Verbs:**
    Directions: Underline the subject once and the correct verb phrase twice.

1. The boy has (chose, chosen) a striped wallpaper.

2. They might have (went, gone) early.

3. Tim should have (driven, drove) his pick-up truck.

4. Their baby had (lain, laid) quietly.

5. I could have (ran, run) farther.

🔀🔀🔀🔀🔀🔀🔀🔀🔀🔀🔀🔀

F. **Subjects, Verbs, and Direct Objects:**
     Directions: Cross out any prepositional phrases. Underline the subject
                  subject once and the verb/verb phrase twice. Label any
                  direct object – **D.O.**

1. A gum wrapper is lying on the floor.

2. I should have written my message.

3. During a flood, those deer must have moved to higher ground.

4. Could you have lost your wallet at the mall?

5. The hammer was not with the other tools.   153

WORKBOOK PAGE 75

Date_____

                        D.O.

6. Will Josh slice the turkey ~~at Thanksgiving~~?

                 D.O.

7. We did**n't** have any coins ~~for a bus ride~~.

                      D.O.

8. Did Neema and you suggest a plan?

                                D.O.

9. One ~~of the bingo players~~ coughed and left the room.

                 D.O.

10. (You) Do **not** close the door.

        ॐॐॐॐॐॐॐॐॐॐॐॐॐ

G. **Sit/Set, Lie/Lay, and Rise/Raise:**

      Directions: Delete any prepositional phrases. Underline the
                      subject once and the verb/verb phrase twice. Label
                      any direct object-**D.O.**

1. I might (sit, set) ~~in the last row~~.

                      D.O.

2. You must have (lay, laid) your paper ~~under your notebook~~.

                   D.O.

3. He (rose, raised) his arm ~~in warning~~.

4. The patient (laid, lay) ~~on a stretcher~~.

                   D.O.

5. Has Sally (set, sat) her umbrella ~~by her front door~~?

        ॐॐॐॐॐॐॐॐॐॐॐॐॐ

H. **Tenses:**

      Directions: Underline the subject once and the verb or verb
                      phrase twice. Write the tense (*present, past,* or *future*).

1. _____**past**_____   He bought sandals yesterday.

2. _____**present**_____   My foot aches.

3. _____**future**_____   Will you finish later?

4. _____**present**_____   Tally dreams often.

5. _____**past**_____   The black Labrador rescued his owner.

6. Will Josh slice the turkey at Thanksgiving?

7. We didn't have any coins for a bus ride.

8. Did Neema and you suggest a plan?

9. One of the bingo players coughed and left the room.

10. Do not close the door.

❧❧❧❧❧❧❧❧❧❧❧❧

G. **Sit/Set, Lie/Lay, and Rise/Raise:**
    Directions: Delete any prepositional phrases. Underline the
                 subject once and the verb/verb phrase twice. Label
                 any direct object-**D.O.**

1. I might (sit, set) in the last row.

2. You must have (lay, laid) your paper under your notebook.

3. He (rose, raised) his arm in warning.

4. The patient (laid, lay) on a stretcher.

5. Has Sally (set, sat) her umbrella by her front door?

❧❧❧❧❧❧❧❧❧❧❧❧

H. **Tenses:**
    Directions: Underline the subject once and the verb or verb
                 phrase twice. Write the tense (*present, past,* or *future*).

1. _____ He bought sandals yesterday.

2. _____ My foot aches.

3. _____ Will you finish later?

4. _____ Tally dreams often.

5. _____ The black Labrador rescued his owner.

Name_____

Date_____

VERBS

Review

<u>Note</u>: Section J, #6 is difficult. Help students to understand that a linking verb must connect the subject with a word after the verb. After deleting the prepositional phrase, there is no word to form the connection.

I. Linking Verbs:

Directions: Write the linking verbs.

1. to **feel**	8. to **remain**	c. **are**
2. to **taste**	9. to **appear**	d. **was**
3. to **look**	10. to **stay**	e. **were**
4. to **smell**	11. to **become**	f. **be**
5. to **seem**	12. to **be**	g. **being**
6. to **sound**	a. **is**	h. **been**
7. to **grow**	b. **am**	

᥈᥈᥈᥈᥈᥈᥈᥈᥈᥈᥈

J. Action Verb or Linking Verb:

Directions: Write **A** if the verb is action; write **L** if the verb is linking.

1. __**A**__ I <u>sneezed</u>.

              is

2. __**L**__ My voice <u>sounds</u> raspy.

3. __**A**__ Our goat <u>bleated</u>.

4. __**A**__ He <u>looked</u> at his map.

              is

5. __**L**__ This apple <u>tastes</u> tart.

6. __**A**__ A cat <u>appeared</u> ~~in the alley~~.

᥈᥈᥈᥈᥈᥈᥈᥈᥈᥈᥈

K. Linking Verbs and Predicate Adjectives:

Directions: Write **L** in the space if the verb is linking. Place a form of
to be above each verb to help determine if the verb is linking.

Remember: Try placing *is, am, are, was,* or *were* in place of the verb. If the meaning of the sentence does not change, the verb is probably linking.

            was

1. __**L**__ She <u>remained</u> quiet.

            are

2. __**L**__ Your ideas <u>sound</u> great.

3. _____ We <u>climbed</u> a tower in Paris.

156

I. Linking Verbs:

Directions: Write the linking verbs.

1. to _____   8.   to _____   c.   _____

2. to _____   9.   to _____   d.   _____

3. to _____   10. to _____   e.   _____

4. to _____   11. to _____   f.   _____

5. to _____   12. to _____   g.   _____

6. to_____   a.   _____   h.   _____

7. to _____   b.   _____

ॐॐॐॐॐॐॐॐॐॐॐॐ

J. Action Verb or Linking Verb?:

Directions: Write **A** if the verb is action; write **L** if the verb is linking.

1. _____   I <u>sneezed</u>.   4. _____   He <u>looked</u> at his map.

2. _____   My voice <u>sounds</u> raspy.   5. _____   This apple <u>tastes</u> tart.

3. _____   Our goat <u>bleated</u>.   6. _____   A cat <u>appeared</u> in the alley.

ॐॐॐॐॐॐॐॐॐॐॐॐ

K. Linking Verbs and Predicate Adjectives:

Directions: Write **L** in the space if the verb is linking. Place a form of *to be*
above each verb to help determine if the verb is linking.

**Remember: Try placing *is, am, are, was,* or *were* in place of the verb. If the meaning
of the sentence does not change, the verb is probably linking.**

1. _____   She <u>remained</u> quiet.

2. _____   Your ideas <u>sound</u> great.

3. _____   We <u>climbed</u> a tower in Paris.

4. _____   That weed <u>grows</u> very rapidly.

                    is
5. __**L**__   Your spiced chicken <u>tastes</u> delicious.

6. _____   Water <u>poured</u> into the gulley.

                    were
7. __**L**__   Those men <u>became</u> business partners.

ঔঔঔঔঔঔঔঔঔঔঔঔ

L. Linking Verbs and Predicate Adjectives:
    Directions: Delete any prepositional phrases. Underline the subject once
                    and the verb twice. Label any predicate adjective – **P.A.**

                                    P.A.
1. That oak <u>chest</u> ~~with white knobs~~ <u>is</u> old.

                            P.A.
2. Your dog's <u>ears</u> <u>seem</u> small ~~for his body size~~.

                            P.A.
3. The <u>corn</u> ~~in those fields~~ <u>looks</u> very dry.

                        P.A.
4. <u>Blueberries</u> <u>taste</u> good ~~on cereal~~.

ঔঔঔঔঔঔঔঔঔঔঔঔ

M. Subject-Verb Agreement:
    Directions: Delete any prepositional phrases. Underline the subject once.
                    Underline the verb or verb phrase that agrees with the subject
                    twice.

1. A <u>mason</u> (<u>places</u>, place) bricks ~~for a wall~~.

2. These <u>dents</u> (looks, <u>look</u>) mild.

3. A <u>shepherd</u> (lead, <u>leads</u>) his sheep.

4. <u>Ham</u> and <u>eggs</u> (<u>are</u>, is) his favorite breakfast.

5. <u>Jim</u> (<u>does</u>(n't), do(n't)) <u>work</u> ~~near the new shopping center~~.

6. Many <u>parents</u> (<u>talk</u>, talks) ~~with school counselors~~.

158

4. _____   That weed <u>grows</u> very rapidly.

5. _____   Your spiced chicken <u>tastes</u> delicious.

6. _____   Water <u>poured</u> into the gulley.

7. _____   Those men <u>became</u> business partners.

ᕮᕮᕮᕮᕮᕮᕮᕮᕮᕮᕮᕮᕮ

L. Linking Verbs and Predicate Adjectives:
   Directions: Delete any prepositional phrases. Underline the subject once
                 and the verb twice. Label any predicate adjective – **P.A.**

1. That oak chest with white knobs is old.

2. Your dog's ears seem small for his body size.

3. The corn in those fields looks very dry.

4. Blueberries taste good on cereal.

ᕮᕮᕮᕮᕮᕮᕮᕮᕮᕮᕮᕮᕮ

M. Subject-Verb Agreement:
   Directions: Delete any prepositional phrases. Underline the subject once.
                 Underline the verb or verb phrase that agrees with the subject
                 twice.

1. A mason (places, place) bricks for a wall.

2. These dents (looks, look) mild.

3. A shepherd (lead, leads) his sheep.

4. Ham and eggs (are, is) his favorite breakfast.

5. Jim (does(n't), do(n't)) work near the new shopping center.

6. Many parents (talk, talks) with school counselor.

Name_____   **VERBS**

WORKBOOK PAGE 78

Date_____   **Review**

Note: In section N, #2, review with students the way to determine if a word after a verb is part of a verb phrase. <u>To sticky</u>: Today, I *sticky* or he *stickies*. Yesterday, I *stickied*. Tomorrow, I *shall sticky*. Obviously, *to sticky* is not an infinitive. *Sticky* is an adjective (predicate adjective) describing the subject, *beans*.

7. Little <u>beads</u> (<u>hang</u>, hangs) ~~from the floral lampshade~~.

8. <u>Kit</u> and <u>Rana</u> (rides, <u>ride</u>) the bus each day.

9. <u>We</u> (<u>deliver</u>, delivers) newspapers ~~on our street~~.

10. <u>One</u> ~~of the baskets~~ (<u>was</u>, were) sold.

11. <u>Clerks</u> ~~at the photo counter~~ (checks, <u>check</u>) pictures.

12. Those <u>volunteers</u> (<u>cover</u>, covers) old tins ~~with fabric~~.

13. The girls' <u>mother</u> (drink, <u>drinks</u>) green tea.

14. <u>He</u> (<u>does</u>[n't]), do[n't]) want a bath.

ॐॐॐॐॐॐॐॐॐॐॐ

N. Transitive and Intransitive Verbs:

Directions: Cross out any prepositional phrases. Underline the subject once and the verb or verb phrase twice. Label any direct object – **D.O.** Write **T** if the verb is transitive; write **I** if the verb is intransitive.

Remember: A transitive verb will have a direct object.

D.O.T. = Direct **O**bject - **T**ransitive

                              D.O.
1. <u>You</u> <u>may grill</u> chicken ~~for dinner~~.   __T__

2. These jelly <u>beans</u> <u>are</u> sticky.   __I__
                    D.O.
3. <u>I</u> <u>collect</u> baseball cards.   __T__

4. A <u>pigeon</u> <u>landed</u> ~~by a fountain~~ ~~in the park~~. __I__
                         D.O.
5. The <u>men</u> ~~at the market~~ <u>sell</u> vegetables.   __T__
                D.O.
6. (<u>You</u>) <u>Dry</u> this sweater ~~on a low setting~~.   __T__

160

7. Little beads (hang, hangs) from the floral lampshade.

8. Kit and Rana (rides, ride) the bus each day.

9. We (deliver, delivers) newspapers on our street.

10. One of the baskets (was, were) sold.

11. Clerks at the photo counter (checks, check) pictures.

12. Those volunteers (cover, covers) old tins with fabric.

13. The girls' mother (drink, drinks) green tea.

14. He (does[n't]), do[n't]) want a bath.

જ્ઞાજ્ઞાજ્ઞાજ્ઞાજ્ઞાજ્ઞાજ્ઞાજ્ઞાજ્ઞાજ્ઞાજ્ઞા

N. Transitive and Intransitive Verbs:
> Directions: Cross out any prepositional phrases. Underline the subject once and the verb or verb phrase twice. Label any direct object – **D.O.** Write **T** if the verb is transitive; write **I** if the verb is intransitive.

Remember: A transitive verb will have a direct object.
D.O.T. = Direct **O**bject - **T**ransitive

1. You may grill chicken for dinner.   _____

2. These jelly beans are sticky.   _____

3. I collect baseball cards.   _____

4. A pigeon landed by a fountain in the park. _____

5. The men at the market sell vegetables.   _____

6. Dry this sweater on a low setting.   _____

IMPORTANT NOTE: You will need to determine how many points you want to assign each item. For example, in Part C, some teachers assign one point per sentence. Others assign two points, one for the subject and one for the verb. Other teachers choose to assign three points for each sentence in this section: one for the subject, one for the correct past participle, and one for the correct verb phrase. This is the reason I recommend that you determine total points for each test.

A.   Directions: Write the contraction.

1. cannot - ___**can't**_____   6. they are - ___**they're**_____

2. he is -___**he's**_____   7. where is - ___**where's**_____

3. have not - ___**haven't**_____   8. is not - ___**isn't**_____

4. who is - ___**who's**_____   9. should not - ___**shouldn't**___

5. did not - ___**didn't**_____   10. he will - ___**he'll**_____

B.   Directions: Circle the correct word.
THE CORRECT WORD IS BOLDFACED.
1.   Do you want (they're, **their**, there) tickets?

2.   I'm not sure that (**you're**, your) on this list.

3.   A little chick ran after (it's, **its**) mother.

4.   Most babies coo at (they're, **their**, there) dads.

5.   (**It's**, Its) good to see you.

6.   (**They're**, Their, There) going to the beach for the weekend.

C.   Directions: Underline the subject once and the correct verb phrase twice.

1. This <u>toy</u> <u>is</u> (broke, <u>broken</u>).

2. <u>Snow</u> <u>had</u> (<u>fallen</u>, fell).

3. <u>She</u> <u>must have</u> (<u>driven</u>, drove) alone.

4. Your <u>shirt</u> <u>is</u> (<u>lying</u>, laying) here.

5. <u>Have</u> <u>you</u> (swam, <u>swum</u>) recently?

162

A.   Directions: Write the contraction.

1. cannot - _____   6. they are - _____

2. he is - _____   7. where is - _____

3. have not - _____   8. is not - _____

4. who is - _____   9. should not - _____

5. did not - _____   10. he will - _____

B.   Directions: Circle the correct word.

1. Do you want (they're, their, there) tickets?

2. I'm not sure that (you're, your) on this list.

3. A little chick ran after (it's, its) mother.

4. Most babies coo at (they're, their, there) dads.

5. (It's, Its) good to see you.

6. (They're, Their, There) going to the beach for the weekend.

C.   Directions: Underline the subject once and the correct verb phrase twice.

1. This toy is (broke, broken).

2. Snow had (fallen, fell).

3. She must have (driven, drove) alone.

4. Your shirt is (lying, laying) here.

5. Have you (swam, swum) recently?

6. The <u>toddler</u> <u>has</u> (blew, <u>blown</u>) bubbles.

7. <u>Models</u> <u>can be</u> (gave, <u>given</u>) the needed information.

8. <u>Nails</u> <u>had been</u> (<u>driven</u>, drove) straight.

9. <u>Ron</u> <u>must have</u> (<u>come</u>, came) late.

10. <u>Have</u> <u>you</u> ever (ran, <u>run</u>) alone?

D.   Directions: Directions: Circle the correct word.

1. (Sit, **Set**) your box here.

2. Steam (**rose**, raised) from the kettle.

3. He must have (lain, **laid**) his cuff links on the dresser.

4. Are we (setting, **sitting**) by ourselves?

5. Several old magazines were (**lying**, laying) beneath an oily rag.

6.   The family (rises, **raises**) money for that charity.

E.   Directions: Underline the subject once and the verb or verb phrase twice.
                      Write the tense (*present, past,* or *future*) in the blank.

1. _____**present**_____   Our <u>kidneys</u> <u>are</u> bean-shaped.

2. _____**present**_____   <u>Hyenas</u> <u>make</u> a strange sound.

3. _____**past**_____   <u>Beth</u> suddenly <u>yawned</u>.

4. _____**future**_____   <u>I</u> <u>shall take</u> your temperature.

5. _____**present**_____   That <u>fan</u> <u>cheers</u> loudly.

6. _____**future**_____   <u>Will</u> your <u>friend</u> <u>agree</u>?

6. The toddler has (blew, **blown**) bubbles.

7. Models can be (gave, **given**) the needed information.

8. Nails had been (**driven**, drove) straight.

9. Ron must have (**come**, came) late.

10. Have you ever (ran, **run**) alone?

D. Directions: Directions: Circle the correct word.

1. (**Sit**, Set) your box here.

2. Steam (**rose**, raised) from the kettle.

3. He must have (lain, **laid**) his cuff links on the dresser.

4. Are we (setting, **sitting**) by ourselves?

5. Several old magazines were (**lying**, laying) beneath an oily rag.

6. The family (rises, **raises**) money for that charity.

E. Directions: Underline the subject once and the verb or verb phrase twice. Write the tense (*present*, *past*, or *future*) in the blank.

1. _____ Our kidneys are bean-shaped.

2. _____ Hyenas make a strange sound.

3. _____ Beth suddenly yawned.

4. _____ I shall take your temperature.

5. _____ That fan cheers loudly.

6. _____ Will your friend agree?

F. Directions: Underline the subject once and the correct verb twice.

Remember: Crossing out any prepositional phrases helps.

1. My grandmother (deliver, delivers) groceries.

2. I (visits, visit) the Alamo each year.

3. Lana (sips, sip) water through a straw.

4. His mother and Bo (buys, buy) old books.

5. She (don't, doesn't) know.

6. Everyone of his friends (eat, eats) breakfast.

7. Those little girls (giggles, giggle) often.

G. Directions. Cross out any prepositional phrases. Underline the subject once and the verb or verb phrase twice.

1. This mail from Grandpa should be opened now.

2. Deb must have gone without us.

4. The mules stood in the shade and brayed.

4. Can you help me with this necklace?

5. Many blankets were lying on the floor.

6. These gumdrops could be stale.

7. I could not have arrived earlier.

8. You may place your feet here.

9. Each person at the fashion show has received a gift.

10. Does Mike shave and shower every day during the summer?

166

F. Directions: Underline the subject once and the correct verb twice.

Remember: Crossing out any prepositional phrases helps.

1. My grandmother (deliver, delivers) groceries.

2. I (visits, visit) the Alamo each year.

3. Lana (sips, sip) water through a straw.

4. His mother and Bo (buys, buy) old books.

5. She (do*n't*, does*n't*) <u>know</u>.

6. Everyone of his friends (eat, eats) breakfast.

7. Those little girls (giggles, giggle) often.

G. Directions. Cross out any prepositional phrases. Underline the subject once and the verb or verb phrase twice.

1. This mail from Grandpa should be opened now.

2. Deb must have gone without us.

3. The mules stood in the shade and brayed.

4. Can you help me with this necklace?

5. Many blankets were lying on the floor.

6. These gumdrops could be stale.

7. I could not have arrived earlier.

8. You may place your feet here.

9. Each person at the fashion show has received a gift.

10.   Does Mike shave and shower every day during the summer?

TO THE TEACHER:

A CUMULATIVE REVIEW IS ON PAGES 170-177.

THIS REVIEW WILL INCLUDE CONCEPTS LEARNED IN THE PREPOSITION UNIT.

BECAUSE THIS IS A LENGTHY REVIEW, YOU MAY WANT TO DIVIDE IT INTO MORE THAN ONE LESSON.

IT MAY BE A GOOD IDEA TO COMPLETE CUMULATIVE REVIEWS PROVIDED IN THIS TEXT <u>IN CLASS</u>.

I SUGGEST THAT YOU HAVE THE STUDENTS DO EACH <u>SECTION</u> ALONE. THEN, GO OVER THE SECTION AND DISCUSS ANSWERS WITH STUDENTS.

I RECOMMEND THAT YOU SPEND A GREAT DEAL OF TIME

COMPLETING CUMULATIVE REVIEWS LOCATED AT THE

END OF EACH UNIT. DON'T RUSH THROUGH THESE.

REVIEW ENHANCES LEARNING!

RETEACH ANY CONCEPTS THAT CAUSE CONFUSION.

AS YOU PROGRESS THROUGH THIS TEXT, THE

CUMULATIVE REVIEWS WILL BECOME LONGER.

HOWEVER, CUMULATIVE TESTS ARE SHORTER THAN

CUMULATIVE REVIEWS.

A. List of Prepositions:

Directions: Write the prepositions by adding missing letters.

A's

1. a b o u t
2. a b o v e
3. a c r o s s
4. a f t e r
5. a g a i n s t
6. a l o n g
7. a m i d
8. a m o n g
9. a r o u n d
10. a t
11. a t o p

B's

12. b e f o r e
13. b e h i n d
14. b e l o w
15. b e n e a t h
16. b e s i d e
17. b e t w e e n
18. b e y o n d

19. b u t (meaning except)
20. b y

C's

21. c o n c e r n i n g

D's

22. d o w n
23. d u r i n g

E's

24. e x c e p t

F's

25. f o r
26. f r o m

I's

27. i n
28. i n s i d e
29. i n t o

L's

30. l i k e

N's

31. n e a r

O's

32. o f
33. o f f
34. i n
35. i n t o
36. o u t
37. o u t s i d e
38. o v e r

P's

39. p a s t

R's

40. r e g a r d i n g

S's

41. s i n c e

T's

42. t h r o u g h
43. t h r o u g h o u t

44. t o
45. t o w a r d

U's

46. u n d e r
47. u n d e r n e a t h
48. u n t i l
49. u p
50. u p o n

W's

51. w i t h
52. w i t h i n
53. w i t h o u t

170

Name_____   **Cumulative Review**

Date_____   **At the End of the Verb Unit**

A. List of Prepositions:

Directions: Write the prepositions by adding missing letters.

A's

1. _ b _ u t

2. _ b o _ _

3. _ _ r _ _ s

4. _ _ t _ r

5. _ g _ i _ _ t

6. _ l _ n _

7. _ m _ d

8. _ m _ _ g

9. _ r _ _ n d

10. a _

11. a _ _ p

B's

12. _ _ f _ r e

13. _ e _ _ n d

14. _ _ l o _

15. _ e n _ _ _ h

16. _ e s _ d _

17. _ e t w _ _ n

18. _ e _ o _ d

19. _ u _ (meaning except)

20. _ y

C's

21. c _ n c _ r _ i _ _

D's

22. _ o _ n

23. _ _ r _ _ g

E's

24. _ _ c _ _ t

F's

25. _ o _

26. _ _ _ m

I's

27. _ n

28. _ n s _ _ _

29. _ n _ _

L's

30. _ i _ _

N's

31. _ e _ r

O's

32. _ f

33. _ _ f

34. _ n

35. _ n _ o

36. _ _ t

37. _ _ _ s i _ e

38. _ _ e r

P's

39. _ a _ t

R's

40. _ e g _ r _ _ n g

S's

41. _ _ _ _ c e

T's

42. _ _ r _ u _ h

43. _ h _ o _ _ h _ u t

44. _ o

45. _ o _ _ _ d

U's

46. _ n _ _ r

47. _ n d _ r n _ _ t h

48. _ n _ _ l

49. u _

50. _ _ o n

W's

51. _ _ t _

52. _ _ _ h i _

53. _ _ t _ _ u _

Note: In Part E-#2, you may wish to discuss why *interesting* is not part of the verb phrase.

B. **Subject/Verb:**

Directions: Cross out any prepositional phrases. Underline the subject once and the verb twice.

1. A wet <u>mop</u> <u><u>lay</u></u> ~~on the damp floor~~.

2. Your dirty <u>socks</u> <u><u>are</u></u> ~~in the hamper~~.

3. <u>Winds</u> ~~from the east~~ <u><u>swept</u></u> ~~through the valley~~.

4. The <u>man</u> ~~at the carnival~~ <u><u>served</u></u> ice cream.

C. **Verb Phrases:**

Directions: Cross out any prepositional phrases. Underline the subject once and the verb phrase twice.

1. Your ice cream <u>cone</u> <u><u>is dripping</u></u>.

2. The <u>race</u> <u><u>must have begun</u></u> ~~at noon~~.

3. <u><u>Did</u></u> <u>Ryan</u> <u><u>take</u></u> his dog ~~with him to the park~~?

D. **Compound Objects of the Preposition:**

Directions: Cross out any prepositional phrases. Underline the subject once and the verb twice.

1. A <u>teacher</u> <u><u>sat</u></u> ~~between Juan and his sister~~.

2. This <u>report</u> ~~about snakes and other reptiles~~ <u><u>is</u></u> long.

3. One <u>camel</u> <u><u>spit</u></u> ~~at its owner and us~~.

E. **Compound Subjects:**

Directions: Cross out any prepositional phrases. Underline the subject once and the verb twice.

1. <u>Joy</u> and her <u>sister</u> <u><u>live</u></u> ~~near a large pond~~.

2. The old <u>mill</u> and <u>waterwheel</u> <u><u>are</u></u> ~~around this bend~~ ~~in the road~~.

172

B. **Subject/Verb:**
   Directions: Cross out any prepositional phrases. Underline the subject once
                 and the verb twice.

1.   A wet mop lay on the damp floor.

2.   Your dirty socks are in the hamper.

3.   Winds from the east swept through the valley.

4.   The man at the carnival served ice cream.

C. **Verb Phrases:**
   Directions: Cross out any prepositional phrases. Underline the subject once
                 and the verb phrase twice.

1.   Your ice cream cone is dripping.

2.   The race must have begun at noon.

3.   Did Ryan take his dog with him to the park?

D. **Compound Objects of the Preposition:**
   Directions: Cross out any prepositional phrases. Underline the subject once
                 and the verb twice.

1.   A teacher sat between Juan and his sister.

2.   This report about snakes and other reptiles is long.

3.   One camel spit at its owner and us.

E. **Compound Subjects:**
   Directions: Cross out any prepositional phrases. Underline the subject once
                 and the verb twice.

1.   Joy and her sister live near a large pond.

2.   The old mill and waterwheel are around this bend in the road.

F. **Compound Verbs:**

    Directions: Cross out any prepositional phrases. Underline the subject once and the verb twice.

1. ~~During exercise class~~, I <u>stopped</u> and <u>rested</u> ~~for five minutes~~.

2. Several <u>tourists</u> <u>walked</u> ~~across the bridge~~ and <u>went</u> ~~inside the castle~~.

G. **Imperative Sentences:**

    Directions: Cross out any prepositional phrases. Underline the subject once and the verb twice.

1. (<u>You</u>) <u>Go</u> ~~without us~~.

2. (<u>You</u>) <u>Wait</u> ~~until Saturday~~.

3. (<u>You</u>) <u>Prop</u> this shovel ~~against the wall~~.

H. **Infinitives:**

    Directions: Cross out any prepositional phrases. Place parentheses ( ) around any infinitive. Underline the subject once and the verb twice.

1. <u>Parker</u> <u>likes</u> (to play) ~~at a playground~~ ~~near her home~~.

2. <u>Uncle Don</u> <u>wants</u> (to go) ~~on a fishing trip~~.

3. <u>Everyone</u> ~~except the man~~ ~~with a broken leg~~ <u>decided</u> (to wade) ~~in the stream~~.

I. **Preposition or Adverb?:**

    Directions: Cross out any prepositional phrases. Underline the subject once and the verb twice. Write **A** if the boldfaced word is an adverb. Write **P** if the boldfaced word is a preposition that begins a prepositional phrase.

1.   **A**   Their ferrets run **around**.
2.   **P**   Their ferrets run **around** their home.

3.   **A**   A bear came **near**.
4.   **P**   A bear came **near** our camp.

174

F. **Compound Verbs:**
    Directions: Cross out any prepositional phrases. Underline the subject once
                 and the verb twice.

1. During exercise class, I stopped and rested for five minutes.

2. Several tourists walked across the bridge and went inside the castle.

G. **Imperative Sentences:**
    Directions: Cross out any prepositional phrases. Underline the subject once
                 and the verb twice.

1. Go without us.

2. Wait until Saturday.

3. Prop this shovel against the wall.

H. **Infinitives:**
    Directions: Cross out any prepositional phrases. Place parentheses ( )
                 around any infinitive. Underline the subject once and the verb
                 twice.

1. Parker likes to play at a playground near her home.

2. Uncle Don wants to go on a fishing trip.

3. Everyone except the man with a broken leg decided to wade in the stream.

I. **Preposition or Adverb?:**
    Directions: Cross out any prepositional phrases. Underline the subject once
                 and the verb twice. Write **A** if the boldfaced word is an adverb.
                 Write **P** if the boldfaced word is a preposition that begins a
                 prepositional phrase.

1. _____ Their ferrets run **around**.
2. _____ Their ferrets run **around** their home.

3. _____ A bear came **near**.
4. _____ A bear came **near** our camp.

WORKBOOK PAGE 82

Cumulative Review

At the End of the Verb Unit

J. **Verb Phrases and *Not*:**

Directions: Cross out any prepositional phrases. Box *not* or *n't*.
Underline the subject once and the verb twice.

1. You may **not** go ~~beyond that blue dot~~.

2. I should **not** have ridden ~~along the busy highway~~.

3. Some baseball fans were**n't** staying ~~through the last inning~~.

K. **General Review:**

Directions: Cross out any prepositional phrases. Underline the subject
once and the verb or verb phrase twice.

Example: Those tadpoles are swimming ~~in a circle~~.

1. They have placed twenty candles ~~atop his birthday cake~~.

2. ~~During high winds~~, the boat pulled ~~into the harbor~~.

3. Our team decided (to stay) ~~inside the gym~~ ~~for practice~~.

4. Several mothers and toddlers met ~~after a puppet show~~.

5. The attorney answers her calls ~~throughout the day~~.

6. I have**n't** seen him ~~since last Friday~~.

7. Five dimes fell ~~off the table~~ and ~~onto a checked sofa~~.

8. We sit ~~by a fountain~~ ~~before school~~.

9. Mary put a hat ~~with a huge feather~~ ~~upon her head~~ and laughed.

10. One ~~of the artists~~ painted a box ~~within a box~~.

11. A man ~~with red suspenders~~ tossed a hay bale ~~into his truck~~.

12. Did her dog trot ~~toward an open door~~?

J. **Verb Phrases and *Not*:**
   Directions: Cross out any prepositional phrases. Box *not* or *n't*.
              Underline the subject once and the verb twice.

1. You may not go beyond that blue dot.

2. I should not have ridden along the busy highway.

3. Some baseball fans weren't staying through the last inning.

K. **General Review:**
   Directions: Cross out any prepositional phrases. Underline the subject
              once and the verb or verb phrase twice.

              Example: Those <u>tadpoles</u> <u>are swimming</u> ~~in a circle~~.

1. They have placed twenty candles atop his birthday cake.

2. During high winds, the boat pulled into the harbor.

3. Our team decided to stay inside the gym for practice.

4. Several mothers and toddlers met after a puppet show.

5. The attorney answers her calls throughout the day.

6. I haven't seen him since last Friday.

7. Five dimes fell off the table and onto a checked sofa.

8. We sit by a fountain before school.

9. Mary put a hat with a huge feather upon her head and laughed.

10. One of the artists painted a box within a box.

11. A man with red suspenders tossed a hay bale into his truck.

12. Did her dog trot toward an open door?

Name_____   **Cumulative Test**

Date_____   **End of Verb Unit**

Directions: Cross out any prepositional phrases. Underline the subject once
and the verb or verb phrase twice.

1. Two <u>children</u> ~~without sunblock~~ <u>made</u> sand castles ~~throughout the day~~.

2. A <u>ball</u> <u>rolled</u> ~~down the sidewalk~~ and ~~into an alley~~.

3. The <u>man</u> ~~beside me~~ <u>jumped</u> ~~across a pile of boards and plaster~~.

4. A <u>jacket</u> ~~with red stripes and white stars~~ <u>lay</u> ~~inside the display window~~.

5. ~~After school~~, <u>one</u> ~~of the students~~ <u>skipped</u> ~~along a path~~.

6. The <u>child</u> <u>stood</u> ~~in his crib~~ and <u>cried</u> ~~for his parents~~.

7. A <u>watercolor</u> ~~by a famous artist~~ <u>hangs</u> ~~over their mantel~~.

8. The women's <u>club</u> <u>listened</u> ~~to a speech~~ ~~concerning good health~~.

9. Each <u>person</u> ~~at the fair~~ <u>wanted</u> (to ride) ~~on the Ferris wheel~~.

10. A <u>container</u> ~~of small plants~~ <u>has been placed</u> ~~on the window ledge~~.

11. ~~During intermission~~, <u>Molly</u> and her <u>sister</u> <u>spoke</u> ~~with the singer's dad~~.

12. (<u>You</u>) <u>Put</u> this old luggage ~~under the bed~~.

13. <u>I</u> <u>did</u>**n't** <u>ask</u> ~~about his trip~~ ~~to Utah~~.

178

Directions: Cross out any prepositional phrases. Underline the subject once
                     and the verb or verb phrase twice.

1.   Two children without sunblock made sand castles throughout the day.

2.   A ball rolled down the sidewalk and into an alley.

3.   The man beside me jumped across a pile of boards and plaster.

4.   A jacket with red stripes and white stars lay inside the display window.

5.   After school, one of the students skipped along a path.

6.   The child stood in his crib and cried for his parents.

7.   A watercolor by a famous artist hangs over their mantel.

8.   The women's club listened to a speech concerning good health.

9.   Each person at the fair wanted to ride on the Ferris wheel.

10.   A container of small plants has been placed on the window ledge.

11.   During intermission, Molly and her sister spoke with the singer's dad.

12.   Put this old luggage under the bed.

13.   I didn't ask about his trip to Utah.

NOUNS

Concrete and Abstract Nouns:

This can be a difficult concept for some students.

   A.   **Teaching Concrete Nouns:**

     Concrete nouns usually can be seen: *car, camera, cat, can*.

     Before introducing concrete and abstract nouns, you may want to ask students to bring a (small) item that is important to them from home.

     On the day that you teach this concept, ask students to hold the item in their hands. Discuss concrete nouns.

     Have students show the item to a neighbor. Ask students to explain to a neighbor why the item is a concrete noun.

NOTE: You may want to provide a writing assignment. Students can explain why their "noun" is important to them.

   B.   **Teaching Abstract Nouns:**

     Abstract nouns are those that cannot be seen.

     Discuss the concept of **abstract nouns** with students. You may want to make a list from students' suggestions.

          Examples: beauty

                     grace

                     charm

                     anger

Some students may want to argue that they can see anger. Ask them to place anger in their hands and show it to you. Obviously, we don't actually see anger; we see *the results* of anger.

182

CONCRETE AND ABSTRACT NOUNS

Do you remember the definition of a noun?

A noun names a person, a place, or a thing.

We will add *idea* to this definition.

A noun names a person, a place, a thing, or an idea.

	Examples:		
	person	-	girl or Tara
	place	-	park or Idaho
	thing	-	spoon or crane
	idea	-	beauty or forgiveness

෨෨෨෨෨෨෨෨෨෨෨෨෨෨෨෨෨෨෨෨

Nouns can be concrete or abstract.

    A.   Concrete Nouns:

        <u>Concrete nouns can be seen</u>.

                Examples: drum

                                 house

                                 moon

                                 skunk

Concrete nouns are made up of atoms. At first, air may not seem concrete. However, using high-powered equipment, you can see atoms.

    B.   Abstract Nouns:

        <u>Abstract nouns cannot be seen</u>.

                Examples: love

                                 gentleness

                                 eternity

                                 anger

Directions: Write **C** in the blank if the noun is concrete and **A** if it is abstract.

1.   __C__   tub

2.   __C__   man

3.   __A__   trust

4.   __C__   toothpaste

5.   __A__   hatred

6.   __C__   steel

7.   __A__   fright

8.   __C__   faucet

9.   __C__   bacon

10.   __A__   laughter

11.   __C__   bulldozer

12.   __A__   stubborness

13.   __C__   rafter

14.   __C__   rattlesnake

15.   __A__   intelligence

16.   __A__   happiness

17.   __A__   justice

18.   __C__   snack

Directions: Write **C** in the blank if the noun is concrete and **A** if it is abstract.

1. _____   tub

2. _____   man

3. _____   trust

4. _____   toothpaste

5. _____   hatred

6. _____   steel

7. _____   fright

8. _____   faucet

9. _____   bacon

10. _____   laughter

11. _____   bulldozer

12. _____   stubborness

13. _____   rafter

14. _____   rattlesnake

15. _____   intelligence

16. _____   happiness

17. _____   justice

18. _____   snack

A noun names a person, place, thing, or idea.

Two types are **common nouns** and **proper nouns**.

    A. Common nouns do not name a specific person, place, or thing.
        Examples: boy   day   planet   dog

Sometimes, a common noun can be classified into types. Types are still common nouns and are not capitalized.
        Example: dog   -   collie
However, if part of a type names a specific place, capitalize that place.
        Examples: **F**rench poodle   (place – France)
                      Bermuda grass   (place – Bermuda)

    B. Proper nouns name a specific person, place, or thing. Capitalize any proper noun.

	Common	**Proper**
Examples:	boy	**D**avid
	day	**M**onday
	planet	**M**ars
	dog	**V**elvet

☙☙☙☙☙☙☙☙☙☙☙☙

Directions: Write **C** if the noun is common and **P** if the noun is proper.

1.	**C**	person	11.	**C**	ranch	21.	**C**	animal
2.	**P**	Bar Harbor	12.	**C**	party	22.	**C**	horse
3.	**P**	Sara	13.	**P**	Mr. Sands	23.	**P**	Mt. Hood
4.	**C**	partner	14.	**C**	state	24.	**C**	doctor
5.	**P**	Vermont	15.	**C**	holiday	25.	**P**	Hawaii
6.	**P**	January	16.	**C**	restaurant	26.	**C**	waitress
7.	**C**	month	17.	**C**	mountain	27.	**C**	dock
8.	**C**	building	18.	**P**	Dr. Small	28.	**C**	flower
9.	**C**	club	19.	**C**	suburb	29.	**C**	daisy
10.	**P**	Dell Bank	20.	**C**	island	30.	**P**	Thanksgiving

Name_____

Date_____

A noun names a person, place, thing, or idea.

Two types are **common nouns** and **proper nouns**.

    A. Common nouns do not name a specific person, place, or thing.
          Examples: boy   day   planet   dog

Sometimes, a common noun can be classified into types. Types are still common nouns and are not capitalized.
          Example: dog   -   collie
However, if part of a type names a specific place, capitalize that place.
          Examples: **F**rench poodle   (place – France)
                     Bermuda grass   (place – Bermuda)

    B. Proper nouns name a specific person, place, or thing. Capitalize any proper noun.

	Common	**Proper**
Examples:	boy	**D**avid
	day	**M**onday
	planet	**M**ars
	dog	**V**elvet

Directions: Write **C** if the noun is common and **P** if the noun is proper.

1. ___	person	11. ___	ranch	21. ___	animal
2. ___	Bar Harbor	12. ___	party	22. ___	horse
3. ___	Sara	13. ___	Mr. Sands	23. ___	Mt. Hood
4. ___	partner	14. ___	state	24. ___	doctor
5. ___	Vermont	15. ___	holiday	25. ___	Hawaii
6. ___	January	16. ___	restaurant	26. ___	waitress
7. ___	month	17. ___	mountain	27. ___	dock
8. ___	building	18. ___	Dr. Small	28. ___	flower
9. ___	club	19. ___	suburb	29. ___	daisy
10. ___	Dell Bank	20. ___	island	30. ___	Thanksgiving

Name_____ **NOUNS**

Date_____ **Common or Proper?**

<u>**Note**</u>: You may want to do this exercise orally. (I suggest that students write in an answer for each item before the class discusses that answer.) Be sure to discuss a *variety* of answers. Stress that "types" are common nouns and, therefore, are not capitalized.

Common nouns do not name a specific person, place, or thing.

Examples: neck   ticket   heart   glue

Sometimes, a common noun can be classified into types. Types are still common nouns and are not capitalized.

<u>**Common**</u>	<u>**Type**</u>	<u>**Proper**</u>
girl	teenager	**L**ani
horse	mare	**L**ady **J**ewel

However, if part of a type names a specific place, capitalize that place.

dog   shepherd   **N**inja

▼

German shepherd   (place – Germany)

Proper nouns name a specific person, place, or thing. Capitalize any proper noun.

<u>**Common**</u>	<u>**Proper**</u>
month	**O**ctober

๛๛๛๛๛๛๛๛๛๛๛

Directions: Write a common noun in Column A, a type of the common noun in Column B, and a proper noun that relates to the common noun in Column C.

ANSWERS MAY VARY/REPRESENTATIVE ANSWERS:

<u>**Column A**</u> COMMON NOUN	<u>**Column B**</u> TYPE (COMMON NOUN)	<u>**Column C**</u> PROPER NOUN
1. **place**	**zoo**	**Baltimore Zoo**
2. **horse**	**pinto**	**Black Beauty**
3. **business**	**salon**	**Echo Hair Salon**
4. **waterform**	**ocean**	**Pacific Ocean**
5. **residence**	**apartments**	**Curry Apartments**
6. **landform**	**island**	**Barren Island**
7. **book**	**cookbook**	*Cooking with Sam*

188

Common nouns do not name a specific person, place, or thing.
Examples: neck   ticket   heart   glue

Sometimes, a common noun can be classified into types. Types are still common nouns and are not capitalized.

Common	**Type**	**Proper**
girl	teenager	Lani
horse	mare	Lady Jewel

However, if part of a type names a specific place, capitalize that place.
dog   shepherd   **N**inja
▼
German shepherd   (place – Germany)

Proper nouns name a specific person, place, or thing. Capitalize any proper noun.

Common	**Proper**
month	**O**ctober

Directions: Write a common noun in Column A, a type of the common noun in Column B, and a proper noun that relates to the common noun in Column C.

Column A COMMON NOUN	**Column B** TYPE (COMMON NOUN)	**Column C** PROPER NOUN
1. __place__	_____	_____
2. __horse__	_____	_____
3. __business__	_____	_____
4. __waterform__	_____	_____
5. __residence__	_____	_____
6. __landform__	_____	_____
7. __book__	_____	_____

NOUNS

Date_____   **Noun or Adjective?**

You have learned that **a noun names a person, place, thing, or idea.**

Sometimes, the same word will be a noun in one sentence and an adjective (describing word) in another sentence.

Examples: A. He planted a **bean** in this cup.

Bean is a noun in this sentence.

B. I don't like this **bean** salad.   _**bean salad**_

Bean is an adjective in this sentence because it describes salad.

Directions: On the line provided, write **N** if the boldfaced word serves as a noun and **A** if the word serves as an adjective (describing word). If your answer is **A**, write the adjective and the word it modifies.

1. __**N**__   I like your **clothes**.   _____

2. __**A**__   A **clothes** brush is lying on the bed.   __**clothes brush**___

3. __**A**__   This **picture** frame is broken.   ___**picture frame**___

4. __**N**__   Our **picture** appeared in the newspaper.   _____

5. __**A**__   We attended a **beauty** pageant.   ___**beauty pageant**___

6. __**N**__   **Beauty** in nature is all around us.   _____

7. __**A**__   He needs a **water** bottle for his backpack. ___**water bottle**___

8. __**N**__   I need **water** for my dog's dish.   _____

9. __**A**__   Jana wants an **egg** sandwich.   ___**egg sandwich**___

10. __**N**__   May I please have an **egg** with cheese?   _____

11. __**N**__   You may use my **telephone** to make a call. _____

12. __**A**__   There are no **telephone** wires in their area. ___**telephone wires**___

190

Name_____

Date_____

You have learned that **a noun names a person, place, thing, or idea.**

Sometimes, the same word will be a noun in one sentence and an adjective (describing word) in another sentence.

Examples: A. He planted a **bean** in this cup.

Bean is a noun in this sentence.

B. I don't like this **bean** salad.   *bean salad*

Bean is an adjective in this sentence because it describes salad.

Directions: On the line provided, write **N** if the boldfaced word serves as a noun and **A** if the word serves as an adjective (describing word). If your answer is **A**, write the adjective and the word it modifies.

1. _____   I like your **clothes**.   _____

2. _____   A **clothes** brush is lying on the bed.   _____

3. _____   This **picture** frame is broken.   _____

4. _____   Our **picture** appeared in the newspaper. _____

5. _____   We attended a **beauty** pageant.   _____

6. _____   **Beauty** in nature is all around us.   _____

7. _____   He needs a **water** bottle for his backpack. _____

8. _____   I need **water** for my dog's dish. _____

9. _____   Jana wants an **egg** sandwich.   _____

10. _____   May I please have an **egg** with cheese? _____

11. _____   You may use my **telephone** to make a call. _____

12. _____   There are no **telephone** wires in their area. _____

WORKBOOK PAGE 88

The same word may serve as a noun in one sentence and as an adjective (describing word) in another sentence.

Example: I put **gas** in my car.   (noun)

They cook on a **gas** range.   *gas* range   (adjective)

☙☙☙☙☙☙☙☙☙☙☙☙☙☙☙☙☙☙☙☙

Directions: Write a sentence using the boldfaced word as a noun in Part A and as an adjective in Part B. In Part B, draw an arrow from your word to what it describes.

ANSWERS MAY VARY/REPRESENTATIVE ANSWERS:

1. **window**

     A. ___**The girls climbed in a low window.**_____

     B. ___**Their family room has a window seat.**_____
                                                  ↻

2. **apple**

     A. ___**Do you want an apple to eat?**_____

     B. ___**Mom makes delicious apple pies.**_____
                                              ↻

3. **beach**

     A. ___**Would you like to go to the beach today?**_____

     B. ___**A beach ball rolled over my blanket.**_____
                  ↻

4. **football**

     A. ___**Throw the football to Amy.**_____

     B. ___**Let's attend our school's football game this afternoon.**_____
                                                          ↻

5. **nose**

     A. ___**My nose is crooked.**_____

     B. ___**Wes has nose drops.**_____
                        ↻

Date_____   **Noun or Adjective?**

The same word may serve as a noun in one sentence and as an adjective (describing word) in another sentence.

Example: I put **gas** in my car.   (noun)

They cook on a **gas** range.   _gas_ range   (adjective)

🐎🐎🐎🐎🐎🐎🐎🐎🐎🐎🐎🐎🐎🐎🐎🐎🐎🐎🐎🐎

Directions: Write a sentence using the boldfaced word as a noun in Part A and as an adjective in Part B. In Part B, draw an arrow from your word to what it describes.

1. **window**

    A. _____

    B. _____

2. **apple**

    A. _____

    B. _____

3. **beach**

    A. _____

    B. _____

4. **football**

    A. _____

    B. _____

5. **nose**

    A. _____

    B. _____

PLURAL NOUNS:

Plural means more than one.

     Singular: (one) dime   **Plural:** (many) dimes

Notice that an apostrophe (') is **not** used when forming the plural.

Rule A: Most nouns simply add **s** to form the plural.

	Examples:	bananA	-	bananas
		curB	-	curbs
		tarmaC	-	tarmacs
		faD	-	fads
		dimplE	-	dimples
		pufF	-	puffs
		ruG	-	rugs
		patH	-	paths
		skI	-	skis
		bacK	-	backs
		dolL	-	dolls
		moM	-	moms
		caN	-	cans

dri**P**	-	drip**s**
sta**R**	-	star**s**
do**T**	-	dot**s**
la**W**	-	law**s**

Note that the following letters are missing from the list:

J, O, Q, S, U, V, X, Y, and Z

J, Q, U, and *V?*

Most English words do not end in these letters.

However, we do have words that have been added to our language via a foreign language. For example, <u>luau</u> is from the Hawaiian language. This word, which means *party,* has become standard in our English language and simply adds **s** to form the plural.

What about *S, X,* and *Z?* These follow Rule B.

Rule B: Nouns ending in <u>**sh**</u>, <u>**ch**</u>, <u>**s**</u>, <u>**x**</u>, and <u>**z**</u> usually add *es* to form the plural.

cla**sh**	clash**es**
pat**ch**	patch**es**
dres**s**	dress**es**
bo**x**	box**es**
fiz**z**	fizz**es**

What about *O* and *Y?*

O and *Y* follow rules that you will learn later in this unit.

Name_____ **NOUNS**

Date_____ **Plurals**

ANSWERS MAY VARY/REPRESENTATIVE ANSWERS:

Directions: Write a noun that ends with the given letter or letters. Then, write the plural of that word.

1. _____pew_____ - _____pews_____

2. _____bib_____ - _____bibs_____

3. _____flood_____ - _____floods_____

4. _____safe_____ - _____safes_____

5. _____whiff_____ - _____whiffs_____

6. _____log_____ - _____logs_____

7. _____rash_____ - _____rashes_____

8. _____winch_____ - _____winches_____

9. _____moth_____ - _____moths_____

10. _____hex_____ - _____hexes_____

11. _____track_____ - _____tracks_____

12. _____coil_____ - _____coils_____

13. _____prom_____ - _____proms_____

14. _____ban_____ - _____bans_____

15. _____crop_____ - _____crops_____

16. _____motor_____ - _____motors_____

17. _____moss_____ - _____mosses_____

18. _____raft_____ - _____rafts_____

Name_____   **NOUNS**

Date_____   **Plurals**

Directions: Write a noun that ends with the given letter or letters. Then, write
the plural of that word.

1.   _____ w   -   _____

2.   _____ b   -   _____

3.   _____ d   -   _____

4.   _____ e   -   _____

5.   _____ f   -   _____

6.   _____ g   -   _____

7.   _____ sh   -   _____

8.   _____ ch   -   _____

9.   _____ th   -   _____

10.   _____ x   -   _____

11.   _____ k   -   _____

12.   _____ l   -   _____

13.   _____ m   -   _____

14.   _____ n   -   _____

15.   _____ p   -   _____

16.   _____ r   -   _____

17.   _____ s   -   _____

18.   _____ t   -   _____

Singular means one.   Plural means more than one.

Rule A: Most nouns add *s* to form the plural.

one garden	two garden**s**
one bolt	many bolt**s**

Rule B: Nouns ending in **sh**, **ch**, **s**, **x**, and **z** usually add *es* to form the plural.

one bru**sh**	two brush**es**
one por**ch**	several porch**es**
one len**s**	three lens**es**
an apartment comple**x**	many apartment complex**es**
buz**z**	buzz**es**

ᏒᏒᏒᏒᏒᏒᏒᏒᏒᏒᏒᏒᏒᏒᏒᏒᏒᏒᏒᏒ

Directions: Write the plural of each noun.

1.   flash - _____**flashes**_____

2.   eagle - _____**eagles**_____

3.   fez - _____**fezes**_____

4.   canvas - _____**canvases**_____

5.   arrival - _____**arrivals**_____

6.   ranch - _____**ranches**_____

7.   hostess - _____**hostesses**_____

8.   sauna - _____**saunas**_____

9.   basic - _____**basics**_____

10.   circus - _____**circuses**_____

Singular means one.   Plural means more than one.

Rule A: Most nouns add *s* to form the plural.

> one garden   two gardens
> one bolt   many bolts

Rule B: Nouns ending in **sh**, **ch**, **s**, **x**, and **z** usually add *es* to form the plural.

> one bru**sh**   two brushes
> one por**ch**   several porches
> one len**s**   three lenses
> an apartment comple**x**   many apartment complexes
> buz**z**   buzzes

Directions: Write the plural of each noun.

1. flash - _____

2. eagle - _____

3. fez - _____

4. canvas - _____

5. arrival - _____

6. ranch - _____

7. hostess - _____

8. sauna - _____

9. basic - _____

10. circus - _____

Name_____   **NOUNS**

Date_____   **Plurals**

Directions: Circle any noun that adds **s** to form the plural; box any noun that
            adds **es** to form the plural.

**Nouns that add _s_ to form the plural have been italicized; nouns adding
_es_ to form the plural have been boldfaced.**

1.	*spa*	19.	**fuzz**
3.	*rib*	20.	*foul*
3.	*tunic*	21.	**wrench**
4.	*flood*	22.	*corral*
5.	*flame*	23.	*tactic*
6.	*flaw*	24.	*weight*
7.	**flush**	25.	**process**
8.	fountain	26.	**reflex**
9.	**brunch**	27.	*mansion*
10.	*prison*	28.	**chorus**
11.	*due*	29.	*trick*
12.	*swirl*	30.	*replica*
13.	**inch**	31.	*hymn*
14.	**gash**	32.	*gondola*
15.	*iceberg*	33.	*legend*
16.	*color*	34.	*caboose*
17.	**cross**	35.	**branch**
18.	*target*	36.	*germ*

Directions: Circle any noun that adds **s** to form the plural; box any noun that adds **es** to form the plural.

1. spa

3. rib

3. tunic

4. flood

5. flame

6. flaw

7. flush

8. fountain

9. brunch

10. prison

11. due

12. swirl

13. inch

14. gash

15. iceberg

16. color

17. cross

18. target

19. fuzz

20. foul

21. wrench

22. corral

23. tactic

24. weight

25. process

26. reflex

27. mansion

28. chorus

29. trick

30. replica

31. hymn

32. gondola

33. legend

34. caboose

35. branch

36. germ

Name_____   **NOUNS**

WORKBOOK PAGE 93

Date_____   **Plurals**

Note: I did not list that *y* could possibly be a consonant due to the confusion it may cause.

Plural means more than one.

Rule C: Nouns ending in **ay**, **ey**, **oy**, and **uy** add *s* to form the plural.

one pathw**ay**	two pathway**s**
one all**ey**	many alley**s**
one dec**oy**	a few decoy**s**
one g**uy**	ten guy**s**

Rule D: Nouns ending in **consonant + y** change the **y** to **i** and add *es* to form the plural.

one pat**ty**	two patt**ies**
one cana**ry**	some canar**ies**
one dol**ly**	three doll**ies**
a ba**by**	bab**ies**

Remember: Consonants are *b, c, d, f, g, h, j, k, l, m, n, p, q, r, s, t, v, w, x,* and *z.*

೧೧೧೧೧೧೧೧೧೧೧೧೧೧೧೧೧೧೧

Directions: Write the plural of each noun.

1.   screenplay -   **screenplays**

2.   county -   **counties**

3.   country -   **countries**

4.   gulley -   **gulleys**

5.   buggy -   **buggies**

6.   lobby -   **lobbies**

7.   alloy -   **alloys**

8.   reply -   **replies**

9.   latchkey -   **latchkeys**

10.   buy -   **buys**

Name_____   **NOUNS**

Date_____   **Plurals**

Plural means more than one.

Rule C: Nouns ending in **ay**, **ey**, **oy**, and **uy** add *s* to form the plural.

one pathw**ay**	two pathway**s**
one all**ey**	many alley**s**
one dec**oy**	a few decoy**s**
one g**uy**	ten guy**s**

Rule D: Nouns ending in **consonant + y** change the **y** to **i** and add *es* to form the plural.

one pat**ty**	two patt**ies**
one cana**ry**	some canar**ies**
one dol**ly**	three doll**ies**
a ba**by**	bab**ies**

Remember: Consonants are *b, c, d, f, g, h, j, k, l, m, n, p, q, r, s, t, v, w, x,* and *z.*

Directions: Write the plural of each noun.

1. screenplay - _____

2. county - _____

3. country - _____

4. gulley - _____

5. buggy - _____

6. lobby - _____

7. alloy - _____

8. reply - _____

9. latchkey - _____

10. buy - _____

203

Plural means more than one.

Rule C: Nouns ending in **ay**, **ey**, **oy**, and **uy** add *s* to form the plural.

w**ay**	way**s**
k**ey**	key**s**
t**oy**	toy**s**

Rule D: Nouns ending in **consonant + y** change the **y** to **i** and add *es* to form the plural.

jet**ty**	jett**ies**
la**dy**	lad**ies**
cr**y**	cr**ies**

෨෨෨෨෨෨෨෨෨෨෨෨෨෨෨෨෨෨෨෨෨෨

Directions: Place a check (✔) in the blank if you change **y** to **i** and add **es** to form the plural.

1. __✔__ battery

2. _____ holiday

3. __✔__ puppy

4. _____ ploy

5. __✔__ nanny

6. _____ bluejay

7. __✔__ dummy

8. _____ abbey

9. __✔__ story

10. __✔__ piggy

204

Plural means more than one.

Rule C: Nouns ending in <u>**ay**</u>, <u>**ey**</u>, <u>**oy**</u>, and <u>**uy**</u> add **s** to form the plural.

w**ay**   way**s**
k**ey**   key**s**
t**oy**   toy**s**

Rule D: Nouns ending in <u>**consonant + y**</u> change the **y** to **i** and add **es** to form the plural.

jet**ty**   jett**ies**
la**dy**   lad**ies**
c**ry**   cr**ies**

૰ૐ૰ૐ૰ૐ૰ૐ૰ૐ૰ૐ૰ૐ૰ૐ૰ૐ૰ૐ૰ૐ૰ૐ૰ૐ

Directions: Place a check (✔) in the blank if you change **y** to **i** and add **es** to form the plural.

1. _____   battery

2. _____   holiday

3. _____   puppy

4. _____   ploy

5. _____   nanny

6. _____   bluejay

7. _____   dummy

8. _____   abbey

9. _____   story

10. _____   piggy

WORKBOOK PAGE 95

Note: A problem arises in that not all dictionaries agree with the plural form for words ending in *o*. Asking students to show you the dictionary entry is one way to determine if they guessed or actually used a dictionary.

Plural means more than one.

Rule E: Some nouns ending in **o** add **s** to form the plural.

hal**o**	halo**s**
buff**o**	buffo**s**

However, some nouns ending in **o** add **es** to form the plural.

tomat**o**   tomato**es**

Some nouns ending in **o** can add **s** or **es**.

USE A DICTIONARY TO DETERMINE THE CORRECT PLURAL ENDING!

If two plural endings are given, the first one is preferred. Use it.

Example: mango (man go) n. pl. es, s 1. The sweet orange-fleshed fruit of an Indian tree...

🐎🐎🐎🐎🐎🐎🐎🐎🐎🐎🐎🐎🐎🐎🐎🐎🐎🐎🐎

Directions: Write the plural of each noun. If necessary, use a dictionary.

1. patio - _____**patios**_____

2. flamingo -_____**flamingos, flamingoes**_____

3. bongo -_____**bongos**_____

4. dingo -_____**dingoes**_____

5. alto - _____**altos**_____

6. dodo - _____**dodos, dodoes**_____

7. zero - _____**zeros, zeroes**_____

8. pimento - _____**pimentos**_____

9. bronco - _____**broncos**_____

10. motto - _____**mottos**_____

Plural means more than one.

Rule E: Some nouns ending in **o** add **s** to form the plural.

halo   halos
buffo   buffos

However, some nouns ending in **o** add **es** to form the plural.

tomato   tomatoes

Some nouns ending in **o** can add **s** or **es**.

USE A DICTIONARY TO DETERMINE THE CORRECT PLURAL ENDING!

If two plural endings are given, the first one is preferred. Use it.

Example: mango (man go) n. pl. es, s 1. The sweet orange-fleshed
fruit of an Indian tree...

🙞🙞🙞🙞🙞🙞🙞🙞🙞🙞🙞🙞🙞🙞🙞🙞🙞🙞🙞🙞🙞

Directions: Write the plural of each noun. If necessary, use a dictionary.

1. patio - _____

2. flamingo - _____

3. bongo - _____

4. dingo - _____

5. alto - _____

6. dodo - _____

7. zero - _____

8. pimento - _____

9. bronco - _____

10. motto - _____

Plural means more than one.

Rule F: Some nouns ending in **f** add **s** to form the plural.

cliff   cliff**s**

However, some nouns ending in **f** change the **f** to **v** and add **es** to form the plural.

loa**f**   loa**ves**

USE A DICTIONARY TO DETERMINE THE CORRECT PLURAL ENDING!

*If no "special" plural ending is stated, simply add **s** to form the plural.*

🙙🙙🙙🙙🙙🙙🙙🙙🙙🙙🙙🙙🙙🙙🙙🙙🙙🙙🙙🙙🙙

Directions: Write the plural of each noun. If necessary, use a dictionary.

1.   cuff - _____**cuffs**_____

2.   leaf - _____**leaves**_____

3.   bluff - _____**bluffs**_____

4.   staff - _____**staffs**_____

5.   hoof - _____**hoofs, hooves**_____

6.   whiff - _____**whiffs**_____

7.   mastiff - _____**mastiffs**_____

8.   wharf - _____**wharves, wharfs**_____

9.   reef - _____**reefs**_____

10.   elf - _____**elves**_____

11.   muff - _____**muffs**_____

208

Name_____

Date_____

Plural means more than one.

Rule F: Some nouns ending in **f** add **s** to form the plural.

cliff   cliff**s**

However, some nouns ending in **f** change the **f** to **v** and add **es** to form the plural.

loa**f**   loa**ves**

USE A DICTIONARY TO DETERMINE THE CORRECT PLURAL ENDING!

*If no "special" plural ending is stated, simply add **s** to form the plural.*

ৡৡৡৡৡৡৡৡৡৡৡৡৡৡৡৡৡৡৡৡৡৡ

Directions: Write the plural of each noun. If necessary, use a dictionary.

1. cuff - _____

2. leaf - _____

3. bluff - _____

4. staff - _____

5. hoof - _____

6. whiff - _____

7. mastiff - _____

8. wharf - _____

9. reef - _____

10. elf - _____

11. muff - _____

NOUNS

Plurals

Plural means more than one.

Rule G: Some nouns completely change to form the plural.

goose   geese

Some nouns that have entered our language from Latin will change to form the plural.

medium (as in television)   media

USE A DICTIONARY TO DETERMINE THE CORRECT PLURAL ENDING!

Rule H: Some nouns do not change to form the plural.

deer   deer

Directions: Write the plural of each noun. If necessary, use a dictionary.

1. fungus - _____**fungi**_____

2. moose - _____**moose**_____

3. mouse - _____**mice**_____

4. louse - _____**lice**_____

5. reindeer - _____**reindeer**_____

6. patriotism - _____**patriotism**_____

7. police - _____**police**_____

8. craftsman - _____**craftsmen**_____

9. woman - _____**women**_____

10. elk - _____**elk**_____

Name_____

Date_____

Plural means more than one.

Rule G: Some nouns completely change to form the plural.

goose   geese

Some nouns that have entered our language from Latin will change to form the plural.

medium (as in television)   media

USE A DICTIONARY TO DETERMINE THE CORRECT PLURAL ENDING!

Rule H: Some nouns do not change to form the plural.

deer   deer

Directions: Write the plural of each noun. If necessary, use a dictionary.

1. fungus - _____

2. moose - _____

3. mouse - _____

4. louse - _____

5. reindeer - _____

6. patriotism - _____

7. police - _____

8. craftsman - _____

9. woman - _____

10. elk - _____

Name_____ **NOUNS**

Date_____ **Plurals**

A. Directions: Write each plural noun. If necessary, use a dictionary.

1. ceremony - _____**ceremonies**_____

2. coach - _____**coaches**_____

3. troop - _____**troops**_____

4. cliff - _____**cliffs**_____

5. circus - _____**circuses**_____

6. jury - _____**juries**_____

7. value - _____**values**_____

8. trench - _____**trenches**_____

B. Directions: Circle the correct spelling of the plural form.
ANSWERS ARE BOLDFACED.

1. **fossils**   fossiles

2. ponys   **ponies**

3. stairwaies   **stairways**

4. **furniture**   furnitures

5. **studios**   studioes

6. datas   **data**

7. **swatches**   swatchs

8. jettys   **jetties**

9. splashs   **spashes**

10. **halos**   haloes

212

Name_____

Date_____

A. Directions: Write each plural noun. If necessary, use a dictionary.

1. ceremony - _____

2. coach - _____

3. troop - _____

4. cliff - _____

5. circus - _____

6. jury - _____

7. value - _____

8. trench - _____

B. Directions: Circle the correct spelling of the plural form.

1. fossils   fossiles

2. ponys   ponies

3. stairwaies   stairways

4. furniture   furnitures

5. studios   studioes

6. datas   data

7. swatches   swatchs

8. jettys   jetties

9. splashs   spashes

10. halos   haloes

TO THE TEACHER:

NOUN DETERMINERS

Although noun determiners are actually **adjectives**, it is better to simply refer to them as determiners. Determiners are yellow lights; slow down and take a look before proceeding. In fact, it's best to actually stop and analyze the word and its usage. **Determiners signal that a noun (or sometimes a pronoun) may follow**.

> For example, **a** is a determiner. When students see **a** in a sentence, they need to examine the words that follow it.

| | *noun* | *noun* |

Example: **A** large white <u>pillow</u> had been tossed in **a** <u>dumpster</u>.

Determiners are provided in this unit to help students identify nouns in a sentence. They serve no other purpose at this moment.

<u>Classification of Determiners</u>:

A. Articles: a, an, the

B. Demonstratives: this, that, those, these

C. Numbers: (**five** hamburgers)

D. Possessive Adjectives (also called **possessive pronouns** used as adjectives)**:**

>   my, his, her, your, its, our, their, whose

E. Possessive Nouns (used as adjectives)**:** (**Phil's** camera) (**dog's** paw)

F. Indefinites: some, few, many, several, no, any*

*There are others.

214

Examples:

noun ⠀⠀⠀⠀⠀⠀⠀⠀ *noun*	
Your briefcase is on **the** lower shelf.	____your *briefcase*____
	____the *shelf*____

noun ⠀⠀⠀⠀⠀⠀⠀⠀ *noun*	
Tom's mom owns **several** stores.	____Tom's *mom*____
	____several *stores*____

⠀⠀⠀⠀⠀⠀ *noun*	
The children's bedroom is yellow.	____The *bedroom*____
	____children's *bedroom*____

noun ⠀⠀⠀⠀⠀⠀⠀⠀ *noun*	
Three worms are crawling on **this** leaf.	____Three *worms*____
	____this *leaf*____

IMPORTANT NOTE:

This can be confusing for students. Introduce each classification slowly and include ample examples. (Examples that are applicable to students' lives are usually best.) Once again, I recommend that the students use white-boards not only to write the examples you provide but also to write their own examples. Engaging students in such activities, I have found, promotes understanding and keeps them interested.

NOUN DETERMINERS

Noun determiners are yellow lights. When you see one, slow down and take a look to see if a noun is following it.

For example, **a** is a determiner. When you see **a** in a sentence, you need to examine the words that follow it.

noun   *noun*   *noun*

Example: **A** fluffy white <u>cloud</u> in **the** <u>shape</u> of **a** <u>balloon</u> appeared.

Note that the noun may have another word or words in front of it.

noun

A *fluffy white* <u>cloud</u>

ೋೋೋೋೋೋೋೋೋೋೋೋೋೋೋೋೋೋೋೋೋೋೋೋೋೋ

Classification of Determiners:

A. Articles: a, an, the

B. Demonstratives: this, that, those, these

C. Numbers: (**two** doors)

D. Possessive Adjectives (also called **possessive pronouns** used as adjectives)**:**

> **my, his, her, your, its, our, their, whose**

E. Possessive Nouns (used as adjectives)**:**   (**Jana's** purse)   (**cat's** claws)

F. Indefinites: some, few, many, several, no, any

ೋೋೋೋೋೋೋೋೋೋೋೋೋೋೋೋೋೋೋೋೋೋೋೋೋೋ

Let's look at each classification:

A. Articles: **A, an,** and **the** will come before a noun. As you have already learned, the noun may have another word in front of it.

> Examples: a <u>pebble</u>   an <u>ant</u>   the dark <u>woods</u>

B. Demonstratives: *This*, *that*, *these*, and *those* MAY come before a noun. However, sometimes they stand alone.

Examples: this <u>photo</u>   that salad <u>fork</u>   these <u>clips</u>   those <u>bugs</u>

If *this*, *that*, *these*, or *those* does NOT have a person, place, thing, or idea following it (closely), it may stand alone and will not be a determiner.

Examples: *This* is great! (*This* stands alone and isn't a determiner here.)
   I want *these*. (*These* stands alone and isn't a determiner here.)

C. Numbers: Numbers **MAY** signal a noun. Other words often come between a number and a noun.

Examples: nine <u>players</u>   twenty-two baseball <u>games</u>

If a *number* does NOT have a person, place, thing, or idea following it (closely), it may stand alone and will not be a determiner:

Examples: I'd like *two*, please. (*Two* stands alone and isn't a determiner here.)

D. Possessive Adjectives (also called possessive pronouns): **My, his, her, your, its, our, their**, and **whose** often signal a noun. Check to see if a noun naming a person, place, thing, or idea is following. *My, your, its, our, their,* and *whose* will usually be followed by a noun. <u>Check *her* carefully</u>.

Examples: my <u>mom</u>   his <u>tongue</u>   her new <u>bike</u>   your <u>video</u>
   its <u>wing</u>   our <u>aunts</u>   their ear <u>drum</u>   whose <u>idea</u>

Do you want to go with ***her***?   (*Her* stands alone and is not a determiner.)

E. Possessive Nouns: Possessive nouns often signal other nouns. Possessive means ownership. Look for a word naming a person, place, thing, or idea after any possessive noun.

Examples: **Bill's** <u>wallet</u>   **girls'** tennis <u>match</u>

F. Indefinites: some, few, many, several, no, any*
Indefinites can be determiners. When you see one of the above words, take a close look to see if a noun follows it. Other words may occur between an indefinite and a noun.

Examples: some cream <u>cheese</u>   few <u>markers</u>   many <u>times</u>

several <u>talks</u>   no fresh <u>water</u>   any soft <u>pretzels</u>

An indefinite may stand alone. If it does, it is not a determiner.
Example: *Several* are going.
   I'll take *several*.

*There are others.   217

Directions: Write the boldfaced determiner and the noun that it modifies
(goes over to) in the blank.

Example: **His** eye hurts.   _____**His eye**_____

1. **This** banjo is out of tune.   _____**This banjo**_____

2. Do you have **an** excuse?   _____**an excuse**_____

3. Tell me **your** funny story.   _____**your story**_____

4. Kammi is selling **her** car.   _____**her car**_____

5. **Ten** customers stood in line.   _____**Ten customers**_____

6. We like **those** oil paintings.   _____**those paintings**_____

7. **Bonnie's** daughter is a pilot.   _____**Bonnie's daughter**_____

8. Bass were caught in **the** lake.   _____**the lake**_____

9. I think that **ten** people won the raffle.   _____**ten people**_____

10. **That** Navajo rug is valuable.   _____**That rug**_____

11. **Many** roads in **their** area are new.   _____**Many roads**_____

                                    _____**their area**_____

12. Do you want to play **these** drums?   _____**these drums**_____

13. **Our** friend modeled **several** times.   _____**Our friend**_____

                                    _____**several times**_____

14.   I don't want **any** prunes.   _____**any prunes**_____

15. That is **Lou's** grandmother.   _____**Lou's grandmother**_____

218

Name_____   **NOUNS**

Date_____   **Determiners**

Directions: Write the boldfaced determiner and the noun that it modifies
               (goes over to) in the blank.

               Example: **His** eye hurts.   _____**His eye**_____

1.   **This** banjo is out of tune.   _____

2.   Do you have **an** excuse?   _____

3.   Tell me **your** funny story.   _____

4.   Kammi is selling **her** car.   _____

5.   **Ten** customers stood in line.   _____

6.   We like **those** oil paintings.   _____

7.   **Bonnie's** daughter is a pilot.   _____

8.   Bass were caught in **the** lake.   _____

9.   I think that **ten** people won the raffle. _____

10. **That** Navajo rug is valuable.   _____

11. **Many** roads in **their** area are new.   _____

                                                 _____

12. Do you want to play **these** drums?   _____

13. **Our** friend modeled **several** times.   _____

                                                 _____

14. I don't want **any** prunes.   _____

15. That is **Lou's** grandmother.   _____

                                                                   219

Name_____   **NOUNS**

WORKBOOK PAGE 101

Date_____   **Determiners**

Directions: Place a ✓ in the blank if the boldfaced word is a determiner. If the word serves as a determiner, write the boldfaced word and the noun that it modifies (goes over to) in the wide blank.

1.   ✓   She ordered **three** sandwiches.   _____three sandwiches_____

2.   ___   The toddler is **three**.   _____

3.   ✓   I want to meet **her** mother.   _____her mother_____

4.   ___   We had to start without **her**.   _____

5.   ___   Are **these** new?   _____

6.   ✓   **These** ideas are good ones.   _____These ideas_____

7.   ___   **Many** were waiting in line.   _____

8.   ✓   **Many** students tried out for the play._____Many students_____

9.   ✓   Todd bought **Tara's** pottery.   _____Tara's pottery_____

10.   ___   Is this **Tara's**?   _____

11.   ___   He chose **those** for their wedding._____

12.   ✓   Please pick up **those** sticks.   _____those sticks_____

13.   ___   We gave **several** to our friends.   _____

14.   ✓   They own **several** stocks.   _____several stocks_____

15.   ___   **Few** need that surgery.   _____

16.   ✓   **Few** people decided to stay.   _____Few people_____

220

Name_____   **NOUNS**

Date_____   **Determiners**

Directions: Place a ✓ in the blank if the boldfaced word is a determiner. If the word serves as a determiner, write the boldfaced word and the noun that it modifies (goes over to) in the wide blank.

1. __   She ordered **three** sandwiches.   _____

2. __   The toddler is **three**.   _____

3. __   I want to meet **her** mother.   _____

4. __   We had to start without **her**.   _____

5. __   Are **these** new?   _____

6. __   **These** ideas are good ones.   _____

7. __   **Many** were waiting in line.   _____

8. __   **Many** students tried out for the play._____

9. __   Todd bought **Tara's** pottery.   _____

10. __   Is this **Tara's**?   _____

11. __   He chose **those** for their wedding.   _____

12. __   Please pick up **those** sticks.   _____

13. __   We gave **several** to our friends.   _____

14. __   They own **several** stocks.   _____

15. __   **Few** need that surgery.   _____

16. __   **Few** people decided to stay.   _____

Name_____   **NOUNS**

WORKBOOK PAGE 102

Date_____   **Determiners**

Determiners:

A. Articles: a, an, the
B. Demonstratives: this, that, those, these
C. Numbers: (**one** block)
D. Possessive Adjectives (possessive pronouns):
       my, his, her, your, its, our, their
E. Possessive Nouns (used as adjectives): (**Bo's** bag) (**boys'** bedroom)
F. Indefinites: some, few, many, several, no, any (and other words)

ৰ৵ৰ৵ৰ৵ৰ৵ৰ৵ৰ৵ৰ৵ৰ৵ৰ৵ৰ৵ৰ৵ৰ৵ৰ৵ৰ৵ৰ৵ৰ৵ৰ৵

Directions: Draw a dotted line under any determiner. Write the determiner
              and the noun that the determiner modifies (goes over to) in the blank.

          Example: Have you lost your backpack?   ___your **backpack**___

1.   Ms. Jones, our music teacher, just arrived.   ___**our teacher**___

2.   Please put this check into my bag.   ___**this check**___

                                                    ___**my bag**___

3.   Several huge owls flew from that tree.   ___**Several owls**___

                                                    ___**that tree**___

4.   Has their favorite game been played?   ___**their game**___

5.   She hit the cymbal with a padded drumstick.   ___**the cymbal**___

                                                    ___**a drumstick**___

6.   Peter's friend owns many horses.   ___**Peter's friend**___

                                                    ___**many horses**___

7.   No reason had been given for his behavior.   ___**no reason**___

                                                    ___**his behavior**___

8.   These muffins are too dry.   ___**These muffins**___

222

Name_____   **NOUNS**

Date_____   **Determiners**

Determiners:
A. **Articles: a, an, the**
B. **Demonstratives: this, that, those, these**
C. **Numbers:**   (**one** block)
D. **Possessive Adjectives** (possessive pronouns):
        my, his, her, your, its, our, their
E. **Possessive Nouns** (used as adjectives):   (**Bo's** bag)   (**boys'** bedroom)
F. **Indefinites: some, few, many, several, no, any** (and other words)

꙾꙾꙾꙾꙾꙾꙾꙾꙾꙾꙾꙾꙾꙾꙾꙾꙾

Directions: Draw a dotted line under any determiner. Write the determiner
        and the noun that the determiner modifies (goes over to) in the blank.

        Example: Have you lost your backpack?   ___your **backpack**___

1.   Ms. Jones, our music teacher, just arrived.   _____

2.   Please put this check into my bag.   _____

        _____

3.   Several huge owls flew from that tree.   _____

        _____

4.   Has their favorite game been played?   _____

5.   She hit the cymbal with a padded drumstick.   _____

        _____

6.   Peter's friend owns many horses.   _____

        _____

7.   No reason had been given for his behavior.   _____

        _____

8.   These muffins are too dry.   _____

Name_____   **NOUNS**

Date_____   **Determiners**

Note: In sentences #5 (*Jan's*), #8 (*city's*), and #9 (*Leah's*), the possessive nouns that serve as determiners are also technically nouns. I suggest that you do not count those wrong if students fail to circle them.

Determiners are yellow lights. When you approach one, slow down and check it carefully. It will help you to identify many nouns.

However, not all nouns have determiners.

Remember that a noun names a person, place, thing, or idea.

Example: Mom asked our neighbor a question about quilts.

Mom asked *our* **neighbor** *a* **question** about **quilts**.

Note that there are no determiners in front of the nouns, Mom or quilts. Determiners definitely help you to identify nouns. *However*, you will need to think about what nouns are when identifying them.

🙌🙌🙌🙌🙌🙌🙌🙌🙌🙌🙌🙌

Directions: Circle any noun. (You may wish to place a wavy line under each determiner as a guide to identifying nouns.)

NOUNS ARE BOLDFACED. (Determiners are italicized.)

1. *One* **puppy** wagged *its* little, curly **tail**.

2. *A* police **car** pulled onto *the* **highway** from *an* **exit**.

3. **Dad** bought *three* **pears**, *two* ripe **bananas**, and *several* **plums**.

4. During *their* **trip** to **Chicago**, **Mark** and his **sister** visited *many* **museums**.

5. Put *Jan's* **stroller**, **playpen**, and **bag** in *that* large **closet**.

6. *Your* **idea** made **money** for *our* **fundraiser** last **winter**.

7. Yesterday, *some* **men** met to discuss *several* important **topics**.

8. *No* **swans** ever glide on *this* **pond** in *the* *city's* **park**.

9. Did you meet *Leah's* **parents** at *her* **wedding** in **June**?

10. *Three* computer **experts** are studying *this* virus **problem**.

Determiners are yellow lights. When you approach one, slow down and check it carefully. It will help you to identify many nouns.

However, not all nouns have determiners.

Remember that a noun names a person, place, thing, or idea.

Example: Mom asked our neighbor a question about quilts.

Mom asked *our* **neighbor** *a* **question** about **quilts**.

Note that there are no determiners in front of the nouns, <u>Mom</u> or <u>quilts</u>. Determiners definitely help you to identify nouns. *However*, you will need to think about what nouns are when identifying them.

ࣟࣟࣟࣟࣟࣟࣟࣟࣟࣟࣟࣟࣟࣟࣟ

Directions: Circle any noun. (You may wish to place a wavy line under each determiner as a guide to identifying nouns.)

1. One puppy wagged its little, curly tail.

2. A police car pulled onto the highway from an exit.

3. Dad bought three pears, two ripe bananas, and several plums.

4. During their trip to Chicago, Mark and his sister visited many museums.

5. Put Jan's stroller, playpen, and bag in that large closet.

6. Your idea made money for our fundraiser last winter.

7. Yesterday, some men met to discuss several important topics.

8. No swans ever glide on this pond in the city's park.

9. Did you meet Leah's parents at her wedding in June?

10. Three computer experts are studying this virus problem.

Name_____   **NOUNS**

Date_____   **Possessives**

Extremely Important Note: **You may be confused because I have omitted the rule that states that singular nouns ending in _s_ add only an apostrophe. The rule actually has changed to the one listed below. However, please feel free to add this rule if you choose.** (Make students aware that nouns they encounter in their reading may appear either way.)

Singular means one.

one boy

Possessive means to possess or to own.

a jacket belonging to a boy

To form the possessive of any singular noun, add '_s_.

boy'**_s_** jacket

This form is called the singular possessive. It is a singular noun showing ownership.

Add '**_s_** even if the word ends in _s_.   Example: Chris'**_s_** jacket

ନ୍ତ ନ୍ତ ନ୍ତ ନ୍ତ ନ୍ତ ନ୍ତ ନ୍ତ ନ୍ତ ନ୍ତ ନ୍ତ ନ୍ତ ନ୍ତ ନ୍ତ ନ୍ତ ନ୍ତ ନ୍ତ

Directions: Write the possessive of each singular noun.

1. a toy belonging to a baby - _____**baby's toy**_____

2. magazines belonging to her sister - _____**sister's magazines**_____

3. a belt belonging to Jasmin - _____**Jasmin's belt**_____

4. a stall for a horse   - _____**horse's stall**_____

5. parties given for an ambassador - _____**ambassador's parties**_____

6. many clients of a hairstylist - _____**hairstylist's clients**_____

7. the shape of an iris - _____**iris's shape   (SEE NOTE ABOVE.)**_____

8. doors on our cupboard - _____**our cupboard's doors**_____

9. a handle on a coffeepot - _____**coffeepot's handle**_____

10.   mail belonging to Mr. Paas - _____**Mr. Paas's mail   (SEE NOTE ABOVE.)**_____

11.   jewelry owned by that woman - _____**that woman's jewelry**_____

226

Date_____

Singular means one.

> one boy

Possessive means to possess or to own.

> a jacket belonging to a boy

To form the possessive of any singular noun, add 's.

> boy's jacket

This form is called the singular possessive. It is a singular noun showing ownership.

Add 's even if the word ends in *s*.   Example: Chris's jacket

๛๛๛๛๛๛๛๛๛๛๛๛๛๛๛๛๛๛๛๛๛๛

Directions: Write the possessive of each singular noun.

1. a toy belonging to a baby - _____

2. magazines belonging to her sister - _____

3. a belt belonging to Jasmin - _____

4. a stall for a horse   - _____

5. parties given for an ambassador - _____

6. many clients of a hairstylist - _____

7. the shape of an iris - _____

8. doors on our cupboard - _____

9. a handle on a coffeepot - _____

10. mail belonging to Mr. Paas - _____

11. jewelry owned by that woman - _____

Plural means more than one.

two boys   several boys

Possessive means to possess or to own.

a tree house belonging to two boys

To form the possessive of any plural noun that ends in *s*, add ʼ.

boysʼ tree house

To form the possessive of any plural noun that does NOT end in *s*, add ʼs.   childrenʼ**s** theater

This form is called the plural possessive. It is a plural noun showing ownership.

ૐૐૐૐૐૐૐૐૐૐૐૐૐૐૐૐૐૐૐૐૐ

Directions: Write the plural noun. Then, write the plural possessive.

1. tadpole - _____**tadpoles**_____

    a creek shared by more than one tadpole - _____**tadpoles**ʼ **creek**_____

2. salesman - _____**salesmen**_____

    a meeting for more than one salesman - _____**salesmen**ʼ**s meeting**_____

3. dancer - _____**dancers**_____

    a teacher belonging to more than one dancer - _____**dancers**ʼ **teacher**_____

4. piglet - _____**piglets**_____

    a pen where more than one piglet lives - _____**piglets**ʼ **pen**_____

5. policeman - _____**policemen**_____

    an office occupied by more than one policeman - **policemen**ʼ**s office**

228

Plural means more than one.

two boys   several boys

Possessive means to possess or to own.

a tree house belonging to two boys

To form the possessive of any plural noun that ends in _s_, add '.

boys' tree house

To form the possessive of any plural noun that does NOT

end in _s_, add '_s_.   children**'s** theater

This form is called the plural possessive. It is a plural noun showing ownership.

ฅ฿ฅ฿ฅ฿ฅ฿ฅ฿ฅ฿ฅ฿ฅ฿ฅ฿ฅ฿ฅ฿ฅ฿ฅ฿

Directions: Write the plural noun. Then, write the plural possessive.

1. tadpole - _____

    a creek shared by more than one tadpole - _____

2. salesman - _____

    a meeting for more than one salesman - _____

3. dancer - _____

    a teacher belonging to more than one dancer - _____

4. piglet - _____

    a pen where more than one piglet lives - _____

5. policeman - _____

    an office occupied by more than one policeman - _____

NOUNS

Possessives

Extremely Important Note: You may be confused because I have omitted the rule that states that singular nouns ending in *s* add only an apostrophe. The rule actually has changed. However, please feel free to add this rule if you choose. (Make students aware that nouns they encounter in their reading may appear either way.)

Singular means one.   one chipmunk

Plural means more than one.   three chipmunks

Possessive means to possess or to own.

1. **To form the possessive of any singular noun, add '*s*.**

    bird'*s* beak

2. **To form the possessive of any plural noun that ends in *s*, add '.**

    birds' nest (a nest belonging to more than one bird)

3. **To form the possessive of any plural noun that does NOT end in *s*, add '*s*.**

    octopus

    octopi's behavior (the behavior of more than one octopus)

🐦🐦🐦🐦🐦🐦🐦🐦🐦🐦🐦🐦🐦🐦🐦🐦🐦🐦🐦

Directions: Write the possessive form in each blank.

1. a bone belonging to one dog - _____**dog's bone**_____

    a bone belonging to more than one dog - _____**dogs' bone**_____

2. a patient attended by one nurse - _____**nurse's patient**_____

    a patient attended by more than one nurse - _____**nurses' patient**_____

3. a boat owned by a woman - _____**woman's boat**_____

    a boat owned by more than one woman - _____**women's boat**_____

4. a campsite used by one family - _____**family's campsite**_____

    a campsite used by more than one family - _____**families' campsite**_____

5. hamsters belonging to a child - _____**child's hamsters**_____

    hamsters belonging to more than one child - _____**children's hamsters**

Date_____

Possessives

Singular means one.   one chipmunk

Plural means more than one.   three chipmunks

Possessive means to possess or to own.

1. **To form the possessive of any singular noun, add 's.**

      bird**'s** beak

2. **To form the possessive of any plural noun that ends in _s_, add '.**

      birds' nest (a nest belonging to more than one bird)

3. **To form the possessive of any plural noun that does NOT end in _s_, add 's.**

      octopus

      octopi's behavior (the behavior of more than one octopus)

ৡৡৡৡৡৡৡৡৡৡৡৡৡৡৡৡৡৡৡৡৡৡ

Directions: Write the possessive form in each blank.

 1. a bone belonging to one dog - _____

      a bone belonging to more than one dog - _____

 2. a patient attended by one nurse - _____

      a patient attended by more than one nurse - _____

 3. a boat owned by a woman - _____

      a boat owned by more than one woman - _____

 4. a campsite used by one family - _____

      a campsite used by more than one family - _____

 5. hamsters belonging to a child - _____

      hamsters belonging to more than one child - _____

Possessive means to possess or to own.

  1. To form the possessive of any singular noun, add _'s_.

      bracelet**'s** clasp

  2. To form the possessive of any plural noun that ends in _s_, add _'_ .

      doctors' conference

  3. To form the possessive of any plural noun that does NOT end in _s_, add _'s_.

      ox

      oxen**'s** barn (a barn belonging to more than one ox)

☙☙☙☙☙☙☙☙☙☙☙☙☙☙☙☙☙☙☙☙☙

Directions: Write the possessive form in each blank.

1. drawings created by one artist - **artist's drawings**

  an exhibit shared by more than one artist - **artists' exhibit**

2. a display done by a florist - **florist's display**

  an expo attended by more than one florist - **florists' expo**

3. plans made by one councilwoman - **councilwoman's plans**

  plans made by more than one councilwoman - **councilwomen's plans**

4. a deal signed by Mr. Nicks - **Mr. Nicks's deal**

  a deal signed by two brothers - **brothers' deal**

5. a hiking trail cleared by a city - **city's hiking trail**

  a hiking trail cleared by more than one city - **cities' hiking trail**

6. shows done by one producer - **producer's shows**

  shows done by more than one producer - **producers' shows**

Possessive means to possess or to own.

1. **To form the possessive of any singular noun, add 's.**

   bracelet**'s** clasp

2. **To form the possessive of any plural noun that ends in s, add '.**

   doctors' conference

3. **To form the possessive of any plural noun that does NOT end in s, add 's.**

   ox

   oxen's barn (a barn belonging to more than one ox)

Directions: Write the possessive form in each blank.

1. drawings created by one artist - _____

   an exhibit shared by more than one artist - _____

2. a display done by a florist - _____

   an expo attended by more than one florist - _____

3. plans made by one councilwoman - _____

   plans made by more than one councilwoman - _____

4. a deal signed by Mr. Nicks - _____

   a deal signed by two brothers - _____

5. a hiking trail cleared by a city - _____

   a hiking trail cleared by more than one city - _____

6. shows done by one producer - _____

   shows done by more than one producer - _____

Possessive means to possess or to own.

1. **To form the possessive of any singular noun, add 's.**

    kite**'s** string

2. **To form the possessive of any plural noun that ends in s, add '.**

    toddlers' exercise class

3. **To form the possessive of any plural noun that does NOT end in s, add 's.**

    goose

    geese's noise

෪෪෪෪෪෪෪෪෪෪෪෪෪෪෪෪෪෪෪෪෪෪

Directions: Write the possessive form in each blank.

1. pastries created by a chef - _____chef**'s** pastries_____

2. a boxcar owned by Rex - _____Rex**'s** boxcar_____

3. tools shared by more than one craftsman - _____craftmen**'s** tools___

4. baseballs signed by several athletes - ____athletes' baseballs_____

5. a bullpen for one team - _____team**'s** bullpen_____

6.   margins on a paper - _____paper**'s** margins_____

7. toe rings owned by my aunt - _____aunt**'s** toe rings_____

8. an apartment shared by two boys - _____boys' apartment_____

9. a shawl knitted by Grandma - _____Grandma**'s** shawl_____

10. bushes purchased by several gardeners - ____gardners' bushes___

11. the tip of an iceberg - _____iceberg**'s** tip_____

12. necklaces designed by Gus - _____Gus**'s** necklaces_____

234

Possessive means to possess or to own.

1. **To form the possessive of any singular noun, add 's.**

    kite**'s** string

2. **To form the possessive of any plural noun that ends in s, add '.**

    toddlers' exercise class

3. **To form the possessive of any plural noun that does NOT end in s, add 's.**

    goose

    geese's noise

෩෩෩෩෩෩෩෩෩෩෩෩෩෩෩෩෩෩෩෩෩

Directions: Write the possessive form in each blank.

1. pastries created by a chef - _____

2. a boxcar owned by Rex - _____

3. tools shared by more than one craftsman - _____

4. baseballs signed by several athletes - _____

5. a bullpen for one team - _____

6. margins on a paper - _____

7. toe rings owned by my aunt - _____

8. an apartment shared by two boys - _____

9. a shawl knitted by Grandma - _____

10. bushes purchased by several gardeners - _____

11. the tip of an iceberg - _____

12. necklaces designed by Gus - _____

NOUNS

Possessives

To form the possessive of any singular noun, add 's.
To form the possessive of any plural noun that ends in s, add '.
To form the possessive of any plural noun that does NOT end in s, add 's.

ᗷᗷᗷᗷᗷᗷᗷᗷᗷᗷᗷᗷᗷᗷᗷᗷᗷᗷᗷᗷ

Directions: Circle the correct possessive form:

1. marbles owned by Sam: **Sam's marbles**   Sams' marbles

2. drums owned by two boys: boy's drums   **boys' drums**

3. an apartment shared by two girls: **girls' apartment** girl's apartment

4. a magnet belonging to Janice: **Janice's magnet**   Janices' magnet

5. a picnic shared by two families: family's picnic   **families' picnic**

6. cap on a radiator: radiators' cap   **radiator's cap**

7. the schedules of several pilots: **pilots' schedules** pilot's schedules

8. pictures drawn by Les: **Les's pictures**   Les pictures

9. cookies baked by Marco: **Marco's cookies**   Marcos' cookies

10. soup made by more than one man: **men's soup**   mens' soup

11. an office shared by two doctors: doctor's office   **doctors' office**

12. menus created by a cook: cooks' menus   **cook's menus**

13. a road used by two ranches: **ranches' road**   ranch's road

14. a stamp on a card: cards' stamp   **card's stamp**

15. damage caused by two storms   storm's damage   **storms' damage**

16. sketches by more than one artist: **artists' sketches** artist's sketches

236

To form the possessive of any singular noun, add 's.
To form the possessive of any plural noun that ends in s, add '.
To form the possessive of any plural noun that does NOT end in s, add 's.

෨෨෨෨෨෨෨෨෨෨෨෨෨෨෨෨෨෨෨෨෨෨෨

Directions: Circle the correct possessive form:

1.	marbles owned by Sam:	Sam's marbles	Sams' marbles
2.	drums owned by two boys:	boy's drums	boys' drums
3.	an apartment shared by two girls:	girls' apartment	girl's apartment
4.	a magnet belonging to Janice:	Janice's magnet	Janices' magnet
5.	a picnic shared by two families:	family's picnic	families' picnic
6.	cap on a radiator:	radiators' cap	radiator's cap
7.	the schedules of several pilots:	pilots' schedules	pilot's schedules
8.	pictures drawn by Les:	Les's pictures	Les pictures
9.	cookies baked by Marco:	Marco's cookies	Marcos' cookies
10.	soup made by more than one man:	men's soup	mens' soup
11.	an office shared by two doctors:	doctor's office	doctors' office
12.	menus created by a cook:	cooks' menus	cook's menus
13.	a road used by two ranches:	ranches' road	ranch's road
14.	a stamp on a card:	cards' stamp	card's stamp
15.	damage caused by two storms	storm's damage	storms' damage
16.	sketches by more than one artist:	artists' sketches	artist's sketches

237

Name_____   **NOUNS**

WORKBOOK PAGE 110

Date_____   **Direct Objects/Indirect Objects**

Note: Teach this concept slowly. Consider doing this worksheet orally.

ANSWERS MAY VARY/REPRESENTATIVE ANSWERS:

Review:

A noun may serve as a **subject** of a sentence.

   Example: **Ginny** <u>bought</u> her husband a tractor for their farm.

A noun may serve as a **direct object** of a sentence.

                                     D.O.

   Example: Ginny bought her husband a **tractor** for their farm. (the object she bought)

A noun may serve as an **object of a preposition**.

                                           O.P.

   Example: Ginny bought her husband a tractor for their **farm**.

                       (*for their farm* = prepositional phrase)

New:

A noun may serve as an **indirect object. An indirect object is the receiver of**
some **direct objects.**

         Example: A dentist gave his patient a new toothbrush.

                                   D.O.

Find the parts of the example: A <u>dentist</u> <u>gave</u> his patient a new toothbrush.

You can mentally insert *to* or *for* **before** an indirect object.

                to   **I.O.**   **D.O.**

   A <u>dentist</u> <u>gave</u> / his patient a new toothbrush.

Look at our original example.

              for   **I.O.**   **D.O.**

   <u>Ginny</u> <u>bought</u> / her husband a tractor for their farm.

When a sentence has a direct object, check to see if it also contains an indirect object.

Remember: You can mentally place *to* or *for* before an indirect object.

       ळ्ळळ्ळळ्ळळ्ळळ्ळळ्ळळ्ळळ्ळळ्ळळ्ळ

Directions: Underline the subject once and the verb twice. Label the direct object-
        D.O. Write a noun that will serve as an indirect object in the blank.

           to   **D.O.**

1. Mom handed / _____**Matt**_____ a rake.

             for   **D.O.**

2. Grandpa baked / his _____**grandchildren**_____ a special dinner.

           to   **D.O.**

3. Parker gave / her _____**cousin**_____ sugarless gum.

                for   **D.O.**

4. A nail technician ordered / a _____**client**_____ some hand cream.

238

Name_____   **NOUNS**

Date_____   **Direct Objects/Indirect Objects**

Review:

A noun may serve as a **subject** of a sentence.

   Example: **Ginny** bought her husband a tractor for their farm.

A noun may serve as a **direct object** of a sentence.
                                   D.O.

   Example: Ginny bought her husband a **tractor** for their farm. (the object she bought)

A noun may serve as an **object of a preposition**.
                                   O.P.

   Example: Ginny bought her husband a tractor for their **farm**.

                            (*for their farm* = prepositional phrase)

New:

A noun may serve as an **indirect object. An indirect object is the receiver of**
some **direct objects.**

                 Example: A dentist gave his patient a new toothbrush.
                                            D.O.

Find the parts of the example: A <u>dentist</u> <u>gave</u> his patient a new toothbrush.

You can mentally insert *to* or *for* **before** an indirect object.

                 to   **I.O.**   **D.O.**
     A <u>dentist</u> <u>gave</u> **/** his patient a new toothbrush.

Look at our original example.

                 for   **I.O.**   **D.O.**
     <u>Ginny</u> <u>bought</u> **/** her husband a tractor for their farm.

When a sentence has a direct object, check to see if it also contains an indirect object.
    Remember: You can mentally place *to* or *for* before an indirect object.

       ॐॐॐॐॐॐॐॐॐॐॐॐॐॐॐॐॐॐ

Directions: Underline the subject once and the verb twice. Label the direct object-
         D.O. Write a noun that will serve as an indirect object in the blank.

       to
1. Mom handed **/** _____ a rake.
       for
2. Grandpa baked / his _____ a special dinner.
       to
3. Parker gave / her _____ sugarless gum.
         for
4. A nail technician ordered / a _____ some hand cream.

                                         239

WORKBOOK PAGE 111

A noun may serve as an **indirect object**. **An indirect object is the receiver of *some* direct objects.**

You can mentally insert ***to*** or ***for* before** an indirect object.

to   **I.O.**   **D.O.**
A <u>painter</u> <u>sent</u> **/** the owner a bill.

for   **I.O.**   **D.O.**
The <u>man</u> <u>fixed</u> **/** his date a nice dinner.

<u>When a sentence has a direct object, check to see if it also contains an indirect object.</u>

<u>Remember: You can mentally place ***to*** or ***for*** before an indirect object.</u>

ୡ୰ୡ୰ୡ୰ୡ୰ୡ୰ୡ୰ୡ୰ୡ୰ୡ୰ୡ୰ୡ୰ୡ୰

Directions: Write ***to*** or ***for*** above the **/**. Circle the indirect object.
NOUNS THAT SERVE AS INDIRECT OBJECTS ARE BOLDFACED HERE.

1. ***to***
    A guide told / the **group** the history of the old mansion.

2. ***for***
    The child drew / his **parents** a picture of their family.

3. ***to***
    Several gallery owners sent / art **buyers** cards concerning a show.

4. ***for***
    Kammi fixed / the **children** grilled-cheese sandwiches.

5. ***to***
    The teacher asked / several **students** the same question.

6. ***for, to***
    Nan printed / her **daughter** a note.

7. ***for, to***
    Mom bought / her **co-worker** lunch today.

8. ***to***
    One French poodle gave / her **master** a lick on his hand.

9. ***for***
    The landlord makes / new **owners** a few extra keys.

10. ***to***
    Dina presented / the **bride** and **groom** a wedding gift.

11. ***for***
    A banker copied / the **couple** three pages of the house contract.

12. ***to***
    Has Mrs. Brau sent / her **godmother** an invitation to the ball?

NOUNS

Direct Objects/Indirect Objects

A noun may serve as an **indirect object**. **An indirect object is the receiver of** *some* **direct objects.**

You can mentally insert **to** or **for before** an indirect object.

                                   to   **I.O.**   **D.O.**

A <u>painter</u> <u>sent</u> **/** the owner a bill.

                                 for   **I.O.**   **D.O.**

The <u>man</u> <u>fixed</u> / his date a nice dinner.

When a sentence has a direct object, check to see if it also contains an indirect object.

<u>Remember: You can mentally place</u> ***to*** <u>or</u> ***for*** <u>before an indirect object.</u>

~~~~~~~~~~~~~~~~~~~~

Directions: Write **to** or **for** above the **/**. Circle the indirect object.

1. A guide told / the group the history of the old mansion.

2. The child drew / his parents a picture of their family.

3. Several gallery owners sent / art buyers cards concerning a show.

4. Kammi fixed / the children grilled-cheese sandwiches.

5. The teacher asked / several students the same question.

6. Nan printed / her daughter a note.

7. Mom bought / her co-worker lunch today.

8. One French poodle gave / her master a lick on his hand.

9. The landlord makes / new owners a few extra keys.

10. Dina presented / the bride and groom a wedding gift.

11. A banker copied / the couple three pages of the house contract.

12. Has Mrs. Brau sent / her godmother an invitation to the ball?

A noun may serve as an **indirect object.** **An indirect object is the receiver of**
some **direct objects.**

You can mentally insert *to* or *for* **before** an indirect object.

for **I.O.**   **D.O.**

Those <u>seamstresses</u> <u>make</u> / children little beanbags.

to **I.O.**   **D.O.**

That <u>teacher</u> <u>mailed</u> / her students cards .

When a sentence has a direct object, check to see if it also contains an indirect object.
Remember: You can mentally place *to* or *for* before an indirect object.

∂∞∂∞∂∞∂∞∂∞∂∞∂∞∂∞∂∞∂∞∂∞∂∞∂∞∂∞∂∞∂∞

Directions: Cross out any prepositional phrases. Underline the subject once
and the verb or verb phrase twice. Label the direct object - **D.O.**
Label the indirect object - **I.O.**

         I.O.   **D.O.**
1. A <u>guide</u> <u>told</u> the group the history ~~of the old mansion~~.
         I.O.   **D.O.**
2. The <u>child</u> <u>drew</u> his parents a picture.
         I.O.   **D.O.**
3. Several gallery <u>owners</u> <u>sent</u> art buyers cards ~~concerning a show~~.
         I.O.   **D.O.**
4. <u>Kammi</u> <u>fixed</u> the children grilled-cheese sandwiches.
         I.O.   **D.O.**
5. The <u>teacher</u> <u>asked</u> several students the same question.
         I.O.   **D.O.**
6. <u>Nan</u> <u>printed</u> her daughter a note.
         I.O.   **D.O.**
7. <u>Mom</u> <u>bought</u> her co-worker lunch today.
         I.O.   **D.O.**
8. One French <u>poodle</u> <u>gave</u> her master a lick ~~on his hand~~.
         I.O.   **D.O.**
9. The <u>landlord</u> makes new owners a few extra keys.
         I.O.   **I.O.**   **D.O.**
10. <u>Tate</u> <u>presented</u> the bride and groom a wedding gift.
         I.O.   **D.O.**
11. A <u>banker</u> <u>copied</u> the couple three pages ~~of the house contract~~.
         I.O.   **D.O.**
12. <u>Has</u> <u>Mrs. Brau</u> <u>sent</u> her godmother an invitation ~~to the ball~~?

242

Name_____   **NOUNS**

Date_____   **Direct Objects/Indirect Objects**

A noun may serve as an **indirect object. An indirect object is the receiver of** *some* **direct objects.**

You can mentally insert *to* or *for* **before** an indirect object.

                              for   **I.O.**   **D.O.**

Those <u>seamstresses</u> <u>make</u> / children little beanbags.

                           to   **I.O.**   **D.O.**

That <u>teacher</u> <u>mailed</u> / her students cards .

When a sentence has a direct object, check to see if it also contains an indirect object.
Remember: You can mentally place *to* or *for* before an indirect object.

Directions: Cross out any prepositional phrases. Underline the subject once and the verb or verb phrase twice. Label the direct object - **D.O.**
Label the indirect object - **I.O.**

1. A guide told the group the history of the old mansion.

2. The child drew his parents a picture.

3. Several gallery owners sent art buyers cards concerning a show.

4. Kammi fixed the children grilled-cheese sandwiches.

5. The teacher asked several students the same question.

6. Nan printed her daughter a note.

7. Mom bought her co-worker lunch today.

8. One French poodle gave her master a lick on his hand.

9. The landlord makes new owners a few extra keys.

10. Tate presented the bride and groom a wedding gift.

11. A banker copied the couple three pages of the house contract.

12. Has Mrs. Brau sent her godmother an invitation to the ball?

243

WORKBOOK PAGE 113
Date_____ **Direct Objects/Indirect Objects**

When a sentence has a direct object, check to see if it also contains an indirect object. Remember: You can mentally place *to* or *for* before an indirect object.

for   **I.O.**   **D.O.**

The <u>chef</u> <u>made</u> / his guests a shrimp salad.

to **I.O.**   **D.O.**

<u>I</u> <u>threw</u> / Jan a football.

ॐॐॐॐॐॐॐॐॐॐॐॐॐॐॐॐॐॐॐॐॐ

A. Directions: Cross out any prepositional phrases. Underline the subject once and the verb or verb phrase twice. Label the direct object – **D.O.**

  D.O.
1. The <u>father</u> <u>ordered</u> a scooter.

  D.O.
2. <u>Marco</u> <u>prepared</u> a spinach dip.

  D.O.
3. <u>Chessa</u> <u>baked</u> a roast ~~with carrots~~.

  D.O.
4. That young <u>woman</u> <u>sends</u> many packages.

  D.O.
5. <u>Miss Sims</u> <u>sewed</u> two ball gowns.

  D.O.
6. A <u>stockbroker</u> <u>bought</u> a thousand shares ~~of stock~~.

B. Directions: Cross out any prepositional phrases. Underline the subject once and the verb or verb phrase twice. Label the direct object – **D.O.** Label the indirect object - **I.O.**

  I.O.   **D.O.**
1. The <u>father</u> <u>ordered</u> his children a scooter.

  I.O.   **D.O.**
2. <u>Marco</u> <u>prepared</u> his wife a spinach dip.

  I.O.   **D.O.**
3. <u>Chessa</u> <u>baked</u> her parents a roast ~~with carrots~~.

  I.O.   **D.O.**
4. The young <u>woman</u> <u>sends</u> the soldier packages.

  I.O.   **D.O.**
5. <u>Miss Sims</u> <u>sewed</u> the mayor's wife two long gowns.

  I.O.   **D.O.**
6. A <u>stockbroker</u> <u>bought</u> Mrs. Hernandez a thousand shares ~~of stock~~.

When a sentence has a direct object, check to see if it also contains an indirect object. Remember: You can mentally place _to_ or _for_ before an indirect object.

                                    for   **I.O.**   **D.O.**
                     The <u>chef</u> <u>made</u> / his guests a shrimp salad.

                            _to_ **I.O.**   **D.O.**
                     I <u>threw</u> / Jan a football.

ৡৡৡৡৡৡৡৡৡৡৡৡৡৡৡৡৡৡৡৡৡৡ

A. Directions: Cross out any prepositional phrases. Underline the subject once and the verb or verb phrase twice. Label the direct object – **D.O.**

1.   The father ordered a scooter.

2.   Marco prepared a spinach dip.

3.   Chessa baked a roast with carrots.

4.   That young woman sends many packages.

5.   Miss Sims sewed two long gowns.

6.   A stockbroker bought a thousand shares of stock.

B. Directions: Cross out any prepositional phrases. Underline the subject once and the verb or verb phrase twice. Label the direct object – **D.O.** Label the indirect object - **I.O.**

1.   The father ordered his children a scooter.

2.   Marco prepared his wife a spinach dip.

3.   Chessa baked her parents a roast with carrots.

4.   The young woman sends the soldier packages.

5.   Miss Sims sewed the mayor's wife two long gowns.

6.   A stockbroker bought Mrs. Hernandez a thousand shares of stock.

PREDICATE NOMINATIVES

A noun may serve as a predicate nominative.

Remember: The complete predicate of a sentence usually begins with the verb and goes to the end of a sentence.

My ball **rolled** down a steep hill.
complete predicate

Last fall, her dad **became** a sports announcer.
complete predicate

A predicate nominative occurs after a linking verb.

ৰ্চ্চৰ্চ্চৰ্চ্চৰ্চ্চৰ্চ্চ

Linking Verbs:

to feel	to smell	to grow	to stay
to taste	to seem	to remain	to become
to look	to sound	to appear	to be (is, am, are, was, were,
			be, being, been)

ৰ্চ্চৰ্চ্চৰ্চ্চৰ্চ্চৰ্চ্চ

A predicate nominative is a noun (or pronoun) that occurs <u>after</u> a

linking verb and <u>means the same as the subject</u>.

P.N.

Example: Their <u>neighbor</u> in Alaska <u>was</u> Mr. Hare.

To determine if a sentence contains a predicate nominative, do the following:

1. Find the subject and verb.

   (Delete any prepositional phrases. A predicate nominative will not appear in a prepositional phrase.)

   Their <u>neighbor</u> ~~in Alaska~~ <u>was</u> Mr. Hare.

2. Ask yourself if the verb is on the linking verb list.

   Was is on the linking verb list. *Was* **may** serve as a linking verb here.

3. If the verb is on that list, see if there is a noun after the verb that means the same as the subject.

   <u>neighbor</u>   =   Mr. Hare

4. Try inverting the sentence to prove a predicate nominative.

   P.N.
   Their <u>neighbor</u> <u>is</u> Mr. Hare.

   Inverted form: *Mr. Hare is their neighbor.*

WORKBOOK PAGE 116

Note: These sentences are relatively simple for students' ease in comprehending the concept. However, # 8 is difficult. Go back to the idea you learned in the verb section. Try inserting *is, am, are, was,* or *were* for other linking verbs to help. I suggest that you do this page orally with your students.

A noun may serve as a predicate nominative. A predicate nominative occurs <u>after</u> a linking verb *<u>and means the same as the subject</u>.*

To determine if a sentence contains a predicate nominative, do the following:

   1.   Delete any prepositional phrases. Find the subject and verb.

The <u>winner</u> <s>of the contest</s> <u>is</u> my collie.

   2.   Ask yourself if the verb is on the linking verb list.   **Yes!** *Is!*

   3.   Is there a noun after the verb that means the same as the subject?

winner   =   collie

   4.   Invert the sentence to prove a predicate nominative.

P.N.

The <u>winner</u> <s>of the contest</s> <u>is</u> my collie.

Inverted form: My collie is the winner (of the contest).

ৡৡৡৡৡৡৡৡৡৡৡৡৡৡৡৡৡৡৡৡ

Directions: Cross out any prepositional phrases. Underline the subject once and the verb twice. Label a predicate nominative – **P.N.** Then, write the inverted form of the sentence in the blank.

               P.N.

1. <u>Miss Shell</u> <u>is</u> our teacher.   **Our teacher is Miss Shell.**

               P.N.

2. My favorite <u>fruit</u> <u>is</u> a pear.   **A pear is my favorite fruit.**

                  P.N.

3. The <u>girl</u> <s>in pigtails</s> <u>is</u> my sister.   **My sister is the girl (in pigtails).**

                 P.N.

4. Their <u>father</u> <u>was</u> the mayor <s>of Ajo</s>.   **The mayor (of Ajo) was their father.**

                P.N.

5. Your best <u>choice</u> <u>is</u> honesty.   **Honesty is your best choice.**

               P.N.

6. <u>Jacob</u> <u>will be</u> your server.   **Your server will be Jacob.**

                 P.N.

7. Our black and white <u>cat</u> <u>is</u> Oreo.   **Oreo is our black and white cat.**

        was   **P.N.**

8. <u>Lani</u> <u>has become</u> the best plumber.   **The best plumber was Lani.**

248

A noun may serve as a predicate nominative. A predicate nominative occurs <u>after</u> a linking verb <u>*and means the same as the subject*</u>.

To determine if a sentence contains a predicate nominative, do the following:
1. Delete any prepositional phrases. Find the subject and verb.

> The <u>winner</u> ~~of the contest~~ <u>is</u> my collie.

2. Ask yourself if the verb is on the linking verb list. **Yes!** <u>*Is*</u>*!*
3. Is there a noun after the verb that means the same as the subject?

> <u>winner</u> = **collie**

4. Invert the sentence to prove a predicate nominative.

> **P.N.**
> The <u>winner</u> ~~of the contest~~ <u>is</u> my collie.

> **Inverted form:** My collie is the winner (of the contest).

🐦🐦🐦🐦🐦🐦🐦🐦🐦🐦🐦🐦🐦🐦🐦

Directions: Cross out any prepositional phrases. Underline the subject once and the verb twice. Label a predicate nominative – **P.N.** Then, write the inverted form of the sentence in the blank.

1. Miss Shell is our teacher. _____

2. My favorite fruit is a pear. _____

3. The girl in pigtails is my sister. _____

4. Their father was the mayor of Ajo. _____

5. Your best choice is honesty. _____

6. Jacob will be your server. _____

7. Our black and white cat is Oreo. _____

was
8. Lani has become the best plumber. _____

Name_____

WORKBOOK PAGE 117

Date_____

NOUNS

Predicate Nominatives

A **predicate nominative** occurs <u>after</u> a linking verb and means the same as the subject.

Remember:
    To determine if a sentence contains a predicate nominative, do the following:
       1.   Delete any prepositional phrases. Find the subject and verb.

           A <u>pansy</u> <u>is</u> a small flower ~~with tiny leaves~~.

       2.   Ask yourself if the verb is on the linking verb list.   Yes! *Is!*
       3.   Is there a noun after the verb that means the same as the subject?

                               P. N.
               <u>**pansy**</u>   **=**   **flower**

       4.   Invert the sentence to prove a predicate nominative.

         Inverted form: A small flower with tiny leaves is a pansy.

         �ϡϡϡϡϡϡϡϡϡϡϡϡϡϡϡϡϡϡϡϡϡ

Directions: Cross out any prepositional phrases. Underline the subject once
               and the verb twice. Label a predicate nominative – **P.N.** Then,
               write the inverted form of the sentence in the blank.

                          P.N.
1. His <u>mother</u> <u>is</u> my piano teacher.

      _____**My piano teacher is his mother.**_____

                       P.N.
2. The <u>person</u> ~~behind the desk~~ <u>is</u> Mrs. Dell.

      _____**Mrs. Dell is the person (behind the desk).**_____

                       P.N.
3. The first bronco <u>rider</u> <u>was</u> Cammi's uncle.

      _____**Cammie's uncle was the first bronco rider.**_____

                       P.N.
4. Our <u>goal</u> ~~for the fundraiser~~ <u>is</u> new playground equipment.

      _____**New playground equipment is our goal (for the fundraiser).**_

         was   **P.N.**
5. <u>Tate</u> <u>remained</u> the wrestling champion ~~for three years~~.

      _____**The wrestling champion (for three years) was Tate.**____

250

A **predicate nominative** occurs <u>after</u> a linking verb and means the same as the subject.

Remember:
> **To determine if a sentence contains a predicate nominative, do the following:**
> 1. Delete any prepositional phrases. Find the subject and verb.
>
> **A <u>pansy</u> <u>is</u> a small flower ~~with tiny leaves~~.**
>
> 2. Ask yourself if the verb is on the linking verb list.   Yes! <u>*Is*</u>*!*
> 3. Is there a noun after the verb that means the same as the subject?
>
> P. N.
> <u>pansy</u>   =   flower
>
> 4. Invert the sentence to prove a predicate nominative.
>
> **Inverted form:**   A small flower with tiny leaves is a pansy.

❧❧❧❧❧❧❧❧❧❧❧❧❧❧❧❧❧❧❧❧❧

Directions: Cross out any prepositional phrases. Underline the subject once and the verb twice. Label a predicate nominative – **P.N.** Then, write the inverted form of the sentence in the blank.

1. His mother is my piano teacher.

   _____

2. The person behind the desk is Mrs. Dell.

   _____

3. The first bronco rider was Cammi's uncle.

   _____

4. Our goal for the fundraiser is new playground equipment.

   _____

              was
5. Tate remained the wrestling champion for three years.

   _____

Name_____   NOUNS

WORKBOOK PAGE 118

Date_____   **Predicate Nominatives**

A **predicate nominative** occurs <u>after</u> a linking verb and means the same as the subject.

🐎🐎🐎🐎🐎🐎🐎🐎🐎🐎🐎🐎🐎🐎🐎🐎

Directions: Cross out any prepositional phrases. Underline the subject once and the verb twice. Label a predicate nominative – **P.N.** Then, write the inverted form of the sentence in the blank.

                                  P.N.

1.   The new <u>coaches</u> <u>were</u> our former history teachers.

         Our former history teachers were the new coaches.

                       P.N.

2.   A <u>platypus</u> <u>is</u> a mammal ~~with webbed feet~~.

         A mammal (with webbed feet) is a platypus.

                       P.N.

3.   The <u>scum</u> ~~on their pool~~ <u>is</u> algae.

         Algae is the scum on their pool.

                       P.N.

4.   Juan's <u>mother</u> <u>is</u> the owner ~~of that Mexican food restaurant~~.

         The owner (of that Mexican food restaurant) is Juan's mother.

            was   **P.N.**

5.   A <u>toddler</u> <u>became</u> the youngest reader in the library's reading program.

      The youngest reader (in the library's reading program) *was* a toddler.

                       P.N.

6.   The bride's last <u>name</u> <u>remained</u> Stellar.

         Stellar remained the bride's last name.

                                  P.N.

7.   The <u>winner</u> ~~in the javelin throw~~ ~~at the first track meet~~ <u>was</u> Parker.

      Parker was the winner (in the javelin throw) (at the first track meet).

                       P.N.

8.   Her <u>reward</u> ~~from the company~~ <u>was</u> a bonus.

         A bonus was her reward (from the company).

A **predicate nominative** occurs <u>after</u> a linking verb and means the same as the subject.

🙦🙦🙦🙦🙦🙦🙦🙦🙦🙦🙦🙦🙦🙦🙦🙦🙦🙦🙦🙦

Directions: Cross out any prepositional phrases. Underline the subject once and the verb twice. Label a predicate nominative – **P.N.** Then, write the inverted form of the sentence in the blank.

1.   The new coaches were our former history teachers.

   _____

2.   A platypus is a mammal with webbed feet.

   _____

3.   The scum on their pool is algae.

   _____

4.   Juan's mother is the owner of that Mexican food restaurant.

   _____

5.   A toddler became the youngest reader in the library's reading program.

   _____

6.   The bride's last name remained Stellar.

   _____

7.   The winner in the javelin throw at the first track meet was Parker.

   _____

8.   Her reward from the company was a bonus.

   _____

A. **Concrete and Abstract Nouns:**

Directions: Write **C** in the blank if the noun is concrete and **A** if it is abstract.

1. __C__ potato   6. __C__ train

2. __C__ factory   7. __A__ courage

3. __A__ love   8. __A__ freedom

4. __C__ bumper   9. __C__ skunk

5. __A__ silliness   10. __A__ fear

B. **Common and Proper Nouns:**

Directions: Place a ◆ if the noun is common.

1. ___ ANNA   5. ◆ STAR   9. ___ CANADA

2. ◆ BANK   6. ___ ALABAMA   10. ◆ ANIMAL

3. ◆ BOTTLE   7. ◆ CARPENTER   11. ◆ CANAL

4. ___ ASIA   8. ◆ FORT   12. ◆ KANGAROO

C. **Noun or Adjective:**

Remember: The same word may serve as a noun in one sentence and as an adjective (describing word) in another sentence.

Examples: A.   I saw a **fish** in a pond.   *Fish* is a noun in this sentence.

B.   I ate a **fish** sandwich.   _fish sandwich_

Fish is an adjective in this sentence because it describes sandwich.

Directions: On the short line provided, write **N** if the boldfaced word serves as a noun and **A** if the word serves as an adjective (describing word). If the word is an adjective, write the word and the noun it modifies.

1. __N__ A farmer planted **corn** in a field.   _____

A. **Concrete and Abstract Nouns:**

Directions: Write **C** in the blank if the noun is concrete and **A** if it is abstract.

1.	_____	potato	6.	_____ train
2.	_____	factory	7.	_____ courage
3.	_____	love	8.	_____ freedom
4.	_____	bumper	9.	_____ skunk
5.	_____	silliness	10.	_____ fear

🍂🍂🍂🍂🍂🍂🍂🍂🍂🍂🍂🍂

B. **Common and Proper Nouns:**

Directions: Place a ◆ if the noun is common.

1.	___ ANNA	5.	___ STAR	9.	___ CANADA
2.	___ BANK	6.	___ ALABAMA	10.	___ ANIMAL
3.	___ BOTTLE	7.	___ CARPENTER	11.	___ CANAL
4.	___ ASIA	8.	___ FORT	12.	___ KANGAROO

🍂🍂🍂🍂🍂🍂🍂🍂🍂🍂🍂🍂

C. **Noun or Adjective:**

Remember: The same word may serve as a noun in one sentence and as an adjective (describing word) in another sentence.

Examples: A.   I saw a **fish** in a pond.   *Fish* is a noun in this sentence.

B.   I ate a **fish** sandwich.   *fish sandwich*

Fish is an adjective in this sentence because it describes sandwich.

Directions: On the short line provided, write **N** if the boldfaced word serves as a noun and **A** if the word serves as an adjective (describing word). If the word is an adjective, write the word and the noun it modifies.

1. _____   A farmer planted **corn** in a field.   _____

2.   **A**   Do you like **corn** chowder?   **corn chowder**
                                                      _____

3.   **A**   **Silk** ties are on sale at that shop.   **Silk ties**
                                                      _____

4.   **N**   **Silk** is a very soft fabric.   _____

෴෴෴෴෴෴෴෴෴෴෴෴෴

D. **Singular and Plural Nouns:**
      Directions: Circle the correct spelling of each plural noun.
                     Use a dictionary if necessary.

ANSWERS ARE BOLDFACED.

1.	**mysteries**	mysterys	9.	**belts**	beltes
2.	torchs	**torches**	10.	**taxes**	taxs
3.	pullies	**pulleys**	11.	**whiffs**	whives
4.	womans	**women**	12.	informations	**information**
5.	tomatos	**tomatoes**	13.	**moths**	mothes
6.	**deer**	deers	14.	troopes	**troops**
7.	calfs	**calves**	15.	replys	**replies**
8.	**lips**	lipses	16.	lens	**lenses**

෴෴෴෴෴෴෴෴෴෴෴෴෴

E. **Determiners:**
      Directions: Place a ✓ in the blank if the boldfaced word is a determiner.
                     If the word serves as a determiner, write the boldfaced word
                     and the noun that it modifies (goes over to) in the wide blank.

1.   ____   May I please have **two** without frosting? _____

2.   ✓   You must order **two** items to get one free.   **two items**
                                                              _____

3.   ____   Do you have **this** in a larger size? _____

2. _____   Do you like **corn** chowder?   _____

3. _____   **Silk** ties are on sale at that shop.   _____

4. _____   **Silk** is a very soft fabric.   _____

෨෨෨෨෨෨෨෨෨෨෨෨

D. **Singular and Plural Nouns:**
    Directions: Circle the correct spelling of each plural noun.
    Use a dictionary if necessary.

1.	mysteries	mysterys	9. belts	beltes
2.	torchs	torches	10. taxes	taxs
3.	pullies	pulleys	11. whiffs	whives
4.	womans	women	12. informations	information
5.	tomatos	tomatoes	13. moths	mothes
6.	deer	deers	14. troopes	troops
7.	calfs	calves	15. replys	replies
8.	lips	lipses	16. lens	lenses

෨෨෨෨෨෨෨෨෨෨෨෨

E. **Determiners:**
    Directions: Place a ✓ in the blank if the boldfaced word is a determiner. If
    the word serves as a determiner, write the boldfaced word and
    the noun that it modifies (goes over to) in the wide blank.

1. ___   May I please have **two** without frosting? _____

2. ___   You must order **two** items to get one free. _____

3. ___   Do you have **this** in a larger size? _____

4.   ✓   Are you fine with **this** decision? _____**this decision**_____

5.   ✓   **Some** business cards have been printed. ___**Some cards**_____

6.   ___   **Some** were excused early. _____

૪ઝ૪ઝ૪ઝ૪ઝ૪ઝ૪ઝ૪ઝ

F. **Possessive Nouns:**
      Directions: Write the possessive form in each blank.

1. pictures belonging to Maddy - _____**Maddy's pictures**_____

2. a home owned by her brother - _____**her brother's home**_____

3. a lease signed by two brothers - _____**(two) brothers' lease**_____

4. pamphlets belonging to a travel agent - ___**a travel agent's pamphlets**___

5. a meeting attended by more than one woman - _____**women's meeting**_____

૪ઝ૪ઝ૪ઝ૪ઝ૪ઝ૪ઝ૪ઝ

G. **Nouns Used as Subject, Direct Object, and Indirect Object:**
      Directions: Write **S.** if the noun serves as a subject.
                          Write **D.O.** if the noun serves as a direct object.
                          Write **I.O.** if the noun serves as an indirect object.

1. **D.O.**   Does an addax drink **water**?

2. **I.O.**   Todd ordered his **family** a grill.

3. **S.**   His black-and-white-striped **flashlight** is too dim.

4. **I.O.**   A teacher read the **students** a story.

5. **D.O.**   Mom placed **candles** on my cake.

4. __   Are you fine with **this** decision? _____

5. __   **Some** business cards have been printed. _____

6. __   **Some** were excused early. _____

❦❦❦❦❦❦❦❦❦❦❦❦

F. **Possessive Nouns:**
    Directions: Write the possessive form in each blank.

1. pictures belonging to Maddy - _____

2. a home owned by her brother - _____

3. a lease signed by two brothers - _____

4. pamphlets belonging to a travel agent - _____

5. a meeting attended by more than one woman - _____

❦❦❦❦❦❦❦❦❦❦❦❦

G. **Nouns Used as Subject, Direct Object, and Indirect Object:**
    Directions: Write **S.** if the noun serves as a subject.
                  Write **D.O.** if the noun serves as a direct object.
                  Write **I.O.** if the noun serves as an indirect object.

1. _____   Does an addax drink **water**?

2. _____   Todd ordered his **family** a grill.

3. _____   His black-and-white-striped **flashlight** is too dim.

4. _____   A teacher read the **students** a story.

5. _____   Mom placed **candles** on my cake.

H. **Predicate Nominatives:**
   Directions: Cross out any prepositional phrases. Underline the subject once
                 and the verb twice. Label a predicate nominative – **P.N.** Then,
                 write the inverted form of the sentence in the blank.

**Remember: A predicate nominative occurs <u>after</u> a linking verb and means the same as
the subject.**

                              P.N.
1.   Their <u>residence</u> <u>is</u> a new apartment ~~on Potter Avenue~~.

   ___**A new apartment (on Potter Avenue) is their new residence.**___

                         P.N.
2.   Those <u>men</u> <u>were</u> the winners ~~of the logging contest~~.

   ___**The winners (of the logging contest) were those men.**___

                                   P.N.
3.   The first <u>settlers</u> ~~in Kentucky~~ <u>were</u> pioneers ~~with Daniel Boone~~.

   ___**Pioneers (with Daniel Boone) were the first settlers (in Kentucky).**___

                         P.N.
4.   That old <u>barn</u> <u>is</u> the oldest building ~~in this village~~.

   ___**The oldest building (in this village) is that old barn.**___

                     ৯৯৯৯৯৯৯৯৯৯৯৯

I. **Identifying Nouns:**
   Directions: Circle any nouns.

   **Remember: Determiners will help you to find some nouns. You may want to
   box them in order to help you.**

1.   *Three* golden **butterflies** with *many* orange **dots** on *its* **wings** flew by.

2.   ***Nan's* daughter** has planted *a* **tree** and *several* rose **bushes** in *her* **yard**.

3.   Will you use *that* paisley **tie** on *a* striped **shirt** with *your* new **suit**?

4.   *Twelve* **charms** hung on *an* unusual **bracelet** without *any* **clasp**.

5.   *On* **Mondays**, *those* **joggers** wind through *the* **park** *before* **dawn**.
260

H. **Predicate Nominatives:**

Directions: Cross out any prepositional phrases. Underline the subject once and the verb twice. Label a predicate nominative – **P.N.** Then, write the inverted form of the sentence in the blank.

Remember: **A predicate nominative occurs after a linking verb and means the same as the subject.**

1. Their residence is a new apartment on Potter Avenue.

     _____

2. Those men were the winners of the logging contest.

     _____

3. The first settlers in Kentucky were pioneers with Daniel Boone.

     _____

4. That old barn is the oldest building in this village.

     _____

ভ্যভ্যভ্যভ্যভ্যভ্যভ্যভ্যভ্যভ্য

I. **Identifying Nouns:**

Directions: Circle any nouns.

Remember: **Determiners will help you to find some nouns. You may want to box them in order to help you.**

1. Three golden butterflies with many orange dots on its wings flew by.

2. Nan's daughter has planted a tree and several rose bushes in her yard.

3. Will you use that paisley tie on a striped shirt with your new suit?

4. Twelve charms hung on an unusual bracelet without any clasp.

5. On Mondays, those joggers wind through the park before dawn.

Name_____   **NOUN TEST**

Date_____
<u>**See note in Section E (page 264) before asking students to complete this test.**</u>

A.   Directions: Write **C** in the blank if the noun is concrete and **A** if it is abstract.

1. __**A**__   peace   5. __**A**__   daze

2. __**C**__   pottery   6. __**C**__   blister

3. __**A**__   fairness   7. __**C**__   shark

4. __**C**__   friend   8. __**A**__   fear

B.   Directions: Write **C** in the blank if the noun is common and **P** if it is proper.

1. _**C**_   WELDER   5. _**C**_   BULLDOG

2. _**C**_   COLLEGE   6. _**C**_   GARAGE

3. _**P**_   PLUTO   7. _**P**_   KANSAS

4. _**P**_   ASIA   8. _**C**_   STADIUM

C.   Directions: Write the plural.

1. cliff - _____**cliffs**_____   7. activity - _____**activities**_____

2. apex - _____**apexes**_____   8. deer - _____**deer**_____

3. jersey - _____**jerseys**_____   9. fun - _____**fun**_____

4. flea - _____**fleas**_____   10. wrench - _____**wrenches**_____

5. wife - _____**wives**_____   11. photo - _____**photos**_____

6. gash - _____**gashes**_____   12. chorus - _____**choruses**_____

262

Name_____   **NOUN TEST**

Date_____

A. Directions: Write **C** in the blank if the noun is concrete and **A** if it is abstract.

1. _____ peace   5. _____ daze

2. _____ pottery   6. _____ blister

3. _____ fairness   7. _____ shark

4. _____ friend   8. _____ fear

B. Directions: Write **C** in the blank if the noun is common and **P** if it is proper.

1. ____ WELDER   5. ____ BULLDOG

2. ____ COLLEGE   6. ____ GARAGE

3. ____ PLUTO   7. ____ KANSAS

4. ____ ASIA   8. ____ STADIUM

C. Directions: Write the plural.

1. cliff - _____   7. activity - _____

2. apex - _____   8. deer - _____

3. jersey - _____   9. fun - _____

4. flea - _____   10. wrench - _____

5. wife - _____   11. photo - _____

6. gash - _____   12. chorus - _____

D. Directions: Write the possessive form in each blank.

1. a business owned by their friend - _____**their friend's business**_____

2. a tearoom belonging to Debra - _____**Debra's tearoom**_____

3. toys shared by more than one child - _____**children's toys**_____

4. a gift presented by three sisters - _____**(three) sisters' gift**_____

5. clients of several companies - _____**(several) companies' clients**_____

E. Directions: Circle any nouns.
> **Remember: Determiners will help you to find some nouns. You may want to box them in order to help you.**

Nouns have been boldfaced. Although identifying determiners has not been required, determiners are italicized.

1. *Many* **members** of *our* **club** are attending *that* national **meeting**.

2. *Loni's* **neighbors** raise **horses** on *a* dude **ranch** in **Wyoming**.

3. May **Tessa** bring *her* **aunt** and *two* **cousins** to *your* **party**?

4. *Those* sleek **boats** at *this* **dock** are **racers** with bright **stripes**.

5. *A few* **students** wrote *an* **essay** about *their* **trip** to **Africa** during *the* **summer**.

F. Directions: Write **S.** if the boldfaced noun serves as a subject.
Write **D.O.** if the boldfaced noun serves as a direct object.
Write **I.O.** if the boldfaced noun serves as an indirect object.
Write **P.N.** if the boldfaced noun serves as a predicate nominative.

NOTE: You may want to ask students to write sentence #1 at the bottom of this worksheet. Have students underline the subject once and verb twice. Ask them to label the direct object. Then, have students return to the directions. This may make this section easier.

1. __**D.O.**__ A guide showed the students a rare **bird**.

2. ___**S.**___ A **guide** showed the students a rare bird.

3. __**P.N.**__ That rare bird is a bald **eagle**.

4. __**I.O.**__ A guide showed the **students** a rare bird.

264

D. Directions: Write the possessive form in each blank.

1. a business owned by their friend - _____

2. a tearoom belonging to Debra - _____

3. toys shared by more than one child - _____

4. a gift presented by three sisters - _____

5. clients of several companies - _____

E. Directions: Circle any nouns.

Remember: Determiners will help you to find some nouns. You may want to box them in order to help you.

1. Many members of our club are attending that national meeting.

2. Loni's neighbors raise horses on a dude ranch in Wyoming.

3. May Tessa bring her aunt and two cousins to your party?

4. Those sleek boats at this dock are racers with bright stripes.

5. A few students wrote an essay about their trip to Africa during the summer.

F. Directions: Write **S.** if the boldfaced noun serves as a subject.
Write **D.O.** if the boldfaced noun serves as a direct object.
Write **I.O.** if the boldfaced noun serves as an indirect object.
Write **P.N.** if the boldfaced noun serves as a predicate nominative.

1. _____ A guide showed the students a rare **bird**.

2. _____ A **guide** showed the students a rare bird.

3. _____ That rare bird is a bald **eagle**.

4. _____ A guide showed the **students** a rare bird.

Name_____

Cumulative Review

Date_____

At the End of the Noun Unit

A. **List of Prepositions:**

Directions: Write the prepositions.

1. about
2. above
3. across
4. after
5. against
6. along
7. amid
8. among
9. around
10. at
11. atop
12. before
13. behind
14. below
15. beneath
16. beside
17. between
18. beyond
19. but

20. by
21. concerning
22. down
23. during
24. except
25. for
26. from
27. in
28. inside
29. into
30. like
31. near
32. of
33. off
34. on
35. onto
36. out
37. outside
38. over

39. past
40. regarding
41. since
42. through
43. throughout
44. to
45. toward
46. under
47. underneath
48. until
49. up
50. upon
51. with
52. within
53. without

266

Name_____   **Cumulative Review**

Date_____   **At the End of the Noun Unit**

A. List of Prepositions:
Directions: Write the prepositions.

1. abo_____	20. b_____	39. pa_____
2. abo_____	21. con_____	40. reg_____
3. acr_____	22. do_____	41. si_____
4. aft_____	23. dur_____	42. th_____
5. aga_____	24. ex_____	43. thr_____
6. alo_____	25. fo_____	44. t_____
7. ami_____	26. fr_____	45. tow_____
8. amo_____	27. i_____	46. un_____
9. aro_____	28. ins_____	47. und_____
10. a_____	29. int_____	48. unt_____
11. ato_____	30. li_____	49. u_____
12. bef_____	31. ne_____	50. upo_____
13. beh_____	32. o_____	51. wi_____
14. bel_____	33. o_____	52. wi_____
15. ben_____	34. o_____	53. wi_____
16. bes_____	35. o_____	
17. bet_____	36. o_____	
18. bey_____	37. ou_____	
19. bu_____	38. ov_____	

B. **Subject/Verb:**

Directions: Cross out any prepositional phrases. Underline the subject once and the verb twice.

1. Monkeys jumped ~~through the branches~~.

2. The travelers drove ~~for three hours~~ ~~without a break~~.

3. Kammie sweeps ~~beneath her bed~~ ~~after dusting~~.

ॐ ॐ ॐ ॐ ॐ ॐ ॐ ॐ ॐ ॐ ॐ ॐ

C. **Compound Objects of the Preposition:**

Directions: Cross out any prepositional phrases. Underline the subject once and the verb twice. Label the object of the preposition – **O.P.**

                           O.P.   **O.P.**

1. Dakota wrote a report ~~concerning hurricanes and tornados~~.

                        O.P.   **O.P.**

2. Our coach sat ~~between Darla and me~~.

                        O.P.   **O.P.**

3. This large envelope is ~~for Tommy or his grandpa~~.

ॐ ॐ ॐ ॐ ॐ ॐ ॐ ॐ ॐ ॐ ॐ ॐ

D. **Compound Subjects:**

Directions: Cross out any prepositional phrases. Underline the subject once and the verb or verb phrase twice.

1. Our phonebook and pens are ~~in the first drawer~~ ~~beside the sink~~.

2. ~~During spring break~~, Tessa and her mother drove ~~to Ohio~~.

3. The host ~~of the television show~~ or his guests will judge the event.

ॐ ॐ ॐ ॐ ॐ ॐ ॐ ॐ ॐ ॐ ॐ ॐ

E. **Imperative Sentences:**

Directions: Cross out any prepositional phrases. Underline the subject once and the verb twice.

1. (You) Press your hand ~~against this board~~.

2. (You) Clean your fingernails ~~with this nailbrush~~.

268

B. **Subject/Verb:**
   Directions: Cross out any prepositional phrases. Underline the subject once
               and the verb twice.

1. Monkeys jumped through the branches.

2. The travelers drove for three hours without a break.

3. Kammie sweeps beneath her bed after dusting.

🙂🙂🙂🙂🙂🙂🙂🙂🙂🙂🙂🙂🙂

C. **Compound Objects of the Preposition:**
   Directions: Cross out any prepositional phrases. Underline the subject once
               and the verb twice. Label the object of the preposition – **O.P.**

1. Dakota wrote a report concerning hurricanes and tornados.

2. Our coach sat between Darla and me.

3. This large envelope is for Tommy or his grandpa.

🙂🙂🙂🙂🙂🙂🙂🙂🙂🙂🙂🙂🙂

D. **Compound Subjects:**
   Directions: Cross out any prepositional phrases. Underline the subject once
               and the verb or verb phrase twice.

1. Our phonebook and pens are in the first drawer beside the sink.

2. During spring break, Tessa and her mother drove to Ohio.

3. The host of the television show or his guests will judge the event.

🙂🙂🙂🙂🙂🙂🙂🙂🙂🙂🙂🙂🙂

E. **Imperative Sentences:**
   Directions: Cross out any prepositional phrases. Underline the subject once
               and the verb twice.

1. Press your hand against this board.

2. Clean your fingernails with this nailbrush.

F. **Infinitives:**
     Directions: Cross out any prepositional phrases. Place parentheses **( )** around
                    any infinitive. Underline the subject once and the verb twice.

1. The <u>children</u> <u><u>want</u></u> **(**to go**)** ~~to a water park~~.

2. <u>She</u> <u><u>plans</u></u> **(**to leave**)** ~~before breakfast~~.

3. <u>I</u> <u><u>need</u></u> **(**to learn**)** ~~about koalas and panda bears~~.

✺✺✺✺✺✺✺✺✺✺✺✺

G. **Preposition or Adverb?:**
     Directions: Cross out any prepositional phrases. Underline the subject once
                    and the verb twice. Write **A** if the boldfaced word is an adverb.
                    Write **P** if the boldfaced word is a preposition that begins a
                    prepositional phrase.

1. __**A**__   Our <u>guest</u> <u><u>came</u></u> **inside**.

2. __**P**__   His <u>horse</u> <u><u>is</u></u> **~~inside~~** ~~the barn~~.

3. __**A**__   One tree <u>trimmer</u> <u><u>crawled</u></u> **out** ~~onto a branch~~.

4. __**P**__   Several <u>wasps</u> <u><u>flew</u></u> **~~out~~** ~~the window~~.

✺✺✺✺✺✺✺✺✺✺✺✺

H. **Verb Phrases and *Not*:**
     Directions: Cross out any prepositional phrases. Box *not* or *n't*.
                    Underline the subject once and the verb phrase twice.
***Not* and *n't* have been boldfaced here.**

1. <u>You</u> <u><u>are</u></u> **not** ~~in this picture~~ ~~with your relatives~~.

2. Our <u>telephone</u> <u><u>had</u>**n't** <u>rung</u></u> all afternoon.

3. <u>She</u> <u><u>may</u></u> **not** <u><u>have been</u></u> ~~at an art show~~.

4. That tractor-trailer <u>driver</u> <u><u>has</u></u> **not** <u><u>driven</u></u> ~~to Buffalo~~.

F. **Infinitives:**
>   Directions: Cross out any prepositional phrases. Place parentheses **( )** around any infinitive. Underline the subject once and the verb twice.

1. The children want to go to a water park.

2. She plans to leave before breakfast.

3. I need to learn about koalas and panda bears.

ঌঌঌঌঌঌঌঌঌঌঌঌ

G. **Preposition or Adverb?:**
>   Directions: Cross out any prepositional phrases. Underline the subject once and the verb twice. Write **A** if the boldfaced word is an adverb. Write **P** if the boldfaced word is a preposition that begins a prepositional phrase.

1. _____   Our guest came **inside**.

2. _____   His horse is **inside** the barn.

3. _____   One tree trimmer crawled **out** onto a branch.

4. _____   Several wasps flew **out** the window.

ঌঌঌঌঌঌঌঌঌঌঌঌ

H. **Verb Phrases and *Not*:**
>   Directions: Cross out any prepositional phrases. Box *not* or *n't*.
>   Underline the subject once and the verb or verb phrase twice.

1. You are not in this picture with your relatives.

2. Our telephone hadn't rung all afternoon.

3. She may not have been at an art show.

4. That tractor-trailer driver has not driven to Buffalo.

271

WORKBOOK PAGE 126

I. **The Verb, *To Be*:**
   Directions: Fill in the blank with the correct form of the infinitive, *to be*.

1. Last week, Sam _____**was**_____ in Idaho on a fishing trip.

2. Presently, I _____**am**_____ here.

3. The other day, we _____**were**_____ near a beach.

4. Tomorrow, Marco _____**will be**_____ in Spain.

ஒ ஒ ஒ ஒ ஒ ஒ ஒ ஒ ஒ ஒ ஒ ஒ

J. **Contractions:**
   Directions: Write the contraction.

1. are not - _____**aren't**_____	6. we are - _____**we're**_____
2. does not - _____**doesn't**_____	7. who is - _____**who's**_____
3. what is - _____**what's**_____	8. cannot - _____**can't**_____
4. they are - _____**they're**_____	9. should not - _____**shouldn't**_____
5. must not - _____**mustn't**_____	10. I shall - _____**I'll**_____

ஒ ஒ ஒ ஒ ஒ ஒ ஒ ஒ ஒ ஒ ஒ ஒ

K. **You're/Your, It's/Its, and They're/Their/There:**
   Directions: Circle the correct word.

1. I think (**it's**, its) too early for a snack.

2. (**You're**, Your) in a very happy mood today.

3. Van went (they're, their, **there**) looking for you.

4. (**They're**, Their, There) going to the hospital to visit (they're, **their**, there) uncle.

5. (**It's**, Its) so hot that (you're, **your**) bananas are overly ripe.

I. **The Verb, *To Be*:**
    Directions: Fill in the blank with the correct form of the infinitive, *to be*.

1.   Last week, Sam _____ in Idaho on a fishing trip.

2.   Presently, I _____ here.

3.   The other day, we _____ near a beach.

4.   Tomorrow, Marco _____ in Spain.

ఇఇఇఇఇఇఇఇఇఇఇఇ

J. **Contractions:**
    Directions: Write the contraction.

1. are not - _____   6. we are - _____

2. does not - _____   7. who is - _____

3. what is - _____   8. cannot - _____

4. they are - _____   9. should not - _____

5. must not - _____   10. I shall - _____

ఇఇఇఇఇఇఇఇఇఇఇఇ

K. **You're/Your, It's/Its, and They're/Their/There:**
    Directions: Circle the correct word.

1. I think (it's, its) too early for a snack.

2. (You're, Your) in a very happy mood today.

3. Van went (they're, their, there) looking for you.

4. (They're, Their, There) going to the hospital to visit (they're, their, there) uncle.

5. (It's, Its) so hot that (you're, your) bananas are overly ripe.

L. Auxiliary (Helping) Verbs:

    Directions: Write the 23 helping verbs.

1. <u>**do**</u>	7. <u>**may**</u>	13. <u>**could**</u>	19. <u>**was**</u>
2. <u>**does**</u>	8. <u>**might**</u>	14. <u>**should**</u>	20. <u>**were**</u>
3. <u>**did**</u>	9. <u>**must**</u>	15. <u>**would**</u>	21. <u>**be**</u>
4. <u>**has**</u>	10. <u>**can**</u>	16. <u>**is**</u>	22. <u>**being**</u>
5. <u>**have**</u>	11. <u>**shall**</u>	17. <u>**am**</u>	23. <u>**been**</u>
6. <u>**had**</u>	12. <u>**will**</u>	18. <u>**are**</u>	

ᔥᔥᔥᔥᔥᔥᔥᔥᔥᔥᔥ

M. Verb Phrases:

    Directions: Cross out any prepositional phrases. Underline the subject once and the verb phrase twice.

1. One <u>rider</u> <u>has washed</u> his bicycle ~~after the race~~.

2. <u>You</u> <u>should have stopped</u> ~~for gas~~.

3. <u>Does</u> your <u>mother</u> <u>cook</u> hamburgers ~~on her new grill~~?

ᔥᔥᔥᔥᔥᔥᔥᔥᔥᔥᔥ

N. Compound Verbs:

    Directions: Cross out any prepositional phrases. Underline the subject once and the verb or verb phrase twice.

1. One <u>cow</u> ~~in the herd~~ <u>lifted</u> its head and <u>mooed</u>.

2. <u>Carlo</u> <u>bought</u> a truck and <u>sold</u> his car ~~to his brother~~.

3. That <u>handyman</u> <u>paints</u>, <u>tiles</u>, and <u>installs</u> lights ~~without a helper~~.

4. <u>Have</u> <u>you</u> <u>heard</u> or <u>seen</u> any news ~~about an earthquake~~?

5. A dessert <u>chef</u> <u>melted</u> chocolate bits ~~in a pan~~ and <u>whipped</u> sugar ~~into it~~.

L. **Auxiliary (Helping) Verbs:**

     Directions: Write the 23 helping verbs.

1. d_____	7. m_____	13. c_____	19. w_____
2. d_____	8. m_____	14. s_____	20. w_____
3. d_____	9. m_____	15. w_____	21. b_____
4. h_____	10. c_____	16. i_____	22. b_____
5. h_____	11. s_____	17. a_____	23. b_____
6. h_____	12. w_____	18. a_____	

↾↾↾↾↾↾↾↾↾↾↾↾

M. **Verb Phrases:**
     Directions: Cross out any prepositional phrases. Underline the subject once and the verb phrase twice.

1. One rider has washed his bicycle after the race.

2. You should have stopped for gas.

3. Does your mother cook hamburgers on her new grill?

↾↾↾↾↾↾↾↾↾↾↾↾

N. **Compound Verbs:**
     Directions: Cross out any prepositional phrases. Underline the subject once and the verb or verb phrase twice.

1. One cow in the herd lifted its head and mooed.

2. Carlo bought a truck and sold his car to his brother.

3. That handyman paints, tiles, and installs lights without a helper.

4. Have you heard or seen any news about an earthquake?

5. A dessert chef melted chocolate bits in a pan and whipped sugar into it.

WORKBOOK PAGE 128

O. **Irregular Verbs:**

   Directions: Underline the subject once and the correct verb phrase twice.

1. I have (ran, run) there.

2. He may have (fell, fallen).

3. Our bell must have (rang, rung).

4. This swing is (broke, broken).

5. Have you (taken, took) a mint?

6. Lou should have (swum, swam) longer.

7. Jo had (did, done) his homework.

8. Has he ever (ate, eaten) clams?

9. Josh might have (flew, flown) alone.

10. We could have (went, gone) with him.

11. Medical kits had been (chosen, chose).

శ్రీశ్రీశ్రీశ్రీశ్రీశ్రీశ్రీశ్రీశ్రీ

P. **Subjects, Verbs, and Direct Objects:**

   Directions: Cross out any prepositional phrases. Underline the subject once
                  and the verb/verb phrase twice. Label any direct object – **D.O.**

                              D.O.
1. She taped her papers together.
                              D.O.
2. Have you cleaned the spots on your shoes?
                                                    D.O.
3. Before the basketball game, the players threw the ball to each other.
                                              D.O.
4. Throughout the winter, workers drove snow plows during blizzards.
                              D.O.
5. One of the lions lifted its head and roared loudly.

276

Name_____   **Cumulative Review**

Date_____   **At the End of the Noun Unit**

O. **Irregular Verbs:**
    Directions: Underline the subject once and the correct verb phrase twice.

1. I have (ran, run) there.

2. He may have (fell, fallen).

3. Our bell must have (rang, rung).

4. This swing is (broke, broken).

5. Have you (taken, took) a mint?

6. Lou should have (swum, swam) longer.

7. Jo had (did, done) his homework.

8. Has he ever (ate, eaten) clams?

9. Josh might have (flew, flown) alone.

10. We could have (went, gone) with him.

11. Medical kits had been (chosen, chose).

৵৵৵৵৵৵৵৵৵৵৵৵৵

P. **Subjects, Verbs, and Direct Objects:**
    Directions: Cross out any prepositional phrases. Underline the subject once
                 and the verb/verb phrase twice. Label any direct object – **D.O.**

1. She taped her papers together.

2. Have you cleaned the spots on your shoes?

3. Before the basketball game, the players threw the ball to each other.

4. Throughout the winter, workers drove snow plows during blizzards.

5. One of the lions lifted its head and roared loudly.

277

Q. **Sit/Set, Lie/Lay, and Rise/Raise:**
   Directions: Delete any prepositional phrases. Underline the subject once
                 and the verb/verb phrase twice. Label any direct object-**D.O.**

                                                    D.O.

1. The best <u>man</u> ~~at the wedding~~ (rose, <u>raised</u>) his glass ~~for a toast~~.

2. <u>She</u> (<u>lay,</u> laid) ~~on a bench with large orange cushions~~.

                               D.O.

3. <u>Ron</u> (<u>set,</u> sat) his cooler ~~outside his back door~~.

4. Your <u>skateboard</u> <u>is</u> (<u>lying,</u> laying) ~~on its side~~.

5. <u>Were</u> <u>you</u> (setting, <u>sitting</u>) ~~on the bleachers before the baseball game~~?

                               D.O.

6. <u>I</u> <u>have</u> (lain, <u>laid</u>) the fabric softener ~~on the washing machine~~.

7. <u>Smoke</u> <u>is</u> (<u>rising,</u> raising) ~~from our small campfire~~.

                           ৡৡৡৡৡৡৡৡৡৡৡৡ

R. **Tenses:**
   Directions: Underline the subject once and the verb or verb phrase
                 twice. Write the tense (*present, past,* or *future*) in the blank.

1. _____**past**_____   <u>We</u> <u>bought</u> fresh vegetables.

2. _____**present**_____   My <u>foot</u> <u>aches</u>.

3. _____**future**_____   <u>Will</u> <u>you</u> <u>finish</u> later?

4. _____**present**_____   <u>Tally</u> <u>dreams</u> often.

5. _____**past**_____   A black <u>Labrador</u> <u>rescued</u> his owner.

6. _____**future**_____   <u>I</u> <u>shall give</u> you my cell phone.

7. _____**present**_____   These <u>cups</u> <u>are</u> silver.

8. _____**present**_____   Large magnolia <u>trees</u> <u>grow</u> nearby.

Q. **Sit/Set, Lie/Lay, and Rise/Raise:**

Directions: Delete any prepositional phrases. Underline the subject once and the verb/verb phrase twice. Label any direct object-**D.O.**

1. The best man at the wedding (rose, raised) his glass for a toast.

2. She (lay, laid) on the bench with large orange cushions.

3. Ron (set, sat) his cooler outside his back door.

4. Your skateboard is (lying, laying) on its side.

5. Were you (setting, sitting) on the bleachers before the baseball game?

6. I have (lain, laid) the fabric softener on the washing machine.

7. Smoke is (rising, raising) from our small campfire.

෨෨෨෨෨෨෨෨෨෨෨෨

R. **Tenses:**

Directions: Underline the subject once and the verb or verb phrase twice. Write the tense (*present, past,* or *future*) in the blank.

1. _____ We bought fresh vegetables.

2. _____ My foot aches.

3. _____ Will you finish later?

4. _____ Tally dreams often.

5. _____ A black Labrador rescued his owner.

6. _____ I shall give you my cell phone.

7. _____ These cups are silver.

8. _____ Large magnolia trees grow nearby.

WORKBOOK PAGE 130

S. Linking Verbs:
    Directions: Write the linking verbs.

1. to **feel**	6. to **seem**	11. to **stay**	d. **was**
2. to **taste**	7. to **sound**	12. to **be**	e. **were**
3. to **look**	8. to **grow**	a. **is**	f. **be**
4. to **smell**	9. to **remain**	b. **am**	g. **being**
5. to **become**	10. to **appear**	c. **are**	h. **been**

ฅ ฅ ฅ ฅ ฅ ฅ ฅ ฅ ฅ ฅ ฅ ฅ ฅ

T. Action Verb or Linking Verb?:

    Directions: Write **A** if the verb is action; write **L** if the verb is linking.

1. **L**   He **appears** calm.

2. **A**   His watch **stopped**.

3. **A**   Our goat **bleats**.

4. **A**   He **looked** at his map.

5. **L**   This apple **tastes** tart.

6. **A**   The cat **jumped** onto a table.

ฅ ฅ ฅ ฅ ฅ ฅ ฅ ฅ ฅ ฅ ฅ ฅ ฅ

U. Linking Verbs and Predicate Adjectives:
    Directions: Write **L** in the space if the verb is linking. Place a form of *to be* above each verb to help determine if the verb is linking.

        Remember: **Try placing** *is, am, are, was,* **or** *were* **in place of the verb. If the meaning of the sentence does not change, the verb is probably linking.**

           was
1. **L**   She <u>seemed</u> confident.   3. _____   Tabby <u>uses</u> a litter box.
          is   *is*
2. **L**   My speech <u>sounds</u> slurred.   4. **L**   This popcorn <u>tastes</u> salty.

S. **Linking Verbs:**
   Directions: Write the linking verbs.

1. to _____   6. to _____   11. to_____   d. _____

2. to _____   7. to _____   12. to _____   e. _____

3. to _____   8. to _____   a. _____   f. _____

4. to _____   9. to _____   b. _____   g. _____

5. to _____   10. to _____   c. _____   h. _____

༼༽༼༽༼༽༼༽༼༽༼༽༼༽

T. **Action Verb or Linking Verb?:**

   Directions: Write **A** if the verb is action; write **L** if the verb is linking.

1. _____   He **appears** calm.

2. _____   His watch **stopped**.

3. _____   Our goat **bleats**.

4. _____   He **looked** at his map.

5. _____   This apple **tastes** tart.

6. _____   The cat **jumped** onto a table.

༼༽༼༽༼༽༼༽༼༽༼༽༼༽

U. **Linking Verbs and Predicate Adjectives**:
   Directions: Write **L** in the space if the verb is linking. Place a form of *to be*
   above each verb to help determine if the verb is linking.

   Remember: Try placing *is, am, are, was,* or *were* in place of the verb. If the meaning of the sentence
   does not change, the verb is probably linking.

1. _____   She <u>seemed</u> confident.   3. _____   Tabby <u>uses</u> a litter box.

2. _____   My speech <u>sounds</u> slurred.   4. _____   This popcorn <u>tastes</u> salty.

V. **Linking Verbs and Predicate Adjectives:**

Directions: Delete any prepositional phrases. Underline the subject once
and the verb twice. Label any predicate adjective – **P.A.**

P.A.
1. That <u>truck</u> ~~with wide mud flaps~~ <u>is</u> new.

P.A.
2. The <u>child</u> <u>is growing</u> sleepy.

P.A.
3. His <u>grandfather</u> <u>became</u> excited ~~about their planned rapids trip~~.

&&&&&&&&&&&&

W. **Subject-Verb Agreement:**

Directions: Delete any prepositional phrases. Underline the subject once.
Underline the verb/verb phrase that agrees with the subject twice.

1. One <u>lizard</u> (<u>hides</u>, hide) ~~under our bushes~~.

2. These <u>actors</u> (learns, <u>learn</u>) lines easily.

3. Some <u>onions</u> (<u>smell</u>, smells) strong.

4. The <u>top</u> ~~of his hands~~ (have, <u>has</u>) a rash.

5. Their <u>butler</u> (<u>does</u>(n't), do(n't)) <u>answer</u> their phone.

6. Our palm <u>trees</u> (<u>sway</u>, sways) ~~in the wind~~.

&&&&&&&&&&&&

X. **Transitive and Intransitive Verbs:**

Directions: Underline the subject once and the verb or verb phrase twice.
Label any direct object - **D.O.** Write **T** if the verb is transitive;
write **I** if the verb is intransitive.

Remember: A transitive verb will have a direct object.

D.O.T. > Direct **O**bject **= T**ransitive

D.O.
1.   __**T**__   We <u>solved</u> the mystery.

D.O.
2.   __**T**__   Mom <u>does</u> crossword puzzles.

D.O.
3.   __**T**__   The <u>server</u> <u>handed</u> us menus.

4.   __**T**__   Jamilla <u>laughed</u> softly.

V. **Linking Verbs and Predicate Adjectives:**
   Directions: Delete any prepositional phrases. Underline the subject once and the verb twice. Label any predicate adjective – **P.A.**

1. That truck with wide mud flaps is new.

2. The child is growing sleepy.

3. His grandfather became excited about their planned rapids trip.

ఆఆఆఆఆఆఆఆఆఆఆ

W. **Subject-Verb Agreement:**
   Directions: Delete any prepositional phrases. Underline the subject once.
   Underline the verb/verb phrase that agrees with the subject twice.

1. One lizard (hides, hide) under our bushes.

2. These actors (learns, learn) lines easily.

3. Some onions (smell, smells) strong.

4. The top of his hands (have, has) a rash.

5. Their butler (does(n't), do(n't)) answer their phone.

6. Our palm trees (sway, sways) in the wind.

ఆఆఆఆఆఆఆఆఆఆఆ

X. **Transitive and Intransitive Verbs:**
   Directions: Underline the subject once and the verb or verb phrase twice.
   Label any direct object - **D.O.** Write **T** if the verb is transitive;
   write **I** if the verb is intransitive.
   Remember: A transitive verb will have a direct object.
   D.O.T. > Direct Object = Transitive

1. _____ We solved the mystery.

2. _____ Mom does crossword puzzles.

3. _____ The server handed us menus.

4. _____ Jamilla laughed softly.

A. Directions: Cross out any prepositional phrases. Underline the subject once and the verb or verb phrase twice.

1. Several <u>bees</u> <u>buzzed</u> ~~around my head~~.

2. A <u>bunch</u> ~~of radishes~~ <u>is lying</u> ~~on the ground~~.

3. (<u>You</u>) <u>Tell</u> us ~~about your trip to Denver~~.

4. A <u>toothbrush</u> and <u>floss</u> <u>are</u> ~~by the bathroom sink~~.

5. Several <u>women</u> ~~at the department store~~ <u>chose</u> (to buy) long coats.

6. <u>I</u> <u>may</u> **not** <u>come</u> ~~without my sister~~.

7. <u>Mario</u> <u>walked</u> ~~toward a police officer~~ and <u>waved</u>.

8. <u>We</u> <u>could**n't**</u> <u>travel</u> ~~through a tunnel~~ ~~near our home~~.

9. <u>Joy</u> <u>buys</u> old jewelry ~~from estate sales~~.

10. A retired <u>athlete</u> <u>sat</u> ~~with his friends and relatives~~ ~~during a game~~.

11. Many <u>fossils</u> <u>have been found</u> ~~in a cave~~ ~~beyond that cliff~~.

12. A <u>line</u> ~~of ants~~ <u>scurried</u> ~~around a pebble~~ ~~outside their front door~~.

B. Directions: Write the contraction.

1. who is - _____**who's**_____   6. I have - _____**I've**_____

2. will not - _____**won't**_____   7. here is - _____**here's**_____

3. are not - _____**aren't**_____   8. I am - _____**I'm**_____

4. they have - _____**they've**_____   9. could not - _____**couldn't**_____

5. you will - _____**you'll**_____   10. is not - _____**isn't**_____

A. Directions: Cross out any prepositional phrases. Underline the subject once
and the verb or verb phrase twice.

1. Several bees buzzed around my head.

2. A bunch of radishes is lying on the ground.

3. Tell us about your trip to Denver.

4. A toothbrush and floss are by the bathroom sink.

5. Several women at the department store chose to buy long coats.

6. I may not come without my sister.

7. Mario walked toward a police officer and waved.

8. We couldn't travel through a tunnel near our home.

9. Joy buys old jewelry from estate sales.

10. A retired athlete sat with his friends and relatives during a game.

11. Many fossils have been found in a cave beyond that cliff.

12. A line of ants scurried around a pebble outside their front door.

B. Directions: Write the contraction.

1. who is - _____

2. will not - _____

3. are not - _____

4. they have - _____

5. you will - _____

6. I have - _____

7. here is - _____

8. I am - _____

9. could not - _____

10. is not - _____

C.   Directions: Circle the correct word.

1.   (They're, **Their**, There) toilet bowl has been cleaned.

2.   (**You're**, Your) a good friend.

3.   (**They're**, Their, There) concerned about cavities.

4.   A raccoon scampered around (it's, **its**) dam.

5.   Gena wants (**your**, you're) advice about this program.

D.   Directions: Underline the subject once and the correct verb phrase twice.

1.   We have (ate, eaten) lunch.

2.   He must have (sang, sung) solo.

3.   This chain is (broke, broken).

4.   I have **not** (saw, seen) them.

5.   Troy may have (taken, took) a trip.

6.   Maria had (beat, beaten) his score.

7.   Lil has (bought, boughten) soap.

8.   The buses have (came, come).

9.   She has (driven, drove) her own car.

10.   Their dad has (went, gone) alone.

E.   Directions: Cross out any prepositional phrases. Underline the subject once and the verb/verb phrase twice. Label any direct object – **D.O.**

                           D.O.
1.   Jenny drew an arrow ~~across her paper~~.

                                     D.O.
2.   ~~Since last Thursday~~, I have earned ten dollars.

                     D.O.
3.   She carried her checkbook ~~into her bank~~.

C. Directions: Circle the correct word.

1. (They're, Their, There) toilet bowl has been cleaned.

2. (You're, Your) a good friend.

3. (They're, Their, There) concerned about cavities.

4. A raccoon scampered around (it's, its) dam.

5. Gena wants (your, you're) advice about this program.

D. Directions: Underline the subject once and the correct verb phrase twice.

1. We have (ate, eaten) lunch.

2. He must have (sang, sung) solo.

3. This chain is (broke, broken).

4. I have not (saw, seen) them.

5. Troy may have (taken, took) a trip.

6. Maria had (beat, beaten) his score.

7. Lil has (bought, boughten) soap.

8. The buses have (came, come).

9. She has (driven, drove) her own car.

10. Their dad has (went, gone) alone.

E. Directions: Cross out any prepositional phrases. Underline the subject once and the verb/verb phrase twice. Label any direct object – **D.O.**

1. Jenny drew an arrow across her paper.

2. Since last Thursday, I have earned ten dollars.

3. She carried her checkbook into her bank.

287

F. Directions: Delete any prepositional phrases. Underline the subject once
                and the verb/verb phrase twice.
**Note: You may want to instruct students to label any direct object to help determine the verb. Decide if you want
to give a point for each correct verb or for each part of a sentence.**
                                        D.O.
1. That <u>club</u> (rises, <u>raises</u>) money ~~for fire victims.~~

2. Our <u>newspaper</u> <u>was</u> (laying, <u>lying</u>) ~~beside our sidewalk.~~

3. <u>You</u> <u>may</u> (<u>sit</u>, set) ~~beside us after your performance.~~
                                        D.O.
4. <u>I</u> <u>must have</u> (<u>laid</u>, lain) my hammer ~~on the garage floor.~~
                                        D.O.
5. The <u>judge</u> (sat, <u>set</u>) his gavel ~~atop her desk.~~

G. Directions: Underline the subject once and the verb or verb phrase
                twice. Write the tense (*present, past,* or *future*) in the blank.

1. _____**past**_____   A <u>feather</u> <u>floated</u> by.

2. _____**present**_____   <u>Tate</u> <u>enjoys</u> fencing.

3. _____**past**_____   <u>Tara</u> <u>seemed</u> confused today.

4. _____**present**_____   Many <u>ducks</u> <u>swim</u> there daily.

5. _____**future**_____   <u>He</u> <u>will keep</u> a journal.

H. Directions: Delete any prepositional phrases. Underline the subject once.
                Underline the verb/verb phrase that agrees with the subject twice.

1. <u>Mom</u> often (buy, <u>buys</u>) us treats.

2. A large <u>goose</u> ~~in the gaggle~~ (<u>leads</u>, lead) the others.

3. His <u>dog</u> and <u>cat</u> (<u>chase</u>, chases) each other.

4. <u>Everyone</u> (are, <u>is</u>) ~~in the pool.~~

5. <u>Tara</u> (<u>does</u>(n't), do(n't)) <u>know</u> me.

6. That <u>man</u> or his <u>wife</u> (run, <u>runs</u>) the business.

7. <u>One</u> ~~of the men~~ (<u>teaches</u>, teach) French.
288

F. Directions: Delete any prepositional phrases. Underline the subject once
                and the verb/verb phrase twice.

1. That club (rises, raises) money for fire victims.

2. Our newspaper was (laying, lying) beside our sidewalk.

3. You may (sit, set) beside us after your performance.

4. I must have (laid, lain) my hammer on the garage floor.

5. The judge (sat, set) his gavel atop her desk.

G. Directions: Underline the subject once and the verb or verb phrase
                twice. Write the tense (*present*, *past*, or *future*) in the blank.

1. _____ A feather floated by.

2. _____ Tate enjoys fencing.

3. _____ Tara seemed confused today.

4. _____ Many ducks swim there daily.

5. _____ He will keep a journal.

H. Directions: Delete any prepositional phrases. Underline the subject once.
                Underline the verb/verb phrase that agrees with the subject twice.

1. Mom often (buy, buys) us treats.

2. A large goose in the gaggle (leads, lead) the others.

3. His dog and cat (chase, chases) each other.

4. Everyone (are, is) in the pool.

5. Tara (does(n't), do(n't)) know me.

6. That man or his wife (run, runs) the business.

7. One of the men (teaches, teach) French.

289

ADJECTIVES

WORKBOOK PAGE 132

Date_____ **Descriptive**

Adjectives describe.

ANSWERS MAY VARY/REPRESENTATIVE ANSWERS:

Directions: Write three adjectives that describe each noun.

1.   peach   2.   parrot

   ripe   colorful

   rotten   rare

   juicy   lively

3.   bin   4.   chips

   plastic   potato

   storage   salty

   clothing   stale

5.   park   6.   skateboard

   national   long

   busy   fast

   city   broken

7.   doctor   8.   bottle

   medical   baby

   young   milk

   foot   water

9.   eggs   10.   car

   burned   race

   scrambled   stolen

   fried   junked

Adjectives describe.

Directions: Write three adjectives that describe each noun.

1.   peach   2.   parrot

    _____   _____

    _____   _____

    _____   _____

3.   bin   4.   chips

    _____   _____

    _____   _____

    _____   _____

5.   park   6.   skateboard

    _____   _____

    _____   _____

    _____   _____

7.   doctor   8.   bottle

    _____   _____

    _____   _____

    _____   _____

9.   eggs   10.   car

    _____   _____

    _____   _____

    _____   _____

Name_____   **ADJECTIVES**

WORKBOOK PAGE 133

Date_____   **Descriptive**

Note: You may want to list answers for several nouns for the class *to see* different thinking. You also may want to take a poll if any students matched the text answers. Keeping students involved is always good!

Adjectives describe.

Directions: Write a descriptive adjective in each blank. Draw an arrow from the descriptive adjective to the noun it modifies (goes over to). Do not use colors. Try not to reuse any adjectives.

ANSWERS MAY VARY/REPRESENTATIVE ANSWERS: The modified noun is in boldfaced print.

1. A. a ____deep____ **hole**   B. a ____muddy____ **hole**

2. A. this ____watery____ **soup**   B. this ____vegetable____ **soup**

3. A. the ____flying____ **bug**   B. the ____gigantic____ **bug**

4. A. many ____rubber____ **tires**   B. many ____large____ **tires**

5. A. ____chocolate____ **milk**   B. ____sour____ **milk**

6. A. a ____digital____ **camera**   B. a ____throw-away____ **camera**

7. A. those ____dirty____ **sheets**   B. those ____flowered____ **sheets**

8. A. a ____full____ **beard**   B. a ____long____ **beard**

9. A. her ____big____ **toe**   B. her ____injured____ **toe**

10. A. some ____cardboard____ **boxes** B. some ____square____ **boxes**

11. A. your ____new____ **shirt**   B. your ____striped____ **shirt**

294

Adjectives describe.

Directions: Write a descriptive adjective in each blank. Draw an arrow from the descriptive adjective to the noun it modifies (goes over to). Do not use colors. Try not to reuse any adjectives.

1. A. a _____ hole   B. a _____ hole

2. A. this _____ soup   B. this _____ soup

3. A. the _____ bug   B. the _____ bug

4. A. many _____ tires   B. many _____ tires

5. A. _____ milk   B. _____ milk

6. A. a _____ camera   B. a _____ camera

7. A. those _____ sheets   B. those _____ sheets

8. A. a _____ beard   B. a _____ beard

9. A. her _____ toe   B. her _____ toe

10. A. some _____ boxes   B. some _____ boxes

11. A. your _____ shirt   B. your _____ shirt

Adjectives describe.

Directions: Write a descriptive adjective in each blank. Draw an arrow from the
descriptive adjective to the noun it modifies (goes over to).

**ANSWERS MAY VARY/REPRESENTATIVE ANSWERS: The modified
noun is in boldfaced print.**

1.   They traveled down a _____dirt_____ **road**.

2.   Ali likes to eat _____wheat_____ **bread** for breakfast.

3.   Those floors were scrubbed with _____soapy_____ **water**.

4.   Two girls joined a _____soccer_____ **team** last week.

5.   _____Strawberry_____ **sundaes** are very tasty.

6.   Miss Dobbs enjoys _____foggy_____ **days**.

7.   This book about _____polar_____ **bears** is interesting.

8.   A _____screeching_____ **sound** can be annoying.

9.   Our family went on a/an _____nature_____ **hike**.

10.   His friend likes _____comic_____ **books**.

11.   A teller spoke with a (an) _____confused_____ **lady** for ten minutes.

12.   What do you think of _____country_____ **music**?

Adjectives describe.

Directions: Write a descriptive adjective in each blank. Draw an arrow from the
descriptive adjective to the noun it modifies (goes over to).

1. They traveled down a _____ road.

2. Ali likes to eat _____ bread for breakfast.

3. Those floors were scrubbed with _____ water.

4. Two girls joined a _____ team last week.

5. _____ sundaes are very tasty.

6. Miss Dobbs enjoys _____ days.

7. This book about _____ bears is interesting.

8. A _____ sound can be annoying.

9. Our family went on a/an _____ hike.

10. His friend likes _____ books.

11. A teller spoke with a (an) _____ lady for ten minutes.

12. What do you think of _____ music?

LIMITING ADJECTIVES

You have learned that many adjectives describe.

There is another type of adjectives called **limiting** or **determining adjectives**.

The good news is that you just learned these as signals in the noun unit. Therefore, you should be able to find and use them easily. Do you remember these classifications?

Classification of Limiting (Determining) Adjectives:

☼ **Articles: a, an, the**

> Example: I ate **an** orange.

> Note: Any time you see *a, an,* or *the*, mark each as an adjective.
> They are also called *articles*.

☼ **Demonstratives: this, that, these, those**

> Example: I met **that** race-car driver.

Use *this* and *that* with <u>singular</u> nouns.   I want this <u>bag</u>.   I want that <u>bag</u>.
Use *these* and *those* with <u>plural</u> nouns.   I want these <u>bags</u>.   I want those <u>bags</u>.

Be careful with demonstratives. If *this, that, these,* or *those* stands alone, it serves as a pronoun.

> Do you want ***these*** shoes?   **(adjective)**
> Do you want ***these***?   **(pronoun)**

☼ **Numbers:**

> Example: We each selected **two** costumes.

Be careful with numbers. If a number stands alone, it serves as a pronoun.

> ***Two*** teams were chosen.   **(adjective)**
> ***Two*** were chosen.   **(pronoun)**

✪ **Possessive Pronouns:**   my, his, her, your, its, our, their, whose

> Example: **My** vest is leather.

These are sometimes referred to as possessive pronouns used as adjectives.

✪ **Possessive Nouns:**

> Examples: I like **Grandpa's** homemade cookies.
>
> The **lions'** den is like a cave.

These are sometimes referred to as possessive nouns used as adjectives.

✪ **Indefinites:**   any, few, no, many, most, several, some

> Example: I want a **few** minutes of your time.

Be careful with indefinites. If an indefinite stands alone, it is a pronoun.

> *Few* floods occur here.   **(adjective)**
>
> I need a *few*.   **(pronoun)**

✪✪✪✪✪✪✪✪✪✪✪✪✪✪✪✪✪✪✪✪✪✪

An adjective modifies another word. *Modifies* means to go over to a word. It answers *what*.

> Example: **This** wagon is lime green.

This is an adjective. This what? This wagon! *This* is an **adjective** modifying *wagon*.

However, a word that can be an adjective will sometimes appear **alone** in a sentence. When this happens, the word will not be an adjective. It will be a **pronoun**.

> Example: **That** is mine.

That what?   You don't know. *That* is a pronoun.

Limiting (Determining) Adjectives:

Articles: a, an, the

Demonstratives: this, that, these, those

Numbers: Example: *seven* points

Possessive Pronouns: my, his, her, your, its, our, their, whose

Possessive Nouns: Example: *Jacy's* comb

Indefinites: any, few, no, many, most, several, some

ะเะเะเะเะเะเะเะเะเะเะเะเะเะเะเ

Directions: Write an appropriate limiting adjective from each category.

ANSWERS MAY VARY/REPRESENTATIVE ANSWERS:

1. **Article** – May I have ____**a**____ penny?

   Demonstratives – May I have ____**that**____ penny?

   Numbers – May I have ____**four**____ pennies?

   Possessive pronouns – May I have ____**your**____ penny?

   Possessive nouns – May I have ____**Lana's**____ penny?

   Indefinites – May I have ____**some**____ pennies?

ะเะเะเ

2. **Article** – ____**The**____ magazines were thrown away.

   Demonstratives – ____**Those**____ magazines were thrown away.

   Numbers – ____**Nine**____ magazines were thrown away.

   Possessive pronouns – ____**Our**____ magazines were thrown away.

   Possessive nouns – ____**Dad's**____ magazines were thrown away.

   Indefinites – ____**Many**____ magazines were thrown away.

Name_____   **ADJECTIVES**

Date_____   **Limiting**

Limiting (Determining) Adjectives:

Articles: a, an, the

Demonstratives: this, that, these, those

Numbers: Example: *seven* points

Possessive Pronouns: my, his, her, your, its, our, their, whose

Possessive Nouns: Example: *Jacy's* comb

Indefinites: any, few, no, many, most, several, some

ৰৈৰৈৰৈৰৈৰৈৰৈৰৈৰৈৰৈৰৈৰৈৰৈ

Directions: Write an appropriate limiting adjective from each category.

1. **Article** – May I have _____ penny?

    Demonstratives – May I have _____ penny?

    Numbers – May I have _____ pennies?

    Possessive pronouns – May I have _____ penny?

    Possessive nouns – May I have _____ penny?

    Indefinites – May I have _____ pennies?

ৰৈৰৈৰৈ

2. **Article** – _____ magazines were thrown away.

    Demonstratives – _____ magazines were thrown away.

    Numbers – _____ magazines were thrown away.

    Possessive pronouns – _____ magazines were thrown away.

    Possessive nouns – _____ magazines were thrown away.

    Indefinites – _____ magazines were thrown away.

Name______________________________ **ADJECTIVES**

WORKBOOK PAGE 138

Date______________________________ **Limiting**

Limiting (Determining) Adjectives:

Articles: a, an, the

Demonstratives: this, that, these, those

Numbers: Example: *three* carrots

Possessive Pronouns: my, his, her, your, its, our, their, whose

Possessive Nouns: Examples: *Jemima's* wish girls' club

Indefinites: any, few, no, many, most, several, some

Directions: Write an appropriate limiting adjective from each category. (Do not use a word twice.) Then, draw an arrow to the noun it modifies (goes over to that word).

ANSWERS WILL VARY/REPRESENTATIVE ANSWERS:

1. (Demonstrative) – You should like **these** ***pictures***.
2. (Possessive pronoun) – That dog is eating **her** ***lunch***.
3. (Number) – We need **ten** ***nails*** to finish the job.
4. (Article) – Do you have **a** ***compass***?
5. (Indefinite) – I have not seen **any** ***turtles*** in this area.
6. (Possessive noun) – A **puppy's** front ***paw*** was hurt.
7. (Possessive pronoun) – **Your** ***backpack*** is like mine.
8. (Indefinite) – I have **no** ***money*** with me.
9. (Demonstrative) – Did Misty write **this** ***story***?
10. (Possessive noun) – **Mom's** ***humor*** amazes me!
11. (Number) – Mrs. Jolly has **six** ***nephews***.
12. (Article) – Do you want **the** ***balloon*** with blue stripes?
13. (Possessive pronoun) – The disc jockey played **our** favorite ***song***.

Limiting (Determining) Adjectives:

<u>**Articles:**</u> **a, an, the**

<u>**Demonstratives:**</u>   **this, that, these, those**

<u>**Numbers:**</u>   Example: *three* carrots

<u>**Possessive Pronouns:**</u>   **my, his, her, your, its, our, their, whose**

<u>**Possessive Nouns:**</u>   Examples: *Jemima's* wish   girls' club

<u>**Indefinites:**</u>   **any, few, no, many, most, several, some**

ഗ്

Directions: Write an appropriate limiting adjective from each category. (Do not use a word twice.) Then, draw an arrow to the noun it modifies (goes over to that word).

1.   (Demonstrative) – You should like _____ pictures.

2.   (Possessive pronoun) – That dog is eating _____ lunch.

3.   (Number) – We need _____ nails to finish the job.

4.   (Article) – Do you have _____ compass?

5.   (Indefinite) – I have not seen _____ turtles in this area.

6.   (Possessive noun) – A _____ front paw was hurt.

7.   (Possessive pronoun) – _____ backpack is like mine.

8.   (Indefinite) – I have _____ money with me.

9.   (Demonstrative) – Did Misty write _____ story?

10.   (Possessive noun) – _____ humor amazes me!

11.   (Number) – Mrs. Jolly has _____ nephews.

12.   (Article) – Do you want _____ balloon with blue stripes?

13.   (Possessive pronoun) – The disc jockey played _____ favorite song.

Directions: Write an appropriate limiting adjective. (Do not use a word twice.)
              Draw an arrow to the noun it modifies (goes over to that word).
ANSWERS MAY VARY/REPRESENTATIVE ANSWERS:

1. (Possessive pronoun) – Divers checked _____**their**_____ *equipment*.

2. (Indefinite) – _____**Few**_____ index *cards* were needed.

3. (Article) – We chose _____**the**_____ small teddy *bear* as a gift.

4. (Demonstrative) – Do you want _____**these**_____ healthy *snacks*?

5. (Number) – They earned _____**forty**_____ *dollars* by mowing yards.

6. (Possessive noun) – _____**Fran's**_____ *lips* are chapped.

7. (Article) – Kim needs _____**a**_____ new winter *jacket*.

8. (Indefinite) – The party planner bought _____**no**_____ *favors*.

9. (Possessive pronoun) – _____**Your**_____ *sunglasses* are on the floor.

10. (Demonstrative) – Please send _____**this**_____ *fax* to your company.

11. (Number) – Tate ordered _____**four**_____ racing *posters*.

12. (Possessive noun) – Have you seen a _____**robin's**_____ *nest*?

13. (Possessive pronoun) – I like _____**her**_____ *attitude*.

14. (Indefinite) – His agent makes _____**many**_____ *decisions*.

15. (Article) – _____**An**_____ *eagle* flew nearby.

16. (Demonstrative) – May I have _____**that**_____ tiny *tangerine*?

17. (Possessive pronoun) – _____**Whose**_____ *wand* is this?

18. (Possessive noun) – Yikes! I lost my _____**sister's**_____ car *keys*!

304

Name_____   **ADJECTIVES**

Date_____   **Limiting**

Directions: Write an appropriate limiting adjective. (Do not use a word twice.)
              Draw an arrow to the noun it modifies (goes over to that word).

1. (Possessive pronoun) – Divers checked _____ equipment.

2. (Indefinite) – _____ index cards were needed.

3. (Article) – We chose _____ small teddy bear as a gift.

4. (Demonstrative) – Do you want _____ healthy snacks?

5. (Number) – They earned _____ dollars by mowing yards.

6. (Possessive noun) – _____ lips are chapped.

7. (Article) – Kim needs _____ new winter jacket.

8. (Indefinite) – The party planner bought _____ favors.

9. (Possessive pronoun) – _____ sunglasses are on the floor.

10. (Demonstrative) – Please send _____ fax to your company.

11. (Number) – Tate ordered _____ racing posters.

12. (Possessive noun) – Have you seen a _____ nest?

13. (Possessive pronoun) – I like _____ attitude.

14. (Indefinite) – His agent makes _____ decisions.

15. (Article) – _____ eagle flew nearby.

16. (Demonstrative) – May I have _____ tiny tangerine?

17. (Possessive pronoun) – _____ wand is this?

18. (Possessive noun) – Yikes! I lost my _____ car keys!

Name_____ **ADJECTIVES**

WORKBOOK PAGE 140

Date_____ **Limiting**

Note: Be sure that students understand that *of the senators* in #10 is a prepositional phrase and can be deleted. The subject is *four*.

Remember: **Some words can be limiting adjectives if they modify a noun or pronoun. That same word will not be a limiting adjective if it stands alone.**

Examples: Please turn on **that** fan.   Adjective – *that* fan

     May I have **that**?   That what? We don't know.
             That is not an adjective.

    ☙☙☙☙☙☙☙☙☙☙☙☙☙☙☙☙☙☙☙☙☙

Directions: Write **Adj.** in the short blank if the boldfaced word serves as a limiting adjective. Write the boldfaced word and the noun it modifies in the blank after the sentence. Write **No** if the boldfaced word does not serve as a limiting adjective.

1.   **Adj.**   I asked **some** friends to help me.   __**some friends**__

2.   **No**   **Some** laughed at the child's remark.   _____

3.   **Adj.**   **Her** exercise class is fun.   __**Her class**__

4.   **No**   Will you go with **her**?   _____

5.   **No**   Please take **these** with you.   _____

6.   **Adj.**   Everyone is amused by **these** gerbils. __**these gerbils**__

7.   **Adj.**   The store had **several** mops on sale. __**several mops**__

8.   **No**   I need **several** for the conference.   _____

9.   **Adj.**   Were **four** bags of nuts purchased? __**four bags**__

10.   **No**   **Four** ~~of the senators~~ voted against the bill.   _____

11.   **Adj.**   I don't know **whose** purse is lost. __**whose purse**__

12.   **No**   Do you know **whose** was chosen?   _____

306

ADJECTIVES

Limiting

Remember: **Some words can be limiting adjectives if they modify a noun or pronoun. That same word will not be a limiting adjective if it stands alone.**

Examples: Please turn on *that* fan.   Adjective – *that* fan

May I have *that*?   That what? We don't know.
That is not an adjective.

෴෴෴෴෴෴෴෴෴෴෴෴෴෴෴෴෴෴෴෴

Directions: Write **Adj.** in the short blank if the boldfaced word serves as a limiting adjective. Write the boldfaced word and the noun it modifies in the blank after the sentence. Write **No** if the boldfaced word does not serve as a limiting adjective.

1. _____   I asked **some** friends to help me.   _____

2. _____   **Some** laughed at the child's remark.   _____

3. _____   **Her** exercise class is fun.   _____

4. _____   Will you go with **her**?   _____

5. _____   Please take **these** with you.   _____

6. _____   Everyone is amused by **these** gerbils.   _____

7. _____   The store had **several** mops on sale.   _____

8. _____   I need **several** for the conference.   _____

9. _____   Were **four** bags of nuts purchased?   _____

10. _____   **Four** of the senators voted against the bill.   _____

11. _____   I don't know **whose** purse is lost.   _____

12. _____   Do you know **whose** was chosen?   _____

A. Directions: Circle any limiting adjectives.

1. **Four** teenagers ordered **a** pizza with **no** cheese.

2. **That** priest visited **several** families in **his** parish.

3. **Mom's** friend sent **some** seeds for **her** garden.

4. **An** engineer presented **the twelve** awards.

5. We like **those** chairs without **any** padding.

ﭏﭏﭏﭏﭏﭏﭏﭏﭏﭏﭏﭏﭏﭏ

B. Directions: Circle any descriptive adjectives.

1. **Stamp** boxes with **green** swirls have been found.

2. **Purple glass** cups with **curved** handles were sold.

3. I want **soft, pleated** drapes for the **bedroom** windows.

4. Elephants have **huge grey** ears and **long** trunks.

5. **Wedding** gifts are often wrapped in **silver** paper with **large white** bows.

ﭏﭏﭏﭏﭏﭏﭏﭏﭏﭏﭏﭏﭏﭏ

C. Directions: Circle limiting <u>and</u> descriptive adjectives.

1. **Many good** cooks use **that old** cookbook for **special** recipes.

2. **A knitted, wool** sweater with **an orange** border was **her birthday** gift.

3. Has **Penny's** horse been given **fresh** water and **several crisp** carrots?

4. **My two** cousins bought **grape** juice from **our school's snack** bar.

5. **This satin** dress with **black polka** dots won **the designer** award.

308

A. Directions: Circle any limiting adjectives.

1. Four teenagers ordered a pizza with no cheese.

2. That priest visited several families in his parish.

3. Mom's friend sent some seeds for her garden.

4. An engineer presented the twelve awards.

5. We like those chairs without any padding.

෧෧෧෧෧෧෧෧෧෧෧෧෧෧

B. Directions: Circle any descriptive adjectives.

1. Stamp boxes with green swirls have been found.

2. Purple glass cups with curved handles were sold.

3. I want soft, pleated drapes for the bedroom windows.

4. Elephants have huge grey ears and long trunks.

5. Wedding gifts are often wrapped in silver paper with large white bows.

෧෧෧෧෧෧෧෧෧෧෧෧෧෧

C. Directions: Circle limiting _and_ descriptive adjectives.

1. Many good cooks use that old cookbook for special recipes.

2. A knitted, wool sweater with an orange border was her birthday gift.

3. Has Penny's horse been given fresh water and several crisp carrots?

4. My two cousins bought grape juice from our school's snack bar.

5. This satin dress with black polka dots won the designer award.

Proper adjectives are descriptive words derived from proper nouns. Let's review common and proper nouns.

Common Noun	Proper Noun	
country	**E**ngland	(name of a specific country)
city	**T**ampa	(name of a specific city)
continent	**A**sia	(name of a specific continent)

A proper adjective is a descriptive word. It is based on a proper noun and is **capitalized**.

Proper Noun	Proper Adjective	
England	**E**nglish	**E**nglish tea
Tampa	**T**ampa	a **T**ampa park
Asia	**A**sian	an **A**sian landscape

Note that *Tampa* does not change when becoming a proper adjective. Some words do not change.

ॐ ॐ

Directions: Write the proper adjective for each proper noun. Then, write a word that it might modify on the line next to it.

ANSWERS MAY VARY/REPRESENTATIVE ANSWERS:

Example: France - _____**French**_____   _____**bread**_____

1. Italy - _____**Italian**_____   _____**pasta**_____

2. Africa - _____**African**_____   _____**desert**_____

3. Mexico - _____**Mexican**_____   _____**citizen**_____

4. America - _____**American**_____   _____**flag**_____

5. Newport Beach - _**Newport Beach**_   _____**street**_____

6. Sweden - _____**Swedish**_____   _____**food**_____

7. Clover Club - _____**Clover Club**_____   _____**meeting**_____

Proper adjectives are descriptive words derived from proper nouns. Let's review common and proper nouns.

Common Noun	Proper Noun	
country	**E**ngland	(name of a specific country)
city	**T**ampa	(name of a specific city)
continent	**A**sia	(name of a specific continent)

A proper adjective is a descriptive word. It is based on a proper noun and is **capitalized**.

Proper Noun	Proper Adjective	
England	**E**nglish	**E**nglish tea
Tampa	**T**ampa	a **T**ampa park
Asia	**A**sian	an **A**sian landscape

Note that *Tampa* does not change when becoming a proper adjective. Some words do not change.

🙰🙰🙰🙰🙰🙰🙰🙰🙰🙰🙰🙰🙰🙰🙰🙰🙰🙰🙰

Directions: Write the proper adjective for each proper noun. Then, write a word that it might modify on the line next to it.

Example: France - _____**French**_____   _____**bread**_____

1. Italy - _____   _____

2. Africa - _____   _____

3. Mexico - _____   _____

4. America - _____   _____

5. Newport Beach - _____   _____

6. Sweden - _____   _____

7. Clover Club - _____   _____

ADJECTIVES

Proper Adjectives

Proper adjectives are descriptive words derived from proper nouns.

Common Noun	*Proper Noun*	
town	**K**ingsdale	(name of a specific town)
state	**A**laska	(name of a specific state)
sea	**B**altic **S**ea	(name of a specific sea)

A proper adjective is a descriptive word based on a proper noun. A proper adjective is **capitalized**.

Proper Noun	*Proper Adjective*	
Kingsdale	**K**ingsdale	a **K**ingsdale carnival
Alaska	**A**laskan	an **A**laskan fishing boat
Baltic **S**ea	**B**altic **S**ea	a **B**altic **S**ea storm

๛๛๛๛๛๛๛๛๛๛๛๛๛๛๛๛๛๛๛๛

Directions: Circle any proper adjective. Draw an arrow to the word it modifies.
PROPER ADJECTIVES ARE UNDERLINED. MODIFIED WORDS ARE BOLDFACED.

1. Her <u>Hawaiian</u> **shirt** is very bright.

2. A <u>French</u> **cottage** is located on a coastal island.

3. The <u>Italian</u> **singer** performed at Sims Hall.

4. A <u>Washington</u> **lawyer** opened a new office.

5. Do you want to go on an <u>African</u> **safari**?

6. We attended a <u>United Nations</u> **meeting**.

7. Have you seen the <u>Long Beach</u> **pier**?

8. His friends visit a <u>Bahamas</u> **beach**.

9. A <u>North American</u> **airline** opened a new <u>Canadian</u> **office**.

10. I collect <u>Kennedy</u> **coins** and <u>Victorian</u> **china**.

312

Proper adjectives are descriptive words derived from proper nouns.

Common Noun	*Proper Noun*	
town	**K**ingsdale	(name of a specific town)
state	**A**laska	(name of a specific state)
sea	**B**altic **S**ea	(name of a specific sea)

A proper adjective is a descriptive word based on a proper noun. A proper adjective is **capitalized**.

Proper Noun	*Proper Adjective*	
Kingsdale	**K**ingsdale	a **K**ingsdale carnival
Alaska	**A**laskan	an **A**laskan fishing boat
Baltic **S**ea	**B**altic **S**ea	a **B**altic **S**ea storm

৵৵৵৵৵৵৵৵৵৵৵৵৵৵৵৵৵৵৵

Directions: Circle any proper adjective. Draw an arrow to the word it modifies.

1. Her Hawaiian shirt is very bright.

2. A French cottage is located on a coastal island.

3. The Italian singer performed at Sims Hall.

4. A Washington lawyer opened a new office.

5. Do you want to go on an African safari?

6. We attended a United Nations meeting.

7. Have you seen the Long Beach pier?

8. His friends visit a Bahamas beach.

9. A North American airline opened a new Canadian office.

10. I collect Kennedy coins and Victorian china.

A complete predicate is the part of a sentence that includes the verb and usually the remainder of a sentence.

> Example: Parachutes **opened in the air**.
>   *complete predicate*

If a sentence is a **question**, make it into a statement before naming the complete predicate.

> Example: Did you speak with that security guard?
>
>   You **did speak with that security guard**.
>   *complete predicate*

🙰🙰🙰🙰🙰🙰🙰🙰🙰🙰🙰🙰🙰🙰🙰🙰🙰🙰🙰🙰🙰

Directions: Place a dotted line under the complete predicate.

1.   An excited puppy **scooted across the kitchen floor**.

2.   They **called the company concerning their loan**.

3.   One kayaker **lifted his oar over his head**.

4.   The drummer **laid his sticks on the floor by his stool**.

5.   The students **write their goals in a notebook**.

6.   My grandparents **attended a musical at a local theater**.

7.   Some of our glue sticks **are dry**.

8.   **Does** Pat **love to walk in the rain**?   Pat **does love to walk in the rain**.

9.   Mrs. Reno and her son **brought several cakes to the picnic**.

10. **Will** a shoemaker **repair your boot**?   A shoemaker **will repair your boot**.

11. Tate's mother and father **remained silent about their decision**.

12. **Has** she **placed a video in her machine**? She **has placed a video in her machine**.

314

A complete predicate is the part of a sentence that includes the verb and usually the remainder of a sentence.

Example: Parachutes **opened in the air**.
complete predicate

If a sentence is a **question**, make it into a statement before naming the complete predicate.

Example: Did you speak with that security guard?

You **did speak with that security guard**.
complete predicate

෴෴෴෴෴෴෴෴෴෴෴෴෴෴෴෴෴෴෴෴෴

Directions: Place a dotted line under the complete predicate.

1.   An excited puppy scooted across the kitchen floor.

2.   They called the company concerning their loan.

3.   One kayaker lifted his oar over his head.

4.   The drummer laid his sticks on the floor by his stool.

5.   The students write their goals in a notebook.

6.   My grandparents attended a musical at a local theater.

7.   Some of our glue sticks are dry.

8.   Does Pat love to walk in the rain?

9.   Mrs. Reno and her son brought several cakes to the picnic.

10.   Will a shoemaker repair your boot?

11.   Tate's mother and father remained silent about their decision.

12.   Has she placed a video in her machine?

315

Name_____   **ADJECTIVES**

WORKBOOK PAGE 145

Date_____   **Predicate Adjectives**

A complete predicate is the part of a sentence that includes the verb and usually the remainder of a sentence.

    Example: Her hair <u>is brown with blonde streaks</u>.
                 complete predicate

φφφφφφφφφφφφφφφφφφ

A. Directions: Place a dotted line under the complete predicate.

1. Sara <u>becomes concerned during storms</u>.   3. My toes <u>are sore and muddy</u>.

2. This shovel <u>has a broken handle</u>.   4. Your hair <u>seems tangled</u>.

φφφφφφφφφφφφφφφφφφ

Sometimes, an adjective occurs in the predicate (after a verb) and describes the subject. This is called a predicate adjective.
                    P.A.
    Example: This <u>ring is shiny</u>.   ___*shiny* ring___

B. Directions: Write an adjective in the first blank. Write the same adjective in the sentence below it. Label it **P.A.** - predicate adjective. Then, place a dotted line under the complete predicate.

ANSWERS MAY VARY/REPRESENTATIVE ANSWERS:

1. a (an) _____**gentle**_____ cat
              P.A.
    The cat <u>is_____**gentle**_____</u>.

2. the ____**brave**____ boys
              P.A.
    The boys <u>are____**brave**____</u>.

3. a (an) ____**windy**____ day
              P.A.
    The day <u>remained____**windy**____</u>.

4. a (an) ____**friendly**____ greeting
              P.A.
    Their greeting <u>was____**friendly**____</u>.

316

A complete predicate is the part of a sentence that includes the verb and usually the remainder of a sentence.

Example: Her hair is brown with blonde streaks.
                                    complete predicate

ʚ̷ɞ ʚ̷ɞ ʚ̷ɞ ʚ̷ɞ ʚ̷ɞ ʚ̷ɞ ʚ̷ɞ ʚ̷ɞ ʚ̷ɞ ʚ̷ɞ ʚ̷ɞ ʚ̷ɞ ʚ̷ɞ ʚ̷ɞ ʚ̷ɞ ʚ̷ɞ

A.   Directions: Place a dotted line under the complete predicate.

1.   Sara becomes concerned during storms.   3.   My toes are sore and muddy.

2.   This shovel has a broken handle.   4.   Your hair seems tangled.

ʚ̷ɞ ʚ̷ɞ ʚ̷ɞ ʚ̷ɞ ʚ̷ɞ ʚ̷ɞ ʚ̷ɞ ʚ̷ɞ ʚ̷ɞ ʚ̷ɞ ʚ̷ɞ ʚ̷ɞ ʚ̷ɞ ʚ̷ɞ ʚ̷ɞ ʚ̷ɞ

Sometimes, an adjective occurs in the predicate (after a verb) and describes the subject. This is called a predicate adjective.
                                             P.A.
Example: This ring is shiny.   **_shiny_** ring

B.   Directions: Write an adjective in the first blank. Write the same adjective in the sentence below it. Label it **P.A.** - predicate adjective. Then, place a dotted line under the complete predicate.

1.   a (an) _____ cat

     The cat is _____.

2.   the _____ boys

     The boys are _____.

3.   a (an) _____ day

     The day remained _____.

4.   a (an) _____ greeting

     Their greeting was _____.

ADJECTIVES

Predicate Adjectives

A complete predicate is the part of a sentence that includes the verb and usually the remainder of a sentence.

Example: A herd of buffalo is roaming in a meadow.
                                    complete predicate

Sometimes an adjective occurs after the verb but describes the subject. This is called a predicate adjective.

🐎🐎🐎🐎🐎🐎🐎🐎🐎🐎🐎🐎🐎🐎🐎🐎

Directions: Write an adjective in the blank provided. Then, underline the complete predicate with a dotted line. Label the predicate adjective – **P.A.**

ANSWERS MAY VARY/REPRESENTATIVE ANSWERS:

                                                    P.A.
1. Our hot dogs tasted _____**delicious**_____.

                                        P.A.
2. These plums are _____**hard**_____.

                                P.A.
3. You look_____**puzzled**_____.

                                        P.A.
4. My teacher seems _____**tired**_____by the end of each week.

                                        P.A.
5. The cartoons were _____**hilarious**_____.

                                P.A.
6. This river is_____**long**_____.

                                        P.A.
7. One beagle became _____**playful**_____.

                                        P.A.
8. The ocean may be _____**choppy**_____during the fierce storm.

                                                P.A.
9. Their movie must have been _____**short**_____.

318

ADJECTIVES

Predicate Adjectives

A complete predicate is the part of a sentence that includes the verb and usually the remainder of a sentence.

Example: A herd of buffalo is roaming in a meadow.
                                    complete predicate

Sometimes an adjective occurs after the verb but describes the subject. This is called a predicate adjective.

&⁊&⁊&⁊&⁊&⁊&⁊&⁊&⁊&⁊&⁊&⁊&⁊&⁊&⁊&⁊&⁊&⁊

Directions: Write an adjective in the blank provided. Then, underline the complete predicate with a dotted line. Label the predicate adjective – **P.A.**

1. Our hot dogs tasted _____.

2. These plums are _____.

3. You look _____.

4. My teacher seems _____ by the end of each week.

5. The cartoons were _____.

6. This river is _____.

7. One beagle became _____.

8. The ocean may be _____ during the fierce storm.

9. Their movie must have been _____.

A predicate adjective occurs after the verb *and* ***goes back to*** <u>***describe***</u> ***the*** <u>***subject***</u> ***of the sentence.***

Remember: To have a predicate adjective, the sentence must contain a linking verb.

Linking Verbs:

to feel	to smell	to grow	to stay
to taste	to seem	to remain	to become
to look	to sound	to appear	to be (is, am, are, was, were, be, being, been)

 P.A.

Example: The <u>skin</u> ~~of a hippopotamus~~ <u>looks</u> thick.   *thick* skin

🙝🙝🙝🙝🙝🙝🙝🙝🙝🙝🙝🙝🙝🙝🙝🙝🙝🙝🙝

Directions: Write a predicate adjective in the blank. Underline the subject once and the verb twice. Label the predicate adjective – **P.A.** Write the predicate adjective and the subject of the sentence in the blank following the sentence.

Example: Your <u>hair</u> <u>is</u> shiny.   ___*shiny* hair___

<u>ANSWERS MAY VARY/REPRESENTATIVE ANSWERS:</u>

1. That <u>man</u> <u>is</u> __**P.A.**__ **tall** .   _____*tall* **man**_____

2. These <u>weights</u> <u>are</u> __**P.A.**__ **heavy** .   _____*heavy* **weights**_____

3. His <u>sister</u> <u>seems</u> __**P.A.**__ **worried** .   _____*worried* **sister**_____

4. Their <u>ideas</u> <u>sound</u> __**P.A.**__ **good** .   _____*good* **ideas**_____

5. Your <u>pet</u> <u>looks</u> __**P.A.**__ **sick** .   _____*sick* **pet**_____

6. This <u>drink</u> <u>tastes</u> __**P.A.**__ **sweet** .   _____*sweet* **drink**_____

7. One <u>child</u> <u>remained</u> __**P.A.**__ **cranky** .   _____*cranky* **child**_____

320

A predicate adjective occurs after the verb and goes back to <u>describe</u> <u>the</u>
<u>subject</u> of the sentence.

Remember: To have a predicate adjective, the sentence must contain a linking verb.

Linking Verbs:

to feel	to smell	to grow	to stay
to taste	to seem	to remain	to become
to look	to sound	to appear	to be (is, am, are, was, were, be, being, been)

P.A.
Example: The <u>skin</u> ~~of a hippopotamus~~ <u>looks</u> thick.   *thick* skin

🦐🦐🦐🦐🦐🦐🦐🦐🦐🦐🦐🦐🦐🦐🦐🦐🦐

Directions: Write a predicate adjective in the blank.   Underline the subject
once and the verb twice. Label the predicate adjective – **P.A.**
Write the predicate adjective and the subject of the sentence in the
blank following the sentence.

Example: Your <u>hair</u> <u>is</u> shiny.   *shiny* hair

1. That man is _____.   _____

2. These weights are _____.   _____

3. His sister seems _____.   _____

4. Their ideas sound _____.   _____

5. Your pet looks _____.   _____

6. This drink tastes _____.   _____

7. One child remained _____.   _____

Take your time in teaching this concept. If students understand degrees of adjectives, the concept of degrees of adverbs in the ensuing unit should be easier.

Language usage (rather than mere identification of nouns, etc.) is very important. The usage of degrees of adjectives will reflect in students' speaking and writing. We want to ascertain that students know how to compare adjectives correctly, even when they encounter new ones as adults.

Emphasize the importance of using a dictionary when not sure.

DEGREES OF ADJECTIVES

We can say that someone is strong.   ꔹ   I am strong.

We may want **to compare two** objects or people.   ꔹ   You are strong**er** than I am.

We may want **to compare more than two**.   ꔹ   You are strong**est** in your family.

We use degrees of adjectives when we compare:
> *strong*
> *stronger*   =   **comparative degree** – comparing **2**
> *strongest*   =   **superlative degree** – comparing **3 or more**

COMPARATIVE DEGREE:

Rule A: **When comparing 2, add <u>er</u> to most one-syllable words.**

> Examples: soft – **softer**   brave – **braver**

Rule B: **When comparing 2, the word may totally change for a <u>few</u> one-syllable words.**

> Examples: good – **better**   bad – **worse**

Rule C: **When comparing 2, use <u>er</u> with some two-syllable words. Use a dictionary if necessary.**

> Examples: happy – **happier**   lively – **livelier**

Rule D: When comparing 2, use <u>more</u> (or *less*) with most words of two or more syllables.

> Examples: handsome – **more** handsome   demanding – **more** demanding

SUPERLATIVE DEGREE:

Rule A: **When comparing 3 or more, add <u>est</u> to most one-syllable words.**

> Examples: soft – **softest**   brave – **bravest**

Rule B: When comparing 3 or more, the word may change for a <u>few</u> one-syllable words.

> Examples: good – **best**   bad – **worst**

Rule C: When comparing 3 or more, use <u>est</u> with some two-syllable words. Use a dictionary if necessary.

> Examples: happy – **happiest**   lively – **liveliest**

Rule D: When comparing 3 or more, use <u>most</u> (or *least*) with many words of two or more syllables. Use a dictionary if necessary.

> Examples: handsome – **most** handsome   demanding – **most** demanding

WORKBOOK PAGE 149

ADJECTIVES

Degrees of Adjectives

ONE-SYLLABLE WORDS:

    <u>Comparing 2</u>: Use **er** most of the time.   ❀Your trophy is bigg**er** than mine.

    <u>Comparing 3 or more</u>: Use **est** most of the time.   ❀Our team's trophy is biggest of all.

TWO-SYLLABLE WORDS:

    <u>Comparing 2</u>: Use **er** some of the time.   ❀The second story was <u>funni**er**</u> than the first.

               Use **more** with many two-syllable words.   ❀I was **more** <u>upset</u> than my friend.

    <u>Comparing 3 or more</u>: Use **est** some of the time.   ❀Of the ten comics, she was <u>funni**est**</u>.

               Use **most** with many two-syllable words.

               ❀Of the four guides, our guide was **most** interesting.

THREE-SYLLABLE WORDS (OR MORE THAN THREE SYLLABLES):

    <u>Comparing 2</u>:   Use **more** with words containing three or more syllables.

           ❀The second math problem was **more** <u>confusing</u> than the first.

    <u>Comparing 3 or more</u>: Use **most** with words containing three or more syllables.

           ❀This math problem was **most** confusing of the entire worksheet.

ठ‍ठ‍ठ‍ठ‍ठ‍ठ‍ठ‍ठ‍ठ‍ठ‍ठ‍ठ‍ठ‍ठ‍ठ‍ठ‍ठ

Directions: Circle the correct adjective.

1. A. This shoe box is (**larger**, largest) than that plastic one.

    B. This shoebox is (larger, **largest**) of all the store's boxes.

2. A. Your horse seems (**calmer**, calmest) than mine.

    B. Your horse seems (calmer, **calmest**) of all the horses in your corral.

3. A. Her diamond ring is (**shinier**, shiniest) than her ruby ring.

    B. Her diamond ring is the (shinier, **shiniest**) jewelry she owns.

4. A. This four-year-old is a (**better**, best) cutter than her little brother.

    B. This four-year-old is the (better, **best**) cutter in her preschool class.

Name_____   **ADJECTIVES**

Date_____   **Degrees of Adjectives**

ONE-SYLLABLE WORDS:

    <u>Comparing 2</u>: Use **er** most of the time.   ❀Your trophy is bigg**er** than mine.

    <u>Comparing 3 or more</u>: Use **est** most of the time. ❀Our team's trophy is biggest of all.

TWO-SYLLABLE WORDS:

    <u>Comparing 2</u>: Use **er** some of the time.   ❀The second story was <u>funnier</u> than the first.

              Use **more** with many two-syllable words.   ❀I was **more** <u>upset</u> than my friend.

    <u>Comparing 3 or more</u>: Use **est** some of the time.   ❀Of the ten comics, she was <u>funniest</u>.

              Use **most** with many two-syllable words.

              ❀Of the four guides, our guide was **most** interesting.

THREE-SYLLABLE WORDS (OR MORE THAN THREE SYLLABLES):

    <u>Comparing 2</u>:   Use **more** with words containing three or more syllables.

      ❀The second math problem was **more** <u>confusing</u> than the first.

    <u>Comparing 3 or more</u>: Use **most** with words containing three or more syllables.

      ❀This math problem was **most** confusing of the entire worksheet.

❧❧❧❧❧❧❧❧❧❧❧❧❧❧❧❧❧❧

Directions: Circle the correct adjective.

1. A. This shoe box is (larger, largest) than that plastic one.

     B. This shoebox is (larger, largest) of all the store's boxes.

2. A. Your horse seems (calmer, calmest) than mine.

     B. Your horse seems (calmer, calmest) of all the horses in your corral.

3. A. Her diamond ring is (shinier, shiniest) than her ruby ring.

     B. Her diamond ring is the (shinier, shiniest) jewelry she owns.

4. A. This four-year-old is a (better, best) cutter than her little brother.

     B. This four-year-old is the (better, best) cutter in her preschool class.

ADJECTIVES

Degrees of Adjectives

ONE-SYLLABLE WORDS:

Comparing 2:   Use **er** most of the time.   ❀Bo is fast**er** than his son.

Comparing 3 or more: Use **est** most of the time.   ❀His son is fast**est** on his team.

TWO-SYLLABLE WORDS:

Comparing 2:   Use **er** some of the time.   ❀This kitten is friski**er** than its mother.

Use **more** with many two-syllable words.   ❀He was **more** careful than I was.

Comparing 3 or more: Use **est** some of the time.   ❀Your costume is scari**est** of all.

Use **most** with many two-syllable words.

❀Of the ten trails, the bike trail is **most** challenging.

THREE-SYLLABLE WORDS (OR MORE THAN THREE SYLLABLES):

Comparing 2:   Use **more** with many two-syllable words.

❀This can opener is **more** dependable than our old one.

Comparing 3 or more: Use **most** with many two-syllable words.

❀Of all of our appliances, our stove is **most** dependable.

৵৵৵৵৵৵৵৵৵৵৵৵৵৵৵৵৵৵৵

Directions: Circle the correct answer.

1.   A.   Jana is the (**more outgoing**, most outgoing) twin.

B.   Tate is the (more outgoing, **most outgoing**) triplet.

2.   A.   This yellow enamel egg is (**lovelier**, loveliest) than a plain glass egg.

B.   This yellow enamel egg is (lovelier, **loveliest**) of the entire egg collection.

3.   A.   This performer seemed (**more confident**, most confident) than the first.

B.   The sixth performer seemed (more confident, **most confident**).

4.   A.   These flat shoes are (**more comfortable**, most comfortable) than heels.

B.   These flat shoes are the (more comfortable, **most comfortable**) I own.

ADJECTIVES

Degrees of Adjectives

ONE-SYLLABLE WORDS:

Comparing 2:   Use **er** most of the time.   ❀Bo is fast**er** than his son.

Comparing 3 or more: Use **est** most of the time.   ❀His son is fast**est** on his team.

TWO-SYLLABLE WORDS:

Comparing 2:   Use **er** some of the time.   ❀This kitten is frisk**ier** than its mother.

Use **more** with many two-syllable words.   ❀He was **more** careful than I was.

Comparing 3 or more: Use **est** some of the time.   ❀Your costume is scari**est** of all.

Use **most** with many two-syllable words.

❀Of the ten trails, the bike trail is **most** challenging.

THREE-SYLLABLE WORDS (OR MORE THAN THREE SYLLABLES):

Comparing 2:   Use **more** with many two-syllable words.

❀This can opener is **more** dependable than our old one.

Comparing 3 or more: Use **most** with many two-syllable words.

❀Of all of our appliances, our stove is **most** dependable.

ఈఈఈఈఈఈఈఈఈఈఈఈఈఈఈఈఈ

Directions: Circle the correct answer.

1. A.   Jana is the (more outgoing, most outgoing) twin.

    B.   Tate is the (more outgoing, most outgoing) triplet.

2. A.   This yellow enamel egg is (lovelier, loveliest) than a plain glass egg.

    B.   This yellow enamel egg is (lovelier, loveliest) of the entire egg collection.

3. A.   This performer seemed (more confident, most confident) than the first.

    B.   The sixth performer seemed (more confident, most confident).

4. A.   These flat shoes are (more comfortable, most comfortable) than heels.

    B.   These flat shoes are the (more comfortable, most comfortable) I own.

327

Directions: Circle the correct degree of adjective.

1. This flavored iced tea is (**tastier**, tastiest) than the regular iced tea.

2. Your suggestion seems (**more workable**, most workable) than mine.

3. This puppy has the (smaller, **smallest**) paws of the entire litter.

4. Of their seven children, Kim is (more athletic, **most athletic**).

5. Of the two solutions, this one is (causticer, **more caustic**).

6. That roast is the (fresher, **freshest**) meat in the market.

7. This dirt trail is (more dangerous, **most dangerous**) of all the trails.

8. Today has been (**hotter**, hottest) than yesterday.

9. This room's carpet is the (more stained, **most stained**) rug in our house.

10. Your last message was (**more concise**, most concise) than your first.

11. My salad dressing seems (**spicier**, spiciest) than your honey-mustard one.

12. That round window appears (**clearer**, clearest) than the square one beside it.

13. A down jacket is (**heavier**, heaviest) than a windbreaker.

14. This china dish has the (more beautiful, **most beautiful**) pattern of the four.

15. Your second choice appears to be (**more acceptable**, most acceptable).

16. Our teacher seems the (quieter, **quietest**) person in the entire school.

17. Chan is the (more outspoken, **most outspoken**) triplet.

18. He is the (better, **best**) speller in our class.

328

Name_____

Date_____

ADJECTIVES

Degrees of Adjectives

Directions: Circle the correct degree of adjective.

1. This flavored iced tea is (tastier, tastiest) than the regular iced tea.

2. Your suggestion seems (more workable, most workable) than mine.

3. This puppy has the (smaller, smallest) paws of the entire litter.

4. Of their seven children, Kim is (more athletic, most athletic).

5. Of the two solutions, this one is (causticer, more caustic).

6. That roast is the (fresher, freshest) meat in the market.

7. This dirt trail is (more dangerous, most dangerous) of all the trails.

8. Today has been (hotter, hottest) than yesterday.

9. This room's carpet is the (more stained, most stained) rug in our house.

10. Your last message was (more concise, most concise) than your first.

11. My salad dressing seems (spicier, spiciest) than your honey-mustard one.

12. That round window appears (clearer, clearest) than the square one beside it.

13. A down jacket is (heavier, heaviest) than a windbreaker.

14. This china dish has the (more beautiful, most beautiful) pattern of the four.

15. Your second choice appears to be (more acceptable, most acceptable).

16. Our teacher seems the (quieter, quietest) person in the entire school.

17. Chan is the (more outspoken, most outspoken) triplet.

18. He is the (better, best) speller in our class.

Name_____

WORKBOOK PAGE 152

Date_____

Degrees of Adjectives

Directions: Write the correct degree of adjective.

   Example: Our second helicopter ride was (bumpy) ___**bumpier**___ .

1.   An apple is a (healthy) _____**healthier**_____ snack than a brownie.

2.   Although I found six sea shells, this one is (good) _____**best**_____ .

3.   The small cut on your arm is (deep) _____**deeper**_____ than the cut on your leg .

4.   Tim is the (popular) ___**most popular**___ uncle of the three.

5.   Of the two drawers, this one is (organized) ___**more organized**___ .

6.   In the pack of rubber bands, this one was (flexible) __**most flexible**__ .

7.   The third garbage can smelled (bad) _____**worst**_____ .

8.   He is the (active) ___**most active**___ member of the club.

9.   An emerald is (precious) ___**more precious**___ than a garnet.

10.   The dentist was (concerned) _**most concerened**_ about her third patient.

11.   Of all the girls in her family, she seems (curious) ___**most curious**___ .

12.   Her parents are (young) __**younger**__ than mine.

13.   Ezra is the (cooperative) ___**most cooperative**___ triplet.

14.   This story is (tragic) ___**more tragic**___ than the poem about the same subject.

15.   I was (thrilled) ___**more thrilled**___ with my science grade than my math grade.

16.   The office manager is (serious) ___**more serious**___ than the owner.

330

Directions: Write the correct degree of adjective.

  Example: Our second helicopter ride was (bumpy) _____*bumpier*_____ .

1. An apple is a (healthy) _____ snack than a brownie.

2. Although I found six sea shells, this one is (good) _____.

3. The small cut on your arm is (deep) _____ than the cut on your leg .

4. Tim is the (popular) _____ uncle of the three.

5. Of the two drawers, this one is (organized) _____.

6. In the pack of rubber bands, this one was (flexible) _____.

7. The third garbage can smelled (bad) _____.

8. He is the (active) _____ member of the club.

9. An emerald is (precious) _____ than a garnet.

10. The dentist was (concerned) _____ about her third patient.

11. Of all the girls in her family, she seems (curious) _____.

12. Her parents are (young) _____ than mine.

13. Ezra is the (cooperative) _____ triplet.

14. This story is (tragic) _____ than the poem about the same subject.

15. I was (thrilled) _____ with my science grade than my math grade.

16. The office manager is (serious) _____ than the owner.

Name_____   **ADJECTIVES**

WORKBOOK PAGE 153

Date_____   **Review**

ANSWERS MAY VARY/REPRESENTATIVE ANSWERS. THE MODIFIED NOUN IS IN ITALICS.

A. **DESCRIPTIVE ADJECTIVES:**

    Directions: Write a descriptive adjective in each blank. Draw an arrow from the descriptive adjective to the noun it modifies (goes over to).

1. This _____**linen**_____ *shirt* looks new.

2. Would you like a (an) _____**dinner**_____ *roll*?

3. A (An) _____**cruise**_____ *ship* anchored off the coast.

4. We found that _____**sleigh**_____ *bed* in the attic.

5. Did you attend a (an) _____**flower**_____ *show*?

6. _____**Neon**_____ *lights* have been installed.

              ꝇꝇꝇꝇꝇꝇꝇꝇꝇꝇꝇꝇ

B. **Limiting (Determining) Adjectives:**

    Articles: a, an, the

    Demonstratives: this, that, these, those

    Numbers: Example: *nine* baskets

    Possessive Pronouns: my, his, her, your, its, our, their, whose

    Possessive Nouns: Example: *animals'* tracks

    Indefinites: any, few, no, many, most, several, some

    Directions: Write an appropriate limiting adjective from each category.

ANSWERS MAY VARY/REPRESENTATIVE ANSWERS:

1. **Article** – _____**A**_____ peach is juicy.

    Demonstratives – May I have _____**this**_____ eraser.

    Numbers – They own _____**fifty**_____ sheep.

    Possessive pronouns – _____**His**_____ ankles are swollen.

    Possessive nouns – Tara drew _____**Hannan's**_____ picture.

    Indefinites – _____**Many**_____ sunflowers have been planted.

332

Name_____   **ADJECTIVES**

Date_____   **Review**

A. **DESCRIPTIVE ADJECTIVES:**

Directions: Write a descriptive adjective in each blank. Draw an arrow from the descriptive adjective to the noun it modifies (goes over to).

1. This _____ shirt looks new.

2. Would you like a (an) _____ roll?

3. A (An) _____ ship anchored off the coast.

4. We found that _____ bed in the attic.

5. Did you attend a (an) _____ show?

6. _____ lights have been installed.

ᴥᴥᴥᴥᴥᴥᴥᴥᴥᴥᴥᴥᴥ

B. **Limiting (Determining) Adjectives:**

Articles: a, an, the

Demonstratives: this, that, these, those

Numbers: Example: *nine* baskets

Possessive Pronouns: my, his, her, your, its, our, their, whose

Possessive Nouns: Example: *animals'* tracks

Indefinites: any, few, no, many, most, several, some

Directions: Write an appropriate limiting adjective from each category.

1. **Article** – _____ peach is juicy.

Demonstratives – May I have _____ eraser.

Numbers – They own _____ sheep.

Possessive pronouns – _____ ankles are swollen.

Possessive nouns – Tara drew _____ picture.

Indefinites – _____ sunflowers have been planted.

Name_____   **ADJECTIVES**

WORKBOOK PAGE 154
Date_____   **Review**

C. **Limiting Adjectives:**

Remember: **Some words can be limiting adjectives if they modify a noun. That same word will not be a limiting adjective if it stands alone.**

Examples: Do you have **any** straws?   Adjective – *any* straws

I don't have **any**.   *Any* what? We don't know. *Any* is not an adjective.

Directions: Place a ✓ in the blank if the boldfaced word is a limiting (determining) adjective. If the word is as an adjective, write the boldfaced word and the noun that it modifies (goes over to) in the wide blank.

1. __✓__   **Your** window is cracked. _____**your window**_____

2. __✓__   He made **few** errors on the test. _____**few errors**_____

3. ____   Did we order **these**? _____

4. __✓__   Have you read **Tim's** newspaper article? _____**Tim's article**_____

5. ____   I would like **four** in the pink color. _____

🙢🙢🙢🙢🙢🙢🙢🙢🙢🙢🙢🙢

D. **Proper Adjectives:**

A proper adjective is a descriptive word. A proper adjective is **capitalized**.

Germany (noun)   a **G**erman watch

Directions: Circle any proper adjective. Draw an arrow to the word it modifies.
A PROPER ADJECTIVE HAS BEEN BOLDFACED; THE WORD IT MODIFIES HAS BEEN ITALICIZED.

1. An **Atlanta** *taxi* took the couple to their hotel.

2. An **Indian** *company* makes these computers.

3. Have you visited a **Jackson Hole** *ranch*?

4. Is a macaw a **South American** *bird*?

334

C. Limiting Adjectives:

Remember: **Some words can be limiting adjectives if they modify a noun. That same word will not be a limiting adjective if it stands alone.**

Examples: Do you have **any** straws?   Adjective – *any* straws

I don't have **any**.   *Any* what? We don't know. *Any* is not an adjective.

Directions: Place a ✓ in the blank if the boldfaced word is a limiting (determining) adjective. If the word is as an adjective, write the boldfaced word and the noun that it modifies (goes over to) in the wide blank.

1. __ **Your** window is cracked. _____

2. __ He made **few** errors on the test. _____

3. __ Did we order **these**? _____

4. __ Have you read **Tim's** newspaper article? _____

5. __ I would like **four** in the pink color. _____

ぴぴぴぴぴぴぴぴぴぴぴ

D. Proper Adjectives:

A proper adjective is a descriptive word. A proper adjective is **capitalized**.

Germany (noun)   a **G**erman watch

Directions: Circle any proper adjective. Draw an arrow to the word it modifies.

1. An Atlanta taxi took the couple to their hotel.

2. An Indian company makes these computers.

3. Have you visited a Jackson Hole ranch?

4. Is a macaw a South American bird?

E. **Predicate Adjectives:**
    Sometimes an adjective occurs after the verb but describes the subject.
    This is called a predicate adjective.

       Directions: Cross out any prepositional phrases. Underline the subject once and the verb twice. Label the predicate adjective – **P.A.**

                          P.A.
1. My tennis <u>shoes</u> <u>are</u> soggy.

                                    P.A.
2. That <u>cottage</u> ~~near the pond~~ <u>is</u> run-down.

                   P.A.
3. The <u>ink</u> <u>is</u> smudged ~~on this paper~~.

                                 P.A.
4. The clown's <u>face</u> <u>looks</u> frightening ~~to some children~~.

                    𝒶𝒶𝒶𝒶𝒶𝒶𝒶𝒶𝒶𝒶𝒶𝒶𝒶

F. **Degrees of Adjectives:**
       Directions: Circle the correct answer.

1. This circular saw seems (**sharper**, sharpest) than my hand saw.

2. This car is (**more compact**, compacter) than the blue one.

3. My cotton shirt is (**more wrinkled**, wrinkleder) than my silk one.

4. Her attitude was (**best**, better) on her third day of work.

5. Emma is the (more active, **most active**) woman in her exercise class.

                    𝒶𝒶𝒶𝒶𝒶𝒶𝒶𝒶𝒶𝒶𝒶𝒶𝒶

G. **Identifying Adjectives:**
       Directions: Circle any adjectives.

1. **No sweet** corn floated in **our chicken** soup.

2. **Rustic, wooden** beams were nailed on **a plastered** ceiling.

3. We prepared **crisp, Belgian** waffles for **those hungry** guests.

4. **A glazed gray** mirror broke into **many jagged** pieces.

E. **Predicate Adjectives:**
    Sometimes an adjective occurs after the verb but describes the subject.
    This is called a predicate adjective.

    Directions: Cross out any prepositional phrases. Underline the subject once
                  and the verb twice. Label the predicate adjective – **P.A.**

1.   My tennis shoes are soggy.

2.   That cottage near the pond is run-down.

3.   The ink is smudged on this paper.

4.   The clown's face looks frightening to some children.

                    ༖༖༖༖༖༖༖༖༖༖༖

F. **Degrees of Adjectives:**
    Directions: Circle the correct answer.

  1.   This circular saw seems (sharper, sharpest) than my hand saw.

  2.   This car is (more compact, compacter) than the blue one.

  3.   My cotton shirt is (more wrinkled, wrinkleder) than my silk one.

  4.   Her attitude was (best, better) on her third day of work.

  5.   Emma is the (more active, most active) woman in her exercise class.

                    ༖༖༖༖༖༖༖༖༖༖༖

G. **Identifying Adjectives:**
    Directions: Circle any adjectives.

1.   No sweet corn floated in our chicken soup.

2.   Rustic, wooden beams were nailed on a plastered ceiling.

3.   We prepared crisp Belgian waffles for those hungry guests.

4.   A glazed gray mirror broke into many jagged pieces.

Name_____ **ADJECTIVES**

Date_____ **Test**

A. Directions: Circle any adjectives.

1. Are **many large** fish in **that rushing** stream?

2. **One** golfer wears **a white leather** glove with **tiny air** holes.

3. **A few** tourists visited **an old railroad** office.

4. **The pouring** rain ruined **their child's paper** hat.

5. **White-chocolate** brownies are in **this gold gift** box.

6. **Pam's spacious, modern** apartment has **no family** room.

B. Directions: Circle any proper adjective. Box any predicate adjective.
PROPER ADJECTIVES ARE BOLDFACED; PREDICATE ADJECTIVES ARE ITALICIZED.
1. Her **Eskimo** friend is *fun-loving*.

2. Our **Italian** guide seemed *pleasant*.

3. A **North Sea** tour begins tomorrow.

4. The **Chicago** skyline is *pretty*.

C. Directions: Write the correct degree of adjective.

1. Your sunglasses are (dark) _____**darker**_____ than mine.

2. Of the triplets, Kayleigh does (bad) _____**worst**_____ in math.

3. Their second website is (unusual) _____**more unusual**_____ than their first.

4. This platinum bracelet is the (expensive) _____**most expensive**_____ piece of jewelry in the store.

5. Of the four forming the new stairway, the top walnut-colored board is (sturdy)
_____**sturdiest**_____.

338

A.   Directions: Circle any adjectives.

1.   Are many large fish in that rushing stream?

2.   One golfer wears a white leather glove with tiny air holes.

3.   A few tourists visited an old railroad office.

4.   The pouring rain ruined their child's paper hat.

5.   White-chocolate brownies are in this gold gift box.

6.   Pam's spacious, modern apartment has no family room.

B.   Directions: Circle any proper adjective.   Box any predicate adjective.

1.   Her Eskimo friend is fun-loving.

2.   Our Italian guide seemed pleasant.

3.   A North Sea tour begins tomorrow.

4.   The Chicago skyline is pretty.

C.   Directions: Write the correct degree of adjective.

1.   Your sunglasses are (dark) _____ than mine.

2.   Of the triplets, Kayleigh does (bad) _____ in math.

3.   Their second website is (unusual) _____ than their
      first.

4.   This platinum bracelet is the (expensive) _____
      piece of jewelry in the store.

5.   Of the four forming the new stairway, the top walnut-colored board is (sturdy)

      _____.

Name_____   **Cumulative Review**
WORKBOOK PAGE 156
Date_____   **At the End of the Adjective Unit**

A. **Prepositions and Object of the Preposition:**
Directions: Cross out any prepositional phrases. Write **<u>O.P.</u>** above any
object of the preposition.

                    O.P.   **O.P.**
1.   The lamp ~~with a leather shade~~ sold ~~for ten dollars~~.

                    O.P.   **O.P.**
2.   That pearl ring ~~with diamonds~~ ~~on each side~~ is pretty.

               O.P.   **O.P.**
3.   She travels ~~without shampoo or hair conditioner~~.

                 ཉ‍ཉ‍ཉ‍ཉ‍ཉ‍ཉ‍ཉ‍ཉ‍ཉ‍ཉ‍ཉ‍ཉ‍ཉ

B. **Subject/Verb:**
Directions: Cross out any prepositional phrases. Underline the subject once
and the verb twice.

1.   A small, steel <u>ball</u> <u>rolled</u> ~~through the machine~~.

2.   <u>One</u> ~~of the drivers~~ <u>stopped</u> ~~before the intersection~~.

3.   ~~During the ice storm~~, several <u>branches</u> <u>fell</u> ~~from a huge tree~~.

                 ཉ‍ཉ‍ཉ‍ཉ‍ཉ‍ཉ‍ཉ‍ཉ‍ཉ‍ཉ‍ཉ‍ཉ‍ཉ

C. **Compound Subjects:**
Directions: Cross out any prepositional phrases. Underline the subject once
and the verb or verb phrase twice.

1.   <u>Sandy</u> and her <u>mother</u> <u>refinish</u> old furniture.

2.   The <u>jockey</u> and the horse <u>owner</u> <u>spoke</u> ~~with the press~~.

3.   <u>Beans</u> and tomato <u>plants</u> <u>had been fertilized</u>.

                 ཉ‍ཉ‍ཉ‍ཉ‍ཉ‍ཉ‍ཉ‍ཉ‍ཉ‍ཉ‍ཉ‍ཉ‍ཉ

D. **Compound Verbs:**
Directions: Cross out any prepositional phrases. Underline the subject once
and the verb or verb phrase twice.

1.   A father <u>penguin</u> <u>sat</u> and <u>protected</u> an egg.

2.   <u>I</u> <u>sprinkled</u> lemon ~~on fish~~ and <u>placed</u> the dish ~~under a broiler~~.

3.   <u>Mr. and Mrs. Ming</u> <u>must accept</u> the offer, <u>write</u> a new contract, or <u>cancel</u> it.
340

A. **Prepositions and Object of the Preposition:**
   Directions: Cross out any prepositional phrases.   Write **O.P.** above any
                 object of the preposition.

1.   The lamp with a leather shade sold for ten dollars.

2.   That pearl ring with diamonds on each side is pretty.

3.   She travels without shampoo or hair conditioner.
   ༥༷༥༷༥༷༥༷༥༷༥༷༥༷༥༷༥༷༥༷༥༷

B. **Subject/Verb:**
   Directions: Cross out any prepositional phrases.   Underline the subject once
                 and the verb twice.

1.   A small, steel ball rolled through the machine.

2.   One of the drivers stopped before the intersection.

3.   During the ice storm, several branches fell from a huge tree.
   ༥༷༥༷༥༷༥༷༥༷༥༷༥༷༥༷༥༷༥༷༥༷

C. **Compound Subjects:**
   Directions: Cross out any prepositional phrases.   Underline the subject once
                 and the verb or verb phrase twice.

1.   Sandy and her mother refinish old furniture.

2.   The jockey and the horse owner spoke with the press.

3.   Beans and tomato plants had been fertilized.
   ༥༷༥༷༥༷༥༷༥༷༥༷༥༷༥༷༥༷༥༷༥༷

D. **Compound Verbs:**
   Directions: Cross out any prepositional phrases.   Underline the subject once
                 and the verb or verb phrase twice.

1.   A father penguin sat and protected an egg.

2.   I sprinkled lemon on fish and placed the dish under a broiler.

3.   Mr. and Mrs. Ming must accept the offer, write a new contract, or cancel it.   341

E. **Infinitives:**
    Directions: Cross out any prepositional phrases. Place parentheses **( )** around
    any infinitive. Underline the subject once and the verb twice.

1. The <u>carpenter</u> <u><u>wants</u></u> **(**to build**)** a cabin ~~by a shallow stream~~.

2. <u>I</u> <u><u>need</u></u> **(**to clean**)** ~~beneath the refrigerator~~.

3. The <u>barber</u> <u><u>decided</u></u> **(**to leave**)** early.
    ཉྫཉྫཉྫཉྫཉྫཉྫཉྫཉྫཉྫཉྫཉྫ

F. **Subject-Verb Agreement:**
    Directions: Delete any prepositional phrases. Underline the subject once.
                   Underline the verb/verb phrase that agrees with the subject twice.

1. That <u>man</u> (buy, <u><u>buys</u></u>) trucks ~~through the Internet~~.

2. <u>Streaks</u> ~~of orange and blue~~ (crosses, <u><u>cross</u></u>) the sky.

3. African <u>art</u> (<u><u>was</u></u>, were) <u><u>displayed</u></u> ~~in the building's lobby~~.

4. An Art Deco <u>hotel</u> (are, <u><u>is</u></u>) <u><u>located</u></u> ~~within Paris~~.

5. My <u>grandma</u> (<u><u>does</u></u>[n't], do[n't]) <u><u>like</u></u> (to swim).

6. <u>Bo</u> and his <u>sister</u> (<u><u>keep</u></u>, keeps) bees ~~for a living~~.

7. <u>Everyone</u> ~~in those shops~~ (work, <u><u>works</u></u>) late.
    ཉྫཉྫཉྫཉྫཉྫཉྫཉྫཉྫཉྫཉྫཉྫ

G. **Verb Phrases and *Not*:**
    Directions: Cross out any prepositional phrases. Box *not* or *n't*.
                 Underline the subject once and the verb or verb phrase twice.

1. <u>I</u> <u><u>can</u></u>**not** <u><u>write</u></u> ~~in this small space~~.

2. <u>Sally</u> <u><u>will</u></u> **not** <u><u>shop</u></u> ~~without her husband~~.

3. This yellow <u>highlighter</u> <u><u>does</u></u>**n't** <u><u>have</u></u> a cap.
342

E. **Infinitives:**
>   Directions: Cross out any prepositional phrases. Place parentheses **( )** around
>   any infinitive. Underline the subject once and the verb twice.

1.   The carpenter wants to build a cabin by a shallow stream.

2.   I need to clean beneath the refrigerator.

3.   The barber decided to leave early.

෨෨෨෨෨෨෨෨෨෨෨෨

F. **Subject-Verb Agreement:**
>   Directions: Delete any prepositional phrases. Underline the subject once.
>   Underline the verb/verb phrase that agrees with the subject twice.

1.   That man (buy, buys) trucks through the Internet.

2.   Streaks of orange and blue (crosses, cross) the sky.

3.   African art (was, were) displayed in the building's lobby.

4.   An Art Deco hotel (are, is) located within Paris.

5.   My grandma (does[n't]), do[n't]) like to swim.

6.   Bo and his sister (keep, keeps) bees for a living.

7.   Everyone in those shops (work, works) late.

෨෨෨෨෨෨෨෨෨෨෨෨

G. **Verb Phrases and *Not*:**
>   Directions: Cross out any prepositional phrases. Box *not* or *n't*.
>   Underline the subject once and the verb or verb phrase twice.

1.   I cannot write in this small space.

2.   Sally will not shop without her husband.

3.   This yellow highlighter doesn't have a cap.

343

H. **Contractions:**
   Directions: Write the contraction.

1. do not - _____**don't**_____   6. is not - _____**isn't**_____

2. I am - _____**I'm**_____   7. I have - _____**I've**_____

3. where is - _____**where's**_____   8. she is - _____**she's**_____

4. you are - _____**you're**_____   9. will not - _____**won't**_____

5. could not - _____**couldn't**_____   10. I would - _____**I'd**_____

&&&&&&&&&&&&&

I. **You're/Your, It's/Its, and They're/Their/There:**
   Directions: Circle the correct word.

1. The door is off (it's, **its**) hinges.

2. (You're, **Your**) knuckle appears bruised.

3. Val and I met (they're, their, **there**).

&&&&&&&&&&&&&

J. **Auxiliary (Helping) Verbs:**
   Directions: Write the 23 helping verbs.

1. *D's*   a. _____**do**_____   b. _____**does**_____   c. _____**did**_____

2. *H's*   a. _____**has**_____   b. _____**have**_____   c. _____**had**_____

3. *M's*   a. _____**may**_____   b. _____**might**_____   c. _____**must**_____

4. *Ould's:* a. _____**could**_____   b. _____**should**_____   c. _____**would**_____

5. *To be:* a. __**is**__   c. __**are**__   e. __**were**__   g. __**being**__

    b. __**am**__   d. __**was**__   f. __**be**__   h. __**been**__

6. *Others:* a. _____**can**_____   b. _____**shall**_____   c. _____**will**_____

344

H. **Contractions:**
Directions: Write the contraction.

1. do not - _____

2. I am - _____

3. where is -_____

4. you are - _____

5. could not - _____

6. is not - _____

7. I have - _____

8. she is - _____

9. will not - _____

10. I would - _____

&&&&&&&&&&&&

I. **You're/Your, It's/Its, and They're/Their/There:**
Directions: Circle the correct word.

1. The door is off (it's, its) hinges.

2. (You're, Your) knuckle appears bruised.

3. Val and I met (they're, their, there).

&&&&&&&&&&&&

J. **Auxiliary (Helping) Verbs:**
Directions: Write the 23 helping verbs.

1. *D's*   a. _____   b. _____   c. _____

2. *H's*   a. _____   b. _____   c. _____

3. *M's*   a. _____   b. _____   c. _____

4. *Ould's*   a. _____   b. _____   c. _____

5. *To be:*   a. _____   c. _____   e. _____   g. _____

    b. _____   d. _____   f. _____   h. _____

6. *Others:*   a. _____   b. _____   c. _____

K. **Irregular Verbs:**

Directions: Underline the subject once and the correct verb phrase twice.

1. A <u>dam</u> <u>must have</u> (<u>burst</u>, bursted).

2. Your <u>pizza</u> <u>has</u> (came, <u>come</u>).

3. <u>Had</u> <u>she</u> (<u>done</u>, did) a science project?

4. <u>I</u> <u>should have</u> (ate, <u>eaten</u>) kiwi.

5. The <u>pond</u> <u>is</u> now (<u>frozen</u>, froze).

6. These guitar <u>strings</u> <u>are</u> (broke, <u>broken</u>).

7. A <u>portrait</u> <u>has been</u> (hanged, <u>hung</u>).

8. That <u>teenager</u> <u>has</u> (drove, <u>driven</u>) his own car.

🙙🙙🙙🙙🙙🙙🙙🙙🙙🙙🙙🙙

L. **Subjects, Verbs, and Direct Objects:**

Directions: Cross out any prepositional phrases. Underline the subject once and the verb/verb phrase twice. Label any direct object – **D.O.**

                                     D.O.
1. The <u>walker</u> <u>crossed</u> a bridge ~~near a waterwheel~~.

                                     D.O.
2. <u>Does</u> <u>Loni</u> <u>make</u> silver rings ~~with emeralds~~?

                          D.O.
3. <u>We</u> <u>placed</u> a wagon wheel ~~by our fireplace~~.

🙙🙙🙙🙙🙙🙙🙙🙙🙙🙙🙙🙙

M. **Sit/Set, Lie/Lay, and Rise/Raise:**

Directions: Delete any prepositional phrases. Underline the subject once and the verb/verb phrase twice. Label any direct object-**D.O.**

                                                            D.O.
1. (<u>You</u>) (<u>Lie</u>, Lay) down.   4. <u>He</u> (sits, <u>sets</u>) barrels ~~on a dock~~.

2. (<u>You</u>) (<u>Sit</u>, Set) here.   5. A <u>box</u> <u>has</u> (laid, <u>lain</u>) there ~~for weeks~~.

                             D.O.
3. (<u>You</u>) (Rise, <u>Raise</u>) your hand.   6. The <u>dog</u> (<u>rose</u>, raised) slowly.

346

K. **Irregular Verbs:**
Directions: Underline the subject once and the correct verb phrase twice.

1. A dam must have (burst, bursted).

2. Your pizza has (came, come).

3. Had she (done, did) a science project?

4. I should have (ate, eaten) kiwi.

5. The pond is now (frozen, froze).

6. These guitar strings are (broke, broken).

7. A portrait has been (hanged, hung).

8. That teenager has (drove, driven) his own car.

ॐॐॐॐॐॐॐॐॐॐॐॐ

L. **Subjects, Verbs, and Direct Objects:**
Directions: Cross out any prepositional phrases. Underline the subject once and the verb/verb phrase twice. Label any direct object – **D.O.**

1. The walker crossed a bridge near a waterwheel.

2. Does Loni make silver rings with emeralds?

3. We placed a wagon wheel by our fireplace.

ॐॐॐॐॐॐॐॐॐॐॐॐ

M. **Sit/Set, Lie/Lay, and Rise/Raise:**
Directions: Delete any prepositional phrases. Underline the subject once and the verb/verb phrase twice. Label any direct object-**D.O.**

1. (Lie, Lay) down.

2. (Sit, Set) here.

3. (Rise, Raise) your hand.

4. He (sits, sets) barrels on a dock.

5. A box has (laid, lain) there for weeks.

6. The dog (rose, raised) slowly.

347

N. Tenses:

Directions: Underline the subject once and the verb or verb phrase twice. Write the tense (*present, past,* or *future*) in the blank.

1. _____**present**_____ He <u>irons</u> well.

2. _____**past**_____ <u>Chris</u> <u>clapped</u> ~~for his favorite wrestler~~.

3. _____**future**_____ A <u>minister</u> <u>will perform</u> the marriage ceremony.

4. _____**present**_____ Several <u>mules</u> <u>are</u> thirsty.

5. _____**present**_____ One polo <u>player</u> <u>leaned</u> ~~over his horse~~.

ৡৡৡৡৡৡৡৡৡৡৡৡ

O. Linking Verbs:

Directions: Unscramble these linking verbs.

1. (to) aminer - **remain**   5. (to) leslm - **smell**   9. (to) mese - **seem**

2. (to) oklo - **look**   6. (to) worg - **grow**   10. (to) prapae - **appear**

3. (to) eatts - **taste**   7. (to) lefe - **feel**   11. (to) ytas - **stay**

4. to emcbeo - **become**   8. (to) dosun - **sound**   12. (to) eb - **be**

a. si - **is**   b. ma - **am**   c. rea - **are**   d. asw - **was**

e. rewe - **were**   f. eb - **be**   g. gnieb - **being**   h. eneb - **been**

ৡৡৡৡৡৡৡৡৡৡৡৡ

P. Action Verb or Linking Verb?:

Directions: Place **X** if the verb is linking.

1. _**X**_ The garlic **smelled** strong. [was]

2. ____ He **smelled** the garlic.

3. _**X**_ Her hair **looks** purple. [is]

4. ____ She **looks** for vintage pins.

348

N. **Tenses:**
>   Directions: Underline the subject once and the verb or verb phrase
>   twice. Write the tense (*present, past,* or *future*) in the blank.

1. _____   He irons well.

2. _____   Chris clapped for his favorite wrestler.

3. _____   A minister will perform the marriage ceremony.

4. _____   Several mules are thirsty.

5. _____   One polo player leaned over his horse.

かかかかかかかかかかか

O. **Linking Verbs:**
>   Directions: Unscramble these linking verbs.

1. (to) aminer - _____   5. (to) leslm - _____   9. (to) mese - _____

2. (to) oklo - _____   6. (to) worg - _____   10. (to) prapae - _____

3. (to) eatts - _____   7. (to) lefe - _____   11. (to) ytas _____

4. to emcbeo - _____   8. (to) dosun -_____   12. (to) eb - _____

>   a. si - _____   b. ma - _____   c. rea - _____   d. asw - _____

>   e. rewe - _____   f. eb - _____   g. gnieb - _____   h. eneb - _____

かかかかかかかかかかか

P. **Action Verb or Linking Verb?:**

>   Directions: Place **X** if the verb is linking.

1. _____   The garlic **smelled** strong.

2. _____   He **smelled** the garlic.

3. _____   Her hair **looks** purple.

4. _____   She **looks** for vintage pins.

349

Cumulative Review

At the End of the Adjective Unit

Q. **Transitive and Intransitive Verbs:**
   Directions: Underline the subject once and the verb or verb phrase twice.
   Label any direct object - **D.O.** Write **T** if the verb is transitive;
   write **I** if the verb is intransitive.
   Remember: **A transitive verb will have a direct object.**
   D.O.T. > Direct **O**bject = **T**ransitive

                                    D.O.
1. ___**T**___   The housecleaner scoured the dirty tub.
                              D.O.
2. ___**T**___   Joy filled a children's swimming pool.

3. ___**I**___   He speaks very softly.

೫೫೫೫೫೫೫೫೫೫೫೫೫

R. **Abstract and Concrete Nouns:**
   Directions: Place a ෆ if the noun is abstract.

1. _____   ANTLER   5. __ෆ__   WELCOME

2. _____   STRAP   6. _____   DOMINO

3. __ෆ__   COMFORT   7. __ෆ__   FONDNESS

4. __ෆ__   STRESS   8. _____   OUTLET

೫೫೫೫೫೫೫೫೫೫೫೫೫

S. **Singular and Plural Nouns:**
   Directions: Write the correct spelling of each plural noun.

1. valley - ____**valleys**____   6. identity - ____**identities**____

2. range - ____**ranges**____   7. crutch - ____**crutches**____

3. chief - ____**chiefs**____   8. news - ____**news**____

4. scene - ____**scenes**____   9. bluff - ____**bluffs**____

5. cargo - ____**cargoes**____   10. harness - ____**harnesses**____

350

Name_____   **Cumulative Review**

Date_____   **At the End of the Adjective Unit**

Q. Transitive and Intransitive Verbs:

Directions: Underline the subject once and the verb or verb phrase twice.
Label any direct object - **D.O.** Write **T** if the verb is transitive;
write **I** if the verb is intransitive.
Remember: A transitive verb will have a direct object.
D.O.T. > Direct Object = Transitive

1. _____   The housecleaner scoured the dirty tub.

2. _____   Joy filled a children's swimming pool.

3. _____   He speaks very softly.

ॐॐॐॐॐॐॐॐॐॐॐॐॐ

R. Abstract and Concrete Nouns:

Directions: Place a ⅄ if the noun is abstract.

1. ____   ANTLER   5. ____   WELCOME

2. ____   STRAP   6. ____   DOMINO

3. ____   COMFORT   7. ____   FONDNESS

4. ____   STRESS   8. ____   OUTLET

ॐॐॐॐॐॐॐॐॐॐॐॐॐ

S. Singular and Plural Nouns:

Directions: Write the correct spelling of each plural noun.

1. valley - _____   6. identity - _____

2. range - _____   7. crutch - _____

3. chief - _____   8. news - _____

4. scene - _____   9. bluff - _____

5. cargo - _____   10. harness - _____

T. **Possessive Nouns:**
    Directions: Write the possessive in each blank.

1. the temperature for today - _____**today's temperature**_____

2. signs owned by a company - _____**company's signs**_____

3. a stroller for two infants - _____**two infants' stroller**_____

         ৡ৹ৡ৹ৡ৹ৡ৹ৡ৹ৡ৹ৡ৹ৡ৹ৡ৹ৡ৹ৡ৹ৡ৹

U. **Nouns Used as Subjects, Direct Objects, and Indirect Objects:**
    Directions: Label any subject (**S.**), direct object (**D.O.**), and indirect object (**I.O.**).

          S.   **I.O.**   **D.O.**
1. An <u>architect</u> handed his client the building plans.

         ৡ৹ৡ৹ৡ৹ৡ৹ৡ৹ৡ৹ৡ৹ৡ৹ৡ৹ৡ৹ৡ৹ৡ৹

V. **Predicate Nominatives:**
    Directions: Underline the subject once and the verb twice. Label a predicate
                   nominative – **P.N.** Write the inverted form in the blank.
Remember: **A predicate nominative occurs <u>after</u> a linking verb and means the same as**
         the subject.
                    P.N.
1. My father's <u>dentist</u> <u><u>was</u></u> Dr. Lucash.

    _____**Dr. Lucash was my father's dentist.**_____
                    P.N.
2. An old <u>inn</u> <u><u>is</u></u> their new home.

    _____**Their new home is an old inn.**_____

         ৡ৹ৡ৹ৡ৹ৡ৹ৡ৹ৡ৹ৡ৹ৡ৹ৡ৹ৡ৹ৡ৹ৡ৹

W. **Identifying Nouns:**
    Directions: Circle any nouns.
Remember: Determiners will help you to find some nouns.
NOUNS ARE BOLDFACED; DETERMINERS ARE ITALICIZED.
1. *Three* **lawnmowers** were sold at *that* pawn **shop**.

2. *Jake's* **uncle** has *no* **mirrors** in *his* **house**.

3. **Nanny** made *thirteen* yellow **costumes** for her *first* dance **performance**.
352

T. **Possessive Nouns:**
    Directions: Write the possessive in each blank.

1. the temperature for today - _____

2. signs owned by a company - _____

3. a stroller for two infants - _____

ᔕᔕᔕᔕᔕᔕᔕᔕᔕᔕᔕᔕ

U. **Nouns Used as Subjects, Direct Objects, and Indirect Objects:**
    Directions: Label any subject (**S.**), direct object (**D.O.**), and indirect object (**I.O.**).

1. An architect handed his client the building plans.

ᔕᔕᔕᔕᔕᔕᔕᔕᔕᔕᔕᔕ

V. **Predicate Nominatives:**
    Directions: Underline the subject once and the verb twice. Label a predicate
                    nominative – **P.N.** Write the inverted form in the blank.
**Remember: A predicate nominative occurs <u>after</u> a linking verb and means the same as
               the subject.**

1. My father's dentist was Dr. Lucash.

    _____

2. An old inn is their new home.

    _____

ᔕᔕᔕᔕᔕᔕᔕᔕᔕᔕᔕᔕ

W. **Identifying Nouns:**
    Directions: Circle any nouns.
Remember: Determiners will help you to find some nouns.

1. Three lawnmowers were sold at that pawn shop.

2. Jake's uncle has no mirrors in his house.

3. Nanny made thirteen yellow costumes for her first dance performance.

Name_____   **Cumulative Test**

Date_____   **End of the Adjective Unit**

A. Directions: Cross out any prepositional phrases. Underline the subject once
                   and the verb or verb phrase twice. Label any direct object – **D.O.**
                   Label any indirect object – **I.O.**

1. A strange <u>noise</u> <u>sounded</u> ~~within the chimney~~.

                                                      D.O.
2. ~~In the afternoon~~, those <u>children</u> <u>read</u> and <u>take</u> a nap.

3. A fashion <u>designer</u> and her <u>assistant</u> <u>spoke</u> ~~regarding fabric~~.

4. Last year, their <u>parents</u> <u>decided</u> **(to learn)** ~~about their ancestors~~.

5. <u>Everyone</u> ~~in the theater~~ <u>applauded</u> ~~after the first act~~.

                      D.O.
6. (<u>You</u>) <u>Use</u> a board ~~without any nails or screws~~.

7. An English <u>bulldog</u> <u>lay</u> ~~beside a fire~~ ~~in the family room~~.

                          I.O.   **D.O.**
8. A <u>hostess</u> <u>handed</u> the laughing customers their menus.

9. ~~Before dawn~~, <u>we</u> <u>rose</u> and <u>drove</u> ~~to a nearby lake~~ ~~for an outing~~.

10. Pink <u>asters</u> <u>have been planted</u> ~~near a birdbath~~.

                    ৵৵৵৵৵৵৵৵৵৵৵

B. Directions: Delete any prepositional phrases. Underline the subject once.
                   Underline the verb/verb phrase that agrees with the subject twice.

1. That <u>nurse</u> (<u>takes</u>, take) blood ~~in a laboratory~~.

2. <u>One</u> ~~of his bosses~~ (want, <u>wants</u>) another computer.

3. Several <u>deputies</u> (patrols, <u>patrol</u>) that area.

4. Their <u>friends</u> (<u>help</u>, helps) ~~during trash pickup~~.

5. <u>She</u> (<u>does</u>(n't), do(n't)) <u>need</u> a passport.

354

A. Directions: Cross out any prepositional phrases. Underline the subject once
                  and the verb or verb phrase twice. Label any direct object – **D.O.**
                  Label any indirect object – **I.O.**

1. A strange noise sounded within the chimney.

2. In the afternoon, those children read and take a nap.

3. A fashion designer and her assistant spoke regarding fabric.

4. Last year, their parents decided to learn about their ancestors.

5. Everyone in the theater applauded after the first act.

6. Use a board without any nails or screws.

7. An English bulldog lay beside a fire in the family room.

8. A hostess handed the laughing customers their menus.

9. Before dawn, we rose and drove to a nearby lake for an outing.

10. Pink asters have been planted near a birdbath.

ॐ ॐ ॐ ॐ ॐ ॐ ॐ ॐ ॐ ॐ ॐ

B. Directions: Delete any prepositional phrases. Underline the subject once.
                  Underline the verb/verb phrase that agrees with the subject twice.

1. That nurse (takes, take) blood in a laboratory.

2. One of his bosses (want, wants) another computer.

3. Several deputies (patrols, patrol) that area.

4. Their friends (help, helps) during trash pickup.

5. She (does(n't), do(n't)) need a passport.

C. Directions: Write the contraction.

1. did not - _____**didn't**_____   6. cannot - _____**can't**_____

2. I have - _____**I've**_____   7. I would - _____**I'd**_____

3. what is - _____**what's**_____   8. I am - _____**I'm**_____

4. you will - _____**you'll**_____   9. must not - _____**mustn't**_____

5. should not - _____**shouldn't**_____   10. you have - _____**you've**_____

🐎🐎🐎🐎🐎🐎🐎🐎🐎🐎🐎

D. Directions: Circle the correct word.

1. (You're, **Your**) television screen is dusty.

2. (They're, Their, **There**) must be a better solution.

3. A chicken is roosting in (it's, **its**) coop.

🐎🐎🐎🐎🐎🐎🐎🐎🐎🐎🐎

E. Directions: Underline the subject once and the correct verb phrase twice.

1. One pool <u>player</u> <u>had</u> (brung, <u>brought</u>) his own cue.

2. <u>Have</u> <u>you</u> ever (rode, <u>ridden</u>) an Arabian horse?

3. <u>Moss</u> <u>must have</u> (<u>grown</u>, grew) there.

4. <u>I</u> <u>should have</u> (ate, <u>eaten</u>) breakfast.

5. The <u>producers</u> <u>might have</u> (<u>spoken</u>, spoke) earlier.

6. The crossing <u>guard</u> <u>may have</u> (went, <u>gone</u>) home.

7. Several <u>gliders</u> <u>have</u> (<u>flown</u>, flew) today.

8. <u>She</u> <u>would</u> **not** <u>have</u> (gave, <u>given</u>) up.

356

C. Directions: Write the contraction.

1. did not - _____

2. I have - _____

3. what is - _____

4. you will - _____

5. should not - _____

6. cannot - _____

7. I would - _____

8. I am - _____

9. must not - _____

10. you have - _____

๛๛๛๛๛๛๛๛๛๛๛๛

D. Directions: Circle the correct word.

1. (You're, Your) television screen is dusty.

2. (They're, Their, There) must be a better solution.

3. A chicken is roosting in (it's, its) coop.

๛๛๛๛๛๛๛๛๛๛๛๛

E. Directions: Underline the subject once and the correct verb phrase twice.

1. One pool player had (brung, brought) his own cue.

2. Have you ever (rode, ridden) an Arabian horse?

3. Moss must have (grown, grew) there.

4. I should have (ate, eaten) breakfast.

5. The producers might have (spoken, spoke) earlier.

6. The crossing guard may have (went, gone) home.

7. Several gliders have (flown, flew) today.

8. She would not have (gave, given) up.

F. Directions: Delete any prepositional phrases. Underline the subject once and the verb/verb phrase twice.

1. You may (lie, lay) ~~on this futon~~.

2. He (rose, raised) his dart.

3. I (laid, lay) my hand ~~over my heart~~.

4. (You) (Sit, Set) ~~by me~~.

5. Joy (set, sat) her car alarm.

6. Bread (rises, raises).

ઌઌઌઌઌઌઌઌઌઌઌઌ

G. Directions: Underline the subject once and the verb or verb phrase twice. Write the tense (*present, past,* or *future*) in the blank.

1. _____**past**_____ A security guard latched the door.

2. _____**present**_____ Chessa and she paint coffee cans.

3. _____**future**_____ Marco will pay my share.

4. _____**present**_____ Their lawyer reads real-estate contracts.

5. _____**present**_____ A yoyo is fun.

ઌઌઌઌઌઌઌઌઌઌઌઌ

H. Directions: Place a ● if the noun is abstract.

1. _____ CREAM

2. _●_ HUNGER

3. _____ FRIEND

4. _●_ FRIENDSHIP

5. _____ PAPERWEIGHT

6. _●_ DELIGHT

ઌઌઌઌઌઌઌઌઌઌઌઌ

I. Directions: Place a ☒ if the noun is proper.

1. ___ MUSTARD

2. _☒_ ALASKA

3. ___ SLUM

4. ___ DEED

5. _☒_ NAPOLEON

6. _☒_ MT. HOOD

7. _☒_ BRIAN

8. ___ QUEEN

9. _☒_ JAPAN

F. Directions: Delete any prepositional phrases. Underline the subject once and the verb/verb phrase twice.

1. You may (lie, lay) on this futon.

2. He (rose, raised) his dart.

3. I (laid, lay) my hand over my heart.

4. (Sit, Set) by me.

5. Joy (set, sat) her car alarm.

6. Bread (rises, raises).

෪෪෪෪෪෪෪෪෪෪෪෪

G. Directions: Underline the subject once and the verb or verb phrase twice. Write the tense (*present, past,* or *future*) in the blank.

1. _____ A security guard latched the door.

2. _____ Chessa and she paint coffee cans.

3. _____ Marco will pay my share.

4. _____ Their lawyer reads real-estate contracts.

5. _____ A yoyo is fun.

෪෪෪෪෪෪෪෪෪෪෪෪

H. Directions: Place a ● if the noun is abstract.

1. ____ CREAM

2. ____ HUNGER

3. ____ FRIEND

4. ____ FRIENDSHIP

5. ____ PAPERWEIGHT

6. ____ DELIGHT

෪෪෪෪෪෪෪෪෪෪෪෪

I. Directions: Place a ☒ if the noun is proper.

1. ____ MUSTARD

2. ____ ALASKA

3. ____ SLUM

4. ____ DEED

5. ____ NAPOLEON

6. ____ MT. HOOD

7. ____ BRIAN

8. ____ QUEEN

9. ____ JAPAN

359

J. Directions: Write the correct spelling of each plural noun.

1. gurney - **gurneys**

2. trout - **trout**

3. cuff - **cuffs**

4. delivery - **deliveries**

5. clue - **clues**

6. chorus - **choruses**

7. flash - **flashes**

8. ox - **oxen**

֍֍֍֍֍֍֍֍֍֍֍֍

K. Directions: Write the possessive form in each blank.

1. a new bus belonging to a city - **(a) city's (new) bus**

2. books written by more than one child - **children's books**

3. locks created by Vikings - **Vikings' locks**

4. guests at a hotel - **hotel's guests**

֍֍֍֍֍֍֍֍֍֍֍֍

L. Directions: Cross out any prepositional phrases. Underline the subject once and the verb twice. Label a predicate nominative – **P.N.** Label a predicate adjective – **P.A.**

P.A.
1. This <u>problem</u> <u>seems</u> complex.

P.N.
2. <u>Dakota</u> <u>was</u> a scholarship winner.

P.A.
3. These <u>pants</u> <u>are</u> too baggy.

P.N.
4. Their <u>mother</u> <u>became</u> a candidate ~~for governor~~.

֍֍֍֍֍֍֍֍֍֍֍֍

M. Directions: Circle any nouns.

1. Many billowy **clouds** blocked the **sun** from our **view**.

2. **Fran** started a **job** at that employment **office** last **Monday**.

360

J. Directions: Write the correct spelling of each plural noun.

1. gurney - _____   5. clue - _____

2. trout - _____   6. chorus - _____

3. cuff - _____   7. flash - _____

4. delivery - _____   8. ox - _____

&&&&&&&&&&&&&

K. Directions: Write the possessive form in each blank.

1. a bus belonging to a city - _____

2. books written by more than one child - _____

3. locks created by Vikings - _____

4. guests at a hotel - _____

&&&&&&&&&&&&&

L. Directions: Cross out any prepositional phrases. Underline the subject once
                 and the verb twice. Label a predicate nominative – **P.N.** Label a
                 predicate adjective – **P.A.**

1. This problem seems complex.

2. Dakota was a scholarship winner.

3. These pants are too baggy.

4. Their mother became a candidate for governor.

&&&&&&&&&&&&&

M. Directions: Circle any nouns.

1. Many billowy clouds blocked the sun from our view.

2. Fran started a job at that employment office last Monday.

Name_____   **ADJECTIVES**

WORKBOOK PAGE 163

Date_____   **Used in Writing**

Note: You may want to ask students to compare their descriptions.

Idea: Have students draw a picture of the dress they described. (This may make an ideal homework assignment.) Place the pictures (with students' permission, of course) on display. Students should enjoy seeing how differently each person described the dress.

Adjectives are extremely important in writing. They add description and detail.

ANSWERS MAY VARY/REPRESENTATIVE ANSWERS:

Directions: Insert an adjective in each blank. Be sure that your adjectives are descriptive. Be creative!

1. The woman is wearing a (an) _____**pink**_____ dress. It has

    _____**sparkling**_____ sequins and _____**shiny**_____ beads on the

    skirt. The hem is trimmed with _____**wide**_____ lace. The sleeves

    are _____**long**_____. What a (an) _____**beautiful**_____

    garment.

2. The hiker is wearing a (an) _____**light**_____ jacket. It has

    _____**corduroy**_____ sleeves and _____**brass**_____ buttons.

    The collar is trimmed with _____**brown**_____ leather. The

    _____**plaid**_____ fabric seems _____**faded**_____.

3. A vehicle has been reported stolen. It is a (an) _____**compact**_____

    car with _____**rusted**_____ paint . It has _____**low**_____ tires

    with _____**wire**_____ rims. The fender is _____**missing**_____. The

    windows are _____**tinted**_____. This vehicle is very _____**shabby**_____.

362

Name_____   **ADJECTIVES**

Date_____   **Used in Writing**

Adjectives are extremely important in writing. They add description and detail.

Directions: Insert an adjective in each blank. Be sure that your adjectives are descriptive. Be creative!

1. The woman is wearing a (an) _____ dress. It has

_____ sequins and _____ beads on the

skirt. The hem is trimmed with _____ lace. The sleeves

are _____. What a (an) _____

garment.

2. The hiker is wearing a (an) _____ jacket. It has

_____ sleeves and _____ buttons.

The collar is trimmed with _____ leather. The

_____ fabric seems _____.

3. A vehicle has been reported stolen. It is a (an) _____

car with _____ paint . It has _____ tires

with _____ rims. The fender is _____. The

windows are _____. This vehicle is very _____.

Name_____   **ADJECTIVES**

WORKBOOK PAGE 164

Date_____   **Used in Writing**

Note: Discuss answers. Lead students to see that words may be very similar in meaning but can express degrees (example: mad, angry, furious, livid).
Question: Does each student have a thesaurus? (I see this as vital!)
Adjectives are extremely important in writing.

ANSWERS MAY VARY/REPRESENTATIVE ANSWERS:

It is important to use a thesaurus. This will help you to find vivid descriptors. It also helps to prevent you from overusing an adjective.

Directions: Use a thesaurus.   Replace each boldfaced adjective.

1. We heard a (**loud**) _____**booming**_____ noise.

2. This blanket is (**dirty**) _____**filthy**_____.

3. A (**wet**) _____**soggy**_____ cloth is lying on the kitchen counter.

4. The child was (**bad**) _____**rude**_____.

5. The teenager seemed (**unhappy**) _____**gloomy**_____ about her friends' decision.

6. May I have a glass of (**cold**) _____**chilled**_____ water?

7. The man was dressed in (**torn**) _____**tattered**_____ denim pants.

8. Take this (**smelly**) _____**reeking**_____ trash out.

9. A (**good**) _____**talented**_____ artist has displayed his work.

10. That rock is (**big**) _____**mammoth**_____.

11. My new calculator is (**small**) _____**minute**_____.

12. His sister is (**nice**) _____**likable**_____.

13. This story is (**interesting**) _____**fascinating**_____.

14. The woman's (**funny**) _____**witty**_____ presentation made us laugh.

15. Your sponge is (**soft**) _____**squishy**_____.

364

Adjectives are extremely important in writing.

It is important to use a thesaurus.   This will help you to find vivid descriptors. It also helps to prevent you from overusing an adjective.

Directions: Use a thesaurus. Replace each boldfaced adjective.

1.   We heard a (**loud**) _____ noise.

2.   This blanket is (**dirty**) _____.

3.   A (**wet**) _____ cloth is lying on the kitchen counter.

4.   The child was (**bad**) _____.

5.   The teenager seemed (**unhappy**) _____ about her friends' decision.

6.   May I have a glass of (**cold**) _____ water?

7.   The man was dressed in (**torn**) _____ denim pants.

8.   Take this (**smelly**) _____ trash out.

9.   A (**good**) _____ artist has displayed his work.

10.   That rock is (**big**) _____.

11.   My new calculator is (**small**) _____.

12.   His sister is (**nice**) _____.

13.   This story is (**interesting**) _____.

14.   The woman's (**funny**) _____ presentation made us laugh.

15.   Your sponge is (**soft**) _____.

ADVERBS

Some texts present the definition of adverbs in this fashion:

> **Adverbs tell when, where, how, and to what extent or how much and modify verbs, adverbs, and adjectives.**

This creates a problem for many students. The confusion arises in telling students that adverbs modify verbs, <u>other adverbs</u>, and <u>adjectives</u>.

It is better to start with this definition:

> **Adverbs tell *how, when, where,* or *to what extent* (*how much*). Most adverbs modify a verb.**

I have divided adverbs into lessons. **Discuss what the adverbs modify on an individual basis in each lesson.** For example, most adverbs that tell *how* modify a verb.   Even saying this will mean little to some students.

Discuss the use of the adverb(s) in each sentence.

Example: The child <u>sobbed</u> loudly.

> **_Loudly_ tells <u>how</u> the child sobbed.**

<u>**Using these concrete examples will help students to understand that an adverb usually modifies a verb.**</u>

(Adverbs that tell *to what extent* frequently modify another adverb or an adjective. Sometimes, an adverb telling *how, when,* or *where* will modify an adverb, but this does not happen often.)

ADVERBS

▼

VERBS

Note that the word, *ADVERBS*, contains the word, *VERBS*. This should help you to remember that most adverbs modify, or go over to, the verb in a sentence.

Adverbs that tell how, when, or where usually modify a verb.

	Adv.	
Examples:	A <u>ladybug</u> <u>moved</u> slowly.	(*how*)
	Adv.	
	A <u>ladybug</u> <u>landed</u> suddenly.	(*when*)
	Adv.	
	A <u>ladybug</u> <u>flew</u> away.	(*where*)

Most adverbs that tell *how* end in <u>ly</u>.

Examples: fresh**ly**   beautiful**ly**   careless**ly**
local**ly**   bold**ly**   sure**ly**

Adverbs such as *hard* and *fast* can be adverbs that tell ***how***.

We worked ***hard*** selling granola bars.
They ate their lunch ***fast***.

Beware: There are some adjectives that end in *ly*: friendly   lovely

Some adverbs tell *to what extent*. There are seven adverbs that are used frequently to tell *to what extent (how much)*.

not   so   very   too   quite   rather   somewhat

<u>If you memorize these, you can easily find them in a sentence.</u>

Of course, other words can tell *to what extent*.

Tate is *totally* frustrated by the unusual directions.
Tate is *completely* frustrated by the unusual directions.

An adverb is a word that can tell <u>when</u>.

Directions: In Part A, delete any prepositional phrase(s). Underline the
               subject once and the verb or verb phrase twice. Label each
               adverb – *Adv.* Fill in the blanks in Part B.

                                    Adv.
        Example: A.   <u>We</u> often <u>swim</u> ~~in a lake~~.

                    B.   ___*Often*___ tells ___*when*___ we ___*swim*___.
                          Adv.
1.   A.   <u>They</u> <u>recently</u> <u>moved</u> ~~to the country~~.

     B.   ___**Recently**___ tells ___**when**___ they ___**moved**___.
                                    Adv.
2.   A.   A <u>band</u> <u>will perform</u> tonight ~~after dark~~.

     B.   ___**Tonight**___ tells ___**when**___ a band ___**will perform**___.
                                    Adv.
3.   A.   <u>We</u> <u>are leaving</u> tomorrow ~~before breakfast~~.

     B.   ___**Tomorrow**___ tells ___**when**___ we ___**are leaving**___.
                                    Adv.
4.   A.   One <u>teacher</u> <u>arrived</u> late ~~to math class~~.

     B.   ___**Late**___ tells ___**when**___ one teacher ___**arrived**___.
                                    Adv.
5.   A.   The <u>board</u> <u>meets</u> <u>daily</u>.

     B.   ___**Daily**___ tells ___**when**___ the board ___**meets**___.
                                    Adv.
6.   A.   Our <u>grandmother</u> <u>occasionally</u> <u>gives</u> a tea ~~for her friends~~.

     B.   ___**Occasionally**___ tells ___**when**___ our grandmother ___**gives (a tea)**___.
                                    Adv.
7.   A.   My <u>doctor</u> <u>frequently</u> <u>laughs</u>.

     B.   ___**Frequently**___ tells ___**when**___ my doctor ___**laughs**___.

Name_____   **ADVERBS**

Date_____   **When**

An adverb is a word that can tell <u>when</u>.

Directions: In Part A, delete any prepositional phrase(s). Underline the
                  subject once and the verb or verb phrase twice. Label each
                  adverb – _Adv._ Fill in the blanks in Part B.

                                    Adv.
     Example: A.   <u>We</u> often <u>swim</u> ~~in a lake~~.

                  B.   ____*Often*____ tells _when_ we ____*swim*____.

1. A.   They recently moved to the country.

    B.   _____ tells _____ they _____.

2. A.   A band will perform tonight after dark.

    B.   _____ tells _____ a band _____.

3. A.   We are leaving tomorrow before breakfast.

    B.   _____ tells _____ we _____.

4. A.   One teacher arrived late to math class.

    B.   _____ tells _____ one teacher _____.

5. A.   The board meets daily.

    B.   _____ tells _____ the board _____.

6. A.   Our grandmother occasionally gives a tea for her friends.

    B.   _____ tells _____ our grandmother _____.

7. A.   My doctor frequently laughs.

    B.   _____ tells _____ my doctor _____.

371

Name_____   **ADVERBS**

Date_____   **When**

<u>Note</u>: **Students may write the adverb and then the verb in each blank.**

An adverb is a word that can tell *when*.

Directions: Delete any prepositional phrases. Underline the subject once
and the verb or verb phrase twice. Label each adverb – *Adv.*
Write the verb and the adverb on the line.

                                                        Adv.
       Example: His <u>dog</u> frequently <u>jumps</u> ~~on visitors~~.   **jumps frequently**
                                           Adv.
 1. <u>Jemima</u> <u>sat</u> ~~by a pool~~ today. _____   **sat today**
                                                    Adv.
 2. <u>He</u> <u>might compete</u> ~~against his cousin~~ later. _____   **might compete later**
                        Adv.
 3. <u>Tara</u> always <u>wears</u> bright colors.   **wears always or always wears**
                  Adv.
 4. <u>Do</u> <u>you</u> ever <u>skate</u> ~~with your cousins~~? _____   **Do skate ever**
                                      Adv.
 5. <u>I</u> <u>must buy</u> my ticket now. _____   **must buy now**
                          Adv.
 6. <u>Pedro</u> sometimes <u>parks</u> his bike ~~by these trees~~.   **parks sometimes**
                                            Adv.
 7. That <u>woman</u> <u>visits</u> her mother monthly. _____   **visits monthly**
                      Adv.
 8. <u>He</u> <u>would</u> never <u>agree</u> (to do) that. _____   **would agree never**
                                    Adv.
 9. Their <u>flight</u> <u>will arrive</u> late. _____   **will arrive late**
                                  Adv.
10. <u>Tim</u> <u>may come</u> ~~with me~~ tomorrow ~~after school~~.   **may come tomorrow**
                        Adv.
11. My <u>uncle</u> often <u>buys</u> old tools ~~at auctions~~. _____   **buys often**
                                    Adv.
12. <u>I</u> <u>should have washed</u> my hair earlier.   **should have washed earlier**
                                      Adv.
13. Her <u>parents</u> <u>write</u> a letter ~~to the editor~~ weekly.   **write weekly**
              Adv.
14. Recently, <u>Emma</u> <u>hiked</u> ~~near a stable~~. _____   **hiked recently**
                    Adv.
15. (<u>You</u>) <u>Call</u> me soon. _____   **Call soon**

372

An adverb is a word that can tell *when*.

Directions: Delete any prepositional phrases. Underline the subject once and the verb or verb phrase twice. Label each adverb – *Adv.* Write the verb and the adverb on the line.

Example: His <u>dog</u> frequently <u>jumps</u> ~~on visitors~~.   **jumps frequently**

1. Jemima sat by a pool today. _____

2. He might compete against his cousin later. _____

3. Tara always wears bright colors. _____

4. Do you ever skate with your cousins? _____

5. I must buy my ticket now. _____

6. Pedro sometimes parks his bike by these trees. _____

7. That woman visits her mother monthly. _____

8. He would never agree to do that. _____

9. Their flight will arrive late. _____

10. Tim may come with me tomorrow after school. _____

11. My uncle often buys old tools at auctions. _____

12. I should have washed my hair earlier. _____

13. Her parents write a letter to the editor weekly. _____

14. Recently, Emma hiked near a stable. _____

15. Call me soon. _____

Name_____   **ADVERBS**

WORKBOOK PAGE 168

Date_____   **Where**

Note: You may want to pair or group students for this exercise. Some teachers will want to add excitement by creating a timed competition.

An adverb is a word that can tell <u>where</u>.

Directions: Think about words that can tell where. Fill in the blanks to spell adverbs that tell *where*.

1. i <u>**n**</u>

2. o <u>**n**</u>

3. u <u>**p**</u>

4. d <u>**o**</u> w <u>**n**</u>

5. i <u>**n**</u> s i d <u>**e**</u>

6. o <u>**f**</u> f

7. o <u>**u**</u> t s i d <u>**e**</u>

8. t h r <u>**o**</u> u <u>**g**</u> h

9. h <u>**e**</u> r <u>**e**</u>

10. t <u>**h**</u> <u>**e**</u> <u>**r**</u> e

11. a <u>**n**</u> y w <u>**h**</u> <u>**e**</u> r e

12. n <u>**o**</u> w <u>**h**</u> <u>**e**</u> r <u>**e**</u>

13. s <u>**o**</u> m e <u>**w**</u> <u>**h**</u> <u>**e**</u> r <u>**e**</u>

14. e <u>**v**</u> e r y <u>**w**</u> <u>**h**</u> <u>**e**</u> r e

15. d <u>**o**</u> w <u>**n**</u> t <u>**o**</u> w <u>**n**</u>

16. <u>**a**</u> w <u>**a**</u> y

17. f <u>**o**</u> r w <u>**a**</u> r d

18. a <u>**r**</u> o <u>**u**</u> <u>**n**</u> d

374

Name_____ **ADVERBS**

Date_____ **Where**

An adverb is a word that can tell <u>where</u>.

Directions: Think about words that can tell where. Fill in the blanks to spell
adverbs that tell *where*.

1. <u>i</u> _

2. <u>o</u> _

3. <u>u</u> _

4. <u>d</u> _ <u>w</u> _

5. <u>i</u> _ <u>s</u> _ <u>d</u> _

6. <u>o</u> _ <u>f</u>

7. <u>o</u> _ <u>t</u> <u>s</u> _ <u>d</u> _

8. <u>t</u> <u>h</u> <u>r</u> _ <u>u</u> _ <u>h</u>

9. <u>h</u> _ <u>r</u> _

10. <u>t</u> _ <u>e</u> _ <u>e</u>

11. <u>a</u> _ _ <u>w</u> _ <u>e</u> _ <u>e</u>

12. <u>n</u> _ <u>w</u> _ <u>e</u> <u>r</u> _

13. <u>s</u> _ <u>m</u> <u>e</u> _ <u>h</u> _ <u>r</u> _

14. <u>e</u> _ <u>e</u> _ <u>y</u> _ <u>h</u> _ <u>r</u> <u>e</u>

15. <u>d</u> _ <u>w</u> _ <u>t</u> _ <u>w</u> <u>n</u>

16. _ <u>w</u> _ <u>y</u>

17. <u>f</u> _ <u>r</u> <u>w</u> _ <u>r</u> <u>d</u>

18. <u>a</u> _ <u>o</u> <u>u</u> _ <u>d</u>

An adverb is a word that can tell where.

Directions: In Part A, delete any prepositional phrase(s). Underline the
subject once and the verb or verb phrase twice. Label each
adverb – *Adv.* Fill in the blanks in Part B.

                                                                    Adv.
Example: A.   The girl ~~with the furry dog~~ plays close ~~to her home~~.

              B.   _____*Close*_____ tells *where* the girl _*plays*_ .

                Adv.
1. A.   A mole lives here.

    B.   ___**Here**___ tells ___**where**___ a mole _____**lives**_____.
                Adv.
2. A.   I went nowhere ~~after my dental appointment~~.

    B.   ___**Nowhere**___ tells ___**where**___ I _____**went**_____.
       Adv.
3. A.   There is Carlos!

    B.   ___**There**___ tells ___**where**___ Carlos _____**is**_____.
                    Adv.
4. A.   That lamp leans forward.

    B.   ___**Forward**___ tells ___**where**___ the lamp _____**leans**_____.
                    Adv.
5. A.   One ~~of the racers~~ threw a towel up ~~in the air~~.

    B.   ___**Up**___ tells ___**where**___ one _____**threw**_____.
                Adv.
6. A.   His grandpa walks downtown ~~for a newspaper~~.

    B.   ___**Downtown**___ tells ___**where**___ his grandpa _____**walks**_____.
                Adv.
7. A.   Her boots are outside ~~beside the back door~~.

    B.   ___**Outside**___ tells ___**where**___ her boots _____**are**_____.
                Adv.
8. A.   A bird flew by ~~with a twig in its beak~~.

    B.   ___**By**___ tells ___**where**___ a bird _____**flew**_____.

376

An adverb is a word that can tell where.

Directions: In Part A, delete any prepositional phrase(s). Underline the subject once and the verb or verb phrase twice. Label each adverb – *Adv.* Fill in the blanks in Part B.

                                                                    Adv.
Example: A.   The <u>girl</u> ~~with the furry dog~~ <u><u>plays</u></u> close ~~to her home~~.

                B.   _____*Close*_____ tells *where* the girl _*plays*_.

1. A. A mole lives here.

    B. _____ tells _____ a mole _____.

2. A. I went nowhere after my dental appointment.

    B. _____ tells _____ I _____.

3. A. There is Carlos!

    B. _____ tells _____ Carlos _____.

4. A. That lamp leans forward.

    B. _____ tells _____ the lamp _____.

5. A. One of the racers threw a towel up in the air.

    B. _____ tells _____ one _____.

6. A. His grandpa walks downtown for a newspaper.

    B. _____ tells _____ his grandpa _____.

7. A. Her boots are outside beside the back door.

    B. _____ tells _____ her boots _____.

8. A. A bird flew by with a twig in its beak.

    B. _____ tells _____ a bird _____.

An adverb is a word that can tell where.

Directions: Delete any prepositional phrase(s). Underline the subject once and the verb or verb phrase twice. Label each adverb – *Adv.*

1. Dr. Silversmith <u>laid</u> his cellular phone **down**.
   Adv.

2. <u>Loni</u> <u>waded</u> **upstream**.
   Adv.

3. His <u>cat</u> <u>rolled</u> **over** ~~on its side~~.
   Adv.

4. <u>You</u> <u>may move</u> **forward**.
   Adv.

5. Their <u>dog</u> <u>runs</u> **around** ~~in circles~~.
   Adv.

6. <u>Does</u> <u>Carla</u> <u>live</u> **nearby**?
   Adv.

7. <u>They</u> <u>went</u> **outside** ~~after the downpour~~.
   Adv.

8. <u>Are</u> <u>you</u> <u>going</u> **far**?
   Adv.

9. Some <u>children</u> <u>hopped</u> **sideways** ~~during the game~~.
   Adv.

10. Two <u>swimmers</u> <u>pushed</u> **away** ~~from the side~~ ~~of a pool~~.
    Adv.

11. <u>You</u> <u>should have come</u> **inside** ~~before the snowstorm~~.
    Adv.

12. Both <u>Gretta</u> and her <u>brother</u> <u>will join</u> us **there**.
    Adv.

13. <u>Many</u> ~~of the surfers~~ <u>rushed</u> **out** (to catch) waves.
    Adv.

14. (<u>You</u>) <u>Come</u> **aboard**.

378

Name_____

Date_____

An adverb is a word that can tell where.

Directions: Delete any prepositional phrase(s). Underline the subject once and
the verb or verb phrase twice. Label each adverb – _Adv._

1. Dr. Silversmith laid his cellular phone down.

2. Loni waded upstream.

3. His cat rolled over on its side.

4. You may move forward.

5. Their dog runs around in circles.

6. Does Carla live nearby?

7. They went outside after the downpour.

8. Are you going far?

9. Some children hopped sideways during the game.

10. Two swimmers pushed away from the side of a pool.

11. You should have come inside before the snowstorm.

12. Both Gretta and her brother will join us there.

13. Many of the surfers rushed out to catch waves.

14. Come aboard.

Name_____   **ADVERBS**

WORKBOOK PAGE 171

Date_____   **How**

Note: You may want to pair or group students for this activity.
Adverbs can tell how.

Directions: Unscramble these adverbs that tell *how*.

1. lystof - **s o f t l y**

2. lyftisw - **s w i f t l y**

3. lygthit - **t i g h t l y**

4. lyldiw - **w i l d l y**

5. lyewets - **s w e e t l y**

6. lysprah - **s h a r p l y**

7. llew - **w e l l**

8. lypeasntla - **p l e a s a n t l y**

9. lylys - **s l y l y**

10. lyuiqte - **q u i e t l y**

11. lypoheful - **h o p e f u l l y**

12. lydlou - **l o u d l y**

13. lyandregsou - **d a n g e r o u s l y**

380

Name_____

Date_____

Adverbs can tell how.

Directions: Unscramble these adverbs that tell *how*.

1. lystof - _ _ _ _ _ _

2. lyftisw - _ _ _ _ _ _ _

3. lygthit - _ _ _ _ _ _ _

4. lyldiw - _ _ _ _ _ _

5. lyewets - _ _ _ _ _ _ _

6. lysprah - _ _ _ _ _ _ _

7. llew - _ _ _ _

8. lypeasntla - _ _ _ _ _ _ _ _ _ _

9. lylys - _ _ _ _ _

10. lyuiqte - _ _ _ _ _ _ _

11. lypoheful - _ _ _ _ _ _ _ _ _

12. lydlou - _ _ _ _ _ _

13. lyandregsou - _ _ _ _ _ _ _ _ _ _ _

381

Name_____   **ADVERBS**

Date_____   **How**

Note: You may want to share answers and tally how many student answers match the ones below. Students will benefit by *hearing* adverbs that tell *how*.

Adverbs can tell *how*.

Directions: Write an adverb that tells *how* in each blank. Do not reuse an adverb.

ANSWERS MAY VARY/REPRESENTATIVE ANSWERS:

1. You did that _____**easily**_____.

2. Those teenage boys are throwing horseshoes _____**well**_____.

3. His neighbor drives _____**cautiously**_____.

4. Stop acting _____**strangely**_____.

5. Tate waved _____**excitedly**_____.

6. We ate _____**hungrily**_____.

7. They build campfires _____**carefully**_____.

8. Jonah rolled a cart _____**fast**_____.

9. A small snake slid _____**slowly**_____ down a rock.

10. Kalani shook the rug _____**vigorously**_____.

11. Those children play _____**happily**_____.

12. That student studies _____**hard**_____.

13. The winner of the contest smiled _____**proudly**_____.

14. Some of the birds flew _____**together**_____.

15. Fry our bacon _____**crisply**_____, please.

16. Press the elevator button _____**gently**_____.

17. A lifeguard yelled _____**loudly**_____ to several swimmers.

382

Adverbs can tell *how*.

Directions: Write an adverb that tells *how* in each blank. Do not reuse an
                adverb.

1. You did that _____.

2. Those teenage boys are throwing horseshoes _____.

3. His neighbor drives _____.

4. Stop acting _____.

5. Tate waved _____.

6. We ate _____.

7. They build campfires _____.

8. Jonah rolled a cart _____.

9. A small snake slid _____ down a rock.

10. Kalani shook the rug _____.

11. Those children play _____.

12. That student studies _____.

13. The winner of the contest smiled _____.

14. Some of the birds flew _____.

15. Fry our bacon _____, please.

16. Press the elevator button _____.

17. A lifeguard yelled _____ to several swimmers.

Name_____ **ADVERBS**

WORKBOOK PAGE 173

Date_____ **How**

Directions: Delete any prepositional phrases. Underline the subject once and the verb or verb phrase twice. Circle any adverb that tells *how*.

ADVERBS ARE BOLDFACED.

1. Rain slid **quietly** down the window.

2. The truck stopped **carefully** at a traffic light.

3. Pierre blew bubbles **gleefully**.

4. One child talked **eagerly** about his hike.

5. Several beagles lay **peacefully** under a tree.

6. My father mixed butter and eggs **together**.

7. A band marched **fast** during the parade.

8. This fire in our fireplace is burning **brightly**.

9. The grandpa rocked the baby **gently** and sang.

10. Dora and Tom scribbled their notes **rapidly**.

11. Sand blew **strongly** across the desert.

12. Carlo sanded wood **smoothly** for a cutting board.

13. One of the bowlers throws her bowling ball **hesitantly**.

14. Did Lars finish the puzzle **completely**?

15. (You) Rinse these dishes **well** with warm water.

384

Date_____

Directions: Delete any prepositional phrases. Underline the subject once and
               the verb or verb phrase twice. Circle any adverb that tells *how*.

1. Rain slid quietly down the window.

2. The truck stopped carefully at a traffic light.

3. Pierre blew bubbles gleefully.

4. One child talked eagerly about his hike.

5. Several beagles lay peacefully under a tree.

6. My father mixed butter and eggs together.

7. A band marched fast during the parade.

8. This fire in our fireplace is burning brightly.

9. The grandpa rocked the baby gently and sang.

10. Dora and Tom scribbled their notes rapidly.

11. Sand blew strongly across the desert.

12. Carlo sanded wood smoothly for a cutting board.

13. One of the bowlers throws her bowling ball hesitantly.

14. Did Lars finish the puzzle completely?

15. Rinse these dishes well with warm water.

ADVERB or ADJECTIVE?

Have you heard anyone say the following sentence?

◆<u>Incorrect</u>:   **You are acting strange.**

Acting is an action verb. You must use an adverb that tells how you are acting.

☺   <u>Correct</u>:   **You *are acting* strangely.**

However, if the verb is a linking verb (not action), use an adjective.

☺   <u>Correct</u>:   **I *look* strange in this costume.**

A review of linking verbs may help you!

Linking verbs do not show action; they usually make a statement.

to feel	to smell	to grow	to stay
to taste	to seem	to remain	to become
to look	to sound	to appear	to be (is, am, are, was, were, be, being, been)

Example: His leg <u>cast</u> <u>looks</u> frayed.

To look is on the linking verb list. Replacing *looks* with *is* does not change the meaning of the sentence.

is

Example: His leg cast <u>looks</u> frayed.

After a linking verb, use an adjective. This adjective will be a <u>describing word</u>.

My soup is **excellent**.   (adjective – excellent soup)
You spell **excellently**.   (adverb – telling *how* you spell)

	Adjective	*Adverb*
Examples:	fine	finely

Examples:

Adjective	*Adverb*

fine   **finely**

My health is <u>fine</u>.

I <u>chopped</u> the celery <u>finely</u>.
action   **how?**
verb

respectful   **respectfully**

The child is very <u>respectful</u>.

<u>Ask</u> me <u>respectfully</u>.
action   **how?**
verb

bad   **badly**

He feels <u>bad</u>.

I <u>played</u> golf <u>badly</u> today.
action   **how?**
verb

good   **well***

Their fort is <u>good</u>.

He <u>races</u> go-carts <u>well</u>.
action   **how?**
Verb

*When using an action verb *and* telling <u>how</u>, use *well*, not *good*.
Kent *makes* pottery well.
Jana *skis* well.
He *speaks* well.
Margie *drove* the speed boat well.

Remember that **fast** and **hard** are the same in the adjective form and the adverb form.

Examples:	<u>fast</u>	That train is **fast**.	(adjective)
		You move **fast**.	(adverb)
	<u>hard</u>	This is a **hard** question.	(adjective)
		You work **hard**.	(adverb)

387

Directions: Write the adverb form of the boldfaced adjective.

1. Jana is a **quick** painter. She painted the room _____**quickly**_____.

2. Josh has a **quiet** voice. He speaks _____**quietly**_____.

3. That girl is very **shy**. She smiles _____**shyly**_____ at us.

4. This wood project is **hard**. I'm working _____**hard**_____ on it.

5. The rider was **silent**. She rode _____**silently**_____.

6. This bench is **solid**. It has been built _____**solidly**_____.

7. The witness was **nervous**. He answered _____**nervously**_____.

8. Our teacher looked **tired**. She nodded _____**tiredly**_____.

9. My neighbor is an **excellent** cook. He cooks _____**excellently**_____.

10. Mario is a **good** dancer. He dances _____**well**_____.

11. The sailboat is a **fast** boat. It moves _____**fast**_____.

12. His doctor is **kind**. He deals _____**kindly**_____ with his patients.

13. Joe and Mona are **brave**. They skydive _____**bravely**_____.

14. The first grader is a **careful** printer. He prints _____**carefully**_____.

15. That vehicle is **slow**. It's moving _____**slowly**_____ up a steep hill.

388

Name_____   **ADVERBS**

Date_____   **How**

Directions: Write the adverb form of the boldfaced adjective.

1. Jana is a **quick** painter. She painted the room _____.

2. Josh has a **quiet** voice. He speaks _____.

3. That girl is very **shy**. She smiles _____ at us.

4. This wood project is **hard**. I'm working _____ on it.

5. The rider was **silent**. She rode _____.

6. This bench is **solid**. It has been built _____.

7. The witness was **nervous**. He answered _____.

8. Our teacher looked **tired**. She nodded _____.

9. My neighbor is an **excellent** cook. He cooks _____.

10. Mario is a **good** dancer. He dances _____.

11. The sailboat is a **fast** boat. It moves _____.

12. His doctor is **kind**. He deals _____ with his patients.

13. Joe and Mona are **brave**. They skydive _____.

14. The first grader is a **careful** printer. He prints _____.

15. That vehicle is **slow**. It's moving _____ up a steep hill.

389

<u>**Note**</u>**: You may want to pair students for this activity.**

Adverbs change the meaning of a sentence.
Directions: Write 2 different adverbs that tell *how* in each blank. Do not
                      reuse an adverb.
ANSWERS MAY VARY/REPRESENTATIVE ANSWERS:

1.   The woman tapped _____**frantically**_____ on the car window.

                                _____**gently**_____

2.   Two workers discussed the problem _____**calmly**_____.

                                                 _____**thoroughly**_____

3.   Many children played _____**together**_____ in a wading pool.

                                     _____**happily**_____

4.   He always rows _____**alone**_____ across the local lake.

                          _____**fast**_____

5.   A bear ate _____**noisily**_____ from a garbage can.

                      _____**greedily**_____

6.   Toni often plays chess _____**well**_____.

                                       _____**slowly**_____

7.   They dress _____**elegantly**_____ for some occasions.

                       _____**up**_____

8.   The shopper crossed the street _____**carefully**_____.

                                                _____**hurriedly**_____

390

Name_____   **ADVERBS**

Date_____   **How**

Adverbs change the meaning of a sentence.

Directions: Write 2 different adverbs that tell *how* in each blank. Do not
reuse an adverb.

1. The woman tapped _____ on the car window.

    _____

2. Two workers discussed the problem _____.

    _____

3. Many children played _____ in a wading pool.

    _____

4. He always rows _____ across the local lake.

    _____

5. A bear ate _____ from a garbage can.

    _____

6. Toni often plays chess _____.

    _____

7. They dress _____ for some occasions.

    _____

8. The shopper crossed the street _____.

    _____

WORKBOOK PAGE 178

Directions: Write the adverb form of the boldfaced adjective.

1. **distinct** ~ The guide speaks _____**distinctly**_____.

2. **proud** ~ They salute the flag _____**proudly**_____.

3. **sad** ~ Several friends said goodbye _____**sadly**_____.

4. **illegal** ~ The driver made a U-turn _____**illegally**_____.

5. **main** ~ Her father works _____**mainly**_____ as a tuna fisher.

6. **good** ~ The teenagers are surfing _____**well**_____.

7. **secure** ~ Your package has been tied _____**securely**_____.

8. **silent** ~ Some workers waited _____**silently**_____ for a bus.

9. **loose** ~ Loose boards hung _____**loosely**_____ on the old barn.

10. **bad** ~ I sprained my ankle _____**badly**_____ yesterday.

11. **hard** ~ Chessa kicked the ball _____**hard**_____ into the
         goal.

12. **furious** ~ Their dog barked _____**furiously**_____ at the passing
         motorists.

13. **complete** ~ Please fill out the form _____**completely**_____.

14. **brilliant** ~ A harvest moon shines _____**brilliantly**_____.

15. **sleepy** ~ The toddler _____**sleepily**_____ mumbled good night.

16. **truthful** ~ He answered the judge _____**truthfully**_____.

17. **awkward** ~ In his first attempt, the new-born colt stood

         _____**awkwardly**_____.

Date_____

Directions: Write the adverb form of the boldfaced adjective.

1. **distinct** ~ The guide speaks _____.

2. **proud** ~ They salute the flag _____.

3. **sad** ~ Several friends said goodbye _____.

4. **illegal** ~ The driver made a U-turn _____.

5. **main** ~ Her father works _____ as a tuna fisher.

6. **good** ~ The teenagers are surfing _____.

7. **secure** ~ Your package has been tied _____.

8. **silent** ~ Some workers waited _____ for a bus.

9. **loose** ~ Loose boards hung _____ on the old barn.

10. **bad** ~ I sprained my ankle _____ yesterday.

11. **hard** ~ Chessa kicked the ball _____ into the goal.

12. **furious** ~ Their dog barked _____ at the passing motorists.

13. **complete** ~ Please fill out the form _____.

14. **brilliant** ~ A harvest moon shines _____.

15. **sleepy** ~ The toddler _____ mumbled good night.

16. **truthful** ~ He answered the judge _____.

17. **awkward** ~ In his first attempt, the new-born colt stood _____.

A. Directions: In Part A, write an adverb telling *how, when,* or *where.*
                 In Part B, write what that adverb tells: *how, when,* or *where.*

ANSWERS MAY VARY/REPRESENTATIVE ANSWERS:

1. Part A: Go _____**today**_____.

   Part B: _____**when**_____

2. Part A: I searched _____**tirelessly**_____.

   Part B: _____**how**_____

3. Part A: A chipmunk scurried _____**everywhere**_____.

   Part B: _____**where**_____

4. Part A: We _____**always**_____ arrive on time.

   Part B: _____**when**_____

B. Directions: Cross out any prepositional phrases. Underline the subject
                 once and the verb or verb phrase twice. Circle the adverb.
                 In the blank, write if the adverb tells *how, when,* or *where.*

1. The department store closed **early**.   _____**when**_____

2. Her charm bracelet rattled **noisily**.   _____**how**_____

3. That mason works **alone** ~~on Mondays~~.   _____**how**_____

4. A crane set a huge crate **down**.   _____**where**_____

5. Everyone exited **immediately**.   _____**when**_____

6. We are going **nowhere** ~~for vacation~~.   _____**where**_____

7. Does this bus travel **downtown**?   _____**where**_____

394

Name_____ **ADVERBS**

Date_____ **How, When, Where**

A. Directions: In Part A, write an adverb telling *how, when,* or *where.*
                  In Part B, write what that adverb tells: *how, when,* or *where.*

1. Part A: Go _____.

    Part B: _____

2. Part A: I searched _____.

    Part B: _____

3. Part A: A chipmunk scurried _____.

    Part B: _____

4. Part A: We _____ arrive on time.

    Part B: _____

B. Directions: Cross out any prepositional phrases. Underline the subject
                  once and the verb or verb phrase twice. Circle the adverb.
                  In the blank, write if the adverb tells *how, when,* or *where.*

1. The department store closed early.   _____

2. Her charm bracelet rattled noisily.   _____

3. That mason works alone on Mondays.   _____

4. A crane set a huge crate down.   _____

5. Everyone exited immediately.   _____

6. We are going nowhere for vacation.   _____

7. Does this bus travel downtown?   _____

ADVERBS

To What Extent

Most adverbs that tell *when, where,* or *how* modify (go over to) a verb.

Miss Arrow moved **there**.	*There tells <u>where</u> Miss Arrow moved.*
She moved **recently**.	*Recently tells <u>when</u> she moved.*
She moved **quickly**.	*Quickly tells <u>how</u> she moved.*

<u>Seven adverbs usually tell *to what extent*. There are others, like *really*, but these 7 are used most often.</u>

1   2   3   4   5   6   7

Not, so, very, too, quite, rather, somewhat

Adverbs that tell *to what extent* are harder to understand because they can modify (go over to) a <u>verb</u>, an <u>adjective</u>, or even another <u>adverb</u>.

Examples:

I did ***not*** go.	(modifies a verb)
This poem is ***rather*** long.	(modifies *long*, an adjective)
She walks ***very*** cautiously on crutches.	(modifies *cautiously*, an adverb that tells <u>how</u>)

෨෨෨෨෨෨෨෨෨෨෨෨෨෨෨෨෨

Directions: Unscramble the seven adverbs that often tell *to what extent*.

1. os - <u>**s o**</u>

2. thsmaweo - <u>**s o m e w h a t**</u>

3. etiqu - <u>**q u i t e**</u>

4. oto - <u>**t o o**</u>

5. herrta - <u>**r a t h e r**</u>

6. revy - <u>**v e r y**</u>

7. ont - <u>**n o t**</u>

396

Most adverbs that tell *when, where,* or *how* modify (go over to) a verb.

Miss Arrow moved **there**.
She moved **recently**.
She moved **quickly**.

There tells <u>where</u> Miss Arrow moved.
Recently tells <u>when</u> she moved.
Quickly tells <u>how</u> she moved.

<u>Seven adverbs usually tell *to what extent*. There are others, like</u> <u>*really*, but these 7 are used most often.</u>

1   2   3   4   5   6   7
Not, so, very, too, quite, rather, somewhat

Adverbs that tell *to what extent* are harder to understand because they can modify (go over to) a <u>**verb**</u>, an <u>**adjective**</u>, or even another <u>**adverb**</u>.

Examples:

I did **not** go.   (modifies a verb)
This poem is **rather** long.   (modifies *long*, an adjective)
She walks **very** cautiously on crutches. (modifies *hesitantly*, an adverb that tells <u>how</u>)

෯෯෯෯෯෯෯෯෯෯෯෯෯෯෯

Directions: Unscramble the seven adverbs that often tell *to what extent*.

1. os - _ _

2. thsmaweo - _ _ _ _ _ _ _ _

3. etiqu - _ _ _ _ _

4. oto - _ _ _

5. herrta - _ _ _ _ _ _

6. revy - _ _ _ _

7. ont - _ _ _

Adverbs that tell _to what extent_ can modify (go over to) a <u>verb</u>, an <u>adjective</u>, or even another <u>adverb</u>.

Not, so, very, too, quite, rather, somewhat

ৡৡৡৡৡৡৡৡৡৡৡৡৡৡৡৡৡৡ

Directions: Write an adverb that tells _to what extent_. Do not reuse an adverb.
ANSWERS MAY VARY/REPRESENTATIVE ANSWERS:

1. The patient's pulse was _____**not**_____ weak.

2. A librarian read _____**rather**_____ softly to the children.

3. Her aim was _____**quite**_____ far to the left.

4. Our city has become _____**too**_____ large.

5. This is _____**very**_____ funny!

6. The fountain bubbles _____**so**_____ gently.

7. Listen to this _____**somewhat**_____ scary tale.

ৡৡৡৡৡৡৡৡৡৡৡৡৡৡৡৡৡৡ

Other words such as _really_ may also tell _to what extent_.

> **Real** is an adjective. That is a <u>real</u> muscle car.
> **Really** tells _to what extent_. Are you <u>really</u> hungry? (to what extent hungry?)

Directions: Circle the correct word:

1. You must remain (real, **really**) quiet.

2. I think that cartoon is (quiet, **quite**) silly.

3. We walk (**really**, real) fast.

4. Are you (real, **really**) strong?

398

Name_____   **ADVERBS**

Date_____   **To What Extent**

Adverbs that tell *to what extent* can modify (go over to) a <u>verb</u>, an <u>adjective</u>, or even another <u>adverb</u>.

Not, so, very, too, quite, rather, somewhat

🙢🙢🙢🙢🙢🙢🙢🙢🙢🙢🙢🙢🙢🙢🙢🙢🙢🙢

Directions: Write an adverb that tells *to what extent*. Do not reuse an adverb.

1. The patient's pulse was _____ weak.

2. A librarian read _____ softly to the children.

3. Her aim was _____ far to the left.

4. Our city has become _____ large.

5. This is _____ funny!

6. The fountain bubbles _____ gently.

7. Listen to this _____ scary tale.

🙢🙢🙢🙢🙢🙢🙢🙢🙢🙢🙢🙢🙢🙢🙢🙢🙢🙢

Other words such as *really* may also tell *to what extent*.

   Real is an adjective. That is a <u>real</u> muscle car.

   Really tells *to what extent*. Are you <u>really</u> hungry? (to what extent hungry?)

Directions: Circle the correct word:

1. You must remain (real, really) quiet.

2. I think that cartoon is (quiet, quite) silly.

3. We walk (really, real) fast.

4. Are you (real, really) strong?

Name_____   **ADVERBS**
WORKBOOK PAGE 182
Date_____   **To What Extent**

Adverbs can tell *to what extent*.

Directions: Circle any adverbs that tell *to what extent*.

Adverbs that tell *to what extent* have been boldfaced.

1. Are you **too** wide-awake to sleep?

2. The insect buzzed **rather** loudly around my head.

3. Do **not** finish your task until tomorrow.

4. We are **really** excited about going with our aunt to Georgia.

5. She is **somewhat** afraid to voice her opinions.

6. The program ended **quite** abruptly.

7. My great-grandmother is **so** witty.

8. I could **barely** hear his voice due to a loud noise.

9. The pilot spoke **very** clearly to her passengers.

10. My sister dresses **quite** smartly for work at her office.

11. Her landlord was **extremely** perturbed about the leak in her roof.

12. My mother is **somewhat** deaf in her left ear.

13. Does**n't** Jasmine go to dance class on Sundays?

14. A **very** shy child peered **quite** timidly into a cardboard box.

15. The creek rose **rather** swiftly during heavy rains.

16. This lamp has been **partially** damaged by sun rays.

17. My oatmeal is **too** thick and **rather** sugary.

400

ADVERBS

To What Extent

Adverbs can tell *to what extent.*

Directions: Circle any adverbs that tell *to what extent.*

1.   Are you too wide-awake to sleep?

2.   The insect buzzed rather loudly around my head.

3.   Do not finish your task until tomorrow.

4.   We are really excited about going with our aunt to Georgia.

5.   She is somewhat afraid to voice her opinions.

6.   The program ended quite abruptly.

7.   My great-grandmother is so witty.

8.   I could barely hear his voice due to a loud noise.

9.   The pilot spoke very clearly to her passengers.

10. My sister dresses quite smartly for work at her office.

11. Her landlord was extremely perturbed about the leak in her roof.

12. My mother is somewhat deaf in her left ear.

13. Doesn't Jasmin go to dance class on Sundays?

14. A very shy child peered quite timidly into a cardboard box.

15. The creek rose rather swiftly during heavy rains.

16. This lamp has been partially damaged by sun rays.

17. My oatmeal is too thick and rather sugary.

Adverbs can tell *how, when, where,* or *to what extent.*

Adverbs that tell ***how, when,*** or ***where*** usually modify (go over to) a **verb**.

Adverbs that tell *to what extent* may modify a **verb**, an **adjective**, or another **adverb**.

୭ଙ୭ଙ୭ଙ୭ଙ୭ଙ୭ଙ୭ଙ୭ଙ୭ଙ୭ଙ

Directions: Circle any adverb in the sentence. The number in parentheses ( ) tells how many adverbs are in that sentence.
Adverbs have been boldfaced.

1. (2) We are going **there today**.

2. (3) **Now** and **then**, a mouse runs **rapidly** from its hole.

3. (2) We worked **hard together** on a social studies project.

4. (3) Omar sang **loudly** to a **very** lively crowd **yesterday**.

5. (2) Jana does **not** feel **well**.

6. (2) Jake kicked the ball **hard** and ran **fast** toward the goal.

7. (2) Several ranchers met **here** for a **very** short conference.

8. (3) **Tomorrow**, you must look **somewhere** for a **rather** old clock.

9. (2) I wrote my name **so carefully** on the dotted line.

Adverbs can tell *how, when, where,* or *to what extent.*

Adverbs that tell ***how, when,*** or ***where*** usually modify (go over to) a **verb**.

Adverbs that tell *to what extent* may modify a **verb**, an **adjective**, or another **adverb**.

᷁᷁᷁᷁᷁᷁᷁᷁᷁᷁᷁᷁᷁᷁᷁᷁

Directions: Circle any adverb in the sentence. The number in parentheses ( ) tells how many adverbs are in that sentence.

1. (2) We are going there today.

2. (3) Now and then, a mouse runs rapidly from its hole.

3. (2) We worked hard together on a social studies project.

4. (3) Omar sang loudly to a very lively crowd yesterday.

5. (2) Jana does not feel well.

6. (2) Jake kicked the ball hard and ran fast toward the goal.

7. (2) Several ranchers met here for a very short conference.

8. (3) Tomorrow, you must look somewhere for a rather old clock.

9. (2) I wrote my name so carefully on the dotted line.

TO THE TEACHER: Comparative and Superlative Degrees of Adverbs

Teach the concept of degrees very carefully. Use many examples. Below are some that might help students to understand this concept.

One-Syllable:

> Joy hits a volley ball <u>hard</u>.   (*Hard* tells **how** Joy hits a volleyball.)
>
> Joy's best friend hits a volleyball <u>hard**er**</u> than Joy.
>
> Of the entire team, Joy's best friend hits the volleyball <u>hard**est**</u>.

Two-Syllable:

> The woman raced <u>quickly</u> to the pond.
>
> Her husband raced ***more*** <u>quickly</u> than his wife.
>
> Their son raced ***most*** <u>quickly</u> of the three.

Three-Syllable (or more):

> Lou reacted <u>positively</u> to the news.
>
> Gayle reacted ***more*** <u>positively</u> than Lou.
>
> Of the three, Milly reacted ***most*** <u>positively</u>.

Other forms:

> I hit the ball ***far***.
>
> Mickey hit the ball ***farther*** than I.
>
> Parker hit the ball ***farthest*** of all the contestants.

Comparative and Superlative Degrees of Adverbs

To compare **2**, we use the **comparative degree**.

A. <u>One-syllable words</u> usually add *er* to compare **2** things or people.

  Jodi runs fast.   Jodi runs fast**er** than her coach.

B. <u>Most two-syllable words</u> use *more* to compare **2**.

  The first speaker spoke loudly to the audience.

  The next speaker spoke *more* loudly than the first.

C. <u>Words of three or more syllables</u> use *more* to compare **2**.

  Joshua climbed carefully.   His sister climbed **more** carefully than he.

D. Some words change forms to compare **2**.

  I played chess *badly* yesterday.   I played *worse* today.

∽∽∽∽∽∽∽∽∽

To compare **3 or more**, we use the **superlative degree**.

A. <u>One-syllable words</u> usually add *est* to compare **<u>3 or more</u>**.

  Jodi runs fast**est** of the entire team.

B. Most <u>two-syllable words</u> use *most* to compare **<u>3 or more</u>**.

  The last speaker spoke *most* loudly of all.

C. <u>Words of three or more syllables</u> use *most* to compare **<u>3 or more</u>**.

  He climbed down *most* carefully during his fifth try.

D. Some words change forms to compare **<u>3 or more</u>**.

  I played chess *worst* during my fourth game.

Directions: In Part A, write the adverb form of the italicized word.
In Part B, write the comparative or superlative form.

Part A: *willing* -   **willingly**

Part B: The fourth worker did the job   **most willingly** .

1. Part A: *sound* -   **soundly**

   Part B: I sleep   **more soundly**   than my brother.

2. Part A: *quick* -   **quickly**

   Part B: I wrote my first email   **more quickly**   than my second one.

3. Part A: *violent* -   **violently**

   Part B: The third volcano erupted   **most violently** .

4. Part A: *close* -   **closely**

   Part B: A jeweler examined the second gem   **more closely** .

5. Part A: *soon* -   **soon**

   Part B: Of the three students, Ellie finished   **soonest** .

6. Part A: *clear* -   **clearly**

   Part B: This large package is labeled   **more clearly**   than the small one.

7. Part A: *dangerous* -   **dangerously**

   Part B: The ship tilted   **most dangerously**   during the third storm.

406

Name_____

Date_____

Directions: In Part A, write the adverb form of the italicized word.
In Part B, write the comparative or superlative form.

Part A: *willing* -   ____**willingly**____

Part B: The fourth worker did the job ____**most willingly**____.

1.   Part A: *sound* -   _____

Part B: I sleep _____ than my brother.

2.   Part A: *quick* -   _____

Part B: I wrote my first email _____ than my
second one.

3.   Part A: *violent* -   _____

Part B: The third volcano erupted _____.

4.   Part A: *close* -   _____

Part B: A jeweler looked at the second gem _____.

5.   Part A: *soon* -   _____

Part B: Of the three students, Ellie finished _____.

6.   Part A: *clear* -   _____

Part B: This large package is labeled _____ than
the small one.

7.   Part A: *dangerous* -   _____

Part B: The ship tilted _____during the third
storm.

Name_____   **ADVERBS**

WORKBOOK PAGE 186

Date_____   **Degrees**

Note: You may want to team students for checking after they have completed this worksheet independently.

Directions: Circle the correct adverb form.

1. Of all the critics, he judges (more fairly, **most fairly**).

2. She laid the second board (**more evenly**, most evenly) than the first.

3. This brown puppy plays (**more eagerly**, most eagerly) than that white one.

4. Their grandpa rocked his fourth grandchild (longer, **longest**).

5. The wind is blowing (**more fiercely**, most fiercely) today than yesterday.

6. Pablo heeded the third signal (more quickly, **most quickly**).

7. The actress discussed her life (**more frankly**, most frankly) during her second interview.

8. Our team worked (**more cooperatively**, most cooperatively) than the other team.

9. Carlo cooks (more expertly, **most expertly**) of all the chefs.

10. The client responded (**more favorably**, most favorably) than her lawyer.

11. Of the two machines, this one spins (**more safely**, most safely).

12. Of the four customs agents, he answers questions (more willingly, **most willingly**).

13. Mr. Lu works (**more steadily**, most steadily) than his son.

14. The tallest triplet plays tennis (more boldly, **most boldly**).

15. Chan dresses (**better**, best) than his brother.

16. The woman petted the third fawn (more gently, **most gently**).

408

Directions: Circle the correct adverb form.

1.   Of all the critics, he judges (more fairly, most fairly).

2.   She laid the second board (more evenly, most evenly) than the first.

3.   This brown puppy plays (more eagerly, most eagerly) than that white one.

4.   Their grandpa rocked his fourth grandchild (longer, longest).

5.   The wind is blowing (more fiercely, most fiercely) today than yesterday.

6.   Pablo heeded the third signal (more quickly, most quickly).

7.   The actress discussed her life (more frankly, most frankly) during her
     second interview.

8.   Our team worked (more cooperatively, most cooperatively) than the other
     team.

9.   Carlo cooks (more expertly, most expertly) of all the chefs.

10.   The client responded (more favorably, most favorably) than her lawyer.

11.   Of the two machines, this one spins (more safely, most safely).

12.   Of the four customs agents, he answers questions (more willingly, most
      willingly).

13.   Mr. Lu works (more steadily, most steadily) than his son.

14.   The tallest triplet plays tennis (more boldly, most boldly).

15.   Chan dresses (better, best) than his brother.

16.   The woman petted the third fawn (more gently, most gently).

Name_____   **ADVERBS**

WORKBOOK PAGE 187

Date_____   **Degrees**

Directions: Circle the correct adverb form.

1. One photographer adjusted her lens (**more exactly**, most exactly) for the second shot.

2. A logger pulled the third rope (more snugly, **most snugly**).

3. The woman climbed (**higher**, highest) during her second try.

4. He swam (better, **best**) during his fourth race.

5. I do my exercises (**more cheerfully**, most cheerfully) than my mother.

6. Patrick spoke (**more plainly**, most plainly) during his second debate.

7. I turned the last of the four screws (more tightly, **most tightly**).

8. Pierre petted the second dog (**more fearlessly**, most fearlessly).

9. This car runs (**more smoothly**, most smoothly) than that van.

10. The taller twin throws a shot put (**farther**, farthest).

11. We rested (**more often**, most often) on our second hike in the state forest.

12. That candidate speaks (**more freely**, most freely) than his opponent.

13. The ambassador smiled (more warmly, **most warmly**) for the fifth picture.

14. Maria walks (**more clumsily**, most clumsily) in heels than in flat shoes.

15. Garth hung the second drape (**more loosely**, most loosely) than the first.

16. Of the triplets, Dakota lives (more simply, **most simply**).

17. Does a racer steer (**better**, best) than an antique roadster?
410

Name_____   **ADVERBS**

Date_____   **Degrees**

Directions: Circle the correct adverb form.

1. One photographer adjusted her lens (more exactly, most exactly) for the second shot.

2. A logger pulled the third rope (more snugly, most snugly).

3. The woman climbed (higher, highest) during her second try.

4. He swam (better, best) during his fourth race.

5. I do my exercises (more cheerfully, most cheerfully) than my mother.

6. Patrick spoke (more plainly, most plainly) during his second debate.

7. I turned the last of the four screws (more tightly, most tightly).

8. Pierre petted the second dog (more fearlessly, most fearlessly).

9. This car runs (more smoothly, most smoothly) than that van.

10. The taller twin throws a shot put (farther, farthest).

11. We rested (more often, most often) on our second hike in the state forest.

12. That candidate speaks (more freely, most freely) than his opponent.

13. The ambassador smiled (more warmly, most warmly) for the fifth picture.

14. Maria walks (more clumsily, most clumsily) in heels than in flat shoes.

15. Garth hung the second drape (more loosely, most loosely) than the first.

16. Of the triplets, Dakota lives (more simply, most simply).

17. Does a racer steer (better, best) than an antique roadster?

411

Name_____   **ADVERBS**

Date_____   **Review**

A. Adjectives and Adverbs:

Directions: Write the adverb form of each adjective.

1. A captain gave a **polite** answer.

    She answered ____**politely**____ .

2. They are **generous** givers.

    They give ____**generously**____ to a charity.

3. It is a **compact** dishwasher.

    It fits ____**compactly**____ between the sink and refrigerator.

4. The actor wore a **shabby** outfit.

    The actor was dressed ____**shabbily**____ .

5. Kiki is a **fast** skier.

    Kiki skis ____**fast**____ .

B. Adjectives and Adverbs:

Directions: Write the adverb form of each adjective.

1. helpful - ____**helpfully**____

2. restless - ____**restlessly**____

3. childish - ____**childishly**____

4. grumpy - ____**grumpily**____

5. awkward - ____**awkwardly**____

412

Name_____ **ADVERBS**

Date_____ **Review**

A. Adjectives and Adverbs:

Directions: Write the adverb form of each adjective.

1. A captain gave a **polite** answer.

    She answered _____.

2. They are **generous** givers.

    They give _____ to a charity.

3. It is a **compact** dishwasher.

    It fits _____ between the sink and refrigerator.

4. The actor wore a **shabby** outfit.

    The actor was dressed _____.

5. Kiki is a **fast** skier.

    Kiki skis _____.

B. Adjectives and Adverbs:

Directions: Write the adverb form of each adjective.

1. helpful - _____

2. restless - _____

3. childish - _____

4. grumpy - _____

5. awkward - _____

413

C. Adjectives and Adverbs:

Directions: Write the adverb form of the boldfaced adjective.

1. **quiet** ~ The child is playing _____**quietly**_____ with her kitten.

2. **silent** ~ A horseman rode _____**silently**_____ into town.

3. **steady** ~ A young gymnast walked _____**steadily**_____ along a beam.

4. **illegal** ~ The person crossed the street _____**illegally**_____.

5. **recent** ~ We received an award _____**recently**_____.

6. **slight** ~ This package is _____**slightly**_____ damaged.

7. **noisy** ~ The group walked _____**noisily**_____ to the ballroom.

8. **slow** ~ You are building your model _____**slowly**_____.

9. **calm** ~ The ducks waddled _____**calmly**_____ toward the pond.

10. **bad** ~ I sprained my ankle _____**badly**_____.

11. **furious** ~ Their dog often barks _____**furiously**_____.

12. **complete** ~ Please fill out this form _____**completely**_____.

13. **brilliant** ~ The sun shone _____**brilliantly**_____.

14. **fast** ~ Several mustangs ran _____**fast**_____ toward the mountains.

15. **usual** ~ He is _____**usually**_____ very talkative in the morning.

414

C. Adjectives and Adverbs:

Directions: Write the adverb form of the boldfaced adjective.

1. **quiet** ~ The child is playing _____ with her kitten.

2. **silent** ~ A horseman rode _____ into town.

3. **steady** ~ A young gymnast walked _____ along
       a beam.

4. **illegal** ~ The person crossed the street _____.

5. **recent** ~ We received an award _____.

6. **slight** ~ This package is _____ damaged.

7. **noisy** ~ The group walked _____ to the ballroom.

8. **slow** ~ You are building your model _____.

9. **calm** ~ The ducks waddled _____ toward the pond.

10. **bad** ~ I sprained my ankle _____.

11. **furious** ~ Their dog often barks _____.

12. **complete** ~ Please fill out this form _____.

13. **brilliant** ~ The sun shone _____.

14. **fast** ~ Several mustangs ran _____ toward the
       mountains.

15. **usual** ~ He is _____ very talkative in the morning.

415

D. Adverbs Telling *When*:

Directions: Write the adverb that means *when*.

> *Helpful Note:*   An antonym is a word that means the opposite.
> A synonym means the same or nearly the same.

ANSWERS MAY VARY/REPRESENTATIVE ANSWERS:

1. an antonym for *sooner* - _____**later**_____

2. means the same as *every day* - _____**daily**_____

3. "It's now or _____**never**_____."

4. a word that means *this day* - _____**today**_____

5. a synonym for always - _____**forever**_____

E. Adverbs Telling *When*:

Directions: Write three adverbs telling *when* that will make sense in each
sentence.

1. I want to go _____**now**_____.

     _____**someday**_____.

     _____**tomorrow**_____.

2. That child _____**never**_____ takes a nap.

     _____**rarely**_____

     _____**sometimes**_____

3. Do you _____**ever**_____ visit your grandparents?

     _____**always**_____

     _____**frequently**_____

416

D. Adverbs Telling *When*:

Directions: Write the adverb that means *when*.

> *Helpful Note:*   An antonym is a word that means the opposite.
> A synonym means the same or nearly the same.

1. an antonym for *sooner* - _____

2. means the same as *every day* - _____

3. "It's now or _____."

4. a word that means *this day* - _____

5. a synonym for always - _____

E. Adverbs Telling *When*:

Directions: Write three adverbs telling *when* that will make sense in each
sentence.

1. I want to go _____.

    _____.

    _____.

2. That child _____ takes a nap.

    _____

    _____

3. Do you _____ visit your grandparents?

    _____

    _____

F. Adverbs Telling *When*:

Directions: Delete (cross out) any prepositional phrases. Underline the subject once and the verb or verb phrase twice. Circle any adverb that tells when.

1. I **never** <u>gargle</u> ~~with salt water~~.

2. A <u>man</u> ~~in a choir gown~~ **suddenly** <u>turned</u> ~~to his neighbor~~.

3. ~~During the World Series~~, her <u>uncle</u> <u>pitched</u> **late** ~~in the last game~~.

4. <u>One</u> ~~of the women at a swap meet~~ **always** <u>sells</u> plastic sunglasses.

5. <u>Jim</u> and his <u>sister</u> <u>deliver</u> newspapers **early**.

G. Adverbs Telling *Where*:

Directions: Write three adverbs that tell *where* to complete each sentence. (Try to use a different adverb in all three sentences.)

1. Come _____**here**_____.

    _____**over**_____.

    _____**in**_____.

2. The jogger runs _____**everywhere**_____.

    _____**by**_____.

    _____**downtown**_____.

3. Stay _____**nearby**_____.

    _____**away**_____.

    _____**there**_____.

418

F. Adverbs Telling *When*:

Directions: Delete (cross out) any prepositional phrases. Underline the subject once and the verb or verb phrase twice. Circle any adverb that tells *when*.

1. I never gargle with salt water.

2. A man in a choir gown suddenly turned to his neighbor.

3. During the World Series, her uncle pitched late in the last game.

4. One of the women at a swap meet always sells plastic sunglasses.

5. Jim and his sister deliver newspapers early.

G. Adverbs Telling *Where*:

Directions: Write three adverbs that tell *where* to complete each sentence. (Try to use a different adverb in all three sentences.)

1. Come   _____.

             _____.

             _____.

2. The jogger runs _____.

             _____.

             _____.

3. Stay   _____.

             _____.

             _____.

H. Adverbs Telling *How*:

Directions: Unscramble the adverb that tells *how*.

1.   Sit (p u) _____**up**_____.

2.   I don't feel (l e w l)_____**well**_____.

3.   The items on the belt at the grocery store moved (s y l w o l)

     _____**slowly**_____.

4.   One fan yelled (l d u o y l) _____**loudly**_____ for the losing

     team.

5.   The group worked (e r t h t o e g) _____**together**_____.

I. Adverbs Telling *How*:

Directions: Delete (cross out) any prepositional phrases. Underline the subject
              once and the verb or verb phrase twice. Circle any adverb that tells
              how.

1.   The <u>waiter</u> <u>greeted us</u> **courteously**.

2.   An ice-cream <u>vendor</u> **quickly** <u>handed</u> a cone ~~to the child~~.

3.   <u>Grandpa</u> <u>cooks</u> and <u>bakes</u> **well**.

4.   An air <u>controller</u> <u>watches</u> his instruments **closely**.

5.   <u>You</u> <u>must clean</u> your drums **thoroughly**.

6.   ~~Before her long trip~~, the <u>traveler</u> <u>studied</u> her map **carefully**.

420

H. Adverbs Telling *How*:

Directions: Unscramble the adverb that tells *how*.

1.   Sit (p u) _____.

2.   I don't feel (l e w l) _____.

3.   The items on the belt at the grocery store moved (s y l w o l)

     _____.

4.   One fan yelled (l d u o y l) _____ for the losing

     team.

5.   The group worked (e r t h t o e g) _____.

I. Adverbs Telling *How*:

Directions: Delete (cross out) any prepositional phrases. Underline the subject
              once and the verb or verb phrase twice. Circle any adverb that tells
              how.

1.   The waiter greeted us courteously.

2.   An ice-cream vendor quickly handed a cone to the child.

3.   Grandpa cooks and bakes well.

4.   An air controller watches his instruments closely.

5.   You must clean your drums thoroughly.

6.   Before her long trip, the traveler studied her map carefully.

421

J. Adverbs Telling _To What Extent_:

Directions: Circle any adverb that tells _to what extent_.
Adverbs telling _to what extent_ are boldfaced.

1.   You are **so** talented.

2.   Press the cookies **rather** lightly with your hand.

3.   The toddler is **not** walking steadily.

4.   This gumbo is **too** thick and **somewha**t over-cooked.

5.   You sound **quite** sure of your decision.

K.   Degrees:

Directions: Circle the correct degree of each adverb.
The correct answer is boldfaced.

1.   I didn't feel well yesterday, but today I feel (**better**, best).

2.   Of the four brothers, Stan visits his parents (more often, **most often**).

3.   The maid vacuumed (**faster**, fastest) on the second day of her new job.

4.   His fifth shirt fit into the luggage (more snugly, **most snugly**).

5.   Of the ten hot air balloons, the striped one climbed (higher, **highest**).

6.   The shortest triplet skips (more happily, **most happily**).

7.   In the law office, Luke types (more quickly, **most quickly**).

8.   Jill cleans the yard (**more completely**, most completely) than her sister.

J. Adverbs Telling *To What Extent*:

Directions: Circle any adverb that tells *to what extent*.

1. You are so talented.

2. Press the cookies rather lightly with your hand.

3. The toddler is not walking steadily.

4. This gumbo is too thick and somewhat over-cooked.

5. You sound quite sure of your decision.

K. Degrees:

Directions: Circle the correct degree of each adverb.

1. I didn't feel well yesterday, but today I feel (better, best).

2. Of the four brothers, Stan visits his parents (more often, most often).

3. The maid vacuumed (faster, fastest) on the second day of her new job.

4. His fifth shirt fit into the luggage (more snugly, most snugly).

5. Of the ten hot air balloons, the striped one climbed (higher, highest).

6. The shortest triplet skips (more happily, most happily).

7. In the law office, Luke types (more quickly, most quickly).

8. Jill cleans the yard (more completely, most completely) than her sister.

A.   Directions: Circle any adverbs.

1.   I do **not** wash windows well.

2.   His little brother hit the ball **hard today**.

3.   Trina leaves her office **early** on Mondays.

4.   They **seldom** work **together** on a project.

5.   Before the storm, we nailed boards **very securely** over our windows.

B.   Directions: Circle the correct word.

1.   My cousin doesn't always clean his room (good, **well**).

2.   The passenger asked the taxi driver to drive (slow, **slowly**).

3.   I like to sing (loud, **loudly**) in the shower.

4.   Stop acting so (weird, **weirdly**).

C.   Directions: Circle the correct degree of adverb.

1.   This new motor runs (**more smoothly**, most smoothly) than the old one.

2.   Of the triplets, Emma dances (more beautifully, **most beautifully**).

3.   The doctor answered the patient's second question (**more calmly**, most calmly).

4.   That clerk responds (more helpfully, **most helpfully**) of all the store's employees.

5.   A rodeo rider performed (more skillfully, **most skillfully**) during the last of the four events.

Name_____   **ADVERBS**

Date_____   **Test**

A. Directions: Circle any adverbs.

1. I do not wash windows well.

2. His little brother hit the ball hard today.

3. Trina leaves her office early on Mondays.

4. They seldom work together on a project.

5. Before the storm, we nailed boards very securely over our windows.

B. Directions: Circle the correct word.

1. My cousin doesn't always clean his room (good, well).

2. The passenger asked the taxi driver to drive (slow, slowly).

3. I like to sing (loud, loudly) in the shower.

4. Stop acting so (weird, weirdly).

C.   Directions: Circle the correct degree of adverb.

1. This new motor runs (more smoothly, most smoothly) than the old one.

2. Of the triplets, Emma dances (more beautifully, most beautifully).

3. The doctor answered the patient's second question (more calmly, most calmly).

4. That clerk responds (more helpfully, most helpfully) of all the store's employees.

5. A rodeo rider performed (more skillfully, most skillfully) during the last of the four events.

425

<u>**NOTE: This review is lengthy; you may want to complete it over a few days.**</u>

A. **Prepositions and Object of the Preposition:**
    Directions: Cross out any prepositional phrases. Write **O.P.** above any
                          object of the preposition.

                                       O.P.   **O.P.**

1.   The <u>teenager</u> ~~in the red shirt~~ <u>works</u> ~~at a bookstore~~.

ॐॐॐॐॐॐॐॐॐॐॐॐॐ

B. **Subject/Verb:**
    Directions: Cross out any prepositional phrases. Underline the subject once
                          and the verb twice.

1.   ~~After shopping during the morning,~~ <u>I</u> <u>ate</u> a salad.

2.   The <u>mayor</u> <u>walked</u> ~~toward the town square~~ ~~with a group of shop owners~~.

ॐॐॐॐॐॐॐॐॐॐॐॐॐ

C. **Compound Subjects and Verbs:**
    Directions: Cross out any prepositional phrases. Underline the subject once
                          and the verb or verb phrase twice.

1.   <u>Sally</u> <u>asked</u> ~~for a glass of water~~ and <u>thanked</u> the waiter.

2.   Their pet <u>hamster</u> <u>ate</u>, <u>drank</u> some water, and <u>ran</u> ~~in circles~~ ~~around its cage~~.

ॐॐॐॐॐॐॐॐॐॐॐॐॐ

D. **Subject-Verb Agreement:**
    Directions: Delete any prepositional phrases. Underline the subject once.
                          Underline the verb/verb phrase that agrees with the subject twice.

1.   His <u>cousins</u> (<u>live</u>, lives) ~~near the Great Lakes~~.

2.   The <u>girl</u> ~~in the white tennis shoes~~ (<u>was</u>, were) the leader.

3.   <u>She</u> (take, <u>takes</u>) a trolley downtown.

ॐॐॐॐॐॐॐॐॐॐॐॐॐ

E. **Contractions:**
    Directions: Write the contraction.

1. cannot - __**can't**__   3. we have - __**we've**__   5. they are - __**they're**__

2. will not - __**won't**__   4. I have - __**I've**__   6. what is - __**what's**__

426

Name_____   **Cumulative Review**

Date_____   **At the End of the Adverb Unit**

<u>**NOTE: This review is lengthy; you may want to complete it over a few days.**</u>

A. **Prepositions and Object of the Preposition:**

Directions: Cross out any prepositional phrases. Write **<u>O.P.</u>** above any object of the preposition.

1.   The teenager in the red shirt works at a bookstore.

 ৵৵৵৵৵৵৵৵৵৵৵৵

B. **Subject/Verb:**

Directions: Cross out any prepositional phrases. Underline the subject once and the verb twice.

1.   After shopping during the morning, I ate a salad.

2.   The mayor walked toward the town square with a group of shop owners.

 ৵৵৵৵৵৵৵৵৵৵৵৵

C. **Compound Subjects and Verbs:**

Directions: Cross out any prepositional phrases. Underline the subject once and the verb or verb phrase twice.

1.   Sally asked for a glass of water and thanked the waiter.

2.   Their pet hamster ate, drank some water, and ran in circles around its cage.

 ৵৵৵৵৵৵৵৵৵৵৵৵

D. **Subject-Verb Agreement:**

Directions: Delete any prepositional phrases. Underline the subject once. Underline the verb/verb phrase that agrees with the subject twice.

1.   His cousins (live, lives) near the Great Lakes.

2.   The girl in the white tennis shoes (was, were) the leader.

3.   She (take, takes) a trolley downtown.

 ৵৵৵৵৵৵৵৵৵৵৵৵

E. **Contractions:**

Directions: Write the contraction.

1. cannot - _____   3. we have - _____   5. they are - _____

2. will not - _____   4. I have - _____   6. what is - _____

F. **You're/Your, It's/Its, and They're/Their/There:**
   Directions: Circle the correct word.

1. (There, **Their**, They're) dog lost (it's, **its**) collar.

2. Do you know (you're, **your**) new address?

3. I know that (**you're**, your) going if (there, their, **they're**) buying the ticket.

   ৯৯৯৯৯৯৯৯৯৯৯৯৯

G. **Auxiliary (Helping) Verbs:**
   Directions: Write the 23 helping verbs.

1. *D's*   a. ____**do**____   b. ____**does**____   c. ____**did**____

2. *H's*   a. ____**has**____   b. ____**have**____   c. ____**had**____

3. *M's*   a. ____**may**____   b. ____**might**____   c. ____**must**____

4. *Ould's* a. ____**could**____   b. ____**should**____   c. ____**would**____

5. *To be:* a. __**is**__   c. __**are**__   e. __**were**__   g. __**being**__

            b. __**am**__   d. __**was**__   f. __**be**__   h. __**been**__

6. *Others:* a. __**can**__   b. __**shall**__   c. __**will**__

   ৯৯৯৯৯৯৯৯৯৯৯৯৯

H. **Irregular Verbs:**
   Directions: Underline the subject once and the correct verb phrase twice.

1. I had (taken, took) extra socks along.

2. Chan should have (drove, driven).

3. You must have (ran, run) fast.

4. Juan could have (went, gone) home.

5. Dad may have (drank, drunk) the milk.

6. Has she (swum, swam) the English Channel?

428

F. **You're/Your, It's/Its, and They're/Their/There:**
   Directions: Circle the correct word.

1. (There, Their, They're) dog lost (it's, its) collar.

2. Do you know (you're, your) new address?

3. I know that (you're, your) going if (there, their, they're) buying the ticket.
   ❧❧❧❧❧❧❧❧❧❧❧❧

G. **Auxiliary (Helping) Verbs:**
   Directions: Write the 23 helping verbs.

1. *D's*   a. _____   b. _____   c. _____

2. *H's*   a. _____   b. _____   c. _____

3. *M's*   a. _____   b. _____   c. _____

4. *Ould's* a. _____   b. _____   c. _____

5. *To be:* a. _____   c. _____   e. _____   g. _____

             b. _____   d. _____   f. _____   h. _____

6. *Others:* a. _____   b. _____   c. _____
   ❧❧❧❧❧❧❧❧❧❧❧❧

H. **Irregular Verbs:**
   Directions: Underline the subject once and the correct verb phrase twice.

1. I had (taken, took) extra socks along.

2. Chan should have (drove, driven).

3. You must have (ran, run) fast.

4. Juan could have (went, gone) home.

5. Dad may have (drank, drunk) the milk.

6. Has she (swum, swam) the English Channel?

Name_____   **Cumulative Review**

WORKBOOK PAGE 196

Date_____   **At the End of the Adverb Unit**

I. Subjects, Verbs, and Direct Objects:
Directions: Cross out any prepositional phrases. Underline the subject once and the verb/verb phrase twice. Label any direct object – **D.O.**

1. A <u>child</u> ~~without a partner~~ ~~for the game~~ <u><u>grabbed</u></u> my hand.

2. <u><u>Do</u></u> <u>you</u> <u>make</u> your campsite ~~by a stream~~?

෴෴෴෴෴෴෴෴෴෴෴෴෴

J. Sit/Set, Lie/Lay, and Rise/Raise:
Directions: Delete any prepositional phrases. Underline the subject once and the verb/verb phrase twice. Label any direct object – **D.O.**

                                D.O.

1. <u>Lily</u> (sits, <u>sets</u>) her books ~~under this shelf.~~   3. <u>They</u> (<u>rise</u>, raise) early.

2. Your <u>pants</u> are (<u>lying</u>, laying) here.   4. <u>(You)</u> (<u>Lie</u>, Lay) still.

෴෴෴෴෴෴෴෴෴෴෴෴෴

K. Tenses:
Directions: Underline the subject once and the verb or verb phrase twice. Write the tense (*present, past,* or *future*) in the blank.

1. _____**future**_____   <u>I</u> <u><u>shall bring</u></u> my horse.

2. _____**present**_____   <u>Sammy</u> <u>collects</u> paperweights.

3. _____**past**_____   A <u>hostess</u> <u>greeted</u> her guests.

෴෴෴෴෴෴෴෴෴෴෴෴෴

L. Linking Verbs:
Directions: Write the 20 linking verbs.

1. (to) **look**   5. (to) **appear**   9. (to) **seem**   13. **is**   17. **were**

2. (to) **feel**   6. (to) **become** 10. (to) **stay**   14. **am**   18. **be**

3. (to) **taste**   7. (to) **grow**   11. (to) **sound** 15. **are** 19. **being**

4. (to) **smell**   8. (to) **remain** 12. (to) **be**   16. **was** 20. **been**

430

Name_____   **Cumulative Review**

Date_____   **At the End of the Adverb Unit**

I. **Subjects, Verbs, and Direct Objects:**
   Directions: Cross out any prepositional phrases. Underline the subject once
              and the verb/verb phrase twice. Label any direct object – **D.O.**

1. A child without a partner for the game grabbed my hand.

2. Do you make your campsite by a stream?

☙☙☙☙☙☙☙☙☙☙☙☙☙

J. **Sit/Set, Lie/Lay, and Rise/Raise:**
   Directions: Delete any prepositional phrases. Underline the subject once
              and the verb/verb phrase twice. Label any direct object – **D.O.**

1. Lily (sits, sets) her books under this shelf.   3. They (rise, raise) early.

2. Your pants are (lying, laying) here.   4. (Lie, Lay) still.

☙☙☙☙☙☙☙☙☙☙☙☙☙

K. **Tenses:**
   Directions: Underline the subject once and the verb or verb phrase
              twice. Write the tense (*present, past,* or *future*) in the blank.

1. _____ I shall bring my horse.

2. _____ Sammy collects paperweights.

3. _____ A hostess greeted her guests.

☙☙☙☙☙☙☙☙☙☙☙☙☙

L. **Linking Verbs:**
   Directions: Write the 20 linking verbs.

1. (to) _l____   5. (to) _a____   9. (to) _s____   13. _i__   17. _w__

2. (to) _f____   6. (to) _b____   10. (to) _s____   14. _a__   18. _b__

3. (to) _t____   7. (to) _g____   11. (to) _s____   15. _a__   19. _b__

4. (to) _s____   8. (to) _r____   12. (to) _b____   16. _w__   20. _b__

M. **Action Verb or Linking Verb?:**
    Directions: Place **X** if the verb is linking.

1. __**X**__   The breeze **feels** good.   3. _____   Clover **grew** in the field.

2. _____   I **feel** sandpaper for texture.   4. __**X**__   Her face **grew** red.

છે છે છે છે છે છે છે છે છે છે છે છે

N. **Infinitives: ANSWERS MAY VARY/REPRESENTATIVE ANSWERS:**
1. Write an infinitive: _____**to polish**_____

છે છે છે છે છે છે છે છે છે છે છે છે

O. **Transitive and Intransitive Verbs:**
    Directions: Underline the subject once and the verb or verb phrase twice.
                   Label any direct object - **D.O.** Write **T** if the verb is transitive;
                   write **I** if the verb is intransitive.
          Remember: A transitive verb will have a direct object.
                   D.O.T. > Direct Object = Transitive
                   D.O.   **D.O.**
1. __**T**__   She soaked her feet.   3. __**T**__   We installed a deadbolt.
                   D.O.
2. __**T**__   Bob closed the blinds.   4. __**I**__   These ladybugs are big.

છે છે છે છે છે છે છે છે છે છે છે છે

P. **Abstract and Concrete Nouns:**
    Directions: Place a ✓ if the noun is abstract.
1. ____   calendar   3. __✓__   glee

2. ____   worm   4. __✓__   dizziness

છે છે છે છે છે છે છે છે છે છે છે છે

Q. **Singular and Plural Nouns:**
    Directions: Write the correct spelling of each plural noun.

1. facility - ____**facilities**____   6. channel - ____**channels**____

2. service - ____**services**____   7. convoy - ____**convoys**____

3. hello - ____**hellos**____   8. child - ____**children**____

4. bonus - ____**bonuses**____   9. arch - ____**arches**____

5. belief - ____**beliefs**____   10. series - ____**series**____

432

M. Action Verb or Linking Verb?:
   Directions: Place **X** if the verb is linking.

1. _____ The breeze **feels** good.   3. _____ Clover **grew** in the field.

2. _____ I **feel** sandpaper for texture.   4. _____ Her face **grew** red.

ᎧᎧᎧᎧᎧᎧᎧᎧᎧᎧᎧᎧᎧ

N. Infinitives:
1. Write an infinitive: _____

ᎧᎧᎧᎧᎧᎧᎧᎧᎧᎧᎧᎧᎧ

O. Transitive and Intransitive Verbs:
   Directions: Underline the subject once and the verb or verb phrase twice.
           Label any direct object - **D.O.** Write **T** if the verb is transitive;
           write **I** if the verb is intransitive.
   Remember: A transitive verb will have a direct object.
           D.O.T. > Direct **O**bject = **T**ransitive

1. _____ She soaked her feet.   3. _____ We installed a deadbolt.

2. _____ Bob closed the blinds.   4. _____ These ladybugs are big.

ᎧᎧᎧᎧᎧᎧᎧᎧᎧᎧᎧᎧᎧ

P. Abstract and Concrete Nouns:
   Directions: Place a ✓ if the noun is abstract.
1. ___ calendar   3. ___ glee

2. ___ worm   4. ___ dizziness

ᎧᎧᎧᎧᎧᎧᎧᎧᎧᎧᎧᎧᎧ

Q. Singular and Plural Nouns:
   Directions: Write the correct spelling of each plural noun.

1. facility - _____   6. channel - _____

2. service - _____   7. convoy - _____

3. hello - _____   8. child - _____

4. bonus - _____   9. arch - _____

5. belief - _____   10. series - _____

433

R. **Possessive Nouns:**
   Directions: Write the possessive in each blank.

1. moss on that tree - _____**(that) tree's moss**_____

2. eggs of penguins - _____**penguins' eggs**_____

3. lace on a dress - _____**dress's lace**_____

   ༚༚༚༚༚༚༚༚༚༚༚༚

S. **Nouns Used as Subjects, Direct Objects, and Indirect Objects:**
   Directions: Label any subject (**S.**), direct object (**D.O.**), and indirect object (**I.O.**).
      S.   **D.O.**
1. Levi lost his baseball card.
      S.   **I.O.**   **D.O.**
2. Kim handed Jasmine a ticket.

   ༚༚༚༚༚༚༚༚༚༚༚༚

T. **Predicate Nominatives:**
   Directions: Underline the subject once and the verb twice. Label a
                   predicate nominative – **P.N.** Write the inverted form in the blank.
   **Remember: A predicate nominative occurs <u>after</u> a linking verb and means the same as
              the subject.**
                    P.N.
1. My <u>father</u> <u><u>was</u></u> the manager <s>of that hockey team</s>.

   _____**The manager was my father.**_____

              P.N.
2. <u>Ginger</u> <u><u>is</u></u> one spice <s>with a yellowish color</s>.

   _____**Ginger is one spice.**_____

   ༚༚༚༚༚༚༚༚༚༚༚༚

U. **Identifying Nouns:**
   Directions: Circle any nouns.
   Remember: Determiners will help you to find some nouns.

1. A **bag** of potato **chips** lay on their kitchen **sink**.

2. **John's* friend** gave his **cousin** several golf **balls** and an old **club**.
<u>*Some consider this usage as an adjective; you may not want to count it incorrect.</u>
434

R. **Possessive Nouns:**
    Directions: Write the possessive in each blank.

1. moss on that tree - _____

2. eggs of penguins - _____

3. lace on a dress - _____
    ᕁᕁᕁᕁᕁᕁᕁᕁᕁᕁᕁᕁ

S. **Nouns Used as Subjects, Direct Objects, and Indirect Objects:**
    Directions: Label any subject (**S.**), direct object (**D.O.**), and indirect object (**I.O.**).

1. Levi lost his baseball card.

2. Kim handed Jasmine a ticket.
    ᕁᕁᕁᕁᕁᕁᕁᕁᕁᕁᕁᕁ

T. **Predicate Nominatives:**
    Directions: Underline the subject once and the verb twice. Label a
                   predicate nominative – **P.N.** Write the inverted form in the blank.
    **Remember: A predicate nominative occurs <u>after</u> a linking verb and means the same as
                   the subject.**

1. My father was the manager of that hockey team.

    _____

2. Ginger is one spice with a yellowish color.

    _____
    ᕁᕁᕁᕁᕁᕁᕁᕁᕁᕁᕁᕁ

U. **Identifying Nouns:**
    Directions: Circle any nouns.
    Remember: Determiners will help you to find some nouns.

1. A bag of potato chips lay on their kitchen sink.

2. John's friend gave his cousin several golf balls and an old club.

V. **Descriptive Adjectives:** <u>ANSWERS MAY VARY/REPRESENTATIVE ANSWERS:</u>
Directions: Write a descriptive adjective in each blank. Draw an arrow from
the descriptive adjective to the noun it modifies (goes over to).

1. That _____**quilted**_____ blanket needs to be washed.

2. Is _____**raw**_____ food delicious?

3. Loni's family used a ____**shopping**____ cart to carry their packages.
🐎🐎🐎🐎🐎🐎🐎🐎🐎🐎🐎🐎🐎

W. **Limiting (Determining) Adjectives:**

🗝 **Articles: a, an, the**
🗝 **Demonstratives: this, that, these, those**
🗝 **Possessive Pronouns: my, his, her, your, its, our, their, whose**
🗝 **Numbers:** Example: *fifty-two* cards
🗝 **Indefinites: any, few, no, many, most, several, some**
🗝 **Possessive Nouns:** Example: a *pig's* snout

Directions: Write an appropriate limiting adjective from each category.

1. Article – __**The**__ drink is cold.   4. Possessive pronouns – __**My**__ drink is cold.

2. Demonstratives – __**These**__ drinks are cold. 5. Possessive nouns – __**Sid's**__ drink is cold.

3. Numbers – __**Eight**__ drinks are cold.   6. Indefinites – __**Some**__ drinks are cold.
🐎🐎🐎🐎🐎🐎🐎🐎🐎🐎🐎🐎🐎

X. **Limiting Adjectives:**
**Remember: Some words can be limiting adjectives if they modify a noun. That
same word will not be a limiting adjective if it stands alone.**
Examples: I need **one** dollar   Adjective – *one* dollar

May I have ***one***?   *One* what? We don't know. *One* is not an
adjective.

Directions: Place a ✓ in the blank if the boldfaced word is a limiting (determining)
adjective. If the word is an adjective, write the boldfaced word and
the noun that it modifies (goes over to) in the wide blank.

1. ✓ **Many** castles were built in 1500. _____**many castles**_____

2. ✓ Do you want **this** balloon? _____**this balloon**_____

3. ___ Do you want **this**? _____

V. **Descriptive Adjectives:**

Directions: Write a descriptive adjective in each blank. Draw an arrow from
the descriptive adjective to the noun it modifies (goes over to).

1.   That _____ blanket needs to be washed.

2.   Is _____ food delicious?

3.   Loni's family used a _____ cart to carry their packages.

ॐॐॐॐॐॐॐॐॐॐॐॐॐ

W. **Limiting (Determining) Adjectives:**

- **Articles: a, an, the**
- **Demonstratives: this, that, these, those**
- **Possessive Pronouns: my, his, her, your, its, our, their, whose**
- **Numbers:** Example: *fifty-two* cards
- **Indefinites: any, few, no, many, most, several, some**
- **Possessive Nouns:** Example: a *pig's* snout

Directions: Write an appropriate limiting adjective from each category.

1. **Article** – _____ drink is cold.   4. **Possessive pronouns** – _____ drink is cold.

2. **Demonstratives** – _____ drinks are cold.   5. **Possessive nouns** – _____ drink is cold.

3. **Numbers** – _____ drinks are cold.   6. **Indefinites** – _____ drinks are cold.

ॐॐॐॐॐॐॐॐॐॐॐॐॐ

X. **Limiting Adjectives:**

**Remember: Some words can be limiting adjectives if they modify a noun. That
same word will not be a limiting adjective if it stands alone.**

Examples: I need **one** dollar   Adjective – *one* dollar

May I have **one**?   *One* what? We don't know. *One* is not an
adjective.

Directions: Place a ✓ in the blank if the boldfaced word is a limiting (determining)
adjective. If the word is an adjective, write the boldfaced word and
the noun that it modifies (goes over to) in the wide blank.

1.   __   **Many** castles were built in 1500. _____

2.   __   Do you want **this** balloon? _____

3.   __   Do you want **this**? _____

Y. Proper Adjectives: <u>**Modified words are italicized.**</u>
   A proper adjective is a descriptive word based on a proper noun.

          Mexico (noun)   the **M**exican hat *dance*

Directions: Circle any proper adjective. Draw an arrow to the word it modifies.

1. I like your **Canadian** *accent.*   3. Do you like **Siamese** *cats?*

2. The **French** *perfume* smells good.   4. Jo climbed a **Rocky Mountain** *slope.*

Z. Predicate Adjectives:
   Sometimes an adjective occurs after the verb but describes the subject.
   This is called a predicate adjective.
   Directions: Cross out any prepositional phrases. Underline the subject once
            and the verb twice. Label the predicate adjective – **P.A.**

                      P.A.   **P.A.**
1. Our watering <u>can</u> <u>looks</u> new.   3. This <u>soda</u> <u>tastes</u> flat.
               P.A.   **P.A.**   **P.A.**
2. His <u>hat</u> <u>is</u> wide and floppy.   4. The table's <u>edge</u> <u>seems</u> sharp.

AA. Degrees of Adjectives:
   Directions: Circle the correct answer.

1. Your voice is (**deeper**, deepest) than mine.

2. My scalp is (**more tender**, tenderer) than the skin on my hands.

3. Mocha is the (more active, **most active**) kitten of the entire litter.

4. Thomas Jefferson was one of the (more educated, **most educated**)
   people in the colonies.

BB. Identifying Adjectives:
   Directions: Circle any adjectives.

1. Dad made **two** pitchers of **fresh**, **sweet** lemonade for **the afternoon** picnic.

2. Val asked **a few** questions about **large**, **fast-running** ostriches.

438

Y. **Proper Adjectives:**
   A proper adjective is a descriptive word based on a proper noun.

   Mexico (noun)   the **M**exican hat *dance*

Directions: Circle any proper adjective. Draw an arrow to the word it modifies.

1. I like your Canadian accent.   3. Do you like Siamese cats?

2. The French perfume smells good.   4. Jo climbed a Rocky Mountain slope.

ॐ ॐ ॐ ॐ ॐ ॐ ॐ ॐ ॐ ॐ ॐ ॐ

Z. **Predicate Adjectives:**
   Sometimes an adjective occurs after the verb but describes the subject.
   This is called a predicate adjective.
   Directions: Cross out any prepositional phrases. Underline the subject once
   and the verb twice. Label the predicate adjective – **P.A.**

1. Our watering can looks new.   3. This soda tastes flat.

2. His hat is wide and floppy.   4. The table's edge seems sharp.

ॐ ॐ ॐ ॐ ॐ ॐ ॐ ॐ ॐ ॐ ॐ ॐ

AA. **Degrees of Adjectives:**
   Directions: Circle the correct answer.

1. Your voice is (deeper, deepest) than mine.

2. My scalp is (more tender, tenderer) than the skin on my hands.

3. Mocha is the (more active, most active) kitten of the entire litter.

4. Thomas Jefferson was one of the (more educated, most educated)
   people in the colonies.

ॐ ॐ ॐ ॐ ॐ ॐ ॐ ॐ ॐ ॐ ॐ ॐ

BB. **Identifying Adjectives:**
   Directions: Circle any adjectives.

1. Dad made two pitchers of fresh, sweet lemonade for the afternoon picnic.

2. Val asked a few questions about large, fast-running ostriches.

439

A. Directions: Cross out any prepositional phrases. Underline the subject once
and the verb or verb phrase twice.

1. A <u>tree</u> ~~along the river~~ <u><u>has fallen</u></u> ~~against a wooden bridge~~.

2. ~~After his bath~~, the <u>baby</u> <u><u>was bundled</u></u> and gently <u><u>dried</u></u>.

3. <u>Everyone</u> ~~except Todd and Lani~~ <u><u>stood</u></u> ~~by a fire pit~~.

ॐॐॐॐॐॐॐॐॐॐॐॐ

B. Directions: Cross out any prepositional phrases. Underline the subject once
and the verb/verb phrase twice. Label any direct object – **D.O.** and
any indirect object – **I.O.** Label any object of the preposition – **O.P.**

                D.O.   **O.P.**

1. Their <u>sister</u> <u><u>ordered</u></u> a video ~~about white-water rafting~~.

               I.O.   **D.O.**   **O.P.**

2. <u><u>Have</u></u> <u>Nikki</u> and <u>he</u> <u><u>sold</u></u> Mrs. Lee logs ~~for her fireplace~~?

ॐॐॐॐॐॐॐॐॐॐॐॐ

C. Directions: Delete any prepositional phrases. Underline the subject once.
Underline the verb/verb phrase that agrees with the subject twice.

1. <u>Jacy</u> and <u>Ben</u> (hauls, <u><u>haul</u></u>) furniture ~~for a moving company~~.

2. ~~After breakfast~~, their <u>mom</u> (<u><u>answers</u></u>, answer) her email.

3. Those <u>cranes</u> (<u><u>stay</u></u>, stays) ~~near the edge of a fish pond~~.

4. No <u>one</u> ~~in the hotel restaurants~~ (<u><u>speaks</u></u>, speak) Spanish.

ॐॐॐॐॐॐॐॐॐॐॐॐ

D. Directions: Write the contraction.

1. cannot - __**can't**__   5. are not - __**aren't**__   9. I would - __**I'd**__

2. will not - __**won't**__   6. I have - __**I've**__   10. she is - __**she's**__

3. here is - __**here's**__   7. we will - __**we'll**__   11. they are - __**they're**__

4. was not - __**wasn't**__   8. is not - __**isn't**__   12. I am - __**I'm**__

A. Directions: Cross out any prepositional phrases. Underline the subject once
       and the verb or verb phrase twice.

1. A tree along the river has fallen against a wooden bridge.

2. After his bath, the baby was bundled and gently dried.

3. Everyone except Todd and Lani stood by a firepit.

🐎🐎🐎🐎🐎🐎🐎🐎🐎🐎🐎

B. Directions: Cross out any prepositional phrases. Underline the subject once
       and the verb/verb phrase twice. Label any direct object – **D.O.** and
       any indirect object – **I.O.** Label any object of the preposition – **O.P.**

1. Their sister ordered a video about white-water rafting.

2. Have Nikki and he sold Mrs. Lee logs for her fireplace?

🐎🐎🐎🐎🐎🐎🐎🐎🐎🐎🐎

C. Directions: Delete any prepositional phrases. Underline the subject once.
       Underline the verb/verb phrase that agrees with the subject twice.

1. Jacy and Ben (hauls, haul) furniture for a moving company.

2. After breakfast, their mom (answers, answer) her email.

3. Those cranes (stay, stays) near the edge of a fish pond.

4. No one in the hotel restaurants (speaks, speak) Spanish.

🐎🐎🐎🐎🐎🐎🐎🐎🐎🐎🐎

D. Directions: Write the contraction.

1. cannot - _____   5. are not - _____   9. I would - _____

2. will not - _____   6. I have - _____   10. she is - _____

3. here is - _____   7. we will - _____   11. they are - _____

4. was not - _____   8. is not - _____   12. I am - _____

E. Directions: Circle the correct word.

1. (They're, **Their**, There) bird has lost some of (it's, **its**) tail feathers.

2. I think that (**they're**, their, there) going to visit (you're, **your**) aunt.

3. It seems odd that (**it's**, its) raining (they're, their, **there**) at this time of year.

❧ ❧ ❧ ❧ ❧ ❧ ❧ ❧ ❧ ❧ ❧ ❧

F. Directions: Underline the subject once and the correct verb phrase twice.

1. I had (went, gone) early.   5. Has he (brung, brought) his hat?

2. Where have you (rode, ridden)?   6. Kannan has (threw, thrown) a ball.

3. A comet had been (saw, seen).   7. I should have (begun, began) earlier.

4. Snow must have (fell, fallen).   8. Have you (given, gave) blood?

❧ ❧ ❧ ❧ ❧ ❧ ❧ ❧ ❧ ❧ ❧ ❧

G. Directions: Delete any prepositional phrases. Underline the subject once and the verb/verb phrase twice.

1. Heat (rises, raises).   4. Dad (laid, lay) the mail by his glasses.

2. A box was (laying, lying) nearby. 5. Lani (set, sat) her alarm.

3. He (set, sat) in the back row.   6. I (lay, laid) on a cot for ten minutes.

❧ ❧ ❧ ❧ ❧ ❧ ❧ ❧ ❧ ❧ ❧ ❧

H. Directions: Underline the subject once and the verb or verb phrase twice. Write the tense (*present, past,* or *future*) in the blank.

1. _____**past**_____   Barbie sketched a map.

2. _____**present**_____   Several streams begin here.

3. _____**future**_____   Jenny will shower soon.

442

E. Directions: Circle the correct word.

1. (They're, Their, There) bird has lost some of (it's, its) tail feathers.

2. I think that (they're, their, there) going to visit (you're, your) aunt.

3. It seems odd that (it's, its) raining (they're, their, there) at this time of year.

જ⁊જ⁊જ⁊જ⁊જ⁊જ⁊જ⁊જ⁊જ⁊જ⁊જ⁊

F. Directions: Underline the subject once and the correct verb phrase twice.

1. I had (went, gone) early.   5. Has he (brung, brought) his hat?

2. Where have you (rode, ridden)?   6. Kannan has (threw, thrown) a ball.

3. A comet had been (saw, seen).   7. I should have (begun, began) earlier.

4. Snow must have (fell, fallen).   8. Have you (given, gave) blood?

જ⁊જ⁊જ⁊જ⁊જ⁊જ⁊જ⁊જ⁊જ⁊જ⁊જ⁊

G. Directions: Delete any prepositional phrases. Underline the subject once and the verb/verb phrase twice.

1. Heat (rises, raises).   4. Dad (laid, lay) the mail by his glasses.

2. A box was (laying, lying) nearby.   5. Lani (set, sat) her alarm.

3. He (set, sat) in the back row.   6. I (lay, laid) on a cot for ten minutes.

જ⁊જ⁊જ⁊જ⁊જ⁊જ⁊જ⁊જ⁊જ⁊જ⁊જ⁊

H. Directions: Underline the subject once and the verb or verb phrase twice. Write the tense (*present, past,* or *future*) in the blank.

1. _____ Barbie sketched a map.

2. _____ Several streams begin here.

3. _____ Jenny will shower soon.

443

I. Directions: Place an **X** if the noun is concrete.

1. **X** CHILI   4. _____ POWER   7. **X** CHALK

2. **X** SOIL   5. **X** JAW   8. _____ IDEA

3. _____ HOPE   6. _____ DOUBT   9. **X** FARM

જાજાજાજાજાજાજાજાજાજાજા

J. Directions: Place a O if the noun is proper.

1. _____ GENERAL   4. _____ ALBUM   7. _O_ LAS VEGAS

2. _____ MASK   5. _O_ THANKSGIVING   8. _____ KING

3. _O_ ILLINOIS   6. _O_ SEA OF CORTEZ   9. _O_ BABE RUTH

જાજાજાજાજાજાજાજાજાજાજા

K. Directions: Write the correct spelling of each plural noun.

1. faculty - **faculties**   6. organ - **organs**

2. globe - **globes**   7. birth - **births**

3. halo - **halos**   8. foot - **feet**

4. marsh - **marshes**   9. press - **presses**

5. cliff - **cliffs**   10. deer - **deer**

જાજાજાજાજાજાજાજાજાજાજા

L. Directions: Write the possessive form in each blank.

1. visitors to a dude ranch - **a dude ranch's visitors**

2. meeting attended by more than one woman - **women's meeting**

3. buses shared by more than one city - **cities' buses**

4. a basketball belonging to two girls - **girls' basketball**

444

I. Directions: Place an **X** if the noun is concrete.

1. ____ CHILI   4. ____ POWER   7. ____ CHALK

2. ____ SOIL   5. ____ JAW   8. ____ IDEA

3. ____ HOPE   6. ____ DOUBT   9. ____ FARM

తతతతతతతతతతతత

J. Directions: Place a ◯ if the noun is proper.

1. ____ GENERAL   4. ____ ALBUM   7. ____ LAS VEGAS

2. ____ MASK   5. ____ THANKSGIVING   8. ____ KING

3. ____ ILLINOIS   6. ____ SEA OF CORTEZ 9. ____ BABE RUTH

తతతతతతతతతతతత

K. Directions: Write the correct spelling of each plural noun.

1. faculty - _____   6. organ - _____

2. globe - _____   7. birth - _____

3. halo - _____   8. foot - _____

4. marsh - _____   9. press - _____

5. cliff - _____   10. deer - _____

తతతతతతతతతతతత

L. Directions: Write the possessive form in each blank.

1. visitors to a dude ranch - _____

2. meeting attended by more than one woman - _____

3. buses shared by more than one city - _____

4. a basketball belonging to two girls - _____

445

M. Directions: Cross out any prepositional phrases. Underline the subject once and the verb twice. Label a predicate nominative – **P.N.** Label a predicate adjective – **P.A.**

                         P.A.
1. Her charm <u>bracelet</u> <u><u>looks</u></u> silver.
               P.N.
2. A <u>laser</u> <u><u>is</u></u> a device ~~with strong light~~.
                   P.N.
3. Their <u>parents</u> <u><u>were</u></u> owners ~~of an old mine~~.

                      ≈≈≈≈≈≈≈≈≈≈≈≈≈

N. Directions: Circle any nouns.
Nouns are boldfaced.
1. **Grammy** pulled several **onions** from the third **row** of her **garden**.

2. An orange **sign** by that old **bridge** warned **people** about **danger**.

                      ≈≈≈≈≈≈≈≈≈≈≈≈≈

O. Directions: Circle any adjectives.

1. I need **four pie** crusts and **fresh red** berries to make **an unusual** dessert.

2. **A few little, frisky** puppies played in **the Brown's* large** yard.
*Some perceive this as a possessive adjective; you may not want to mark it incorrect.

                      ≈≈≈≈≈≈≈≈≈≈≈≈≈

P. Directions: Circle any proper adjective. Box any predicate adjective.
Proper adjectives are boldfaced. Predicate adjectives are boldfaced and italicized.
1. **Belgian** waffles are ***tasty***.

2. Is a grizzly a **North American** bear?

Q. Directions: Write the correct degree of adjective.

1. That elephant is the (large) _____**largest**_____ animal in our zoo.

2. These red lights are (shiny) _____**shinier**_____ than the green ones.

3. The winds during the second storm were (forceful) _____**more forceful**_____ than during the first.

4. She is the (serious) _____**most serious**_____ triplet.
446

M. Directions: Cross out any prepositional phrases. Underline the subject once
                  and the verb twice. Label a predicate nominative – **P.N.** Label a
                  predicate adjective – **P.A.**

1. Her charm bracelet looks silver.

2. A laser is a device with strong light.

3. Their parents were owners of an old mine.

めめめめめめめめめめめめ

N. Directions: Circle any nouns.

1. Grammy pulled several onions from the third row of her garden.

2. An orange sign by that old bridge warned people about danger.

めめめめめめめめめめめめ

O. Directions: Circle any adjectives.

1. I need four pie crusts and fresh red berries to make an unusual dessert.

2. A few little, frisky puppies played in the Brown's large yard.

めめめめめめめめめめめめ

P. Directions: Circle any proper adjective. Box any predicate adjective.

1. Belgian waffles are tasty.

2. Is a grizzly a North American bear?

Q.   Directions: Write the correct degree of adjective.

1. That elephant is the (large) _____ animal in our zoo.

2. These red lights are (shiny) _____ than the green ones.

3. The winds during the second storm were (forceful) _____
    than during the first.

4. She is the (serious) _____ triplet.

TO THE TEACHER:

Please teach pronouns with great care. Many of the concepts such as indirect objects and direct objects will now be used to teach proper usage.

🙶🙶🙶🙶🙶🙶🙶🙶🙶🙶🙶🙶🙶🙶🙶🙶🙶🙶🙶🙶

PRONOUNS

PERSONAL PRONOUNS:

Pronouns take the place of NOUNS. <u>Sally</u> likes berries.

She likes berries.

She (pronoun) takes the place of *Sally* (noun).

Pronouns agree in number and gender.

Number: Two comics told **their** jokes. (*Two* requires ***their***.)

Gender (male or female): A princess walked to **her** car.

(Use a female pronoun [she, her] with a girl or a woman. Use a male pronoun [he, him] with a boy or man.)

Note: If you aren't sure if the noun is female or male, you may use his/her.
However, *his* has become acceptable in this situation.

Nominative Pronouns (also called Subjective Pronouns)	**Objective Pronouns**	**Possessive Pronouns**
I	me	my, mine
he	him	his
she	her	her, hers
you	you	your, yours
it	it	its
we	us	our, ours
they	them	their, theirs
who	whom	whose

Use in a sentence:	**Use in a sentence:**	**Use in a sentence:**
1. Subject	1. Object of a Preposition	Shows Ownership
2. Predicate Nominatives	2. Direct Object	
	3. Indirect Object	

451

☼

Nominative Pronouns: **I, he, she, you, it, we, they, who**

A nominative pronoun can serve as a **subject** or a **predicate nominative**.

Subject:

You have learned that a subject of a sentence tells the *who* or *what* of a sentence.

The **boy** rode a skateboard.   The subject of the sentence is *boy*.

He rode a skateboard.   The subject is *he*.

Look at the ☼ above. *He* is on the list of nominative pronouns.

Nominative pronouns are also called **subjective** pronouns.

🙥🙥🙥🙥🙥🙥🙥🙥🙥🙥🙥🙥🙥🙥🙥🙥🙥🙥🙥🙥🙥

Directions: Insert a nominative pronoun for the boldfaced noun or nouns.

1. **Jake** delivers pizza in the evening.   _____**He**_____ delivers pizza in the evening.

2. **Lana** and **her brother** hike in the Smokey Mountains.   _____**They**_____ hike in the Smokey Mountains.

3. **Bo** and (your name) **Student's Name** look at pictures. Bo and ____**I**___ look at pictures.

4. That **bear** is huge.   _____**It**_____ is huge.

5. **Levi and** (your name) **Student's Name** eat ketchup on fries.   _____**We**_____ eat ketchup on fries.

6. Which **person** needs a ride?   ____**Who**_____ needs a ride?

7. His **mother** is the woman with red hair.   _____**She**_____ is the woman with red hair.

8. (Your friend's name) **Student's Name**, do _____**you**_____ want a drink?

452

✿

Nominative Pronouns: **I, he, she, you, it, we, they, who**

A nominative pronoun can serve as a **subject** or a **predicate nominative**.

Subject:

You have learned that a subject of a sentence tells the *who* or *what* of a sentence.

The **boy** rode a skateboard.   The subject of the sentence is *boy*.

He rode a skateboard.   The subject is *he*.

Look at the ° above. ***He*** is on the list of nominative pronouns.

Nominative pronouns are also called **subjective** pronouns.

🙠🙠🙠🙠🙠🙠🙠🙠🙠🙠🙠🙠🙠🙠🙠🙠🙠🙠

Directions: Insert a nominative pronoun for the boldfaced noun or nouns.

1. **Jake** delivers pizza in the evening.   _____ delivers pizza in the evening.

2. **Lana** and **her brother** hike in the Smokey Mountains.   _____ hike in the Smokey Mountains.

3. **Bo** and (your name)_____ look at pictures. Bo and _____ look at pictures.

4. That **bear** is huge. _____ is huge.

5. **Levi and** (your name)_____ eat ketchup on fries.   _____ eat ketchup on fries.

6. Which **person** needs a ride? _____ needs a ride?

7. His **mother** is the woman with red hair. _____ is the woman with red hair.

8. (Your friend's name) _____, do _____ want a drink?

Name_____   **PRONOUNS**

Date_____   **Predicate Nominatives**

<u>**Note:**</u> **Teach students the easy process of inverting a sentence as a proof.**

✿

  Nominative Pronouns: **I, he, she, you, it, we, they, who**

A nominative pronoun can serve as a subject or a **predicate nominative**.

Predicate Nominative:

  You have learned that a predicate nominative occurs after a (linking) verb and means the same as the subject.

    Their dad is the **surfer** with black hair.

                    P.N.
    Their <u>dad</u> <u>is</u> the **surfer** ~~with black hair~~.

  Invert the sentence to offer a proof:

    Proof: <u>The surfer (with black hair) is their dad.</u>

  ✿To replace *surfer* with a pronoun is tricky. First, the pronoun has to be on the nominative pronoun list: **I, he, she, you, it, we, they, who**

    Their dad is the **surfer** with black hair.

 Could we use *him*? Their dad is that surfer (him) with gray hair. No! *Him* is not on the nominative pronoun list. We must use **he**! **He** is on the list of nominative pronouns.

    Their dad is **he** ~~with black hair~~.

    Proof: <u>He is their dad.</u>
    ෨෨෨෨෨෨෨෨෨෨

Directions: Circle the correct pronoun. Write the proof on the line.

1. The winners were (us, **we**).   Proof: _____ **We were the winners.** ___

2. Her dad is (him, **he**) ~~in a suit~~. Proof: _____ **He is her dad.** ___

3. The champs are (**they**, them). Proof: _____ **They are the champs.** ___

4. My friend is (**she**, her) ~~with bangs~~.   Proof: ___ **She is my friend.** ___

5. The first person ~~in line~~ was (me, **I**). Proof: ___ **I was the first person.** ___
454

✿
Nominative Pronouns: **I, he, she, you, it, we, they, who**

A nominative pronoun can serve as a subject or a **predicate nominative**.

Predicate Nominative:

You have learned that a predicate nominative occurs after a (linking) verb and means the same as the subject.

Their dad is the **surfer** with black hair.

P.N.
Their <u>dad</u> <u>is</u> the **surfer** ~~with black hair~~.

Invert the sentence to offer a proof.

Proof: <u>The surfer (with black hair) is their dad.</u>

✿To replace *surfer* with a pronoun is tricky. First, the pronoun has to be on the nominative pronoun list: **I, he, she, you, it, we, they, who**

Their dad is the **surfer** with black hair.

Could we use *him*?   Their dad is that surfer (him) with gray hair. No! *Him* is not on the nominative pronoun list. We must use **he**! **He** is on the list of nominative pronouns.

Their dad is **he** ~~with black hair~~.

Proof: <u>He is their dad.</u>

ৡৡৡৡৡৡৡৡৡ

Directions: Circle the correct pronoun. Write the proof on the line.

1. The winners were (us, we).   Proof: _____

2. Her dad is (him, he) ~~in a suit~~. Proof: _____

3. The champs are (they, them). Proof: _____

4. My friend is (she, her) ~~with bangs~~.   Proof: _____

5. The first person in line was (me, I). Proof: _____

PRONOUNS

Date_____

Subjects
Predicate Nominatives

Nominative Pronouns: **I, he, she, you, it, we, they, who**

A nominative pronoun can serve as a **subject** or a **predicate nominative**.

ॐॐॐॐॐॐॐॐॐॐॐॐॐॐॐॐॐॐ

A.   Directions: Delete any prepositional phrase. Underline the subject once and
the verb twice. In the blank, replace the subject with a nominative
pronoun and write the verb with it.

Example: A <u>bug</u> <u><u>flew</u></u> ~~around our tent~~.

_____It flew._____

1.   A <u>fisherman</u> <u><u>cast</u></u> his line.

_____**He cast.**_____

2.   Several café <u>owners</u> <u><u>met</u></u>.

_____**They met.**_____

3.   My <u>friends</u> and <u>I</u> <u><u>played</u></u> ~~at a park~~.

_____**We played.**_____

ॐॐॐॐॐॐॐॐॐॐ

B.   Directions: Delete any prepositional phrase. Underline the subject once and
the verb twice. Write **P.N.** above the predicate nominative.
Write the proof.

           P.N.
1.   The <u>senator</u> <u><u>is</u></u> she ~~with the briefcase~~.

   Proof: _____**She is the senator.**_____

              P.N.
2.   The first <u>person</u> ~~through the door~~ <u><u>was</u></u> I.

   Proof: _____**I was the first person.**_____

            P.N.
3.   His <u>brothers-in-law</u> <u><u>are</u></u> they ~~in polo shirts~~.

   Proof: _____**They are his brothers-in-law.**_____

     P.N.
4.   Your <u>uncle</u> <u><u>is</u></u> who?

   Proof: _____**Who is your uncle?**_____

Nominative Pronouns: **I, he, she, you, it, we, they, who**

A nominative pronoun can serve as a **subject** or a **predicate nominative**.

ॐ-ॐ-ॐ-ॐ-ॐ-ॐ-ॐ-ॐ-ॐ-ॐ-ॐ-ॐ-ॐ-ॐ-ॐ-ॐ-ॐ-ॐ-ॐ

A.   Directions: Delete any prepositional phrase. Underline the subject once and the verb twice. In the blank, replace the subject with a nominative pronoun and write the verb with it.

Example: A <u>bug</u> <u>flew</u> ~~around our tent~~.

<u>   It flew.   </u>

1.   A fisherman cast his line.

      _____

2.   Several café owners met.

      _____

3.   My friends and I played at a park.

      _____

ॐ-ॐ-ॐ-ॐ-ॐ-ॐ-ॐ-ॐ-ॐ-ॐ

B.   Directions: Delete any prepositional phrase. Underline the subject once and the verb twice. Write **P.N.** above the predicate nominative. Write the proof.

1.   The senator is she with the briefcase.

      Proof: _____

2.   The first person through the door was I.

      Proof: _____

3.   His brothers-in-law are they in polo shirts.

      Proof: _____

4.   Your uncle is who?

      Proof: _____

457

Objective Pronouns: **me, him, her, you, it, us, them, whom**
Objective pronouns can serve as an ***object* of a preposition**, a **direct *object***, or an **indirect *object***.

Remember that an object of a preposition is a noun or pronoun that ends a prepositional phrase.

O.P.
Lean against <u>**me**</u>.   prepositional phrase ~ *against me*

object of the preposition = *me*. ***Me*** is an objective pronoun.

A. Directions: Circle the prepositional phrase.
PREPOSITIONAL PHRASES ARE BOLDFACED.

1. Sit **beside us**.

2. Hannah went **with him**.

3. **With whom** are you going?

~~~~~~

Remember that a direct object receives the action of a verb.

<p style="text-align:center">D.O.
A bug bit **her**.   ***Her*** is a direct object. ***Her*** is an objective pronoun.</p>

B. Directions: Underline the subject once and the verb twice. Label the direct Object – **D.O.**

D.O.	D.O.
1. A paper <u>airplane</u> <u>hit</u> me.	3. Their <u>sister</u> <u>joined</u> her.
D.O.	D.O.
2. <u>I</u> <u>enjoyed</u> it!	4. <u>Mrs. Crabb</u> <u>called</u> them.

~~~~~~

Remember that an indirect object is a noun or pronoun that indirectly receives the action of a verb. You can put *to* or *for* in front of an indirect object.

I.O.   D.O.
My niece drew us a picture.   ***Us*** is an indirect object.

C. Directions: Underline the subject once and the verb/verb phrase twice. Label the direct object – **D.O.** and the indirect object – **I. O.**

        I.O.   D.O.

1. <u>He</u> <u>handed</u> me a tall, striped cup.

                I.O.   D.O.

2. A shoe <u>shiner</u> <u>handed</u> us his card.

        I.O.   D.O.

3. <u>Tara</u> <u>gave</u> them her apology.

Objective Pronouns: **me, him, her, you, it, us, them, whom**
Objective pronouns can serve as an *object* **of a preposition,** a **direct** *object,* or
an **indirect** *object.*

Remember that an object of a preposition is a noun or pronoun that ends a prepositional phrase.

O.P.
Lean against **me**.   prepositional phrase ~ *against me*

object of the preposition = *me*. ***Me*** is an objective pronoun.

A. Directions: Circle the prepositional phrase.

1. Sit beside us.

2. Hannah went with him.

3. With whom are you going?

Remember that a direct object receives the action of a verb.

D.O.
A bug bit **her**.   ***Her*** is a direct object. ***Her*** is an objective pronoun.

B. Directions: Underline the subject once and the verb twice. Label the direct
                Object – **D.O.**

1. A paper airplane hit me.   3. Their sister joined her.

2. I enjoyed it!   4. Mrs. Crabb called them.

**Remember that an indirect object is a noun or pronoun that indirectly receives the action
of a verb. You can put *to* or *for* in front of an indirect object.**

I.O.   D.O.
My niece drew us a picture.   ***Us*** is an indirect object.

C. Directions: Underline the subject once and the verb/verb phrase twice. Label
                the direct object – **D.O.** and the indirect object – **I. O.**

1. He handed me a tall, striped cup.

2. A shoe shiner handed us his card.

3. Tara gave them her apology.

Name_____ **PRONOUNS**

WORKBOOK PAGE 206

Date_____ **Objective Pronouns**

An objective pronoun can serve as an *object* of a preposition, a **direct object**, or an **indirect object**.   (me, him, her, you, it, us, them, whom)

A.   Directions: Tell if the boldfaced pronoun serves as a direct object (**D.O.**), indirect object (**I.O.**), or an object of the preposition (**O.P.**).

1.   __D.O.__   I like **you**.

2.   __I.O.__   Ken handed **us** a pen.

3.   __D.O.__   Stop **them**!

4.   __O.P.__   There is a wasp near **you**.

5.   __D.O.__   Gretta greeted **me**.

6.   __I.O.__   The grocer handed **him** a sack of oranges.

7.   __O.P.__   The wind is blowing; walk against **it**.

8.   __O.P.__   For **whom** are you waiting?

⅋⅋⅋⅋⅋⅋⅋⅋⅋⅋⅋⅋⅋⅋⅋⅋⅋⅋⅋⅋⅋⅋⅋⅋⅋⅋

A nominative pronoun can serve as a **subject** or as a **predicate nominative.**
I, he, she, you, it, we, they, who

A.   Directions: Tell if the boldfaced pronoun serves as a subject - **S.** or a predicate nominative - **P.N.**

1.   __S.__   **You** have a scar on your arm.

2.   __S.__   Along the way, **we** dropped crumbs for the ducks.

3.   __S.__   Are **they** finished with their project?

4.   __P.N.__   His first neighbor is **she** in the blue dress.

5.   __P.N.__   Their choice was **I**.

6.   __S.__   Mario, Dana, Jana, Tate, and **he** met at a pizza parlor.
460

An objective pronoun can serve as an *object* of a preposition, a **direct object**, or an **indirect *object*.** (me, him, her, you, it, us, them, whom)

A. Directions: Tell if the boldfaced pronoun serves as a direct object (**D.O.**), indirect object (**I.O.**), or an object of the preposition (**O.P.**).

1. _____ I like **you**.

2. _____ Ken handed **us** a pen.

3. _____ Stop **them**!

4. _____ There is a wasp near **you**.

5. _____ Gretta greeted **me**.

6. _____ The grocer handed **him** a sack of oranges.

7. _____ The wind is blowing; walk against **it**.

8. _____ For **whom** are you waiting?

❧❧❧❧❧❧❧❧❧❧❧❧❧❧❧❧❧❧❧❧❧❧❧❧❧❧❧

A nominative pronoun can serve as a **subject** or as a **predicate nominative.**
I, he, she, you, it, we, they, who

A. Directions: Tell if the boldfaced pronoun serves as a subject - **S.** or a predicate nominative - **P.N.**

1. _____ **You** have a scar on your arm.

2. _____ Along the way, **we** dropped crumbs for the ducks.

3. _____ Are **they** finished with their project?

4. _____ His first neighbor is **she** in the blue dress.

5. _____ Their choice was **I**.

6. _____ Mario, Dana, Jana, Tate, and **he** met at a pizza parlor.

WORKBOOK PAGE 207

Date_____   **Nominative and Objective**

Note: **You may want to do at least half of this page with students. It would be good to guide them to understand that a direct object, indirect object, or object of the preposition requires an objective pronoun (me, him, her, us, them, whom). A subject or predicate nominative requires a nominative pronoun (I, he, she, we, they, who).** *You* **and** *it* **apply to both.**

Directions: Circle the correct pronoun. **(The boldfaced information tells how the pronoun functions.)**

1. Come with (I, **me**).   – object of the preposition

2. A puppy licked (**us**, we).   – direct object

3. (**I**, me) enjoy scuba diving.   – subject

4. Micah handed (they, **them**) towels.   – indirect object

5. The last person to enter the room was (him, **he**).   – predicate nominative

6. Take (I, **me**) with you.   – direct object

7. To (**whom**, who) did you send that email?   – object of the preposition

8. A jogger ran by (**her**, she).   – object of the preposition

9. A safety expert handed (he, **him**) an orange cone.   – indirect object

10. Glenda and (her, **she**) agree.   – subject

11. The symphony leader chose (**them**, they) to help.   – direct object

12. A tornado passed near (**us**, we).   – object of the preposition

13. May Jamil and (**we**, us) stand here?   – subject

14. Mom baked (they, **them**) cookies for a bake sale.   – indirect object

15. That matter does not concern (I, **me**).   – direct object

16. His dad is (**he**, him) in the red tie.   – predicate nominative

17. (**Who**, Whom) has a good idea?   – subject

Directions: Circle the correct pronoun. **(The boldfaced information tells how the pronoun functions.)**

1. Come with (I, me).   – **object of the preposition**

2. A puppy licked (us, we).   – **direct object**

3. (I, me) enjoy scuba diving.   – **subject**

4. Micah handed (they, them) towels.   – **indirect object**

5. The last person to enter the room was (him, he).   – **predicate nominative**

6. Take (I, me) with you.   – **direct object**

7. To (whom, who) did you send that email?   – **object of the preposition**

8. A jogger ran by (her, she).   – **object of the preposition**

9. A safety expert handed (he, him) an orange cone.   – **indirect object**

10. Glenda and (her, she) agree.   – **subject**

11. The symphony leader chose (them, they) to help.   – **direct object**

12. A tornado passed near (us, we).   – **object of the preposition**

13. May Jamil and (we, us) stand here?   – **subject**

14. Mom baked (they, them) cookies for a bake sale.   – **indirect object**

15. That matter does not concern (I, me).   – **direct object**

16. His dad is (he, him) in the red tie.   – **predicate nominative**

17. (Who, Whom) has a good idea?   – **subject**

Compound means more than one. To make a decision about pronoun usage in compounds, think about <u>how</u> the pronoun is used in the sentence.

If the pronoun serves as a subject or predicate nominative, use *I, he, she, we, they,* or *who*.

If the pronoun serves as a direct object, indirect object, or object of the preposition, use *me, him, her, us, them,* or *whom*.

FINGER TRICK: If you are unsure, try placing your finger over the first part of the compound. Then make the decision.

Example: John and (I, me) want to attend a boxing match.
---------- (**I**, me) want to attend a boxing match.

<small>Place finger here.</small>

☙☙☙☙☙☙☙☙☙☙☙☙☙☙☙☙☙☙☙

CORRECT PRONOUNS ARE BOLDACED.
Directions: Circle the correct pronoun.

1. Joe and (**we**, us) went to the dentist.

2. My friend and (**I**, me) will wax the floor.

3. The X-ray person gave Josh and (they, **them**) several films.

4. Please sit beside Tate and (**us**, we).

5. The clerk handed Marta and (**her**, she) some change.

6. Do you want to go with my brother and (I, **me**)?

7. Our cousins are Dirk and (**he**, him).

8. Many students and (them, **they**) went to a pep rally.

9. The coach presented her teammates and (**her**, she) a trophy.

10. Don't put Jake and (**him**, he) in the first row.

11. A shoe-repair lady and (him, **he**) will put new heels on our shoes.

12. Please give your parents and (we, **us**) your answer.

Name_____   **PRONOUNS**

Date_____   **Compounds**

Compound means more than one. To make a decision about pronoun usage in compounds, think about how the pronoun is used in the sentence.

If the pronoun serves as a subject or predicate nominative, use *I, he, she, we, they,* or *who.*

If the pronoun serves as a direct object, indirect object, or object of the preposition, use *me, him, her, us, them,* or *whom.*

FINGER TRICK: If you are unsure, try placing your finger over the first part of the compound. Then make the decision.

Example: John and (I, me) want to attend a boxing match.
---------- (**I**, me) want to attend a boxing match.

Place finger here.

ை ை ை ை ை ை ை ை ை ை ை ை ை ை ை ை ை ை

Directions: Circle the correct pronoun.

1.   Joe and (we, us) went to the dentist.

2.   My friend and (I, me) will wax the floor.

3.   The X-ray person gave Josh and (they, them) several films.

4.   Please sit beside Tate and (us, we).

5.   The clerk handed Marta and (her, she) some change.

6.   Do you want to go with my brother and (I, me)?

7.   Our cousins are Dirk and (he, him).

8.   Many students and (them, they) went to a pep rally.

9.   The coach presented her teammates and (her, she) a trophy.

10.   Don't put Jake and (him, he) in the first row.

11.   A shoe-repair lady and (him, he) will put new heels on our shoes.

12.   Please give your parents and (we, us) your answer.

465

Reflexive pronouns end with **self** or **selves**. Reflexive pronouns are <u>myself</u>, <u>himself</u>, <u>herself</u>, <u>itself</u>, <u>yourself</u>, <u>ourselves</u>, and <u>themselves</u>. A reflexive pronoun reflects back to another noun or pronoun in a sentence. The word to which a reflexive pronoun refers back is called an ***antecedent***.

   Examples: Taylor did the whole job by herself.
         The antecedent is **Taylor**. *Herself* refers back to **Taylor**.

      A cat licked itself.
         The antecedent is **cat**. *Itself* refers back to **cat**.

DO NOT USE hisself or theirselves. They are incorrect.

    ৡৡৡৡৡৡৡৡৡৡৡৡৡৡৡৡৡৡ

Directions: Circle the reflexive pronoun. Write the antecedent in the blank
      after the sentence.
REFLECTIVE PRONOUNS ARE BOLDFACED.
  Remember: The word to which a reflexive pronoun refers back is called an ***antecedent***.

1. Josh checked the equipment **himself**. _____**Josh**_____

2. I want to do the project by **myself**. _____**I**_____

3. You must do it **yourself**.   _____**You**_____

4. The guests helped **themselves** to food. _____**guests**_____

5. A kitten looked at **itself** in a mirror. _____**kitten**_____

6. Julie painted the entire scene **herself**. _____**Julie**_____

7. Bo and I will make pizza **ourselves**. _____**Bo/I**_____

8. The sisters planned a trip **themselves**. _____**sisters**_____

9. Toni, **herself**, was not hurt.   _____**Toni**_____

10. Do you want to sit by **yourself**? _____**you**_____

Name_____   **PRONOUNS**

Date_____   **Reflexive**

Reflexive pronouns end with **self** or **selves**. Reflexive pronouns are <u>myself</u>, <u>himself</u>, <u>herself</u>, <u>itself</u>, <u>yourself</u>, <u>ourselves</u>, and <u>themselves</u>. A reflexive pronoun reflects back to another noun or pronoun in a sentence. The word to which a reflexive pronoun refers back is called an ***antecedent.***

> Examples: Taylor did the whole job by herself.
>> The antecedent is **Taylor**. *Herself* refers back to **Taylor**.

>> A cat licked itself.
>>> The antecedent is **cat**. *Itself* refers back to **cat**.

DO NOT USE hisself or theirselves. They are incorrect.

Directions: Circle the reflexive pronoun. Write the antecedent in the blank after the sentence.

Remember: The word to which a reflexive pronoun refers back is called an ***antecedent.***

1. Josh checked the equipment **himself**.   _____

2. I want to do the project by **myself**.   _____

3. You must do it **yourself**.   _____

4. The guests helped **themselves** to food. _____

5. A kitten looked at **itself** in a mirror.   _____

6. Julie painted the entire scene **herself**.   _____

7. Bo and I will make pizza **ourselves**.   _____

8. The sisters planned a trip **themselves**.   _____

9. Toni, **herself**, was not hurt.   _____

10. Do you want to sit by **yourself**?   _____

Name_____   **PRONOUNS**

WORKBOOK PAGE 210

Date_____   **Demonstrative**

The demonstrative pronouns are **this, that, these, those**.

    Examples: I want **this**.   Do you want **these**?
                   That is my favorite!   **Those** are yours.

This and **that** are singular. **These** and **those** are plural and refer to two or more.

    Them is not a demonstrative pronoun.

        Incorrect: Them is for sale.   Correct: Those are for sale.

If *this, that, those,* or *these* modify (go over to) another word, they function as adjectives, not pronouns.

    Examples: This is old.   (pronoun)
                  This bucket is old. (adjective- *this bucket.*)

NOUNS THAT ARE MODIFIED (WITH AN ARROW) ARE IN ITALICS.

Directions: Write **P** if the boldfaced word serves as a pronoun. Write **A** if the boldfaced word serves as an adjective and draw an arrow to the noun it modifies (goes over to).

1. **P** **This** is awful.

2. **A** Do you want **these** potato *skins*?

3. **A** We put **that** towel in the hamper.

4. **P** I believe that **those** are mine.

5. **P** I can't believe **that**.

6. **A** Is **this** *bag* heavy?

7. **P** Put more salt on **this**, please.

8. **P** Who brought **these** to the classroom?

9. **A** I need to remove **this** *gum* from my shirt.

10. **A** **These** *rugs* must be cleaned.

468

The demonstrative pronouns are **this, that, these, those**.

Examples: I want **this**.   Do you want **these**?
            That is my favorite!   **Those** are yours.

This and **that** are singular. **These** and **those** are plural and refer to two or more.

Them is not a demonstrative pronoun.

Incorrect: Them is for sale.   Correct: Those are for sale.

If *this, that, those,* or *these* modify (go over to) another word, they function as adjectives, not pronouns.

Examples: This is old.   (pronoun)
            This bucket is old.   (adjective- *this bucket.*)

ৰ্কৰ্কৰ্কৰ্কৰ্কৰ্কৰ্কৰ্কৰ্কৰ্কৰ্ক

Directions: Write **P** if the boldfaced word serves as a pronoun. Write **A** if the boldfaced word serves as an adjective and draw an arrow to the noun it modifies (goes over to).

1. _____   **This** is awful.

2. _____   Do you want **these** potato skins?

3. _____   We put **that** towel in the hamper.

4. _____   I believe that **those** are mine.

5. _____   I can't believe **that**.

6. _____   Is **this** bag heavy?

7. _____   Put more salt on **this**, please.

8. _____   Who brought **these** to the classroom?

9. _____   I need to remove **this** gum from my shirt.

10. _____   **These** rugs must be cleaned.

Interrogative pronouns ask questions.
The interrogative pronouns are **who**, **whom**, **whose**, **which**, and **what**.

Whose, *which*, and *what* are pronouns when they stand alone.

Examples: **Whose** is this?
Which do you want?
What do you know about the flight?

Whose, *which*, and *what* are adjectives when they modify another word.

Examples: **Whose** coat is on the floor?   (**whose** *coat*)
Have you decided **which** pattern you like? (**which** *pattern*)
What answer do you expect?   (**what** *answer*)

🙞🙞🙞🙞🙞🙞🙞🙞🙞🙞🙞🙞

Directions: Write **P** if the boldfaced word serves as a pronoun. Write **A** if the
boldfaced word serves as an adjective and draw an arrow to the
noun it modifies (goes over to).

NOUNS THAT ARE MODIFIED (WITH AN ARROW) ARE IN ITALICS.

1. __P__ **What** is the answer?

2. __A__ Do you know **which** *apartment* is his?

3. __P__ **Whose** might be chosen?

4. __A__ **What** *fern* is this?

5. __P__ **Which** do you need?

6. __A__ **Whose** *car* is in the driveway?

7. __P__ I don't know **which** is the best.

8. __A__ Have you determined **which** *flight* is leaving?

9. __P__ **What** did you say?

10. __A__ Are you aware **which** *story* is mine?

470

Name_____   **PRONOUNS**

Date_____   **Interrogative**

Interrogative pronouns ask questions.
The interrogative pronouns are **who, whom, whose, which,** and **what.**

Whose, which, and *what* are pronouns when they stand alone.

Examples: ***Whose*** is this?
                    Which do you want?
                    What do you know about the flight?

Whose, which, and *what* are adjectives when they modify another word.

Examples: ***Whose*** coat is on the floor?   (**whose** *coat*)
                    Have you decided ***which*** pattern you like?   (**which** *pattern*)
                    What answer do you expect?   (**what** *answer*)

きゃきゃきゃきゃきゃきゃきゃきゃきゃきゃきゃ

Directions: Write **P** if the boldfaced word serves as a pronoun. Write **A** if the
                    boldfaced word serves as an adjective and draw an arrow to the
                    noun it modifies (goes over to).

1. _____   **What** is the answer?

2. _____   Do you know **which** apartment is his?

3. _____   **Whose** might be chosen?

4. _____   **What** fern is this?

5. _____   **Which** do you need?

6. _____   **Whose** car is in the driveway?

7. _____   I don't know **which** is the best.

8. _____   Have you determined **which** flight is leaving?

9. _____   **What** did you say?

10. _____   Are you aware **which** story is mine?

Indefinite pronouns take the place of nouns.
Indefinite pronouns include **anyone**, **everybody**, **everyone**, **nobody**, **none**,
somebody, and **someone**.

Examples: Has **anyone** seen my notebook?
              She has **none**.

Indefinite pronouns also include **any**, **both**, **each**, **either**, **few**, **many**,
neither, and **no**. When these words stand alone, they are pronouns. However,
they are adjectives when they modify another word.

Examples: **Both** are going.   (***Both*** is a pronoun here; it stands alone.)
              Both girls are going.   (***Both*** is an adjective here; ***both*** girls.)

              I don't like **either**.   (***Either*** is a pronoun here; it stands alone.)
              I don't like **either** CD. (***Either*** is an adjective here; ***either*** CD.)

ॡॡॡॡॡॡॡॡॡॡॡॡ

A.   Directions: Write an indefinite pronoun that makes sense in each blank.
ANSWERS MAY VARY/REPRESENTATIVE ANSWERS:

1. Did _____**anyone**_____ buy milk?

2. _____**Somebody**_____ left the top off the peanut butter.

3. Sarah asked _____**everybody**_____ to vote for her.

4. _____**Everyone**_____ wants to know.

B.   Directions: Write **P** if the boldfaced word serves as a pronoun. Write **A** if
                   the boldfaced word serves as an adjective and draw an arrow to
                   the noun it modifies (goes over to). **MODIFIED WORDS ARE ITALICED.**

1. __**P**__ **Some** helped.

2. __**A**__ He had hoped for **some** *rain*.

3. __**P**__ Do you want **any**?

4. __**A**__ Does she have **any** *horses*?

5. __**P**__ Chan bought **several** ~~for his bike~~.

6. __**A**__ During the storm, **several** *trees* had fallen.

472

Indefinite pronouns take the place of nouns.
Indefinite pronouns include **anyone**, **everybody**, **everyone**, **nobody**, **none**,
somebody, and **someone**.

       Examples: Has **anyone** seen my notebook?
                    She has **none**.

Indefinite pronouns also include **any**, **both**, **each**, **either**, **few**, **many**,
neither, and **no**. When these words stand alone, they are pronouns. However,
they are adjectives when they modify another word.

       Examples: **Both** are going.   (*Both* is a pronoun here; it stands alone.)
                   Both girls are going.   (*Both* is an adjective here; *both* girls.)

                   I don't like **either**.   (*Either* is a pronoun here; it stands alone.)
                   I don't like **either** CD.   (*Either* is an adjective here; *either* CD.)

                 ᖷᖷᖷᖷᖷᖷᖷᖷᖷᖷᖷᖷᖷ

A. Directions: Write an indefinite pronoun that makes sense in each blank.

1. Did _____ buy milk?

2. _____ left the top off the peanut butter.

3. Sarah asked _____ to vote for her.

4. _____ wants to know.

B. Directions: Write **P** if the boldfaced word serves as a pronoun. Write **A** if
                       the boldfaced word serves as an adjective and draw an arrow to
                       the noun it modifies (goes over to).

1. _____ **Some** helped.

2. _____ He had hoped for **some** rain.

3. _____ Do you want **any**?

4. _____ Does she have **any** horses?

5. _____ Chan bought **several** for his bike.

6. _____ During the storm, **several** trees had fallen.

TO THE TEACHER: *PAGE 475 = WORKBOOK PAGE 213*

Teach the lesson explaining possessive pronouns carefully.

The lesson concerning antecedents will be more difficult than some

other lessons. However, your students have already been introduced

to the concept of antecedents. I recommend that you

do half of the lesson orally with students. This guidance and

reinforcement should help them greatly.

POSSESSIVE PRONOUNS

The possessive pronouns are:

my, mine
his
her, hers
your, yours
its
our, ours
their, theirs
whose

My, his, her, your, its, our, their, and *whose* are placed before nouns or other pronouns.

Examples: **my** cart   **her** name   **its** beak   **their** flight

            his hats   **your** dad   **our** desks   **whose** bat

Mine, hers, yours, ours, and *theirs* are not placed before nouns or other pronouns (usually). They refer back to a noun or a pronoun in a sentence.

Examples: This drawing is **mine**.

                         That suitcase with the checked lining is **hers**.

                         The gift is **yours** to keep.

                         One of the cars is **ours**.

                         Is the puppy **theirs**?

Do you see that you can write possessive pronouns in two ways?

My cat is gray and white.   The gray and white cat is **mine**.

●Note that *his* does not change.

His cat is black.   The black cat is **his**.

●Notice that *its* does not have an apostrophe (').

The possessive pronouns are **my, mine, his, her, hers, your, yours, its, our, ours, their, theirs,** and **whose**.

Examples: **my** friend   **her** lips   **its** paw   **their** parents
                his brother   **your** lungs   **our** trip   **whose** truck

Mine, hers, yours, ours, and *theirs* go to a noun or pronoun earlier in the sentence.

Examples: I think that those *raisins* are **mine**.
                   Is that *marker* **hers**?
                   Are these *blueprints* **yours**?
                   That *motorcycle* is **ours**.
                   Are these *baskets* **theirs**?

You can write most possessive pronouns in two ways:

       Our house is yellow.   The yellow house is **ours**.

ক্তক্তক্তক্তক্তক্তক্তক্তক্তক্তক্ত

Directions: Write a possessive pronoun that makes sense in each blank.
ANSWERS MAY VARY/REPRSENTATIVE ANSWERS:

1. ____**Our**_____ friends agree with you.

2. Are ____**your**_____ shoes new?

3. Marta and Lee rushed toward ____**their**_____ mom.

4. ____**Her**_____ score was high.

5. Does ____**my**_____ toe look bruised?

6. Before lunch, the librarian talked with ____**his**_____ helpers.

7. Hans called, but ____**his**_____ message was not clear.

8. A kangaroo hopped near ____**its**_____ mother.

9. Has anyone seen ____**my**_____ backpack?

10. ____**Whose**_____ sandwich is this?

The possessive pronouns are **my**, **mine**, **his**, **her**, **hers**, **your**, **yours**, **its**, **our**, **ours**, **their**, **theirs**, and **whose**.

Examples: **my** friend   **her** lips   **its** paw   **their** parents
          his brother   **your** lungs   **our** trip   **whose** truck

Mine, hers, yours, ours, and *theirs* go to a noun or pronoun earlier in the sentence.

Examples: I think that those *raisins* are **mine**.
                Is that *marker* **hers**?
                Are these *blueprints* **yours**?
                That *motorcycle* is **ours**.
                Are these *baskets* **theirs**?

You can write most possessive pronouns in two ways:

Our house is yellow.   The yellow house is **ours**.

෴෴෴෴෴෴෴෴෴෴෴෴෴

Directions: Write a possessive pronoun that makes sense in each blank.

1.   _____ friends agree with you.

2.   Are _____ shoes new?

3.   Marta and Lee rushed toward _____ mom.

4.   _____ score was high.

5.   Does _____ toe look bruised?

6.   Before lunch, the librarian talked with _____ helpers.

7.   Hans called, but _____ message was not clear.

8.   A kangaroo hopped near _____ mother.

9.   Has anyone seen _____ backpack?

10.   _____ sandwich is this?

<u>**Its**</u>, <u>**their**</u>, and <u>**your**</u> are possessive pronouns. They are **not** spelled with an apostrophe ('). They modify (go over to) a noun or another pronoun.

A cub snuggled next to **its** momma. (**its** momma)
They like **their** new apartment. (**their** apartment)
Is **your** chain new? (**your** chain)

<u>**It's**</u>, <u>**they're**</u>, and <u>**you're**</u> are contractions. They use an apostrophe (').

it's = it is **It's** sunny today.
they're = they are **They're** eating strawberries on their cereal.
you're = you are I know that **you're** excited about the fair.

ঔঔঔঔঔঔঔঔঔঔঔঔঔঔঔ

Directions: Circle the correct word.

1. What is (**your**, you're) address?

2. (Their, **They're**) waiting until the rain stops.

3. (Its, **It's**) time for lunch.

4. Are (**your**, you're) computer skills good?

5. (**Their**, They're) moving boxes are wet.

6. A prairie dog ran into (**its**, it's) hole.

7. My dad and (**your**, you're) grandfather are golfing.

8. Have you seen (they're, **their**) video game?

9. My fishing pole has tangled line and (**its**, it's) pole is bent.

10. In the late afternoon, (**you're**, your) expected to cut the grass.

11. (Their, **They're**) always in a hurry.

12. (**It's**, Its) not polite to burp at (**your**, you're) dinner table.
478

<u>**Its**</u>, <u>**their**</u>, and <u>**your**</u> are possessive pronouns. They are **not** spelled with an apostrophe (’). They modify (go over to) a noun or another pronoun.

     A cub snuggled next to **its** momma.   (**its** momma)
     They like **their** new apartment.   (**their** apartment)
     Is **your** chain new?   (**your** chain)

<u>**It's**</u>, <u>**they're**</u>, and <u>**you're**</u> are contractions. They use an apostrophe (’).

     it's = it is   **It's** sunny today.
     they're = they are   **They're** eating strawberries on their cereal.
     you're = you are   I know that **you're** excited about the fair.

Directions: Circle the correct word.

1. What is (your, you're) address?

2. (Their, They're) waiting until the rain stops.

3. (Its, It's) time for lunch.

4. Are (your, you're) computer skills good?

5. (Their, They're) moving boxes are wet.

6. A prairie dog ran into (its, it's) hole.

7. My dad and (your, you're) grandfather are golfing.

8. Have you seen (they're, their) video game?

9. My fishing pole has a tangled line and (its, it's) pole is bent.

10. In the late afternoon, (you're, your) expected to cut the grass.

11. (Their, They're) always in a hurry.

12. (It's, Its) not polite to burp at (your, you're) dinner table.

Possessive pronouns are **my**, **mine**, **his**, **her**, **hers**, **your**, **yours**, **its**, **our**, **ours**, **their**, **theirs**, and **whose**.

Possessive pronouns reflect back to another noun or pronoun in a sentence. The word to which a possessive pronoun refers back is called an ***antecedent***.

Example: Bill sent **his** cousin a yoyo.
(**Bill's**)

His refers back to Bill. ***Bill*** is the <u>antecedent</u> of *his*.

~ **You wouldn't use *her*; in this case, Bill is a boy.**

Example: Manny and Susan went to **their** karate class.
(**Manny and Susan's**)

Their refers back to Manny and Susan. ***Manny and Susan*** is the <u>antecedent</u> of *their*.

~ **You wouldn't use *his* or *her*; you are referring to both Manny and Susan.**

This is what is meant when the rule says that the possessive pronoun must agree in gender (boy-girl) and number.

Directions: Circle the possessive pronoun. Write the antecedent in the blank after the sentence.

Remember: The word to which a possessive pronoun refers back is called an ***antecedent***.
POSSESSIVE PRONOUNS ARE IN BOLDFACED ITALICS.

1. Jake likes *his* new teacher.   <u>__Jake_____</u>

2. The teachers met in *their* office.   <u>___teachers_____</u>

3. That printer gave *her* bid at once.   <u>___printer_____</u>

4. I like *my* watch.   <u>___I_____</u>

5. Someone left *his* sunglasses.   <u>___Someone_____</u>

6. Tyler and Loni want *their* lunch.   <u>___Tyler/Loni_____</u>

7. A monkey scratched *its* arm.   <u>___monkey_____</u>

8. Jenny and I cleaned for *our* mother.<u>___Jenny/I_____</u>

480

Possessive pronouns are **my, mine, his, her, hers, your, yours, its, our, ours, their, theirs,** and **whose**.

Possessive pronouns reflect back to another noun or pronoun in a sentence. The word to which a possessive pronoun refers back is called an ***antecedent***.

      Example: Bill sent **his** cousin a yoyo.
                  (**Bill's**)

    His refers back to Bill. ***Bill*** is the <u>antecedent</u> of *his*.
    ~ You wouldn't use *her*; in this case, Bill is a boy.

      Example: Manny and Susan went to **their** karate class.
                  (**Manny and Susan's**)

Their refers back to Manny and Susan. ***Manny and Susan*** is the <u>antecedent</u> of *their*.
    ~ You wouldn't use *his* or *her*; you are referring to both Manny and Susan.

This is what is meant when the rule says that the possessive pronoun must agree in gender (boy-girl) and number.

ৡৡৡৡৡৡৡৡৡৡৡৡৡৡৡৡৡৡৡ

Directions: Circle the possessive pronoun. Write the antecedent in the blank after the sentence.

Remember: The word to which a possessive pronoun refers back is called an ***antecedent***.

1. Jake likes his new teacher.   _____

2. The teachers met in their office.   _____

3. That printer gave her bid at once.   _____

4. I like my watch.   _____

5. Someone left his sunglasses.   _____

6. Tyler and Loni want their lunch.   _____

7. A monkey scratched its arm.   _____

8. Jenny and I cleaned for our mother. _____

Name_____   **PRONOUNS**

Date_____   **Review**

<u>Note</u>: **It may help to have students delete prepositional phrases, underline the subject once, and underline the verb/verb phrase twice. Be sure to discuss these exercises orally with students.**

A. Nominative Pronouns:

Remember: Nominative pronouns can serve as a subject or a predicate nominative.
I, he, she, it, you, we, they, who

Directions: Write **S.** if the boldfaced pronoun serves as a subject; write **P.N.** if the boldfaced pronoun serves as a predicate nominative.

1. ___**S.**___   Throughout the evening, **they** watched television.

2. ___**P.N.**___   The chief engineer is **she** with the hard hat.

3. ___**S.**___   During the last quarter of the game, **we** decided to leave.

4. ___**P.N.**___   One winner of the funny car race was **he** in the blue car.

෧෧෧෧෧෧෧෧෧෧෧෧෧෧෧෧

B. Objective Pronouns:

Remember: Objective pronouns can serve as a direct object, an indirect object, or an object of a preposition.
me, him, her, it, you, us, them, whom

Directions: Write **D.O.** if the boldfaced pronoun serves as a direct object, write **I.O** if the boldfaced pronoun serves as an indirect object, and write **O.P.** if the boldfaced pronoun serves as an object of the preposition.

1. ___**D.O.**___   Her elbow jabbed **me** in the side.

2. ___**O.P.**___   Go without **us**, please.

3. ___**I.O.**___   Don't give **them** any more peanuts.

4. ___**I.O.**___   Paula baked **him** wheat bread.

5. ___**D.O.**___   Marco fielded the ball and threw **it** to first base.

6. ___**O.P.**___   To **whom** did you give your note?

A. Nominative Pronouns:

Remember: Nominative pronouns can serve as a subject or a predicate nominative.
I, he, she, it, you, we, they, who

Directions: Write **S.** if the boldfaced pronoun serves as a subject; write **P.N.** if the boldfaced pronoun serves as a predicate nominative.

1. _____   Throughout the evening, **they** watched television.

2. _____   The chief engineer is **she** with the hard hat.

3. _____   During the last quarter of the game, **we** decided to leave.

4. _____   One winner of the funny car race was **he** in the blue car.

B. Objective Pronouns:

Remember: Objective pronouns can serve as a direct object, an indirect object, or an object of a preposition.
me, him, her, it, you, us, them, whom

Directions: Write **D.O.** if the boldfaced pronoun serves as a direct object, write **I.O** if the boldfaced pronoun serves as an indirect object, and write **O.P.** if the boldfaced pronoun serves as an object of the preposition.

1. _____   Her elbow jabbed **me** in the side.

2. _____   Go without **us**, please.

3. _____   Don't give **them** any more peanuts.

4. _____   Paula baked **him** wheat bread.

5. _____   Marco fielded the ball and threw **it** to first base.

6. _____   To **whom** did you give your note?

C. Pronoun Usage:

Directions: Circle the correct pronoun.

1. (**I**, Me) have dug a hole for a bush.

2. Did you receive a letter from (we, **us**)?

3. Give (**them**, they) your name.

4. The first to arrive at the party was (her, **she**).

5. To (**whom**, who) are you sending this box?

6. (**He**, Him) is studying Spanish.

7. Hans wants to do the job (**himself**, hisself).

8. A tray of muffins was placed between (**us**, we).

ৰ্চৰ্চৰ্চৰ্চৰ্চৰ্চৰ্চৰ্চৰ্চৰ্চৰ্চৰ্চৰ্চৰ্চ

D. Compound Pronoun Usage:

Reminder: Don't forget the finger trick.

Directions: Circle the correct pronoun.

1. Would you like to come with Deka and (**me**, I)?

2. The janitor, the window washer, and (him, **he**) met for a meeting.

3. Gabe and (us, **we**) need to redo our homework.

4. The president of her company and (her, **she**) discussed her new job.

5. Pass Grammy and (**them**, they) the mashed potatoes.

6. The winners of the game were Sid and (**I**, me).

484

C. Pronoun Usage:

Directions: Circle the correct pronoun.

1. (I, Me) have dug a hole for a bush.

2. Did you receive a letter from (we, us)?

3. Give (them, they) your name.

4. The first to arrive at the party was (her, she).

5. To (whom, who) are you sending this box?

6. (He, Him) is studying Spanish.

7. Hans wants to do the job (himself, hisself).

8. A tray of muffins was placed between (us, we).

శ్రీశ్రీశ్రీశ్రీశ్రీశ్రీశ్రీశ్రీశ్రీశ్రీశ్రీశ్రీశ్రీశ్రీశ్రీ

D. Compound Pronoun Usage:

Reminder: Don't forget the finger trick.

Directions: Circle the correct pronoun.

1. Would you like to come with Deka and (me, I)?

2. The janitor, the window washer, and (him, he) met for a meeting.

3. Gabe and (us, we) need to redo our homework.

4. The president of her company and (her, she) discussed her new job.

5. Pass Grammy and (them, they) the mashed potatoes.

6. The winners of the game were Sid and (I, me).

Name_____   **PRONOUNS**

WORKBOOK PAGE 219

Date_____   **Review**

E. Reflexive Pronouns:

Directions: Write six reflexive pronouns. **(also themselves)**

1. ____**myself**____   4. ____**yourself**____

2. ____**himself**____   5. ____**itself**____

3. ____**herself**____   6. ____**ourselves**____

ૐ ૐ ૐ ૐ ૐ ૐ ૐ ૐ ૐ ૐ ૐ ૐ ૐ ૐ ૐ ૐ

F. Pronoun or Adjective?:

Directions: Write **PRO.** in the blank if the boldfaced word serves as a pronoun.

1. **PRO.**   Did you find **that**?

2. _____   **Which** knob is copper?

3. _____   **Both** boys laughed and waved to us.

4. **PRO.**   After basketball practice, **some** stayed to shoot hoops.

5. _____   Put **these** stickers on your book cover.

6. **PRO.**   **Many** ~~of the band members~~ march in every parade.

ૐ ૐ ૐ ૐ ૐ ૐ ૐ ૐ ૐ ૐ ૐ ૐ ૐ ૐ ૐ ૐ

G. Indefinite Pronouns: ANSWERS MAY VARY/REPRESENTATIVE ANSWERS:

Directions: Write an indefinite pronoun that makes sense in each blank.

1. Did ____**anyone**____ hear that?

2. The announcer asked ____**everyone**____ to stand.

3. ____**Nobody**____ answered the telephone.

486

E. Reflexive Pronouns:

Directions: Write six reflexive pronouns.

1. _____   4. _____

2. _____   5. _____

3. _____   6. _____

🐿🐿🐿🐿🐿🐿🐿🐿🐿🐿🐿🐿🐿🐿🐿🐿🐿

F. Pronoun or Adjective?:

Directions: Place **PRO.** in the blank if the boldfaced word serves as a pronoun.

1. _____   Did you find **that**?

2. _____   **Which** knob is copper?

3. _____   **Both** boys laughed and waved to us.

4. _____   After basketball practice, **some** stayed to shoot hoops.

5. _____   Put **these** stickers on your book cover.

6. _____   **Many** of the band members march in every parade.

🐿🐿🐿🐿🐿🐿🐿🐿🐿🐿🐿🐿🐿🐿🐿🐿🐿

G. Indefinite Pronouns:

Directions: Write an indefinite pronoun that makes sense in each blank.

1. Did _____ hear that?

2. The announcer asked _____ to stand.

3. _____ answered the telephone.

WORKBOOK PAGE 220

H. Possessive Pronouns:

Directions: Unscramble these possessive pronouns.

1. s h i - __**his**__   6. t e r i h - __**their**__

2. y m - __**my**__   7. u r o - __**our**__

3. s r h e - __**hers**__   8. u y r o - __**your**__

4. r u o s y - __**yours**__   9. e n i m - __**mine**__

5. s t i - __**its**__   10. o s h e w - __**whose**__

కాకాకాకాకాకాకాకాకాకాకాకాకాకాకాకా

I. Possessive Pronoun Usage:

Directions: Circle the correct pronoun.

1. Mr. Jones carried a cane and (**his**, her) own luggage.

2. I like (them, **their**) scooters.

3. The guides showed (his, **their**) groups through the museum.

4. Carrie likes the dog that she bought; it is (her, **hers**).

కాకాకాకాకాకాకాకాకాకాకాకాకాకాకాకా

J. Antecedents:

Directions: Circle the possessive pronoun; write its antecedent in the blank.

1. __**children**__ Some children brought **their** marbles to the playground.

2. __**Mary**__ Mary lifted **her** baton and began.

3. __**Mario/Jan**__ Did Mario and Jan lead **their** team to victory?

4. __**We**__ We must use **our** talents to solve this puzzle.

488

H. Possessive Pronouns:

Directions: Unscramble these possessive pronouns.

1. s h i - _____   6. t e r i h - _____

2. y m - _____   7. u r o - _____

3. s r h e - _____   8. u y r o - _____

4. r u o s y - _____   9. e n i m - _____

5. s t i - _____   10. o s h e w - _____

I. Possessive Pronoun Usage:

Directions: Circle the correct pronoun.

1. Mr. Jones carried a cane and (his, her) own luggage.

2. I like (them, their) scooters.

3. The guides showed (his, their) groups through the museum.

4. Carrie likes the dog that she bought; it is (her, hers).

J. Antecedents:

Directions: Circle the possessive pronoun; write its antecedent in the blank.

1. _____   Some children brought their marbles to the playground.

2. _____   Mary lifted her baton and began.

3. _____   Did Mario and Jan lead their team to victory?

4. _____   We must use our talents to solve this puzzle.

489

Name_____   **PRONOUNS**

Date_____   **Test**

A.   Directions: Circle the correct pronoun.

 1.   My friends and (**I**, me) are meeting at four o'clock.

 2.   The new teacher is (**he**, him) by the copy machine.

 3.   Do you want to sit between Jim and (I, **me**).

 4.   Those girls asked to water the lawn by (**themselves**, theirselves).

 5.   Jill doesn't drive (his, **her**) own car to work.

 6.   A judge and (**she**, her) will marry soon.

 7.   Please allow your brother to do the task (**himself**, hisself).

 8.   Some bowlers left (his, **their**) bowling balls at home.

 9.   Misty asked (I, **me**) to help with the prom.

10.   For (**whom**, who) did you buy a present?

11.   Our friends agreed with (we, **us**).

12.   Josh and (me, **I**) made dinner.

13.   Will you give (we, **us**) a donation?

14.   Someone left (their, **his**) sunglasses on the table. **(Someone = 1 person)**

15.   (**Who**, Whom) has washed the dishes?

B   Directions: Circle the possessive pronoun. Write the antecedent in the blank.

1.   Did the bee go into *its* hive?   _____**bee**_____

2.   The mechanic finished *his* test.   _____**mechanic**_____

3.   Patty wanted *her* mother to wait.   _____**Patty**_____

4.   A few managers gave *their* reports. _____**managers**_____

490

Name_____   **PRONOUNS**

Date_____   **Test**

A. Directions: Circle the correct pronoun.

1. My friends and (I, me) are meeting at four o'clock.

2. The new teacher is (he, him) by the copy machine.

3. Do you want to sit between Jim and (I, me).

4. Those girls asked to water the lawn by (themselves, theirselves).

5. Jill doesn't drive (his, her) own car to work.

6. A judge and (she, her) will marry soon.

7. Please allow your brother to do the task (himself, hisself).

8. Some bowlers left (his, their) bowling balls at home.

9. Misty asked (I, me) to help with the prom.

10. For (whom, who) did you buy a present?

11. Our friends agreed with (we, us).

12. Josh and (me, I) made dinner.

13. Will you give (we, us) a donation?

14. Someone left (their, his) sunglasses on the table.

15. (Who, Whom) has washed the dishes?

B Directions: Circle the possessive pronoun. Write the antecedent in the blank.

1. Did the bee go into its hive?   _____

2. The mechanic finished his test.   _____

3. Patty wanted her mother to wait.   _____

4. A few managers gave their reports. _____   491

A. **Subject/Verb:**
   Directions: Cross out any prepositional phrases. Underline the subject once and the verb or verb phrase twice. Place any infinitive in parentheses **( )**. Label any direct object – **D.O.**

1. Three <u>horses</u> ~~from a local farm~~ <u><u>will enter</u></u> a horserace ~~near Portland~~.
   (D.O. above "horserace")

2. ~~Within an hour of her father's call~~, <u>Mom</u> <u><u>left</u></u> ~~for the airport~~.

3. <u>One</u> ~~of the singers~~ <u><u>stepped</u></u> ~~behind a microphone~~ **(** to sing **)** a solo.

4. Rustic <u>logs</u> <u><u>are lying</u></u> ~~behind their office building~~ ~~at a small airport~~.

5. ~~Before lunch or dinner~~, <u>ranchers</u> <u><u>wash</u></u> and <u><u>dry</u></u> their hands ~~at an outdoor sink~~.
   (D.O. above "hands")

ঔঔঔ

B. **Compound Subjects and Verbs:**
   Directions: Cross out any prepositional phrases. Underline the subject once and the verb or verb phrase twice.

1. A <u>chef</u> and his <u>assistant</u> <u><u>stirred</u></u> sauce ~~into the noodles~~.

2. ~~During a pep rally~~, <u>girls</u> and <u>boys</u> <u><u>sang</u></u> songs and <u><u>cheered</u></u> ~~for their team~~.

3. The <u>newsman</u> and the weather <u>reporter</u> <u><u>talked</u></u> ~~about a tornado~~ ~~in the area~~.

4. <u>(You)</u> <u><u>Move</u></u> that purple sofa here but <u><u>keep</u></u> the pillows ~~on it~~.

ঔঔঔ

C. **Subject-Verb Agreement:**
   Directions: Delete any prepositional phrases. Underline the subject once. Underline the verb that agrees with the subject twice.

1. <u>Ms. Link</u> (**<u><u>works</u></u>**, work) ~~near a bus station~~.

2. Your <u>shirt</u> ~~with blue buttons~~ (are, **<u><u>is</u></u>**) beside the white one.

3. <u>One</u> ~~of the buses~~ (arrive, **<u><u>arrives</u></u>**) ~~at noon~~.

4. Their <u>father</u> and <u>mother</u> (**<u><u>grow</u></u>**, grows) herbs ~~for cooking~~.

492

A. **Subject/Verb:**
    Directions: Cross out any prepositional phrases. Underline the subject once and the verb or verb phrase twice. Place any infinitive in parentheses **( )**. Label any direct object – **D.O.**

1. Three horses from a local farm will enter a horserace near Portland.

2. Within an hour of her father's call, Mom left for the airport.

3. One of the singers stepped behind a microphone to sing a solo.

4. Rustic logs are lying behind their office building at a small airport.

5. Before lunch or dinner, ranchers wash and dry their hands at an outdoor sink.

                                             ❧❧❧

B. **Compound Subjects and Verbs:**
    Directions: Cross out any prepositional phrases. Underline the subject once and the verb or verb phrase twice.

1. A chef and his assistant stirred sauce into the noodles.

2. During a pep rally, girls and boys sang songs and cheered for their team.

3. The newsman and the weather reporter talked about a tornado in the area.

4. Move that purple sofa here but keep the pillows on it.

                                             ❧❧❧

C. **Subject-Verb Agreement:**
    Directions: Delete any prepositional phrases. Underline the subject once. Underline the verb that agrees with the subject twice.

1. Ms. Link (works, work) near a bus station.

2. Your shirt with blue buttons (are, is) beside the white one.

3. One of the buses (arrive, arrives) at noon.

4. Their father and mother (grow, grows) herbs for cooking.

D. **Contractions:**
   Directions: Write the contraction.

1. did not - ____**didn't**____   5. I am - ____**I'm**____   9. do not - ____**don't**____

2. he is - ____**he's**____   6. who is - ____**who's**____   10. I have - ____**I've**____

3. cannot - ____**can't**____   7. they have - **they've**   11. they are -____**they're**____

4. we are - ____**we're**____   8. will not - ____**won't**____   12. would not - **wouldn't**

☙☙☙

E. **You're/Your, It's/Its, and They're/Their/There:**
   Directions: Circle the correct word.

1. Is (**there**, their, they're) a problem?

2. I want (you're, **your**) help.

3. If (its, **it's**) raining, let's use (there, **their**, they're) umbrella.

☙☙☙

F. **Irregular Verbs:**
   Directions: Underline the subject once and the correct verb phrase twice.

1. <u>Has</u> <u>Tara</u> (brung, <u>brought</u>) some water?

2. <u>Cal</u> <u>must have</u> (spoke, <u>spoken</u>) early.

3. <u>I</u> <u>should have</u> (ran, <u>run</u>) further.

4. <u>Hannah</u> <u>might have</u> (<u>come</u>, came) alone.

5. <u>Have</u> your new <u>pigs</u> (ate, <u>eaten</u>) anything?

6. The <u>painter</u> <u>must have</u> (<u>fallen</u>, fell).

7. That stable <u>boy</u> <u>has</u> (went, <u>gone</u>) home.

8. This <u>hose</u> <u>may have</u> (sprang, <u>sprung</u>) a leak.

9. <u>You</u> <u>should have</u> (<u>drunk</u>, drank) more juice.

494

D. **Contractions:**
   Directions: Write the contraction.

1. did not - _____   5. I am - _____   9. do not - _____

2. he is - _____   6. who is - _____   10. I have - _____

3. cannot - _____   7. they have - _____   11. they are - _____

4. we are - _____   8. will not - _____   12. would not - _____

ॐॐॐ

E. **You're/Your, It's/Its, and They're/Their/There:**
   Directions: Circle the correct word.

1. Is (there, their, they're) a problem?

2. I want (you're, your) help.

3. If (its, it's) raining, let's use (there, their, they're) umbrella.

ॐॐॐ

F. **Irregular Verbs:**
   Directions: Underline the subject once and the correct verb phrase twice.

1. Has Tara (brung, brought) some water?

2. Cal must have (spoke, spoken) early.

3. I should have (ran, run) further.

4. Hannah might have (come, came) alone.

5. Have your new pigs (ate, eaten) anything?

6. The painter must have (fallen, fell).

7. That stable boy has (went, gone) home.

8. This hose may have (sprang, sprung) a leak.

9. You should have (drunk, drank) more juice.   495

G. **Sit/Set, Lie/Lay, and Rise/Raise:**
    Directions: Delete any prepositional phrases. Underline the subject once
    and the verb/verb phrase twice. Label any direct object – **D.O.**

                                                                    D.O.
1. <u>We</u> <u>had been</u> (<u>lying</u>, laying) ~~near a fire~~.   3. <u>Mia</u> (rises, <u>raises</u>) ostriches.

2. <u>Are</u> <u>they</u> (setting, <u>sitting</u>) ~~with Stan~~?   4. (<u>You</u>) (<u>Lie</u>, Lay) here.

                                    ❧ ❧ ❧

H. **Tenses:**
    Directions: Underline the subject once and the verb or verb phrase
    twice. Write the tense (*present, past*, or *future*) in the blank.

1. _____**present**_____   His <u>puppy</u> <u>yelps</u> constantly.

2. _____**present**_____   <u>Chan</u> and <u>Janie</u> <u>enjoy</u> chess.

3. _____**past**_____   <u>Fireworks</u> <u>shot</u> into the air.

4. _____**past**_____   <u>Marta</u> <u>asked</u> me to stay.

5. _____**future**_____   <u>Toby</u> <u>will join</u> the Army soon.

                                    ❧ ❧ ❧

I. **Action Verb or Linking Verb?:**

    Directions: Place **X** if the verb is linking.

1. __**X**__ This oatmeal **<u>smells</u>** good.   3. __**X**__ My bare toes **are** dirty.

2. __**X**__ Tate **<u>appeared</u>** breathless.   4. _____ She **<u>remained</u>** in her seat.

                                    ❧ ❧ ❧

J. **Transitive and Intransitive Verbs:**

    Directions: Place a ✓ if the verb is transitive.

            Remember: A transitive verb will have a direct object.
                   D.O.T. > Direct Object = Transitive

1. _____ Lu stood up.   3. __✓__ Do you like mysteries?

2. __✓__ We planted apple trees.   4. _____ One camel spit at me.
496

G. **Sit/Set, Lie/Lay, and Rise/Raise:**

Directions: Delete any prepositional phrases. Underline the subject once
and the verb/verb phrase twice. Label any direct object – **D.O.**

1. We had been (lying, laying) near a fire.   3.   Mia (rises, raises) ostriches.

2. Are they (setting, sitting) with Stan?   4.   (Lie, Lay) here.

&ҩ҂҂

H. **Tenses:**

Directions: Underline the subject once and the verb or verb phrase
twice. Write the tense (*present, past,* or *future*) in the blank.

1. _____   His puppy yelps constantly.

2. _____   Chan and Janie enjoy chess.

3. _____   Fireworks shot into the air.

4. _____   Marta asked me to stay.

5. _____   Toby will join the Army soon.

&ҩ҂҂

I. **Action Verb or Linking Verb?:**

Directions: Place **X** if the verb is linking.

1. _____   This oatmeal **smells** good.   3.   _____   My bare toes **are** dirty.

2. _____   Tate **appeared** breathless.   4.   _____   She **remained** in her seat.

&ҩ҂҂

J. **Transitive and Intransitive Verbs:**

Directions: Place a ✓ if the verb is transitive.

Remember: A transitive verb will have a direct object.
D.O.T. > Direct Object = Transitive

1. _____   Lu stood up.   3.   _____   Do you like mysteries?

2. _____   We planted apple trees.   4.   _____   One camel spit at me.

K. **Abstract and Concrete Nouns:**

Directions: Place a ✓ if the noun is abstract.

1. _✓_ love   3. _✓_ harm   5. ___ hubcap

2. _✓_ kindness   4. ___ pin   6. _✓_ grace

∜∜∜

L. **Common and Proper Nouns:**

Directions: Place a ✓ if the noun is proper.

1. ___ MOUNTAIN   3. ___ ELBOW   5. ___ BANKER

2. _✓_ TENNESSEE   4. _✓_ OZARKS   6. _✓_ CHINA

∜∜∜

M. **Singular and Plural Nouns:**

Directions: Write the correct spelling of each plural noun.

1. halo - _____**halos**_____   6. goose - _____**geese**_____

2. march - _____**marches**_____   7. touch - _____**touches**_____

3. charity - _____**charities**_____   8. railway - _____**railways**_____

4. airbus - _____**airbuses**_____   9. skiff - _____**skiffs**_____

5. penknife - _____**penknives**_____ 10. laughter - _____**laughter**_____

∜∜∜

N. **Nouns Used as Subjects, Direct Objects, Indirect Objects, and Objects of the Preposition:**

Directions: Label any subject (**S.**), direct object (**D.O.**), indirect object (**I.O.**), and object of the preposition (**O.P.**).

  S.   D.O.   O.P.   S.   I.O.   D.O.
1. We added milk to our sliced bananas.   3. Jack told us the truth.
  S.   D.O.   S.   D.O.   O.P.
2. I am searching a database.   4. Did you find a toad near our tent?

498

K. **Abstract and Concrete Nouns:**

   Directions: Place a ✓ if the noun is abstract.

1. ____   love   3. ____   harm   5. ____   hubcap

2. ____   kindness   4. ____   pin   6. ____   grace

ॐॐॐ

L. **Common and Proper Nouns:**

   Directions: Place a ✓ if the noun is proper.

1. ____   MOUNTAIN   3. ____   ELBOW   5. ____   BANKER

2. ____   TENNESSEE   4. ____   OZARKS   6. ____   CHINA

ॐॐॐ

M. **Singular and Plural Nouns:**

   Directions: Write the correct spelling of each plural noun.

1. halo - _____   6. goose - _____

2. march - _____   7. touch - _____

3. charity - _____   8. railway - _____

4. airbus - _____   9. skiff - _____

5. penknife - _____   10. laughter - _____

ॐॐॐ

N. **Nouns Used as Subjects, Direct Objects, Indirect Objects, and Objects of the Preposition:**

   Directions: Label any subject (**S.**), direct object (**D.O.**), indirect object (**I.O.**), and object of the preposition (**O.P.**).

1. We added milk to our sliced bananas.   3. Jack told us the truth.

2. I am searching a database.   4. Did you find a toad near our tent?

499

Name_____   **Cumulative Review**
WORKBOOK PAGE 225
Date_____   **At the End of the Pronoun Unit**

O. **Possessive Nouns:**

  Directions: Write the possessive in each blank.

1. carvings on a desk - _____**desk's carvings**_____

2. a check received by Ross - _____**Ross's (Ross') check**_____

3. bags carried by a traveler - _____**traveler's bags**_____

4. a moat belonging to a castle - _____**castle's moat**_____

5. competition of more than one poodle - _____**poodles' competition**_____

6. dance class attended by more than one child - ___**children's dance class**___

       ☙☙☙

P. **Predicate Nominatives:**

  Directions: Underline the subject once and the verb twice. Label a
       predicate nominative – **P.N.** Write the inverted form in the blank.
       P.N.
1. A <u>bay</u> <u>is</u> an evergreen tree with laurel leaves.

  ____**An evergreen tree (with laurel leaves) is a bay.**____
       P.N.
2. That <u>blizzard</u> <u>was</u> our worst storm.

  ____**Our worst storm was that blizzard.**_____
    P.N.
3. <u>Nightingales</u> <u>are</u> birds with a pretty song.

  ____**Birds (with a pretty song) are nightingales.**____

       ☙☙☙

Q. **Identifying Nouns:**

  Directions: Circle any nouns.

Remember: Determiners will help you to find some nouns.

1. I bought two **pints** of **milk**, **bread**, several **tomatoes**, and **bacon** for my
 lunch.

2. The **conductor** on that **train** collects **tickets** from many **passengers**.
500

O. **Possessive Nouns:**

Directions: Write the possessive in each blank.

1. carvings on a desk - _____

2. a check received by Ross - _____

3. bags carried by a traveler - _____

4. a moat belonging to a castle - _____

5. competition of more than one poodle - _____

6. dance class attended by more than one child - _____

ॐॐॐ

P. **Predicate Nominatives:**

Directions: Underline the subject once and the verb twice. Label a
                    predicate nominative – **P.N.** Write the inverted form in the blank.

1. A bay is an evergreen tree with laurel leaves.

_____

2. That blizzard was our worst storm.

_____

3. Nightingales are birds with a pretty song.

_____

ॐॐॐ

Q. **Identifying Nouns:**

Directions: Circle any nouns.

Remember: Determiners will help you to find some nouns.

1. I bought two pints of milk, bread, several tomatoes, and bacon for my lunch.

2. The conductor on that train collects tickets from many passengers.

R. **Descriptive Adjectives:**

   Directions: Write a descriptive adjective in each blank.

1. _____**gentle**_____ deer   3. _____**checked**_____ tie

2. _____**thriving**_____ plant   4. _____**sleek**_____ snowboard

ৰ৵ৰ৵ৰ৵

S. **Proper Adjectives:**

   Directions: Circle a proper adjective. Underline any predicate adjective.
PROPER ADJECTIVES ARE BOLDFACED; PREDICATE ADJECTIVES ARE ITALICIZED.

1. That **African** nation is *powerful*.

2. Her hair was once *red*.

3. Her brother is dating a **British** model.

ৰ৵ৰ৵ৰ৵

T. **Limiting (Determining) Adjectives:**

   ▪ **Articles: a, an, the**
   ▪ **Demonstratives: this, that, these, those**
   ▪ **Possessive Pronouns: my, his, her, your, its, our, their, whose**
   ▪ **Numbers:** Example: *one* sign
   ▪ **Indefinites: any, few, no, many, most, several, some**
   ▪ **Possessive Nouns:** Example: an *elephant's* trunk

   Directions: Write an appropriate limiting adjective from each category.

1. Article – **The** house is old.   4. Possessive pronouns – **Her** house is old.

2. Demonstratives – **These** houses are old.   5. Possessive nouns – **Pat's** house is old.

3. Numbers – **Five** houses are old.   6. Indefinites – **Some** houses are old.

ৰ৵ৰ৵ৰ৵

U. **Identifying Adjectives:**

   Directions: Circle any adjectives.

1. **Fifteen** plates of **spicy chicken** wings were placed on **a long**, **wooden** table.

2. **Several** reporters asked **the** thief about **his female** partner in **a petty** crime.

502

R. **Descriptive Adjectives:**

   Directions: Write a descriptive adjective in each blank.

1. _____ deer   3. _____ tie

2. _____ plant   4. _____ snowboard

ॐॐॐ

S. **Proper Adjectives:**

   Directions: Circle a proper adjective. Underline any predicate adjective.

1. That African nation is powerful.

2. Her hair was once red.

3. Her brother is dating a British model.

ॐॐॐ

T. **Limiting (Determining) Adjectives:**

   ▯ **Articles: a, an, the**
   ▯ **Demonstratives: this, that, these, those**
   ▯ **Possessive Pronouns: my, his, her, your, its, our, their, whose**
   ▯ **Numbers:** Example: *one* sign
   ▯ **Indefinites: any, few, no, many, most, several, some**
   ▯ **Possessive Nouns:** Example: an *elephant's* trunk

   Directions: Write an appropriate limiting adjective from each category.

1. Article – _____ house is old.   4. Possessive pronouns – _____ house is old.

2. Demonstratives – _____ houses are old.   5. Possessive nouns – _____ house is old.

3. Numbers – _____ houses are old.   6. Indefinites – _____ houses are old.

ॐॐॐ

U. **Identifying Adjectives:**

   Directions: Circle any adjectives.

1. Fifteen plates of spicy chicken wings were placed on a long, wooden table.

2. Several reporters asked the thief about his female partner in a petty crime.

V. **Degrees of Adjectives:**

Directions: Circle the correct answer.

1. This large peach is (**jucier**, juciest) than the small one.

2. His second fable was (**more creative**, creativer) than his first.

3. Micah is the (more curious, **most curious**) triplet.

4. Of all the lifeguards, Mickey was (more dependable, **most dependable**).

๛ ๛ ๛

W. **Adverbs Telling *How, When, Where, and To What Extent*:**

Directions: Delete any prepositional phrases. Underline the subject once and the verb or verb phrase twice. Circle any adverb that tells *how, when, where, or to what extent.*

1. <u>Mom</u> **always** <u>reads</u> that newsletter **completely**.

2. The <u>toddler</u> <u>tends</u> to stumble **rather frequently**.

3. **Yesterday**, some <u>teachers</u> <u>went</u> **downtown** ~~after school~~.

4. <u>Tessa</u> <u>sweeps</u> **quite quickly** but **well**.

5. **Later**, <u>they</u> <u>went</u> **down** ~~into the cellar~~ and <u>walked</u> **around**.

๛ ๛ ๛

X. **Degrees of Adverbs:**

Directions: Circle the correct answer.

1. She checked her blood pressure (more carefully, **most carefully**) the third time.

2. Chessa skates (**more easily**, most easily) than her sister.

3. Fido jumps (higher, **highest**) of the five dogs.

4. The tall athlete shot (more accurately, **most accurately**) in the final game.

5. Of the two lions, the first paced (**more restlessly**, most restlessly).

V.   **Degrees of Adjectives:**

   Directions: Circle the correct answer.

1.   This large peach is (jucier, juciest) than the small one.

2.   His second fable was (more creative, creativer) than his first.

3.   Micah is the (more curious, most curious) triplet.

4.   Of all the lifeguards, Mickey was (more dependable, most dependable).

ॐॐॐ

W.   **Adverbs Telling *How, When, Where, and To What Extent*:**

Directions: Delete any prepositional phrases. Underline the subject once and the verb or verb phrase twice. Circle any adverb that tells *how, when, where, or to what extent.*

1.   Mom always reads that newsletter completely.

2.   The toddler tends to stumble rather frequently.

3.   Yesterday, some teachers went downtown after school.

4.   Tessa sweeps quite quickly but well.

5.   Later, they went down into the cellar and walked around.

ॐॐॐ

X.   **Degrees of Adverbs:**

   Directions: Circle the correct answer.

1.   She checked her blood pressure (more carefully, most carefully) the third time.

2.   Chessa skates (more easily, most easily) than her sister.

3.   Fido jumps (higher, highest) of the five dogs.

4.   The tall athlete shot (more accurately, most accurately) in the final game.

5.   Of the two lions, the first paced (more restlessly, most restlessly).   505

Name_____   **Cumulative Test**

Date_____   **End of Pronoun Unit**

A. Directions: Cross out any prepositional phrases. Underline the subject once
                 and the verb or verb phrase twice.

1. ~~In their living room,~~ they <u>placed</u> a hall clock ~~near a bay window~~.

2. <u>Jose</u> <u>took</u> a deep breath and <u>dived</u> ~~into the water~~.

3. That <u>jacket</u> ~~with red cuffs~~ <u>is</u> ~~within my price range~~.

4. ~~During the summer,~~ <u>tugboats</u> and <u>sailboats</u> <u>travel</u> ~~along the coast~~.

5. An <u>essay</u> ~~concerning New York~~ <u>should be written</u> ~~by Monday~~.

6. (<u>You</u>) <u>Trim</u> the white border ~~from this poster~~ ~~about rocks~~.

7. <u>Everyone</u> ~~except Mary~~ <u>crawled</u> ~~through a cave~~ ~~behind the waterfall~~.

8. ~~During a party~~ ~~at a beach house,~~ some <u>guests</u> <u>walked</u> ~~across the sand~~.

ক্সক্সক্স

B. Directions: Underline the subject once. Underline the verb/verb phrase that
                 agrees with the subject twice.

1. One <u>chef</u> (cook, <u>cooks</u>) delicious gumbo.

2. Their <u>mothers</u> (buys, <u>buy</u>) vintage linens.

3. <u>Mo</u> and his <u>brother</u> (<u>raise</u>, raises) goats.

4. <u>One</u> ~~of the reporters~~ (<u>asks</u>, ask) good questions.

ক্সক্সক্স

C. Directions: Write the contraction.

1. cannot - __**can't**__   5. do not - __**don't**__   9. I would - __**I'd**__

2. will not - __**won't**__   6. I have - __**I've**__   10. he is - __**he's**__

3. where is - __**where's**__   7. we will - __**we'll**__   11. they are - **they're**

4. was not - __**wasn't**__   8. is not - __**isn't**__   12. I am - __**I'm**__

506

A. Directions: Cross out any prepositional phrases. Underline the subject once
              and the verb or verb phrase twice.

1. In their living room, they placed a hall clock near a bay window.

2. Jose took a deep breath and dived into the water.

3. That jacket with red cuffs is within my price range.

4. During the summer, tugboats and sailboats travel along the coast.

5. An essay concerning New York should be written by Monday.

6. Trim the white border from this poster about rocks.

7. Everyone except Mary crawled through a cave behind the waterfall.

8. During a party at a beach house, some guests walked across the sand.

ॐ ॐ ॐ

B. Directions: Underline the subject once. Underline the verb/verb phrase that
              agrees with the subject twice.

1. One chef (cook, cooks) delicious gumbo.

2. Their mothers (buys, buy) vintage linens.

3. Mo and his brother (raise, raises) goats.

4. One of the reporters (asks, ask) good questions.

ॐ ॐ ॐ

C. Directions: Write the contraction.

1. cannot - _____   5. do not - _____   9. I would - _____

2. will not - _____   6. I have - _____   10. he is - _____

3. where is - _____   7. we will - _____   11. they are - _____

4. was not - _____   8. is not - _____   12. I am - _____

507

D. Directions: Circle the correct word.

1. If (**you're**, your) going to the South, visit (they're, their, **there**).

2. (They're, **Their**, There) school will hold (it's, **its**) carnival soon.

3. Do you know if (**they're**, their, there) hiking near (you're, **your**) cabin?

જ⁀જ⁀જ⁀જ⁀જ⁀જ⁀જ⁀જ⁀જ⁀જ⁀જ⁀

E. Directions: Circle the correct verb.

1. He has (went, **gone**) to the creek.   10. The bell must have (**rung**, rang).

2. We have (rode, **ridden**) here alone.   11. Lou has (ate, **eaten**) a snack.

3. My balloon has (busted, **burst**).   12. A patient (laid, **lay**) on a gurney.

4. I had (saw, **seen**) him at the store.   13. She has (**given**, gave) us a gift.

5. Has your watch (**broken**, broke)?   14. Mike may have (**done**, did) that.

6. One racer has (drove, **driven**) fast.   15. She has (threw, **thrown**) a curve.

7. Have you (brung, **brought**) water?   16. I should have (**begun**, began) early.

8. The horse had (ran, **run**) far.   17. Our bus had (came, **come**) late.

9. The sun has (**risen**, raised).   18. A dog is (**lying**, laying) by my door.

જ⁀જ⁀જ⁀

F. Directions: Underline the subject once and the verb or verb phrase
                    twice. Write the tense (*present, past,* or *future*) in the blank.

1. _____**past**_____   Rough <u>waters</u> <u>scared</u> us.

2. _____**present**_____   <u>Dad</u> <u>sells</u> cars.

3. _____**past**_____   The <u>travelers</u> <u>ate</u> tilefish.

4. _____**present**_____   <u>I</u> <u>like</u> crackers and cheese.

5. _____**future**_____   <u>Sara</u> <u>will chop</u> wood.

D. Directions: Circle the correct word.

1. If (you're, your) going to the South, visit (they're, their, there).

2. (They're, Their, There) school will hold (it's, its) carnival soon.

3. Do you know if (they're, their, there) hiking near (you're, your) cabin?

ঔঔঔঔঔঔঔঔঔঔঔ

E. Directions: Circle the correct verb.

1. He has (went, gone) to the creek.   10. The bell must have (rung, rang).

2. We have (rode, ridden) here alone.   11. Lou has (ate, eaten) a snack.

3. My balloon has (busted, burst).   12. A patient (laid, lay) on a gurney.

4. I had (saw, seen) him at the store.   13. She has (given, gave) us a gift.

5. Has your watch (broken, broke)?   14. Mike may have (done, did) that.

6. One racer has (drove, driven) fast.   15. She has (threw, thrown) a curve.

7. Have you (brung, brought) water?   16. I should have (begun, began) early.

8. The horse had (ran, run) far.   17. Our bus had (came, come) late.

9. The sun has (risen, raised).   18. A dog is (lying, laying) by my door.

ঔঔঔ

F. Directions: Underline the subject once and the verb or verb phrase
                   twice. Write the tense (*present, past,* or *future*) in the blank.

1. _____ Rough waters scared us.

2. _____ Dad sells cars.

3. _____ The travelers ate tilefish.

4. _____ I like crackers and cheese.

5. _____ Sara will chop wood.

509

G. Directions: Place an **X** if the noun is concrete.

1. __X__ chalk   4. ____ faith   7. ____ bickering

2. __X__ moss   5. __X__ gum   8. __X__ pore

3. ____ love   6. ____ weakness   9. __X__ flame

ॐॐॐ

H. Directions: Place a ± if the noun is proper.

1. _+_ PLUM ISLAND   4. _+_ MT. ETNA   7. ____ COAST

2. _+_ LABOR DAY   5. ____ TROUT   8. _+_ NANCY

3. _+_ PUGET SOUND   6. _+_ NEW ENGLAND   9. _+_ BOSTON

ॐॐॐ

I. Directions: Write the correct spelling of each plural noun.

1. omnibus - __**omnibuses**__   6. crutch - __**crutches**__

2. dairy - __**dairies**__   7. studio - __**studios**__

3. virus - __**viruses**__   8. mouse - __**mice**__

4. moose - __**moose**__   9. waffle - __**waffles**__

5. thief - __**thieves**__   10. reflex - __**reflexes**__

ॐॐॐ

J. Directions: Write the possessive form in each blank.

1. the doors of our house - __**(our) house's doors**__

2. a bus used by more than one traveler - __**travelers' bus**__

3. a bird refuge belonging to more than one county - __**counties' bird refuge**__

4. a cabin belonging to a captain - __**captain's cabin**__

5. events planned by more than one woman - __**women's events**__

510

G. Directions: Place an **X** if the noun is concrete.

1. ___ chalk   4. ___ faith   7. ___ bickering

2. ___ moss   5. ___ gum   8. ___ pore

3. ___ love   6. ___ weakness   9. ___ flame

ৰৈৰৈৰৈ

H. Directions: Place a ± if the noun is proper.

1. ___ PLUM ISLAND   4. ___ MT. ETNA   7. ___ COAST

2. ___ LABOR DAY   5. ___ TROUT   8. ___ NANCY

3. ___ PUGET SOUND   6. ___ NEW ENGLAND   9. ___ BOSTON

ৰৈৰৈৰৈ

I. Directions: Write the correct spelling of each plural noun.

1. omnibus - _____   6. crutch - _____

2. dairy - _____   7. studio - _____

3. virus - _____   8. mouse - _____

4. moose - _____   9. waffle - _____

5. thief - _____   10. reflex - _____

ৰৈৰৈৰৈ

J. Directions: Write the possessive form in each blank.

1. the doors of our house - _____

2. a bus used by more than one traveler - _____

3. a bird refuge belonging to more than one county - _____

4. a cabin belonging to a captain - _____

5. events planned by more than one woman - _____
511

K. Directions: Circle any nouns.

1. The **cook** and I heated our olive **oil** in an enamel **pan** over medium **heat**.

2. Many **breezes** and **sounds** of the **ocean** come through the **house** on that **cliff**.

ৰ৾৾ৰ৾৾ৰ৾৾

L. Directions: Circle any adjectives.

1. **A comfortable wicker** chair is next to **one small trestle** table in **their dining** room.

2. **That blonde** lady bought **hollow**, **glass** vases in **several** sizes and **bright** colors.

ৰ৾৾ৰ৾৾ৰ৾৾

M. Directions: Write the correct degree of adjective.

1. This new hair dryer is (**more powerful**, most powerful) than the old one.

2. Chessa is the (funnier, **funniest**) student in her class.

3. We chose the (more colorful, **most colorful**) poster of the five.

4. This leather cube is (**more durable**, most durable) than the sea-grass cube.

ৰ৾৾ৰ৾৾ৰ৾৾

N. Directions: Circle the correct pronoun.

1. Mr. Jones gave (we, **us**) his word.

2. The winner was (me, **I**).

3. Lars and (them, **they**) drove to a pier.

4. Take this to Mario and (**her**, she).

5. From (**whom**, who) did you receive the email?

6. His brother, sisters, and (**he**, him) should have come in out of the rain.

7. The girls want to complete the project (**themselves**, theirselves).

8. A doorman greeted (**us**, we) with a huge smile.

9. Each of the boys must take (**his**, their) gear to the locker room.

K. Directions: Circle any nouns.

1. The cook and I heated our olive oil in an enamel pan over medium heat.

2. Many breezes and sounds of the ocean come through the house on that cliff.

২৯২৯২৯

L. Directions: Circle any adjectives.

1. A comfortable wicker chair is next to one small trestle table in their dining room.

2. That blonde lady bought hollow, glass vases in several sizes and bright colors.

২৯২৯২৯

M. Directions: Write the correct degree of adjective.

1. This new hair dryer is (more powerful, most powerful) than the old one.

2. Chessa is the (funnier, funniest) student in her class.

3. We chose the (more colorful, most colorful) poster of the five.

4. This leather cube is (more durable, most durable) than the sea-grass cube.

২৯২৯২৯

N. Directions: Circle the correct pronoun.

1. Mr. Jones gave (we, us) his word.

2. The winner was (me, I).

3. Lars and (them, they) drove to a pier.

4. Take this to Mario and (her, she).

5. From (whom, who) did you receive the email?

6. His brother, sisters, and (he, him) should have come in out of the rain.

7. The girls want to complete the project (themselves, theirselves).

8. A doorman greeted (us, we) with a huge smile.

9. Each of the boys must take (his, their) gear to the locker room.   513

O. Directions: Place **X** in the blank if the boldfaced word serves as an adjective.

1. _____ **Several** decided to go.

2. _____ **What** do you know?

3. __X__ **This** hut was built last year.

4. __X__ With two days' notice, **many** sailors returned to their ship.

5. __X__ Cal has decided **which** pogo stick he wants.

❦❦❦

P. Directions: Fill in the blank.

1. Write a possessive pronoun: __my, mine, his, her, hers, your, yours, its,__
                                __our, ours, their, theirs, whose__

2. Write an infinitive: **to skip**   (ANSWER MAY VARY/REPRESENTATIVE ANSWER)

3. Write a reflexive pronoun: __myself, himself, herself, yourself, itself,__
                              __ourselves, themselves__

4. Write an indefinite pronoun: __no, any, some, several, many, none,__
                                __few, *or other indefinite pronouns*__

5. What is the antecedent of the possessive pronoun of this sentence?
   Lee has taken his dog to a doggie park. _____**Lee**_____

❦❦❦

Q. Directions: Circle any adverb.

1. Tessa **never** goes **anywhere alone** after dark.

2. One golfer did **not** score **very high yesterday**.

3. The couple **recently** walked **downtown together**.

❦❦❦

R. Directions: Circle the correct word.

1. I don't feel (**well**, good).

2. That person always drives (slow, **slowly**).

3. Stop acting (**weirdly**, weird) in front of your friends.

514

O. Directions: Place **X** in the blank if the boldfaced word serves as an adjective.

1. _____   **Several** decided to go.

2. _____   **What** do you know?

3. _____   **This** hut was built last year.

4. _____   With two days' notice, **many** sailors returned to their ship.

5. _____   Cal has decided **which** pogo stick he wants.
ॐॐॐ

P. Directions: Fill in the blank.

1. Write a possessive pronoun: _____

2. Write an infinitive: _____

3. Write a reflexive pronoun: _____

4. Write an indefinite pronoun: _____

5. What is the antecedent of the possessive pronoun of this sentence?

    Lee has taken his dog to a doggie park. _____
ॐॐॐ

Q. Directions: Circle any adverb.

1. Tessa never goes anywhere alone after dark.

2. One golfer did not score very high yesterday.

3. The couple recently walked downtown together.
ॐॐॐ

R. Directions: Circle the correct word.

1. I don't feel (well, good).

2. That person always drives (slow, slowly).

3. Stop acting (weirdly, weird) in front of your friends.

515

S.   Directions: Write the correct degree of adverbs.

1.   Tessa skates (smoothly) _____**most smoothly**_____ of anyone in her family.

2.   Of the twins, Brian gave his speech (clearly) _____**more clearly**_____.

3.   Ross brushes the mare (briskly) _____**more briskly**_____ than the colt.

4.   At the fourth hole, the golfer hit his ball (hard) _____**hardest**_____.

❧❧❧

T.   Directions: Look at the boldfaced word in each sentence. Label how it
                          functions in the sentence.

    S.   = subject

    P.N. = predicate nominative

    D.O. =   direct object

    I.O. = indirect object

    O.P. = object of the preposition

1.   **D.O.**   Do not scare **me**.

2.   **P.N.**   His purchase was a **bottle** from India.

3.   **S.**   At the beginning of the day, **Dad** cleaned out our car.

4.   **D.O.**   The tight end caught the **football** in the end zone.

5.   **S.**   Marco and **she** are rocking on a horse.

6.   **O.P.**   Ham and eggs were served for **breakfast**.

7.   **I.O.**   Dee built her **children** a fort in their backyard.

8.   **O.P.**   The performer received applause for his **acting**.

9.   **D.O.**   Have you ever seen a **raccoon**?

10. **P.N.**   Our uncle is that **man** in the blue and white bulky sweater.

S.   Directions: Write the correct degree of adverbs.

1.   Tessa skates (smoothly) _____ of anyone in her family.

2.   Of the twins, Brian gave his speech (clearly) _____.

3.   Ross brushes the mare (briskly) _____ than the colt.

4.   At the fourth hole, the golfer hit his ball (hard) _____.

ॐॐॐ

T.   Directions: Look at the boldfaced word in each sentence. Label how it
                           functions in the sentence.

               S.   = subject

               P.N. = predicate nominative

               D.O. =   direct object

               I.O. = indirect object

               O.P. = object of the preposition

1.   _____   Do not scare **me**.

2.   _____   His purchase was a **bottle** from India.

3.   _____   At the beginning of the day, **Dad** cleaned out our car.

4.   _____   The tight end caught the **football** in the end zone.

5.   _____   Marco and **she** are rocking on a horse.

6.   _____   Ham and eggs were served for **breakfast**.

7.   _____   Dee built her **children** a fort in their backyard.

8.   _____   The performer received applause for his **acting**.

9.   _____   Have you ever seen a **raccoon**?

10. _____   Our uncle is that **man** in the blue and white bulky sweater.

Date_____

The four types of sentences are declarative, interrogative, imperative, and exclamatory.

1. A **declarative** sentence makes a statement; it ends in a period (.).
   Example: His hair is black**.**

2. An **interrogative** sentence asks a question; it ends in a question mark (**?**).
   Example: Is Tom sick**?**

3. An **imperative** sentence gives a command; it ends in a period (.).
   Example: Tear this into pieces.

4. An **exclamatory** sentence shows emotion; it ends in an exclamation point (**!**).
   Example: Look out**!**

&&&&&&&&&&&&&

A.   Directions: Write the sentence type on the line.

1. _____**exclamatory**_____   Stop that car!

2. _____**imperative**_____   Put a leash on your dog.

3. _____**declarative**_____   This book has many pictures.

4. _____**interrogative**_____   Do you wear a helmet?

B.   Directions: Write the sentence type on the line. Place a period, question mark, or exclamation point at the end of the sentence.

1. _____**interrogative**_____   Do you have a ruler**?**

2. _____**declarative**_____   Mafalde is a type of pasta.

3. _____**exclamatory**_____   Wow! We did it**!**

4. _____**imperative**_____   Go to recess.

5. _____**declarative**_____   We asked if we could stay.

6. _____**imperative**_____   Be sure to exit here.

518

The four types of sentences are declarative, interrogative, imperative, and exclamatory.

1. A **declarative** sentence makes a statement; it ends in a period (.).
    Example: His hair is black**.**

2. An **interrogative** sentence asks a question; it ends in a question mark (**?**).
    Example: Is Tom sick**?**

3. An **imperative** sentence gives a command; it ends in a period (.).
    Example: Tear this into pieces**.**

4. An **exclamatory** sentence shows emotion; it ends in an exclamation point (**!**).
    Example: Look out**!**

   ৯৯৯৯৯৯৯৯৯৯৯৯৯

A.   Directions: Write the sentence type on the line.

1. _____   Stop that car!

2. _____   Put a leash on your dog.

3. _____   This book has many pictures.

4. _____   Do you wear a helmet?

B.   Directions: Write the sentence type on the line. Place a period, question
                mark, or exclamation point at the end of the sentence.

1. _____   Do you have a ruler

2. _____   Mafalde is a type of pasta

3. _____   Wow! We did it

4. _____   Go to recess

5. _____   We asked if we could stay

6. _____   Be sure to exit here

519

Name_____   **SENTENCE TYPES**
WORKBOOK PAGE 229
Date_____

The four types of sentences are declarative, interrogative, imperative, and exclamatory.

1. A **declarative** sentence makes a statement; it ends in a period (**.**).

2. An **interrogative** sentence asks a question; it ends in a question mark (**?**).

3. An **imperative** sentence gives a command; it ends in a period (**.**).

4. An **exclamatory** sentence shows emotion; it ends in an exclamation point (**!**).

చాచాచాచాచాచాచాచాచాచాచా

A.   Directions: Write the type of sentence. Place a punctuation mark at the end of each sentence.

1. _____**imperative**_____   Put putty in this hole**.**

2. _____**declarative**_____   This has a fruity flavor**.**

3. _____**interrogative**_____   How do I make fondue**?**

4. _____**declarative**_____   Let's play checkers**.**

5. _____**imperative**_____   Divide your paper into two columns**.**

6. _____**declarative**_____   A buran is a type of storm**.**

7. _____**exclamatory**_____   Yikes! We're lost**!**

చాచాచాచాచాచా

B.   Directions: Write the sentence type required.
ANSWERS MAY VARY/REPRESENTATIVE ANSWERS:
1. declarative: _____**My eye is twitching.**_____

2. interrogative: _____**Do you like poetry?**_____

3. exclamatory: _____**No! I refuse!**_____

4. imperative: _____**Touch your toes.**_____
520

Name_____

Date_____

The four types of sentences are declarative, interrogative, imperative, and exclamatory.

1. A **declarative** sentence makes a statement; it ends in a period (**.**).

2. An **interrogative** sentence asks a question; it ends in a question mark (**?**).

3. An **imperative** sentence gives a command; it ends in a period (**.**).

4. An **exclamatory** sentence shows emotion; it ends in an exclamation point (**!**).

࿐࿐࿐࿐࿐࿐࿐࿐࿐࿐࿐࿐࿐

A. Directions: Write the type of sentence. Place a punctuation mark at the end of each sentence.

1. _____   Put putty in this hole

2. _____   This has a fruity flavor

3. _____   How do I make fondue

4. _____   Let's play checkers

5. _____   Divide your paper into two columns

6. _____   A buran is a type of storm

7. _____   Yikes! We're lost

࿐࿐࿐࿐࿐

B. Directions: Write the sentence type required.

1. declarative: _____

2. interrogative: _____

3. exclamatory: _____

4. imperative: _____

ENVELOPE

The envelope for a friendly letter usually is in **block form**. That means that each line begins exactly below the first letter in the line before it.

YOUR NAME
HOUSE NUMBER AND STREET ADDRESS   **RETURN ADDRESS**
CITY, STATE   ZIP CODE

PERSON TO WHOM YOU ARE SENDING LETTER
HOUSE NUMBER AND STREET ADDRESS
CITY, STATE   ZIP CODE

Sample:

Misty Storm   ************
10031 North 90th Lane   STAMP
Scottsdale, AZ   85258   ************

Mr. and Mrs. James Tuley
288222 NW Boones Ferry Road
Wilsonville, OR   97070

IMPORTANT NOTES:

1. In a formal envelope, abbreviations are not used.

2. A variation of the block style allows for indenting each line. If this is chosen, both the return address and the regular address must be indented.

FRIENDLY LETTER

The parts of a friendly letter are the **heading**, the **salutation** (greeting), the **body**, the **closing**, and the **signature**.

A three-lined formal heading will be used. In informal letters, the date is frequently the only item included.

In a formal letter, as in all formal writing, abbreviations are not used. The exception to this is the postal code for states. A postal code is capitalized, and no punctuation is used.

Examples: Vermont = VT   Missouri = MO
North Dakota = ND   Idaho = ID

FRIENDLY LETTER PARTS:

	HOUSE NUMBER AND STREET NAME
	or POST OFFICE BOX
HEADING	CITY, STATE ZIP CODE
	COMPLETE DATE (no abbreviations)

GREETING Dear _____,

BODY The message is written here. Indent at least five letters. You may skip a line between the greeting and the body. Maintain margins on both sides of the paper. Be sure to start a new paragraph each time you change topics.

CLOSING Sincerely,
SIGNATURE Writer's Name

Important Notes:

A. Note the use of commas. Place a comma between the city and state in the heading. Place one after the greeting. Place one at the end of the closing. Do **NOT** place a comma between the state and zip code in the heading.

B. Note that the heading, the closing, and the signature are lined up. You should be able to draw a straight line down the page.

C. Capitalize only the **first word** of a closing. Be sure that you spell *sincerely* and *truly* correctly.

D. Space a letter down a page; don't clump it at the top half.

E. Maintain margins. Set up your heading so that your longest line does not flow into the margin area.

Name_____ **FRIENDLY LETTERS/**

Date_____ **ENVELOPES**

NOTE: Give students many opportunities to write friendly letters and envelopes throughout the school year.

Write a friendly letter to someone. Label the parts of your friendly letter.

LETTERS AND ENVELOPES MAY VARY BUT SHOULD BE ACCURATE.

	STUDENT'S STREET ADDRESS
HEADING	**TOWN (CITY), STATE ZIP CODE**
	TODAY'S DATE

Dear Leo,   SALUTATION (GREETING)

Hi! Did your family go to the East to visit Maryland, Delaware, and Washington, D. C., again this year? Were you able to get tickets to tour the White House? Did you go to Arlington Cemetery one day? Did you visit the Jefferson Memorial and the Washington Monument? (When my BODY **grandmother was young, she walked up every step of the Washington Monument. She must have been in great shape!) Did you take a boat on the Chesapeake Bay on a windy day? Where in Delaware did you and your family go? Did you stay at the beach?**

Your friend, CLOSING

Sandy   SIGNATURE

B. Directions: Write your return address; then, address the envelope to a friend.

STUDENT'S NAME   **STAMP**

STUDENT'S STREET ADDRESS

TOWN (CITY), STATE   ZIP CODE

NAME OF RECIPIENT

STREET ADDRESS OF RECIPIENT

TOWN (CITY), STATE   ZIP CODE

Note: Some put the zip code at the same location but on the next line.

Name_____   **FRIENDLY LETTERS/**

Date_____   **ENVELOPES**

Write a friendly letter to a friend. Label the parts of your friendly letter.

_____
_____
_____
_____
_____
_____
_____
_____
_____
_____
_____
_____
_____
_____
_____
_____
_____
_____
_____
_____
_____

B. Directions: Write your return address; then, address the envelope to a friend.

_____
_____   **STAMP**
_____
_____

                    _____
                    _____
                    _____

_____

WORKBOOK PAGE 233
Date_____

An **interjection is a word or phrase that shows strong emotion.**

A *phrase* is just a group of words. It does **not** express a complete thought.

An interjection ends with an exclamation point (**!**).

Word: Yeah!

Phrase: Far out!

A sentence that expresses strong emotion is called an exclamatory sentence.

A sentence contains both a subject and verb; it expresses a complete thought.

Example: Look out!   (You) <u>Look</u> out!

This expresses a complete thought. It is an exclamatory sentence, **not** an interjection.

ॐॐॐॐॐॐॐ

A.   Directions: Circle any interjection.

1. **Yikes!** I see a bear!

2. The elderly hippie smiled and said, "**Right on!**"

3. **Ouch!** That hurt!

4. "**Oh dear!**" Grandma murmured.

5. We're leaving now! **Yeah!**

B.   Directions: Write an appropriate interjection in the blank.

1. _____**Sh!**_____ Be quiet!

2. You're wet! _____**Oh no!**_____

3. I'm winning! _____**Yippee!**_____
526

An **interjection is a word or phrase that shows strong emotion.**

A *phrase* is just a group of words. It does **not** express a complete thought.

An interjection ends with an exclamation point (**!**).

Word: Yeah!

Phrase: Far out!

A **sentence** that expresses strong emotion is called an **exclamatory sentence**.

A sentence contains both a subject and verb; it expresses a complete thought.

Example: Look out!   (You) Look out!

This expresses a complete thought. It is an exclamatory sentence, **not** an interjection.

෴෴෴෴෴෴෴

A. Directions: Circle any interjection.

1. Yikes! I see a bear!

2. The elderly hippie smiled and said, "Right on!"

3. Ouch! That hurt!

4. "Oh dear!" Grandma murmured.

5. We're leaving now! Yeah!

B. Directions: Write an appropriate interjection in the blank.

1. _____ Be quiet!

2. You're wet! _____

3. I'm winning! _____

527

And, but, and *or* are called coordinating **conjunctions.** They **connect** two or more items.

>Mark **and** I played basketball.

>You **or** Will must finish this job.

>He skis, **but** he doesn't snowboard.

However, *but* is a preposition, not a conjunction, when it means *except.*

☙☙☙☙☙

A. Directions: Circle any coordinating conjunction in each sentence.

1. Please bring a water bottle **or** a canteen.

2. The salesman spoke with a customer **but** looked in another direction.

3. Her mouse pad **and** note box are bright pink leather.

4. One student didn't run **and** play **but** sat alone.

5. You may choose vanilla **or** chocolate **but** not strawberry.

B. Directions: Two coordinating conjunctions might fit in each blank. Write the first in the blank and the second in the parentheses.

1. Randy __**and/or**__ his sister worked in the school carnival booth.

2. The man climbed the tower __**but/and**__ became dizzy.

3. Lars, Peter, __**and/or**__ Julian played football on Saturday.

C. Directions: Write a sentence using the indicated coordinating conjunction.
ANSWERS MAY VARY/REPRESENTATIVE ANSWERS:
1. (or) ____**You may ride the palomino or the pinto.**_____

2. (and) ____**Their house is between Adams Street and First Avenue.**__

3. (but) ____**Soldiers rested but stayed alert.**_____

And, but, and *or* are called coordinating **conjunctions.** They **connect** two or more items.

> Mark **and** I played basketball.

> You **or** Will must finish this job.

> He skis, **but** he doesn't snowboard.

However, *but* is a preposition, not a conjunction, when it means *except.*

ॐॐॐॐॐ

A. Directions: Circle any coordinating conjunction in each sentence.

1. Please bring a water bottle or a canteen.

2. The salesman spoke with a customer but looked in another direction.

3. Her mouse pad and note box are bright pink leather.

4. One student didn't run and play but sat alone.

5. You may choose vanilla or chocolate but not strawberry.

B. Directions: Two coordinating conjunctions might fit in each blank. Write the first in the blank and the second in the parentheses.

1. Randy _____ (_____) his sister worked in the school carnival booth.

2. The man climbed the tower _____ (_____) became dizzy.

3. Lars, Peter, _____ (_____) Julian played football on Saturday.

C. Directions: Write a sentence using the indicated coordinating conjunction.

1. (or) _____

2. (and) _____

3. (but) _____

<u>Sentences</u>:   A sentence expresses a **complete thought**.
            This can also be called an **independent clause**.
            A sentence begins with a **capital letter** and ends with a
            punctuation mark.

<u>Fragments</u>: A fragment does **not** express a complete thought.

~ Sometimes, a subject is missing.   **Example:** My likes to snowboard.

~ Sometimes, a verb is missing.   **Example:** Jan, Sara, and Chan to snowboard.

~ Some fragments have neither subject nor verb.

                    Example: In a hurry on the way to the bus after school.

Do not confuse an imperative sentence with a fragment.

    Example: Go.   This has the subject, (You) – you understood. (You) Go.
                  ᏽᏽᏽᏽᏽᏽᏽᏽᏽᏽᏽᏽᏽᏽ

Directions: Read each fragment. Using the fragment, write a sentence.
ANSWERS MAY VARY/REPRESENTATIVE ANSWERS:

1. Your is torn.   **Your shirt is torn.**

2. Next time.   **You may want to come with us next time.**

3. A purred at our feet.   **A white fluffy kitty purred at our feet.**

4. Old oak tree down.   **An old oak tree blew down during a storm.**

5. Grass in their yard.   **Antonio mowed the grass in their yard.**

6. A photo album in the drawer.

    A photo album containing her college pictures is in the drawer.

7. Grease all over.   **We put grease all over our bicycle chains.**

8. The vineyard on the hill.   **Abe owns the vineyard on the hill.**
530

Sentences: A sentence expresses a **complete thought**.
                    This can also be called an **independent clause**.
                    A sentence begins with a **capital letter** and ends with a
                    punctuation mark.

Fragments: A fragment does **not** express a complete thought.

~ Sometimes, a subject is missing.   **Example:** My likes to snowboard.

~ Sometimes, a verb is missing.   **Example:** Jan, Sara, and Chan to snowboard.

~ Some fragments have neither subject nor verb.

                    Example: In a hurry on the way to the bus after school.

Do not confuse an imperative sentence with a fragment.

Example: Go.   This has the subject, (You) – you understood. (You) Go.

🐎🐎🐎🐎🐎🐎🐎🐎🐎🐎🐎🐎

Directions: Read each fragment. Using the fragment, write a sentence.

1. Your is torn. _____

2. Next time. _____

3. A purred at our feet. _____

4. Old oak tree down. _____

5. Grass in their yard. _____

6. A photo album in the drawer. _____

_____

7. Grease all over. _____

8. The vineyard on the hill. _____

WORKBOOK PAGE 236

Date_____

Note: Spend ample time teaching various ways to correct run-ons!

Sentences: A sentence expresses a **complete thought**. This can also be called an **independent clause**. A sentence begins with a **capital letter** and ends with a **punctuation mark**.

Run-Ons: A run-on may consist of two or more sentences run together.
Example: This ring is silver my brother made it.

If two complete sentences are separated by a comma, it is still a run-on.

Example: This ring is silver, my brother made it.

A run-on may consist of a group of sentences combined with too many conjunctions (*and, but, or*).

Example: Later, the girl did a crossword puzzle ***and*** ate popcorn ***and*** then watched a television show ***but*** didn't like it.

ॐॐॐॐॐॐॐॐॐॐॐ

A.   Directions: Write **S** if the words form a sentence. Write **R-O** if the words form a run-on.

1.   __**S**__   Franny threw dice onto the game board.

2.   __**R-O**__   Nanny stooped, she picked up her poodle.

3.   __**R-O**__   I want juice my friend wants milk.

4.   __**R-O**__   Joe nodded but didn't smile and he waved but didn't come over.

5.   __**S**__   Mom went to the gym to work out.

B.   Directions: Rewrite and change these run-on sentences.
ANSWERS MAY VARY/REPRESENTATIVE ANSWERS:

1. Penny is an artist she draws cards. **Penny is an artist who draws cards.**

2. Wrap this present, put a bow on it. **Wrap this present and put a bow on it.**

3. She took a bath then went to bed. **After she took a bath, she went to bed.**

4. Bo swung and he yelled and he missed the ball but he grinned.

   When Bo swung, yelled, and missed the ball, he grinned.

Sentences: A sentence expresses a **complete thought**. This can also be
                    called an **independent clause**. A sentence begins with a **capital
                    letter** and ends with a **punctuation mark**.

Run-Ons: A run-on may consist of two or more sentences run together.
                    Example: This ring is silver my brother made it.

If two complete sentences are separated by a comma, it is still a run-on.

Example: This ring is silver, my brother made it.

A run-on may consist of a group of sentences combined with too many
conjunctions (*and, but, or*).

Example: Later, the girl did a crossword puzzle *and* ate popcorn *and*
                    then watched a television show *but* didn't like it.

≈≈≈≈≈≈≈≈≈≈≈≈≈

A.   Directions: Write **S** if the words form a sentence. Write **R-O** if the words
                    form a run-on.

1. ____   Franny threw dice onto the game board.

2. ____   Nanny stooped, she picked up her poodle.

3. ____   I want juice my friend wants milk.

4. ____   Joe nodded but didn't smile and he waved but didn't come over.

5. ____   Mom went to the gym to work out.

B.   Directions: Rewrite and change these run-on sentences.

1. Penny is an artist she draws cards. _____

2. Wrap this present, put a bow on it. _____

3. She took a bath then went to bed. _____

4. Bo swung and he yelled and he missed the ball but he grinned.

CAPITALIZATION

NOTES

Rule 1: **Capitalize the first word of any sentence.**

A **declarative sentence** makes a statement.

The balloon is silver.

An **imperative sentence** gives a command.

Blow up this balloon.

An **interrogative sentence** asks a question.

Does this balloon have a hole in it?

An **exclamatory sentence** shows emotion or excitement.

You brought us balloons!

Rule 2: **Capitalize a person's name and initials for names.**

Jenny Victoria Smith   Jenny V. Smith   J. V. S.

Rule 3: **Capitalize a formal or an informal title.**

Formal Title:
Mrs. Jenny Smith   Doctor Jenny Smith   Mayor Jenny Smith
Captain Jenny Smith   Senator Jenny Smith   Judge Jenny Smith

Informal Title:
Aunt Jenny   Grandma Jenny

Capitalize a title standing alone if a person's name can be inserted.

Did **Dad** give you that?
Insert Dad's name: Did **Tony** give you that?

My **dad** takes us hiking.
You would not say *My Tony takes us hiking*. Do not capitalize the informal title standing alone here.

Do not capitalize a title if it is a career choice.

Jenny wants to become a doctor.

Rule 4: **Capitalize the pronoun, I.**
(A pronoun takes the place of a noun.)

May **I** show you?

WORKBOOK PAGE 240

Date_____

<u>Note</u>: Be sure to share answers. Students could also write answers to Part A on their white-boards. In A-#6, discuss that career choices are not capitalized.

A. Directions: Write your answers on the line:

ANSWERS MAY VARY/REPRESENTATIVE ANSWERS:

1. Write you first, middle, and last names.

   ____**Michael**____   ____**Brody**____   ____**Timms**____

2. Write your initials. ____**M. B. T.**____

3. Write a relative's first name. ____**Ralph**____

4. Write your relative's first name with his or her informal title.

          Example: Grammy Tammy ____**Uncle Ralph**____

5. Write how your name would appear if you were to become governor of your

   state. ____**Governor (Student's last name)**____

6. Write a sentence stating a career choice that you may choose. Use the

   pronoun, *I*. ____**I want to be a paramedic.**____

                    ❧ ❧ ❧ ❧ ❧

B. Directions: Write the capital letter above any word that needs to be capitalized.

1. **M**ay **C**arlos and **I** speak with the manager?

2. **L**ast week **M**iss **L**aura **S**. **F**inn was hired as a teacher.

3. **W**as **P**resident **R**ichard **M**. **N**ixon's middle name **M**illhouse?

4. **G**ive **U**ncle **T**roy a hug, **P**arker **V**ictoria.

5. **I** think that **D**r. **M**inski and **M**om won the raffle.

6. **M**y grandmother's title and name is **R**epresentative **M**aria **A**. **T**rueblood.

7. **W**ill **D**ad be interviewing **D**. **T**. **H**ooker who is a fire chief?

8. **B**rian and **C**ousin **A**llen bought a tire from **M**r. **P**amsky, our neighbor.

9. **H**er uncle and **I** work in **S**enator **S**hyer's office.

538

Name_____   **CAPITALIZATION**

Date_____

A. Directions: Write your answers on the line:

1. Write you first, middle, and last names.

   _____ _____ _____

2. Write your initials. _____

3. Write a relative's first name. _____

4. Write your relative's first name with his or her informal title.

      Example: Grammy Tammy   _____

5. Write how your name would appear if you were to become governor of your

   state. _____

6. Write a sentence stating a career choice that you may choose. Use the

   pronoun, *I.* _____

                              ∂∂∂∂∂

B. Directions: Write the capital letter above any word that needs to be capitalized.

1. may carlos and i speak with the manager?

2. last week miss laura s. finn was hired as a teacher.

3. was president richard m. nixon's middle name millhouse?

4. give uncle troy a hug, parker victoria.

5. i think that dr. minski and mom won the raffle.

6. my grandmother's title and name is representative maria a. trueblood.

7. will dad be interviewing d. t. hooker who is a fire chief?

8. brian and cousin allen bought a tire from mr. pamsky, our neighbor.

9. her uncle and i work in senator shyer's office.

539

NOTES

Rule 5:   **Capitalize days of the week and the months.**

      Examples: Thursday   June

Rule 6:   **Capitalize holidays and special days.**

      Examples: Presidents' Day   Arbor Day

Rule 7:   **Capitalize the proper names of a geographic place.**

      Remember: A common noun names a general topic and is not capitalized.
      A proper noun names a specific person or place.

Examples:

bay - Buzzards Bay	spring - Hot Springs
beach - Delray Beach	sound - Vineyard Sound
canyon - Bighorn Canyon	state - Idaho
cape - Cape Charles	swamp - Congaree Swamp
cave - Jewel Cave	town - Pedlar Mills
city - Honolulu	township - Hope Township
creek - White Run	valley - Green Valley
continent - South America	waterfalls - Angel Falls
county - Essex County	
dam - Coulee Dam	
desert - Great Salt Lake Desert	
forest - Wayne National Forest	
fort - Fort Raleigh	
gorge - New River Gorge	
gulf - Persian Gulf	
harbor - Bar Harbor	
island - Fire Island	
lake - Lake Chelean	
mountain - Mount Rainier	
ocean - Pacific Ocean	
park - Olympic National Park	
pass - Deer Lodge Pass	
province - British Columbia	
range - Grand Tetons	
recreation area - Lake Mead Recreation Area	
region - West	
river - Knife River	
ruins - Case Grande Ruins	
sea - Caribbean Sea	
seashore - Padre Island National Seashore	

Name_____   **CAPITALIZATION**

WORKBOOK PAGE 243

Date_____

A. Directions: Write your answers on the line.
ANSWERS MAY VARY/REPRESENTATIVE ANSWERS:

1. Write the name of a city that you would like to visit. ____**Nashville**_____

2. In what state would you like to live someday? ____**South Dakota**_____

3. Name a famous lake. ____**Lake Champlain**_____

4. Name a country that borders the United States. ____**Mexico**_____

5. On what continent do you live? ____**North America**_____

6. Name a mountain range. ____**Ozark Mountains**_____

7. What is your favorite park? ____**Horizon Park**_____

8. Name a place in Canada. ____**Quebec**_____

୨୦୨୦୨୦୨୦୨୦

B. Directions: Write the capital letter above any word that needs to be capitalized.

1. **I**s **D**olphin **I**sland in **G**reat **S**alt **L**ake?

2. **T**hey live near the **Y**ew **M**ountains in the **E**ast.

3. **W**e visited **C**rystal **O**nyx **C**ave near **B**eaver **R**iver in **K**entucky.

4. **L**ast year, we studied about the **C**umberland **F**alls in **D**aniel **B**oone **N**ational **F**orest.

5. **I**s **I**ndian **S**prings near **A**margosa **D**esert in **N**evada?

6. **T**he **F**ox **R**iver empties into **G**reen **B**ay.

7. **D**id you know that **H**umbug **M**ountain is located near the **P**acific **O**cean?

8. **T**hey live in **S**traban **T**ownship in **A**dams **C**ounty, **P**ennsylvania.

9. **D**oes she visit **K**ure **B**each near **C**ape **F**ear each summer?

542

Name_____   **CAPITALIZATION**

Date_____

A. Directions: Write your answers on the line.

1. Write the name of a city that you would like to visit. _____

2. In what state would you like to live someday? _____

3. Name a famous lake. _____

4. Name a country that borders the United States. _____

5. On what continent do you live? _____

6. Name a mountain range. _____

7. What is your favorite park? _____

8. Name a place in Canada. _____

&&&&&

B. Directions: Write the capital letter above any word that needs to be capitalized.

1. is dolphin island in great salt lake?

2. they live near the yew mountains in the east.

3. we visited crystal onyx cave near beaver river in kentucky.

4. last year, we studied about the cumberland falls in daniel boone national forest.

5. is indian springs near amargosa desert in nevada?

6. the fox river empties into green bay.

7. did you know that humbug mountain is located near the pacific ocean?

8. they live in straban township in adams county, pennsylvania.

9. does she visit kure beach near cape fear each summer?

NOTES

Rule 8: Capitalize the name of canals, tunnels, roads, bridges, monuments, and other structures.

Examples: Fort Myers
Fisher Freeway
Blatnik Bridge
Washington Monument
Harry Grove Stadium
Woodlake Nature Center

Do not capitalize a TYPE of building. However, if the name of that building is given, capitalize it.

Examples:
building - bank - Bordon Bank
building - museum - Herritt's Museum
building - library - Mercury Library
building - hospital - Memorial Hospital

Rule 9: Capitalize the name of a school, college, or other place of learning.

Examples:
Liberty Preschool   Mercer University
Taft Elementary School   Kirk Day School
West Middle School   Tri Vocational School

Do not capitalize a school, college, or other place of learning if it does not give a specific name.

Examples: Their sister left for college.
Is Jack attending an art school?

Rule 10: Capitalize the name of a business.

Examples:
Halo Hair Salon   Turbo Bowling Alley
Gentle Giant Maid Service   Lakeside Inn
Gift Baskets to You, Inc.   Apple Car Company
Deluxe Tire Store   Raintree Mall
Elco Enterprises   Arc Airlines
Happy Trails Restaurant   Hal's Ranch Supplies
Whitman Towing   Pride-Lee Corporation
Sharon's Carpet Cleaning   Key Computer Services

Name_____   **CAPITALIZATION**

WORKBOOK PAGE 246

Date_____

A. Directions: Write your answers on the line.
ANSWERS MAY VARY/REPRESENTATIVE ANSWERS:

1. Write the name of the nearest hospital. _____**Mayo Clinic**_____

2. Write the name of your school. _____**Best Elementary School**_____

3. Create a name for a library. _____**Patriot Library**_____

4. What business is closest to your home? _____**Planet Hardware Store**_____

5. If you owned your own store, what would you name it?

_____**Teddy Bear Tea Party Birthday House**_____

ᄃᄋᄃᄋᄃᄋᄃᄋᄃᄋ

B. Directions: Write the capital letter above any word that needs to be capitalized.

1. **I**s **E**gleston **C**hildren's **H**ospital near **A**tlanta **C**hristian **C**ollege?

2. **W**e crossed **M**emorial **B**ridge instead of taking **B**ismarck **E**xpressway.

3. **I**s **A**rmstrong **T**unnel near **P**ittsburgh **C**ivic **A**rena?

4. **T**hey ate at **B**rookside **R**estaurant before going to **B**elcourt **C**astle in **N**ewport.

5. **S**ammy attends **M**uffits **P**reschool on **S**trawberry **L**ane.

6. **I**s **Q**uaker **H**ills **H**igh **S**chool near **R**ock **F**ord **P**lantation?

7. **H**ow far is **S**ilver **S**tadium from **S**trong **M**useum?

8. **T**heir son is a teacher at **T**aft **E**lementary **S**chool on **R**ye **D**rive.

9. **S**he flew into **B**ishop **A**irport and drove to **B**aker **C**ollege.

10. **T**he family stayed at **H**erald **H**otel near **M**ayfair **M**all.

11. **T**ake **I**nterstate 65 to **J**ackson **O**ak **M**onument in **M**obile, **A**labama.

12. **M**icah's mom works at **B**irk **E**lectric **C**ompany near his middle school.

546

Name_____   **CAPITALIZATION**

Date_____

A. Directions: Write your answers on the line.

1. Write the name of the nearest hospital. _____

2. Write the name of your school. _____

3. Create a name for a library. _____

4. What business is closest to your home? _____

5. If you owned your own store, what would you name it?

_____

ॐ ॐ ॐ ॐ ॐ

B. Directions: Write the capital letter above any word that needs to be capitalized.

1. is egleston children's hospital near atlanta christian college?

2. we crossed memorial bridge instead of taking bismarck expressway.

3. is armstrong tunnel near pittsburgh civic arena?

4. they ate at brookside restaurant before going to belcourt castle in newport.

5. sammy attends muffits preschool on strawberry lane.

6. is quaker hills high school near rock ford plantation?

7. how far is silver stadium from strong museum?

8. their son is a teacher at taft elementary school on rye drive.

9. she flew into bishop airport and drove to baker college.

10. the family stayed at herald hotel near mayfair mall.

11. take interstate 65 to jackson oak monument in mobile, alabama.

12. micah's mom works at birk electric company near his middle school.

547

Name_____   **CAPITALIZATION**

WORKBOOK PAGE 247

Date_____   **Using Rules 1 - 10**

Directions: Write the capital letter above any word that needs to be capitalized.

1.   **M**arco and **I** went to **S**ilver **S**trand **S**tate **B**each last **L**abor **D**ay.

2.   **W**e crossed the **H. P. L**ong **B**ridge and drove along **O**ld **S**panish **T**rail.

3.   **H**ave you seen **L**umbermen's **M**onument in **S**ilver **V**alley on **L**ake **H**uron?

4.   **T**he **H**appy **H**en **R**estaurant is located in **R**iverside **M**all.

5.   **J**ana and **A**unt **L**ulu traveled by **C**icero **S**wamp to reach **E**verson **M**useum

     of **A**rt.

6.   **N**ext year, **G**overnor **K**aas will visit the **G**reat **T**ower in **I**taly.

7.   **D**id **M**ichelangelo paint the ceiling of the **S**istine **C**hapel in **V**atican **C**ity?

8.   **L**ast **A**ugust, my father began to work for **S**unshine **T**ile **C**ompany in **C**lay

     County.

9.   **T**he town of **I**conium is near **H**oney **C**reek **S**tate **P**ark and **R**athbun **D**am.

10. **J**ack attended his cousin's wedding at **S**t. **M**ark's **C**hurch on **S**aturday,

     March 21.

11. **O**n **N**urses' **D**ay, we visited **D**iamond **C**averns and picnicked along **B**eaver

     River.

12. **D**id **G**randpa **G**anzi attend **N**ew **J**ersey **T**raining **S**chool near **I**nterstate 80?

13. **C**andace and her uncle camped near **F**ish **C**reek in **M**ount **H**ood **N**ational

     Forest.

548

Directions: Write the capital letter above any word that needs to be capitalized.

1. marco and i went to silver strand state beach last labor day.

2. we crossed the h. p. long bridge and drove along old spanish trail.

3. have you seen lumbermen's monument in silver valley on lake huron?

4. the happy hen restaurant is located in riverside mall.

5. jana and aunt lulu traveled by cicero swamp to reach everson museum of

    art.

6. next year, governor kaas will visit the great tower in italy.

7. did michelangelo paint the ceiling of the sistine chapel in vatican city?

8. last august, my father began to work for sunshine tile company in clay

    county.

9. the town of iconium is near honey creek state park and rathbun dam.

10. jack attended his cousin's wedding at st. mark's church on saturday,

    march 21.

11. on nurses' day, we visited diamond caverns and picnicked along beaver

    river.

12. did grandpa ganzi attend new jersey training school near interstate 80?

13. candace and her uncle camped near fish creek in mount hood national

    forest.

NOTES

Rule 11: **Capitalize the name of a language.**

English	**D**utch
Latin	**G**reek

Rule 12: **Capitalize the name of an organization.**

Vermont **A**ssociation of **H**ome **E**ducators

Children's **C**harities **F**oundation

American **C**ancer **S**ociety

Paradise **H**ills **R**iding **A**ssociation

Rule 13: **Capitalize the first word of a salutation (greeting) and of a closing of a letter.**

<u>Salutation</u>	<u>Closing</u>
Dear Darby,	**S**incerely yours,
My dearest auntie,	**Y**our best friend,

Rule 14: **Capitalize the name of a special event.**

Prescott **P**ioneer **D**ays	**M**anayunk **A**rts **F**estival
Harney **H**orse **S**how	**G**lendale **D**oll and **B**ear **S**how
American **R**oyal **R**odeo	**B**rown **C**ounty **F**air

Do NOT capitalize the event <u>unless</u> a specific name is given.

We attended a bluegrass festival.
Katrina enjoyed that baby-massage workshop.

Rule 15: **Capitalize the first word in a line of poetry.**

Fame is fickle food
Upon a shifting plate...
　　　　　　-Emily Dickinson

Date_____

A. Directions: Write the capital letter above any word that needs to be capitalized.

1. **D**ear **R**eba,

   Nicki and **I** went to **C**lear **C**hannel **J**ob **F**air on **S**aturday.

                              Love forever,

                              Luana

2. **D**o you want to join **G**oldwing **R**iders' **C**lub?

3. **M**om is going to **D**anish **D**ays celebration in **S**anta **B**arbara.

4. **T**he **C**ountry **P**eddler **C**raft **S**how was held in **P**ennsylvania.

5. **J**asmine speaks only **S**panish during the **O**akwood **L**anguage **C**lub meetings.

6. **W**e attended **N**apa **V**alley **F**air and **S**ilverado **P**arade last week.

7. **T**he **R**ussian **C**hildren's **W**elfare **S**ociety will meet next **W**ednesday.

8. **L**ord **A**lfred **T**ennyson wrote in a poem:

   On either side the river lie,

   Long fields of barley and of rye,

9. **M**y friend donated a car to the **N**ational **K**idney **F**oundation last year.

10. **S**ome people attending the **R**ed **P**oppy **F**estival spoke **C**hinese.

                    ✌✌✌✌✌

B. Directions: Write your answer on the line. ANSWERS MAY VARY/REPRESENTATIVE ANSWERS:

1. What language would you like to learn? _____**French**_____

2. Write a closing of a letter. _____**Your pal,**_____

A. Directions: Write the capital letter above any word that needs to be capitalized.

1. dear reba,

    nicki and i went to clear channel job fair on saturday.

                                    love forever,

                                    luana

2. do you want to join goldwing riders' club?

3. mom is going to danish days celebration in santa barbara.

4. the country peddler craft show was held in pennsylvania.

5. jasmine speaks only spanish during the oakwood language club meetings.

6. we attended napa valley fair and silverado parade last week.

7. the russian children's welfare society will meet next wednesday.

8. lord alfred tennyson wrote in a poem:

    on either side the river lie,

    long fields of barley and of rye,

9. my friend donated a car to the national kidney foundation last year.

10. some people attending the red poppy festival spoke chinese.
                    ☙☙☙☙☙

B. Directions: Write your answer on the line.

1. What language would you like to learn? _____

2. Write a closing of a letter. _____

NOTES

Rule 16: **Capitalize the name of any historical document.**

> **G**ettysburg **A**ddress
>
> **V**oting **R**ights **A**ct

Rule 17: **Capitalize the name of any historical event.**

> **B**attle of **Q**uebec
>
> **W**hiskey **R**ebellion

Rule 18: **Capitalize the name of a government body or organization.**

Supreme **C**ourt	**H**ouse of **R**epresentatives
Congress	**D**epartment of **T**reasury

Rule 19: **Capitalize the name of a program.**

> **G**reat **F**rontier
>
> **H**ead **S**tart
>
> **O**peration **S**mile

Rule 20: **Capitalize the name of a colony, empire, or other governments.**

Plymouth **C**olony	**X**ia **D**ynasty
Bear **F**lag **R**epublic	**U**nited **S**tates of **A**merica

Rule 21: **Capitalize the name of a political party and members of a political party.**

Progressive **P**arty	a **D**emocrat
a **R**epublican candidate	

Rule 22: **Capitalize the name of a period of time.**

> **A**ir **A**ge
>
> **E**ra of **G**ood **F**eelings

Name_____   **CAPITALIZATION**
WORKBOOK PAGE 253
Date_____

Directions: Write the capital letter above any word that needs to be capitalized.

1.   **D**id congress pass the **H**epburn **A**ct to regulate railroads?

2.   **A**fter the **L**one **S**tar **R**epublic became **T**exas, the **M**exican war was fought.

3.   **W**here people could not read in **A**merica, the *Constitution* was read to them.

4.   **T**he **V**irginia **C**olony was first a part of the **B**ritish **E**mpire.

5.   **D**uring the **R**evolutionary **W**ar, the **B**attle of **S**avannah was fought in **G**eorgia.

6.   **T**he **D**epartment of **H**ousing and **U**rban **D**evelopment was created to aid cities.

7.   **I**n 1956, the **I**nterstate **H**ighway **P**rogram was started to build 41,000 miles of

divided highways.

8.   **D**uring the **M**iddle **A**ges, **M**arco **P**olo visited the **C**hinese **E**mpire.

9.   **T**he **N**orth **A**tlantic **T**reaty **O**rganization was formed in 1949.

10.   **T**he members of the **P**opulist **P**arty joined **D**emocrats in nominating **W**illiam **J.**

Bryan.

11.   **T**he **Q**ing **D**ynasty was followed by the **R**epublic of **C**hina in 1912.

12.   **A**fter **W**orld **W**ar II, the government of **P**uerto **R**ico started a project called

"**O**peration **B**ootstrap" to help the people.

13.   **A**fter the **F**rench and **I**ndian **W**ar, **B**ritain and **F**rance signed the **T**reaty of

Paris.

14.   **D**id the **J**efferson **P**arent **O**rganization sponsor the **H**elping **C**hildren **P**rogram?
556

Name_____   **CAPITALIZATION**

Date_____

Directions: Write the capital letter above any word that needs to be capitalized.

1. did congress pass the hepburn act to regulate railroads?

2. after the lone star republic became texas, the mexican war was fought.

3. where people could not read in america, the *constitution* was read to them.

4. the virginia colony was first a part of the british empire.

5. during the revolutionary war, the battle of savannah was fought in georgia.

6. the department of housing and urban development was created to aid cities.

7. in 1956, the interstate highway program was started to build 41,000 miles of

    divided highways.

8. during the middle ages, marco polo visited the chinese empire.

9. the north atlantic treaty organization was formed in 1949.

10. the members of the populist party joined democrats in nominating william j.

    bryan.

11. the qing dynasty was followed by the republic of china in 1912.

12. after world war II, the government of puerto rico started a project called

    "operation bootstrap" to help the people.

13. after the french and indian war, britain and france signed the treaty of

    paris.

14. did the jefferson parent organization sponsor the helping children program?

Directions: Write the capital letter above any word that needs to be capitalized.

1. Tthe Roman Empire began when the Roman Senate named a leader.

2. Was the Geneva Agreement of 1954 also written in Japanese?

3. poetry: Pink clouds

     Light blue sky

     Sunset on the horizon

4. We attend the Merritt Mountain Music Festival each year.

5. President Johnson belonged to the Whig Party after the Civil War.

6. His family went to the San Jose Air Show.

7. She belongs to the Buckles and Bows Square Dance Club.

8. The Peace Corps was started under Kennedy's program called the New

     Frontier.

9. Is the head of Children's Toy Foundation speaking at a meeting tonight?

10. During the Space Age, a woman from the Soviet Union went into orbit.

11. Does the leader of the International Trade Organization speak German?

12. The National Defense Education Act helped young people go to college.

13. Dear Wyatt,

     Did you go to the Dover Film Festival recently? I heard they

     showed a film about the War of 1812.

                                    Your buddy,
                                    Than

Directions: Write the capital letter above any word that needs to be capitalized.

1. the roman empire began when the roman senate name a leader.

2. was the geneva agreement of 1954 also written in Japanese?

3. poetry: pink clouds

    light blue sky

    sunset on the horizon

4. we attend the merritt mountain music festival each year.

5. president johnson belonged to the whig party after the civil war.

6. his family went to the san jose air show.

7. she belongs to the buckles and bows square dance club.

8. the peace corps was started under kennedy's program called the "new

    frontier."

9. is the head of children's toy foundation speaking at a meeting tonight?

10. during the space age, a woman from the soviet union went into orbit.

11. does the leader of the international trade organization speak german?

12. the national defense education act helped young people go to college.

13. dear wyatt,

    did you go to the dover film festival recently? i heard they

    showed a film about the war of 1812.

                your buddy,
                than   559

NOTES

Rule 23: **Capitalize the first word of a direct quotation** (that which a person says). **The person who said it must also be included.**

Example: Selena said, "**M**y science project fizzled."

Note that the word after the direct quotation is *not* capitalized unless it is a person's name or another proper noun.

Example: "**W**here is your dog?" **a**sked Julio.

Rule 24: **Capitalize the first word, the last word, and all important words of a title.**

Examples: <u>**N**ight **F**lying</u>
"**M**y **B**ig **T**eddy **B**ear"

How do you know if a word is **important** and should be capitalized?

This will help you: **Do not capitalize *a, an, the, and, but, or, nor,* or prepositions of four or less letters (unless the word is first or last).**

Examples: <u>**B**abe, the **G**allant **P**ig</u>
"**T**he **K**ing and **H**is **H**arp"

Rule 25: **Capitalize the Roman numerals and the letters of the major topics in an outline.**

     I.
        A.
        B.
        C.

    II.
        A.
        B.
        C.

Capitalize the first word in an outline. If other words in the outline are proper nouns, capitalize them. Otherwise, no other words are capitalized.

    I.   **A**dvertising in print
        A.   **D**irect mail
        B.   **I**n stores
    II.   **C**ommercials in **E**nglish

Name_____   **CAPITALIZATION**

WORKBOOK PAGE 257

Date_____

A. Directions: Capitalize these titles.

1. <u>**H**atchet</u>   5. <u>**T**he **B**oxcar **C**hildren</u>

2. <u>**N**ational **V**elvet</u>   6. "**T**he **F**armer in the **D**ell"

3. "**A**merica the **B**eautiful"   7. <u>**A**nne of **G**reen **G**ables</u>

4. <u>**N**o **D**ogs **A**llowed</u>   8. "**T**he **L**and and the **P**eople"

෩෩෩෩෩

B. Directions: Capitalize this outline.

    I.   **E**vening clothing

        A.   **F**ormal wear

            1.   **T**uxedos

            2.   **C**ocktail dresses

        B.   **C**asual clothes

    II.   **S**pecial attire

        A.   **B**ridal gowns

        B.   **P**rom gowns

෩෩෩෩෩

C. Directions: Write the capital letter where needed.

1. **M**arsha asked, "**W**hat would you like to drink?"

2. "**Y**ou must sit down," said **P**aco.

3. **C**aptain **J**ohn **S**mith said, "**I**f you don't work, you don't eat."

4. "**T**his is my best project!" exclaimed **H**unter.

5. **W**illiam **S**hakespeare wrote the line, "**T**o be or not to be…"

Name_____

Date_____

A. Directions: Capitalize these titles.

1. hatchet

2. national velvet

3. "america the beautiful"

4. no dogs allowed

5. the boxcar children

6. "the farmer in the dell"

7. anne of green gables

8. "the land and the people"

ๆ ๆ ๆ ๆ ๆ

B. Directions: Capitalize this outline.

    i. evening clothing

       a. formal wear

          1. tuxedos

          2. cocktail dresses

       b. casual clothes

    ii. special attire

       a. bridal gowns

       b. prom gowns

ๆ ๆ ๆ ๆ ๆ

C. Directions: Write the capital letter where needed.

1. marsha asked, "what would you like to drink?"

2. "you must sit down," said paco.

3. captain john smith said, "if you don't work, you don't eat."

4. "this is my best project!" exclaimed hunter.

5. william shakespeare wrote the line, "to be or not to be..."

563

NOTES

Rule 26: **Capitalize a brand name but not the product.**

  Examples: **P**opo paper towels

  Stonybrook bread

Rule 27: **Capitalize the name of a religion and the name for a supreme being.**

  Examples: **J**udaism **G**od
  Christianity **H**eavenly **F**ather
  Hindu **B**uddha

Rule 28: **Capitalize the name of a church, temple, or other place of worship.**

  Examples: **I**glesia de **D**ios
  Tempe **C**alvary **C**hurch
  Mt. **S**inai **T**emple

Rule 29: **Capitalize the name of a religious denomination.**

  Examples: **P**resbyterian **L**utheran

If the name of a specific church is **not** given, capitalize only the denomination.

  Example: a **M**ormon mission

Rule 30: **Capitalize a proper adjective but not the noun it modifies.**

  Remember: A proper adjective comes from a proper noun.

PROPER NOUN	**PROPER ADJECTIVE**
France	**F**rench
Asia	**A**sian

  Examples: a **F**rench inn
  an **A**sian country

Rule 31: **Capitalize a direction when it refers to a region of a country or a region of the world. Capitalize a direction when it is used with a specific geographic place.**

  Examples: He lives in the **N**orthwest.
  Their daughter is in the **M**iddle **E**ast.
  My address is 12 **N**orth Elm Lane 565

Name_____   **Capitalization**

WORKBOOK PAGE 260

Date_____

ANSWERS MAY VARY/REPRESENTATIVE ANSWERS:

A. Directions: Write your answers on the line.

1. Make up a name for a brand of milk. _____**Moocha Milk**_____

2. Name a church, synagogue, or other place of worship in your area.

_____**St. Mary's Basilica**_____

3. What is the proper adjective for *Alaska*? _____**Alaskan**_____

4. In which region of the country do you live? _____**West**_____

5. Name a religion of the world. _____**Hinduism**_____

6. Do you live in the Eastern Hemisphere or Western Hemisphere?

_____**Western Hemisphere**_____

ൟൟൟൟൟൟൟൟൟൟൟ

B. Directions: Place capital letters where needed.

1. **M**y aunt bought a **W**islow* tractor for her **V**irginia home.

2. **I**s **S**t. **P**eter's **E**piscopal **C**hurch located at 509 **E**ast **O**range **A**venue?

3. **K**ami purchased an **A**frican table and a **R**isca* baking dish at a yard sale.

4. **H**er **E**uropean friend visited the **S**outh recently.

5. **A** quilt sale was held at a **B**aptist church on **W**est **A**dams **S**treet.

6. **H**is uncle visited a **S**hinto temple on an **A**merican island.

7. **S**al grew up in a **G**erman neighborhood in the **E**ast.

8. **D**oes **B**uddhism include a belief about goddesses?

9. **I**s **Z**eus a god in **G**reek or **R**oman mythology?

*a brand name

566

Name_____

Date_____

A. Directions: Write your answers on the line.

1. Make up a name for a brand of milk. _____

2. Name a church, synagogue, or other place of worship in your area.

_____

3. What is the proper adjective for *Alaska*? _____

4. In which region of the country do you live? _____

5. Name a religion of the world. _____

6. Do you live in the Eastern Hemisphere or Western Hemisphere?

_____

ฝฝฝฝฝฝฝฝฝฝฝ

B. Directions: Place capital letters where needed.

1. my aunt bought a wislow* tractor for her virginia home.

2. is st. peter's episcopal church located at 509 east orange avenue?

3. kami purchased an african table and a risca* baking dish at a yard sale.

4. her european friend visited the south recently.

5. a quilt sale was held at a baptist church on west adams street.

6. his uncle visited a shinto temple on an american island.

7. sal grew up in a german neighborhood in the east.

8. does buddhism include a belief about goddesses?

9. is zeus a god in greek or roman mythology?
*a brand name

DO NOT CAPITALIZE

animals: **frog**   **fox**

However, capitalize a proper adjective with an animal.

Example: Shawn has an **I**rish setter.   (country - **I**reland)

dances: **tap dance**   **waltz**

However, capitalize a proper adjective with a dance.

Example: We like the **M**exican hat dance. (country - **M**exico)

directions: **north**   **southeast**

However, capitalize a direction if it is a region of the country or a region of the world.

Examples: They visit the **N**ortheast.

Lebanon is in the **N**ear **E**ast.

In addition, capitalize a direction when it appears with a geographic place.

Examples: His father went to **N**orth **K**orea.

They live at 20 **E**ast **C**obbler **S**treet

diseases: **cold**   **cancer**

However, capitalize a proper adjective with a disease.

Examples: My grandma once had the **A**sian flu.

(continent - **A**sia)

The patient has **A**lzheimer's disease.

(**A**lzheimer was the one who "discovered" the disease.)

568

foods: ham   peach

> **However**, capitalize a proper adjective with a food.
>> Example: May I have a **D**anish pastry?
>>> (country - **D**enmark)

career choices: nurse   police officer

games: checkers   puzzles

> **However**, capitalize a trademarked game.
>> Example: We played **R**ummicub.

musical instruments: drum   clarinet

> **However**, capitalize a proper adjective with a musical instrument.
>> Example: Mrs. Boca plays the **F**rench horn.   (country - **F**rance)

seasons: autumn   summer

school subjects: reading   history

> **However**, capitalize a proper adjective with a school subject.
>> Example: **A**merican history

> **In addition**, capitalize a subject if it is a language or has a number.
>> Examples: **E**nglish
>>   **A**lgebra II

plants: pansy   bush

> **However**, capitalize a proper adjective with a plant.

>> Example: **E**nglish tea rose

Name_____   **CAPITALIZATION**

WORKBOOK PAGE 263
Date_____

Directions: You have learned that there are certain categories that we do not
capitalize. Unscramble the words that name these.

Do not capitalize:

1. aesssno - **s e a s o n s**

2. esssidae - **d i s e a s e s**

3. uscamli notrsnsitem - **m u s i c a l   i n s t r u m e n t s**

4. ncodetriis - **d i r e c t i o n s**

5. eerrac oiehccs - **c a r e e r   c h o i c e s**

6. adnsec - **d a n c e s**

7. snamisal - **a n i m a l s**

8. emgsa - **g a m e s**

9. closho butscejs - **s c h o o l   s u b j e c t s**

10. odosf - **f o o d s**

11. saplnt - **p l a n t s**

570

Name_____

Date_____

Directions: You have learned that there are certain categories that we do not
capitalize. Unscramble the words that name these.

Do not capitalize:

1. aesssno - _ _ _ _ _ _ _

2. esssidae - _ _ _ _ _ _ _ _

3. uscamli notrsnsitem - _ _ _ _ _ _ _   _ _ _ _ _ _ _ _ _ _ _

4. ncodetriis - _ _ _ _ _ _ _ _ _ _

5. eerrac oiehccs - _ _ _ _ _ _   _ _ _ _ _ _ _

6. adnsec - _ _ _ _ _ _

7. snamisal - _ _ _ _ _ _ _

8. emgsa - _ _ _ _ _

9. closho butscejs - _ _ _ _ _ _   _ _ _ _ _ _ _ _

10. odosf - _ _ _ _ _

11. saplnt - _ _ _ _ _ _

Directions: Write the capital letter above any word that needs to be capitalized.

1.   **M**y favorite subjects are **E**nglish and arithmetic.

2.   **O**ne of her uncles who has tonsillitis lives in the **S**outh.

3.   **H**is **G**erman shepherd was playing under a weeping willow tree.

4.   **S**he dances the polka while her uncle plays the accordion.

5.   **H**ave you every played chess during your summer vacation?

6.   **C**han lives at 647 **S**outh **R**itz **A**venue in the **N**ortheast.

7.   **T**heir dad became district manager of a **S**outhwest company.

8.   **O**ur little beagle should never be fed chocolate candy.

9.   **G**randpa planted cherry tomatoes and **B**ermuda onions in his garden.

10.   **T**he couple danced the tango as the man played a **P**ortuguese mandolin.

11.   **T**he principal of that school also teaches earth science and **B**iology I.

12.   **A** **S**cottish chef made crepes and used a **G**erman caramel sauce.

13.   **L**ast autumn, **A**llie visited her grandparents in **W**est **V**irginia.

14.   **I**n music class, we learned about the **F**rench horn, the trombone, and the

oboe.

Directions: Write the capital letter above any word that needs to be capitalized.

1. my favorite subjects are english and arithmetic.

2. One of her uncles who has tonsillitis lives in the south.

3. his german shepherd was playing under a weeping willow tree.

4. she dances the polka while her uncle plays the accordion.

5. have you every played chess during your summer vacation?

6. chan lives at 647 south ritz avenue in the northeast.

7. their dad became district manager of a southwest company.

8. our little beagle should never be fed chocolate candy.

9. grandpa planted cherry tomatoes and bermuda onions in his garden.

10. the couple danced the tango as the man played a portuguese mandolin.

11. the principal of that school also teaches earth science and biology I.

12. a scottish chef made crepes and used a german caramel sauce.

13. last autumn, allie visited her grandparents in west virginia.

14. in music class, we learned about the french horn, the trombone, and the

    oboe.

Name_____   CAPITALIZATION
WORKBOOK PAGE 265
Date_____   **Review**

Directions: Write the capital letter above any word that needs to be capitalized.

1. a. "**B**aby **T**ortoise"   c. **M**istakes **T**hat **W**orked

    b. **T**he **D**ark **S**tories   d. **D**anger at the **F**air

2. **M**any people who live in **M**ontreal, **C**anada, speak **F**rench.

3. **T**he **R**omanov **D**ynasty in **R**ussia ruled for over three hundred years.

4. **T**he **F**ederalist **P**apers were written by **J**ames **M**adison and **J**ohn **J**ay.

5. **D**ear **U**ncle **M**ario,

        The **S**ports **C**ar **C**lub of **G**ermany will meet in **N**ovember at **B**raun

    House.

                                        Sincerely yours,

                                        Anthony

6. "**G**ive your speech on **A**rmed **F**orces' **D**ay,"   said his granddad.

7. **D**id the **P**ullman **C**ompany fire workers join the **A**merican **R**ailway

    Union?

8. **I**s the **M**onsoon **G**olf **T**ournament held at **G**raystone **C**ountry **C**lub?

9. **T**hey went to **S**t. **V**incent **I**sland near **C**ape **S**aint **G**eorge.

10. **I**n **D**ecember, **D**ad traveled to **H**ighland **L**ake along the **M**aine **T**urnpike.

11. **T**he **A**rctic **C**ircle is south of the **B**rooks **R**ange and near the **B**ering **S**ea.

12. **D**r. **A**llison **R**. **J**ones asked, "**H**ave you had hay fever or a sinus infection?"
574

Directions: Write the capital letter above any word that needs to be capitalized.

1. a. "baby tortoise"   c. <u>mistakes that worked</u>

    b. <u>the dark stories</u>   d. <u>danger at the fair</u>

2. many people who live in montreal, canada, speak french.

3. the romanov dynasty in russia ruled for over three hundred years.

4. the <u>federalist papers</u> were written by james madison and john jay.

5. dear uncle mario,

        the sports car club of germany will meet in november at braun

    house.
                                                sincerely yours,

                                                anthony

6. "give your speech on armed forces day,"   said his granddad.

7. did the pullman company fire workers join the american railway

    union?

8. is the monsoon golf tournament held at graystone country club?

9. they went to st. vincent island near cape saint george.

10. In december, dad traveled to highland lake along the maine turnpike.

11. the arctic circle is south of the brooks range and near the bering sea.

12. dr. allison r. jones asked, "have you had hay fever or a sinus infection?"

Name_____   **CAPITALIZATION**

Date_____   **Test**

Directions: Write the capital letter above any word that needs to be capitalized.

1. **A F**rench explorer brought fruit trees from **C**hile to **M**onterey **C**ounty.

2. **H**is uncle, a pilot, entered **F**reeland **C**linic on **E**ast **R**ome **S**treet for typhoid

     fever tests.

3. **D**oes **G**randma **M**ontez belong to the **C**armel **S**titchers **C**lub?

4. **D**id you eat **G**erman sausage at **G**oose **C**reek **I**nn near **M**arina **S**tate **B**each?

5. **D**ear **T**ate,

      In **A**ugust, we enjoy the **S**trawberry **F**estival in **W**atsonville, a town in the
      West.
                                               Love always,
                                               Tessa

6. **M**iss **L**u said, "**L**ee and **I** attended a craft fair at **S**t. **J**ames **C**hurch on **W**ebb
     Lane."

7. **H**e traveled south on **H**ighway 1 to **B**ig **S**ur **N**ational **P**ark on the **P**acific
     Ocean.

8. **J**asmine met me at **A**rlington **N**ational **C**emetery on **I**ndependence **D**ay.

9. **T**hey met **G**eneral **B**argas at a **R**epublican meeting at **B**ayview **C**ultural **C**enter.

10. **H**as **M**om read <u>Roll of **T**hunder, **H**ear **M**y **C**ry</u> to her reading and **E**nglish classes?

11. the **A**rctic **C**ircle is south of the **B**rooks **R**ange and near the **B**ering **S**ea.

12. **S**enator **J**ones asked, "**H**ave you visited the **U**nited **N**ations in **N**ew **Y**ork **C**ity?"

13. **I**n 1864, **J**ohn **F**reemont proclaimed **C**alifornia to be the **B**ear **F**lag **R**epublic.

14. **I** studied the **L**ouisiana **P**urchase and the **T**rail of **T**ears at **W**ilson **C**ollege.

576

CAPITALIZATION

Test

Directions: Write the capital letter above any word that needs to be capitalized.

1. a french explorer brought fruit trees from chile to monterey county.

2. his uncle, a pilot, entered freeland clinic on east rome street for typhoid fever tests.

3. does grandma montez belong to the carmel stitchers club?

4. did you eat german sausage at goose creek inn near marina state beach?

5. dear tate,

      in august, we enjoy the strawberry festival in watsonville, a town in the west.

                              love always,

                              tessa

6. miss lu said, "lee and i attended a craft fair at st. james church on webb lane."

7. he traveled south on highway 1 to big sur national park on the pacific ocean.

8. jasmine met me at arlington national cemetery on independence day.

9. they met general bargas at a republican meeting at bayview cultural center.

10. has mom read <u>roll of thunder, hear my cry</u> to her reading and english classes?

11. the arctic circle is south of the brooks range and near the bering sea.

12. senator jones asked, "have you visited the united nations in new york city?"

13. in 1864, john freemont proclaimed california to be the bear flag republic.

14. i studied the louisiana purchase and the trail of tears at wilson college.

NOTES

PUNCTUATION

NOTES

PERIOD: (.)

Rule 1: **Place a period at the end of a declarative sentence.**

A **declarative sentence** makes a statement.

This wrench is rusted.

Rule 2: **Place a period at the end of an imperative sentence.**

An **imperative sentence** gives a command.

Stand up.

Rule 3: **Place a period after most abbreviations.**

A. Days of the Week:

Sunday — **Sun.**
Monday — **Mon.**
Tuesday — **Tues., Tue.**＊
Wednesday — **Wed.**

Thursday — **Thurs., Thur.**＊
Friday — **Fri.**
Saturday — **Sat.**

＊The first listing is preferred.

B. Months of the Year:

January — **Jan.**
February — **Feb.**
March — **Mar.**
April — **Apr.**
May
June

July
August — **Aug.**
September — **Sept.**
October — **Oct.**
November — **Nov.**
December — **Dec.**

C. Titles and Initials:

Ms. — title that does not show if a woman is married or unmarried

Mrs. — (plural = Mmes.) title before a married woman's name

Mr. — Mister

Juan Victor Sanchez — **J. V. S.**   **Mr. J. V. S**anchez

Pres. (**P**resident) Sanchez   **Gov.** (**G**overnor) Sanchez

D. Places (general):

Drive — **Dr.**   Street — **St.**   Highway — **Hwy.**
Avenue — **Ave.**   Lane — **Ln.**   Boulevard — **Blvd.**

CHECK A DICTIONARY IF YOU ARE UNSURE OF AN ABBREVIATION.

NOTES

PERIOD: (.) cont.

    E. Places (specific):

Saint Paul — **St. Paul**	Mount Fox — **Mt. Fox**
Minnesota — **Minn.**	North America — **N. Am.**

However, do not place a period after a postal code: Minnesota - **MN**

    F. Directions:

        North — **N.**   southwest — **sw.**

    G. Organizations:

        Some organizations use periods with their abbreviations.
        American Dairy Science Association — **A. D. S. A.**

        The abbreviation of many organizations no longer require periods.
        County Dance and Song Society — **CDSS**
        Association of Christian Schools International — **ACSI**

        When the abbreviation spells a word (acronym), periods are not used.
        Educational Concerns for Hunger Organization — **ECHO**

    H. Others:

abbreviation — **abbrev.**	approximately — **approx.**
Swedish — **Swed.**	Before Christ — **B.C.**
adverb — **adv.**	Anno Domino (Latin = in the year of the Lord) — **A.D.**

NOTE: **If a sentence ends with an abbreviation that requires a period, do not place another period.**   He addressed me as Mrs.

Rule 4: Place a period after the letters and numbers in outlines.

    I. Marine animals
      A. Squid
      B. Starfish
    II. Land animals
      A. Camels
        1. One-Humped
        2. Two-Humped
      B. Elephants

Name_____   **PUNCTUATION**

WORKBOOK PAGE 272

Date_____   **Periods**

Directions: Write your answer on each line.
ANSWERS MAY VARY/REPRESENTATIVE ANSWERS:

1. Write your first, middle, and last names.   ____**Noah Tuley Bencze**____

2. Write your initials.   ____**N. T. B.**____

3. Write your state's postal code.   __**RI**__

4. Using abbreviations, write 13 West Ark Street.   ____**13 W. Ark St.**____

5. Write the abbreviation for each day of the week: __**Sun.**__   __**Mon.**__

     __**Tues.**__   __**Wed.**__   __**Thurs.**__   __**Fri.**__   __**Sat.**__

6. Write the abbreviation for each month: January - __**Jan.**__   February - __**Feb.**__

     March - __**Mar.**__   April - __**Apr.**__   August - __**Aug.**__   September - __**Sept.**__

     October - __**Oct.**__   November - __**Nov.**__   December - __**Dec.**__

7. Using the abbreviation for doctor, write a friend's name if he or she were to

     become a physician.   _____**Dr. Parker Panella**_____

8. Write an abbreviation for the National Hockey League.   __**NHL or N. H. L.**__

9. Using an abbreviation, name a mountain.   ____**Mt. Elden**____

10. Place periods in this outline: I.   North America
                                                              A.   Canada
                                                                    1.   Government
                                                                    2.   Tourism
                                                              B.   Mexico
                                                      II.   South America
                                                              A.   Peru
                                                              B.   Argentina
                                                              C.   Chile
                                                                    1.   Geography
                                                                    2.   Resources

Name_____   **PUNCTUATION**

Date_____   **Periods**

Directions: Write your answer on each line.

1.   Write your first, middle, and last names.   _____

2.   Write your initials.   _____

3.   Write your state's postal code.   _____

4.   Using abbreviations, write 13 West Ark Street.   _____

5.   Write the abbreviation for each day of the week: _____   _____

     _____   _____   _____   _____   _____

6.   Write the abbreviation for each month: January - _____   February - _____

     March - _____   April - _____   August - _____   September - _____

     October - _____   November - _____   December - _____

7.   Using the abbreviation for doctor, write a friend's name if he or she were to

     become a physician.   _____

8.   Write an abbreviation for the National Hockey League.   _____

9.   Using an abbreviation, name a mountain.   _____

10. Place periods in this outline: I   North America
                                              A   Canada
                                                  1   Government
                                                  2   Tourism
                                              B   Mexico
                                         II   South America
                                              A   Peru
                                              B   Argentina
                                              C   Chile
                                                  1   Geography
                                                  2   Resources

585

Name_____   **PUNCTUATION**

WORKBOOK PAGE 273
Date_____   **Periods**

Directions: Place a period where needed.

1.   Turn on the light.

2.   Mrs. Tang and Gov. Reed will meet soon.

3.   His home is at 125 S. Denver St.

4.   They traveled to Ft. McDowell last week.

5.   I lived in St. Louis, MO, when I was a child.

6.   Lieut. Deanna P. Vanderhall is stationed in Eur. for two years.

7.   On Sat., Jan. 1, they'll release a new album.

8.   I.   Pioneer men

    A.   Daniel Boone

       1.   Life

       2.   Travels

    B.   Davy Crockett

   II.   Pioneer women

    A.   Jenny Wiley

    B.   Abigail Dunway

    C.   Elizabeth Hamrick

9.   The Battle of Hastings occurred in 1066 A.D.

10.   Ms. Lyon, do you live on E. Princess Dr.?
586

Name_____

Date_____

Directions: Place a period where needed.

1. Turn on the light

2. Mrs Tang and Gov Reed will meet soon

3. His home is at 125 S Denver St

4. They traveled to Ft McDowell last week

5. I lived in St Louis, MO, when I was a child

6. Lieut Deanna P Vanderhall is stationed in Eur for two years

7.   On Sat , Jan 1, they'll release a new album

8. I   Pioneer men

    A   Daniel Boone

      1   Life

      2   Travels

    B   Davy Crockett

  II   Pioneer women

    A   Jenny Wiley

    B   Abigail Dunway

    C   Elizabeth Hamrick

9. The Battle of Hastings occurred in 1066 A D

10. Ms Lyon, do you live on E Princess Dr ?

COMMA: (,)

Rule 1: **Place a comma between the day and year in a date.**

November 30, 2010

Rule 2: **Place a comma between a day and date.**

Tuesday, April23, 2002

Rule 3: **Place a comma after a date if the date doesn't end a sentence.**

They married on May 15, 2004, in Boston.

ఛఛఛఛఛఛఛఛఛఛఛఛ

A. Directions: Write the answer.

ANSWERS MAY VARY/REPRESENTATIVE ANSWERS:

1. Write the month, day, and year that you were born (in words and numbers):

_____**January 2, 2005**_____

2. Write the name of the day, month, day (number) and year of tomorrow's date.

_____**Thursday, April 14, 2005**_____

3. Look at *Rule 3*. Write a date within a sentence.

_____**On October 3, 2004, we drove to New Mexico.**_____

ఛఛఛఛఛఛఛఛఛఛఛఛ

B. Directions: Insert commas where needed.

1. Are you attending their wedding on December 2, 2008?

2. Katie graduated on Friday, June 7, 2002.

3. On March 4, 2011, our neighbors will celebrate their twenty-fifth wedding anniversary.

COMMA: (,)

Rule 1:   Place a comma between the day and year in a date.

November 30, 2010

Rule 2:   Place a comma between a day and date.

Tuesday, April23, 2002

Rule 3:   Place a comma after a date if the date doesn't end a sentence.

They married on May 15, 2004, in Boston.

ॐॐॐॐॐॐॐॐॐॐॐॐ

A.   Directions: Write the answer.

1.   Write the month, day, and year that you were born (in words and numbers).

_____

2.   Write the name of the day, month, day (number) and year of tomorrow's date.

_____

3.   Look at *Rule 3*. Write a date within a sentence.

_____

ॐॐॐॐॐॐॐॐॐॐॐॐ

B.   Directions: Insert commas where needed.

1.   Are you attending their wedding on December 2 2008?

2.   Katie graduated on Friday June 7 2002.

3.   On March 4 2011 our neighbors will celebrate their twenty-fifth wedding anniversary.

COMMA: (,)

> **Rule 4: Place a comma between a town or city and a state.**
>
>   Orlando, Florida
>
> **Rule 5: Place a comma between a town and a county.**
>
>   Gettysburg, Adams County
>
> **Rule 6: Place a comma between a city and a country.**
>
>   Madrid, Spain
>
> **Rule 7: In a street address, place a comma after the street and after the city. Do not place a comma between a state and zip code.**
>
>   Their address is 34 Rice Lane, Lenexa, KS   66215.

Do **not** place a comma *if* a word appears between the street address and city.

>   Their address is 34 Rice Lane **in** Lenexa, KS   66215.

Note that a comma is **not** placed between the *house address* and the street address.

>   Their address is *34* Rice Lane, Lenexa, KS   66215.

> **Rule 8: Place a comma after the state or country if it appears before the end of a sentence.**
>
>   Min lived in Fairfax, Virginia, for ten years.

✧✧✧✧✧✧✧✧✧✧✧

Directions: Write the answer.

ANSWERS MAY VARY/REPRESENTATIVE ANSWERS:

1.   Write a sentence stating your complete address. (Include your zip code.)

        I live at 12345 South 90th Street, Columbus, Ohio   43215.

2.   Using *Rule 5,* write a sentence with your town (city) and state appearing within the sentence.

        Scottsdale, Arizona, is very hot in the summer.

COMMA: (,)

Rule 4: Place a comma between a town or city and a state.

Orlando, Florida

Rule 5: Place a comma between a town and a county.

Gettysburg, Adams County

Rule 6: Place a comma between a city and a country.

Madrid, Spain

Rule 7: In a street address, place a comma after the street and after the city. Do not place a comma between a state and zip code.

Their address is 34 Rice Lane, Lenexa, KS   66215.

Do **not** place a comma *if* a word appears between the street address and city.

Their address is 34 Rice Lane **in** Lenexa, KS   66215.

Note that a comma is **not** placed between the *house address* and the street address.

Their address is *34* Rice Lane, Lenexa, KS   66215.

Rule 8: Place a comma after the state or country if it appears before the end of a sentence.

Min lived in Fairfax, Virginia, for ten years.

ào ào ào ào ào ào ào ào ào ào ào

Directions: Write the answer.

1.   Write a sentence stating your complete address. (Include your zip code.)

_____

2.   Using *Rule 5,* write a sentence with your town (city) and state appearing within the sentence.

_____

Name_____

WORKBOOK PAGE 276

Date_____

Using Comma Rules 1 - 8

Directions: Insert commas where needed.

1. Jemima moved to Fairbanks, Alaska.

2. Mrs. Remus was hired on July 5, 2004.

3. Was President George W. Bush sworn into office on Monday, January 2, 2000?

4. Jacob's friend moved to 5 Mill Road in Mount Laurel, New Jersey.

5. Their uncle lives at 12 Wilmot Road, Tucson, Arizona   85711.

6. The mayor resigned on Tuesday, October 5, 2004.

7. The museum will open in Orange County, California.

8. The conference was held on November 2, 2004, in Casper, Wyoming.

9. Miss Firth's office is at 4 Marsh Road, Wilmington, DE 19810.

10. The board meeting was held on Friday, August 22, 2004, at noon.

11. Marco and Anne live in Miami, Dade County, Florida.

12. We traveled to Toledo, Ohio, last winter.

592

Directions: Insert commas where needed.

1. Jemima moved to Fairbanks Alaska.

2. Mrs. Remus was hired on July 5 2004.

3. Was President George W. Bush sworn into office on Monday January 2
    2000?

4. Jacob's friend moved to 5 Mill Road in Mount Laurel New Jersey.

5. Their uncle lives at 12 Wilmot Road Tucson Arizona   85711.

6. The mayor resigned on Tuesday October 5 2004.

7. The museum will open in Orange County California.

8. The conference was held on November 2 2004 in Casper Wyoming.

9. Miss Firth's office is at 4 Marsh Road Wilmington DE 19810.

10. The board meeting was held on Friday August 22 2004 at noon.

11. Marco and Anne live in Miami Dade County Florida.

12. We traveled to Toledo Ohio last winter.

COMMA: (,)

Rule 9: **Place a comma after three or more items in a series. Do not place a comma <u>after the last item</u>.**

I'll buy boots, a ski jacket, and gloves for our trip.

Rule 10: **Place a comma after an introductory word.**

No, I'm not ready.   Yes, I can hear you.   Well, I think so.

Rule 11: **Place a comma after the greeting of a friendly letter.**

Dear Tate,

Rule 12: **Place a comma after the closing of a friendly letter.**

Yours truly,

Rule 13: **Place a comma to set off a noun of direct address**
(a person spoken "to").

Carla, may I go with you?   May I go with you, Carla?

If a noun of direct address is within a sentence, place a comma **before** and **after** it.

May I, Carla, go with you?

ฬฬฬฬฬฬฬฬฬฬฬฬฬ

Directions: Insert needed commas.

1. No, we aren't leaving at noon.

2. Hannah, will you show me your picture?

3. Dear Rob,

I am glad that you are bringing juice, rolls, and hot dogs to our picnic. Yes, you may bring your friend along. I'll see you there, Cousin Rob.

Always,

Chan

594

COMMA: (,)

Rule 9: **Place a comma after three or more items in a series. Do not place a comma <u>after the last item</u>.**

I'll buy boots, a ski jacket, and gloves for our trip.

Rule 10: **Place a comma after an introductory word.**

No, I'm not ready.   Yes, I can hear you.   Well, I think so.

Rule 11: **Place a comma after the greeting of a friendly letter.**

Dear Tate,

Rule 12: **Place a comma after the closing of a friendly letter.**

Yours truly,

Rule 13: **Place a comma to set off a noun of direct address** (a person spoken "to").

Carla, may I go with you?   May I go with you, Carla?

If a noun of direct address is within a sentence, place a comma **before** and **after** it.

May I, Carla, go with you?

🐎🐎🐎🐎🐎🐎🐎🐎🐎🐎🐎🐎

Directions: Insert needed commas.

1. No we aren't leaving at noon.

2. Hannah will you show me your picture?

3. Dear Rob
    I am glad that you are bringing juice rolls and hot dogs to our picnic. Yes you may bring your friend along. I'll see you there Cousin Rob.

        Always
        Chan   595

COMMA: (,)

Rule 9: Place a comma after three or more items in a series. Do not place a comma <u>after the last item</u>.

Fruit pops, water, and yogurt were sold at the fair.

Rule 10: Place a comma after an introductory word.

Yes, we are sure.

Rule 11: Place a comma after the greeting of a friendly letter.

My friend,

Rule 12: Place a comma after the closing of a friendly letter.

Truly yours,

Rule 13: Place a comma to set off a noun of direct address (a person spoken "to").

Jenny, sit with us.   Sit with us, Jenny.

If a noun of direct address is within a sentence, place a comma **before** and **after** it.

Sit, Jenny, with us.

☙☙☙☙☙☙☙☙☙☙☙☙

Directions: Insert needed commas.

1.   Dear Nan,

Yes, I can come with you to Yellowstone.

Your best friend,
Devi

2.   Micah, will you compete in Brazilian jujitsu?

3.   The dancer placed her tap shoes, her ballet shoes, and a comb in her bag.

596

COMMA: (,)

Rule 9:   **Place a comma after three or more items in a series. Do not place a comma <u>after the last item</u>.**

Fruit pops, water, and yogurt were sold at the fair.

Rule 10:   **Place a comma after an introductory word.**

Yes, we are sure.

Rule 11:   **Place a comma after the greeting of a friendly letter.**

My friend,

Rule 12:   **Place a comma after the closing of a friendly letter.**

Truly yours,

Rule 13:   **Place a comma to set off a noun of direct address** (a person spoken "to").

Jenny, sit with us.   Sit with us, Jenny.

If a noun of direct address is within a sentence, place a comma **before** and **after** it.

Sit, Jenny, with us.

🍃🍃🍃🍃🍃🍃🍃🍃🍃🍃🍃🍃

Directions: Insert needed commas.

1. Dear Nan

      Yes I can come with you to Yellowstone.

            Your best friend
            Devi

2. Micah will you compete in Brazilian jujitsu?

3. The dancer placed her tap shoes her ballet shoes and a comb in her bag.

PUNCTUATION

WORKBOOK PAGE 279

Date_____   **Commas**

Note: Be sure to teach this with many examples. Best practices include students writing personal examples. Using white-boards is recommended.

COMMA: (,)

> **Rule 14:   Use a comma to clarify (make clear) a sentence.**
>
> > After the party favors were given.
> > After the party, favors were given.
>
> **Rule 15:   Use a comma to invert a name. Place the last name, a comma, and the first name.**
>
> > Tom J. Lee   =   Lee, Tom J.
>
> **Rule 16:   If two complete sentences are joined by a conjunction** *(and, but, or)*, **place a comma before the conjunction.**
>
> > His motorcycle is old, but it looks new and shiny.
>
> **Rule 17:   Use a comma after a direct quotation that is followed by a verb like "said" and a speaker.** (It will not ask a question or show emotion.)
>
> > "This avocado is too ripe," said Lars.
>
> **If the person who is making the statement is given first, place a comma after the person's name + verb.** (This may use "asked" or "exclaimed.")
>
> > > Lars said, "This avocado is too ripe."
> > > Emma asked, "Is this avocado too ripe?"
>
> **Rule 18:   Use a comma to set off an appositive.** (An appositive is a word or group of words that explains a noun in a sentence. Often, an appositive will give additional information about the noun.
>
> > Bo likes to sit on the front step.   (Who is *Bo*?)
> > Bo, <u>our kitty</u>, likes to sit on the front step.

రెరెరెరెరెరెరెరెరెరెరె

Directions: Insert needed commas.

1.   The mechanic asked, "Where's my wrench?"

2.   Mrs. Hart, our neighbor, has been elected mayor.

3.   Before dinner, plates must be set on this table.

4.   "Please come in," said Emily.

598

COMMA: (,)

Rule 14:   Use a comma to clarify (make clear) a sentence.

> After the party favors were given.
> After the party, favors were given.

Rule 15:   Use a comma to invert a name. Place the last name, a comma, and the first name.

> Tom J. Lee   =   Lee, Tom J.

Rule 16:   If two complete sentences are joined by a conjunction *(and, but, or)*, place a comma before the conjunction.

> His motorcycle is old, but it looks new and shiny.

Rule 17:   Use a comma after a direct quotation that is followed by a verb like "said" and a speaker. (It will not ask a question or show emotion.)

> "This avocado is too ripe," said Lars.

If the person who is making the statement is given first, place a comma after the person's name + verb. (This may use "asked" or "exclaimed.")

> Lars said, "This avocado is too ripe."

> Emma asked, "Is this avocado too ripe?"

Rule 18:   Use a comma to set off an appositive. (An appositive is a word or group of words that explains a noun in a sentence. Often, an appositive will give additional information about the noun.

> Bo likes to sit on the front step.   (Who is *Bo*?)

> Bo, <u>our kitty,</u> likes to sit on the front step.

ɷɷɷɷɷɷɷɷɷɷɷ

Directions: Insert needed commas.

1.   The mechanic asked "Where's my wrench?"

2.   Mrs. Hart our neighbor has been elected mayor.

3.   Before dinner plates must be set on this table.

4.   "Please come in " said Emily.

<u>**Note: Be sure to review these rules and ask for different students' examples.**</u>

COMMA: (,)

Rule 14: Use a comma to clarify (make clear) a sentence.

After the party favors were given.
After the party, favors were given.

Rule 15: Use a comma to invert a name. Place the last name, a comma, and the first name.

Tom J. Lee   =   Lee, Tom J.

Rule 16: If two complete sentences are joined by a conjunction (*and, but, or*), place a comma before the conjunction.

His motorcycle is old, but it looks new and shiny.

Rule 17: Use a comma after a direct quotation that is followed by a verb like "said" and a speaker. (It will not ask a question or show emotion.)

"This avocado is too ripe," said Lars.

If the person who is making the statement is given first, place a comma after the person's name + verb. (This may use "asked" or "exclaimed.")

Lars said, "This avocado is too ripe."

Emma asked, "Is this avocado too ripe?"

Rule 18: Use a comma to set off an appositive. (An appositive is a word or group of words that explains a noun in a sentence. Often, an appositive will give additional information about the noun.

Bo likes to sit on the front step.   (Who is *Bo*?)

Bo, <u>our kitty</u>, likes to sit on the front step.

ॐॐॐॐॐॐॐॐॐॐॐ

Directions: Insert needed commas.

1. Brad's name on the list appeared as Smith, Brad.

2. "I want up," said the toddler.

3. Give this hat to Miss Lant, the lady in the red hat.

4. The bride walked down the aisle, and she waved to her nephews.

600

COMMA: (,)

Rule 14: **Use a comma to clarify (make clear) a sentence.**

After the party favors were given.
After the party, favors were given.

Rule 15: **Use a comma to invert a name. Place the last name, a comma, and the first name.**

Tom J. Lee   =   Lee, Tom J.

Rule 16: **If two complete sentences are joined by a conjunction (*and, but, or*), place a comma before the conjunction.**

His motorcycle is old, but it looks new and shiny.

Rule 17: **Use a comma after a direct quotation that is followed by a verb like "said" and a speaker.** (It will not ask a question or show emotion.)

"This avocado is too ripe," said Lars.

If the person who is making the statement is given first, place a comma after the person's name + verb. (This may use "asked" or "exclaimed.")

Lars said, "This avocado is too ripe."

Emma asked, "Is this avocado too ripe?"

Rule 18: **Use a comma to set off an appositive.** (An appositive is a word or group of words that explains a noun in a sentence. Often, an appositive will give additional information about the noun.

Bo likes to sit on the front step.   (Who is *Bo*?)

Bo, our kitty, likes to sit on the front step.

ৰ৵ৰ৵ৰ৵ৰ৵ৰ৵ৰ৵ৰ৵ৰ৵ৰ৵ৰ৵ৰ৵

Directions: Insert needed commas.

1. Brad's name on the list appeared as Smith Brad.

2. "I want up " said the toddler.

3. Give this hat to Miss Lant the lady in the red hat.

4. The bride walked down the aisle and she waved to her nephews.

601

Directions: Insert needed commas.

1.   Lindy,

Shari's wedding is on Sunday, December 21, 2006.

Love,
Annie

2.   You look like your mother, and your brother looks like your dad.

3.   Johnson, Ricky T.

4.   The car attendant asked, "May I have your keys?"

5.   My new home is at 12 Ruby Lane, Rockford, IL 61102.

6.   No, I won't be flying to Rome, Italy.

7.   Mrs. Reed, do you want to buy a cookbook?

8.   Her family's pets include a ferret, a hamster, a cat, and three dogs.

9.   Ted arrived from Memphis, Tennessee, this morning.

10.   In the middle of the storm, clouds billowed overhead.

11.   "You stepped in some mud," said his mother.

12.   Mom said, "We must go to the grocery store, Kim."

13.   Chessa, my little sister in the white dress, is a flower girl.

14.   Jessica has bought a new bike, but she will ride it only on trails.

15.   "The wood on this gate needs to be replaced," said the carpenter.

16.   Mark will attend Baylor University, or he will go to a college in his state.

17. Her dog, a small Scotch terrier, is groomed at La Pierre's.

602

Directions: Insert needed commas.

1. Lindy

    Shari's wedding is on Sunday December 21 2006.

                          Love
                          Annie

2. You look like your mother and your brother looks like your dad.

3. Johnson Ricky T.

4. The car attendant asked "May I have your keys?"

5. My new home is at 12 Ruby Lane Rockford IL 61102.

6. No I won't be flying to Rome Italy.

7. Mrs. Reed do you want to buy a cookbook?

8. Her family's pets include a ferret a hamster a cat and three dogs.

9. Ted arrived from Memphis Tennessee this morning.

10. In the middle of the storm clouds billowed overhead.

11. "You stepped in some mud " said his mother.

12.   Mom said "We must go to the grocery store Kim."

13. Chessa my little sister in the white dress is a flower girl.

14. Jessica has bought a new bike but she will ride it only on trails.

15. "The wood on this gate needs to be replaced " said the carpenter.

16.   Mark will attend Baylor University or he will go to a college in his state.

17. Her dog a small Scotch terrier is groomed at La Pierre's.

Question Mark:

Rule: **Use a question mark (?) at the end of an interrogative sentence. (An interrogative sentence asks a question.)**

Did Madison find her hockey stick**?**
Will you come with me**?**

Exclamation Mark:

Rule 1: **Use an exclamation point (!) after an exclamatory sentence.** (An *exclamatory sentence* shows strong feeling.)

We're the first-place winners!
Mom, I just saw a snake!

Rule 2: **Use an exclamation point (!) after an interjection.**
(An *interjection* is a word <u>or</u> phrase that shows strong feeling.)

Cool! Let's do it!
I lost my wallet! *Oh no!*

phrase – two or more words that do not
form a complete sentence

ᐓᐓᐓᐓᐓᐓᐓᐓᐓᐓᐓᐓᐓᐓᐓᐓᐓᐓᐓᐓᐓ

Part A: Place question marks or exclamation marks where needed.

1. Yikes**!** I almost stepped on a toad**!**

2. Have you eaten lunch**?**

3. You're the champion**!**

Part B: Write a sentence using the required ending punctuation.
ANSWERS MAY VARY/REPRESENTATIVE ANSWERS:

1. (question mark) ___**Would you like banana?**___

    _____

2. (exclamation point) ___**Whew! I nearly fell into the creek!**___

    _____

Question Mark:

Rule: Use a question mark (?) at the end of an interrogative sentence. (An interrogative sentence asks a question.)

Did Madison find her hockey stick**?**
Will you come with me**?**

Exclamation Mark:

Rule 1: Use an exclamation point (!) after an exclamatory sentence. (An *exclamatory sentence* shows strong feeling.)

We're the first-place winners!
Mom, I just saw a snake!

Rule 2: Use an exclamation point (!) after an interjection.
(An *interjection* is a word or phrase that shows strong feeling.)

Cool! Let's do it!
I lost my wallet! *Oh no!*

phrase – two or more words that do not
form a complete sentence

🐎🐎🐎🐎🐎🐎🐎🐎🐎🐎🐎🐎🐎🐎🐎🐎🐎🐎🐎🐎

Part A: Place question marks or exclamation marks where needed.

1. Yikes I almost stepped on a toad

2. Have you eaten lunch

3. You're the champion

Part B: Write a sentence using the required ending punctuation.

1. (question mark)

   _____

   _____

2. (exclamation point)

   _____

   _____

605

Name_____   **PUNCTUATION**

Date_____   **Apostrophe**

<u>Important:</u> <u>You may want to provide a fourth rule for possessives.</u>

<u>Rule: A singular word ending in *s* and showing ownership, simply adds an</u>

<u>apostrophe. Example: Chris' boat This rule has actually been replaced with</u>

<u>rule 2-A. However, many parents prefer this to the newer rule: Chris's boat.</u>

Apostrophe:

Rule 1: Use an apostrophe (') in a contraction to show where a letter or letters have been left out.

can't - cannot
I'm - I am

Rule 2: Use an apostrophe (') to show possession (ownership).

A. If the word showing ownership is singular (one), add ' + s.

a kitten**'s** pillow
the book**'s** cover
one model**'s** smile

B. If the word showing ownership is plural (more than one) and ends in s, just add an apostrophe (') after the s.

one lady - many ladies: ladies' tea rooms
one bee - two bees: bees' hive

C. If the word showing ownership is plural (more than one) and does NOT end in s, add ' + s.

one mouse - two mice: mice**'s** nest
one child - many children: children**'s** books

ઝઝઝઝઝઝઝઝઝઝઝઝ

Directions: Write the following.

ANSWERS MAY VARY/REPRESENTATIVE ANSWERS:

1. a contraction - ____**couldn't**____

2. watercolors belonging to a boy - ____**boy's watercolors**____

3. cakes from several bakeries - ____**bakeries' cakes**____

4. shoes belonging to more than one repairman - ____**repairmen's shoes**____

5. a wagon belonging to Les - ____**Les's wagon**____

606

Apostrophe:

Rule 1: **Use an apostrophe (') in a contraction to show where a letter or letters have been left out.**

can't - cannot
I'm - I am

Rule 2: **Use an apostrophe (') to show possession (ownership).**

A. **If the word showing ownership is singular (one), add ' + s.**

a kitten's pillow
the book's cover
one model's smile

B. **If the word showing ownership is plural (more than one) and ends in s, just add an apostrophe after the s.**

one lady - many ladies: ladies' tea rooms
one bee - two bees: bees' hive

C. **If the word showing ownership is plural (more than one) and does NOT end in s, add ' + s.**

one mouse - two mice: mice's nest
one child   - many children: children's books

ॐॐॐॐॐॐॐॐॐॐॐॐ

Directions: Write the following.

1. a contraction - _____

2. watercolors belonging to a boy - _____

3. cakes from several bakeries - _____

4. shoes belonging to more than one repairman - _____

5. a wagon belonging to Les - _____

Apostrophe:

Rule 1:   Use an apostrophe (') in a contraction to show where a letter or letters have been left out.

> they're - they are
> don't - do not

Rule 2:   Use an apostrophe to show possession (ownership).

A. If the word showing ownership is singular (one), add ' + s.

> a tassle on a rope - rope**'s** tassle
> one cowgirl**'s** boots

B. If the word showing ownership is plural (more than one) and ends in s, just add an apostrophe after the s.

> a trailer - many trailers: trailers' hitches
> one boy - many boys: boys' club

C. If the word showing ownership is plural (more than one) and does NOT end in s, add ' + s.

> one goose - two geese: geese**'s** meadow
> businesswoman - two businesswomen: businesswomen**'s** meeting

When two people own the *same* item, add an apostrophe after the second name.

> Example: Katie and Lani's new apartment

When two people own *separate* items, add an apostrophe after both names.

> Example: Tim's and Tate's cars

ॐॐॐॐॐॐॐॐॐॐॐ

Directions: Insert needed apostrophes.

1.   My bicycle's tire is flat.

2.   If you're ready to leave, I'll drive you home.

3.   Mary and Jonah's aunt wouldn't go on the ride.

4.   Women's dresses and toddlers' shoes are on sale today.

5.   Didn't her mother buy a man's suit?

608

Apostrophe:

Rule 1: Use an apostrophe (') in a contraction to show where a letter or letters have been left out.

> they're - they are
> don't - do not

Rule 2: Use an apostrophe (') to show possession (ownership).

    A. If the word showing ownership is singular (one), add ' + s.

> a tassle on a rope - rope**'s** tassle
> one cowgirl**'s** boots

    B. If the word showing ownership is plural (more than one) and ends in s, just add an apostrophe (') after the s.

> a trailer - many trailers: trailers' hitches
> one boy   - many boys: boys' club

    C. If the word showing ownership is plural (more than one) and does NOT end in s, add ' + s.

> one goose - two geese: geese**'s** meadow
> businesswoman - two businesswomen: businesswomen**'s** meeting

When two people own the *same* item, add an apostrophe after the second name.

> Example: Katie and Lani's new apartment

When two people own *separate* items, add an apostrophe after both names.

> Example: Tim's and Tate's cars

Directions: Insert needed apostrophes.

1. My bicycles tire is flat.

2. If youre ready to leave, Ill drive you home.

3. Mary and Jonahs aunt wouldnt go on the ride.

4. Womens dresses and toddlers shoes are on sale today.

5. Didnt her mother buy a mans suit?   609

Name_____

WORKBOOK PAGE 285

Date_____

Rule 1: Use a colon in writing the time.

        4:30 A.M.   9:19 P.M.

Rule 2: Use a colon to break down larger units to smaller ones.

        Genesis 1:1   Unit 5: Chapter 3

Rule 3: Place a colon after divisions of topics in writing.

        Animals**:**

         Jungle Animals**:**

Rule 4: Place a colon after the greeting of a business letter.

        Dear Senator Kane**:**   Gentlemen**:**

Rule 5: Use a colon after the heading of a list.

        Things to do**:**
- Walk the dog
- Do homework

The clerk ordered the following: lipstick, eye shadow, blush, and liner.

   ﬄ

Directions: Write an example for each rule.

ANSWERS MAY VARY/REPRESENTATIVE ANSWERS

Rule 1:   __8:00 A.M._____

Rule 2:   __Acts 3:28_____

Rule 3:   __Native Americans:_____
         __Iroquois:__

Rule 4:   __Dear Miss Segal:_____

Rule 5:   __I bought these items: watercolors, pastels, and brushes.__

610

Name_____

Date_____

Rule 1:   Use a colon in writing the time.

4:30 A.M.   9:19 P.M.

Rule 2:   Use a colon to break down larger units to smaller ones.

Genesis 1:1   Unit 5: Chapter 3

Rule 3:   Place a colon after divisions of topics in writing.

Animals:

Jungle Animals:

Rule 4:   Place a colon after the greeting of a business letter.

Dear Senator Kane: Gentlemen:

Rule 5:   Use a colon after the heading of a list.

Things to do:
- Walk the dog
- Do homework

The clerk ordered the following: lipstick, eye shadow, blush, and liner.

ल्ल

Directions: Write an example for each rule.

Rule 1: _____

Rule 2: _____

Rule 3: _____

Rule 4: _____

Rule 5: _____

WORKBOOK PAGE 286

Colon:

Rule 1: Use a colon in writing the time.   7:05 P.M.

Rule 2: Use a colon to break down larger units to smaller ones.

       Numbers 3:1   Chapter 2: Part 1

Rule 3: Place a colon after divisions of topics in writing.

       Battles:
         Battle of Bull Run:

Rule 4: Place a colon after the greeting of a business letter.   Madam:

Rule 5: Use a colon after the heading of a list.

       Things I want:
          - Video
          - CD
          - Vinyl

     Did you buy these items: cereal, milk, bread, butter, and grapes?

ᕭᕭᕭᕭᕭᕭᕭᕭᕭᕭᕭᕭᕭᕭᕭᕭᕭᕭᕭᕭ

Directions: Place a colon where needed.

1. Names of my dogs:
      - Rex
      - Sugar
      - Force

2. Dear Mr. Benson:

3. You must return these items to the public library: a video, a book and a DVD.

4. Things to remember:
      - Call my friend
      - Meet my brother after school
      - Help wash the car

5. Please be ready by 4:00 in the afternoon.

Rule 1: Use a colon in writing the time.   7:05 P.M.

Rule 2: Use a colon to break down larger units to smaller ones.

       Numbers 3:1   Chapter 2: Part 1

Rule 3: Place a colon after divisions of topics in writing.

       Battles:
        Battle of Bull Run:

Rule 4: Place a colon after the greeting of a business letter. Madam:

Rule 5: Use a colon after the heading of a list.

       Things I want:
         - Video
         - CD
         - Vinyl

    Did you buy these items: cereal, milk, bread, butter, and grapes?

Directions: Place a colon where needed.

1. Names of my dogs
      - Rex
      - Sugar
      - Force

2. Dear Mr. Benson

3. You must return these items to the public library a video, a book and a DVD.

4. Things to remember
      - Call my friend
      - Meet my brother after school
      - Help wash the car

5. Please be ready by 4 00 in the afternoon.

Name_____   **PUNCTUATION**

WORKBOOK PAGE 287

Date_____   **Semicolon**

> **Reminder:** A **complete sentence** can stand alone as a **complete thought.**

Semicolon:

Rule: Use a semicolon (;) to join two complete sentences. These must be about a similar topic.

> **Correct:** Jana is on a swim team; she practices at a nearby pool.

> **Incorrect:** Jana is on a swim team; her uncle lives in Nebraska.

> **complete sentence   complete sentence**

Note: Place the semicolon after the last word of the first thought. Place the first word of the second complete thought a space after the semicolon.

> Example: The boys went fishing; they didn't catch any fish.

෬෬෬෬෬෬෬෬෬෬෬෬෬෬෬෬෬෬෬෬෬

Part A: Place a semicolon after the first complete thought. Write a complete sentence that is about the same topic on the line.

ANSWERS MAY VARY/REPRESENTATIVE ANSWERS:

1. Lee is a carpenter**; he works for R & J Builders.**_____

2. They have a new puppy**; he is a German shepherd.**_____

3. Lana and I saw little lambs on a farm**; we petted them.**_____

4. I can't find my pen**; it's blue with red polka dots.**_____

5. Their mom is a good baker**; she makes chewy nut cookies.**_____

Part B: Place a semicolon between the complete thoughts.

1. A rooster crowed loudly; it woke me.

2. Bo and I are going to the beach; we are leaving at nine o'clock in the morning.

3. Lynx Lake is in Arizona; it is located near the city of Prescott.

4. These glass vases are colorful; they are considered works of art.

614

Reminder: A **complete sentence** can stand alone as a **complete thought.**

<u>**Semicolon:**</u>
Rule: Use a semicolon (;) to join two complete sentences. These must be about a similar topic.

Correct: Jana is on a swim team; she practices at a nearby pool.

Incorrect: Jana is on a swim team; her uncle lives in Nebraska.

complete sentence   complete sentence

Note: Place the semicolon after the last word of the first thought. Place the first word of the second complete thought a space after the semicolon.

Example: The boys went fishing; they didn't catch any fish.

ରେ ରେ ରେ ରେ ରେ ରେ ରେ ରେ ରେ ରେ ରେ ରେ ରେ ରେ ରେ ରେ ରେ ରେ ରେ

Part A: Place a semicolon after the first complete thought. Write a complete sentence that is about the same topic on the line.

1. Lee is a carpenter _____.

2. They have a new puppy _____.

3. Lana and I saw little lambs on a farm _____.

4. I can't find my pen _____.

5. Their mom is a good baker _____.

Part B: Place a semicolon between the complete thoughts.

1. A rooster crowed loudly it woke me.

2. Bo and I are going to the beach we are leaving at nine o'clock in the morning.

3. Lynx Lake is in Arizona it is located near the city of Prescott.

4. These glass vases are colorful they are considered works of art.

PUNCTUATION

Date_____   **Semicolon**

Semicolon:

Rule: **Use a semicolon (;) to join two complete sentences. These must be about a similar topic. Do <u>not</u> place a conjunction (*and, but, or*) with a semicolon.**

   Correct: Lars is a toddler; he just learned to walk.

   Incorrect: Lars is a toddler; and he just learned to walk.

   Correct: Katie found a quarter on the floor; she didn't spend it.

   Incorrect: Katie found a quarter on the floor; but she didn't spend it.

☙☙☙☙☙☙☙☙☙☙☙☙☙☙☙☙☙☙☙☙☙

Part A: Place a semicolon after the first complete thought. Write a complete sentence that is about the same topic after the semicolon.

Remember: *Place the semicolon after the last word of the first thought.*
            Place the first word of the second complete thought a space after the semicolon.

1. They placed a fan on their patio; **the breeze it creates cools them.**

2. The child scraped her knee; **her mother gave her a wet cloth to use.**

3. The day had turned cold; **workers put on their heavy jackets.**

4. We put pink light bulbs in our lamp; **our family room has a pink glow.**

5. Grandma lives in a gated house; **she uses a special code to enter.**

Part B: Place a semicolon between the complete thoughts.

1. Tom bought a new tub; it is round with jet sprays.

2. A stagecoach ran along that route; someone built a hotel for travelers.

3. These flowers are drooping; they need water.

4. Several farmers are growing figs; others are growing olives.

Semicolon:
Rule: **Use a semicolon (;) to join two complete sentences. These must be about a similar topic. Do _not_ place a conjunction (_and, but, or_) with a semicolon.**

    Correct: Lars is a toddler; he just learned to walk.

    Incorrect: Lars is a toddler; and he just learned to walk.

    Correct: Katie found a quarter on the floor; she didn't spend it.

    Incorrect: Katie found a quarter on the floor; but she didn't spend it.

🦜🦜🦜🦜🦜🦜🦜🦜🦜🦜🦜🦜🦜🦜🦜🦜🦜

Part A: Place a semicolon after the first complete thought. Write a complete sentence that is about the same topic after the semicolon.

Remember: *Place the semicolon after the last word of the first thought.*
Place the first word of the second complete thought a space after the semicolon.

1. They placed a fan on their patio _____.

2. The child scraped her knee _____.

3. The day had turned cold _____.

4. We put pink light bulbs in our lamp _____.

5. Grandma lives in a gated house _____.

Part B: Place a semicolon between the complete thoughts.

1. Tom bought a new tub it is round with jet sprays.

2. A stagecoach ran along that route someone built a hotel for travelers.

3. These flowers are drooping they need water.

4. Several farmers are growing figs others are growing olives.

REVIEW

Semicolon:
**Rule: Use a semicolon (;) to join two complete sentences.
          These must be about a similar topic.**

Colon:
Rule 1: Use a colon (:) in writing the time.   12:00 A.M.

Rule 2: Use a colon (:) to break down units.   Mark 3:10
                                                           Chapter 3: Part 2

Rule 3: Place a colon (:) after divisions of topics in writing.   Lakes:
                                                                             Salt:

Rule 4: Place a colon after the greeting of a business letter.   Dear Sir:

Rule 5: Use a colon after the heading of a list.   Camping List:
                                                        - flashlight
                                                        - sleeping bag
                                                        - water bottles

This is my camping list **(:)** a flashlight, a sleeping bag, and water bottles.

🐎🐎🐎🐎🐎🐎🐎🐎🐎🐎🐎🐎🐎🐎🐎🐎🐎🐎🐎🐎

Directions: Place semicolons and colons where needed.

1. Rule 1: Wait your turn.

2. You will need the following items by noon: a sack lunch, snacks, and drinks.

3. This hat is old; it belonged to my poppa.

4. Dad read Psalm 10:3 at the 11:00 church service.

5. Landforms:
      Islands:
      Coves:

6. Members of the Board:

7. Her poodle has a bow on its collar; it must have been groomed.

REVIEW

Semicolon:
Rule: Use a semicolon (;) to join two complete sentences.
**   These must be about a similar topic.**

Colon:
Rule 1:   Use a colon (:) in writing the time.   12:00 A.M.

Rule 2:   Use a colon (:) to break down units.   Mark 3:10
                                                                                          Chapter 3: Part 2

Rule 3:   Place a colon (:) after divisions of topics in writing.   Lakes:
                                                                                                                        Salt:

Rule 4:   Place a colon after the greeting of a business letter.   Dear Sir:

Rule 5:   Use a colon after the heading of a list.   Camping List:
                                                                                                   - flashlight
                                                                                                   - sleeping bag
                                                                                                   - water bottles
This is my camping list **(:)** a flashlight, a sleeping bag, and water bottles.

🙟🙟🙟🙟🙟🙟🙟🙟🙟🙟🙟🙟🙟🙟🙟🙟🙟🙟🙟🙟

Directions: Place semicolons and colons where needed.

1.   Rule 1 Wait your turn.

2.   You will need the following items by noon   a sack lunch, snacks, and drinks.

3.   This hat is old it belonged to my poppa.

4.   Dad read Psalm 10 3 at the 11 00 church service.

5.   Landforms
        Islands
        Coves

6.   Members of the Board

7.   Her poodle has a bow on its collar it must have been groomed.

Hyphen:

Rule 1: **Use a hyphen (-) to combine some closely related words.**

half-moon   top-notch

Use a dictionary to determine if words should use a hyphen.

Rule 2: **Use a hyphen (-) between fractions.**

one-third   three-fourths

Rule 3: **Use a hyphen (-) between two-digit word numbers from 21 to 99.**

twenty-one   eighty-five

Rule 4: **Use a hyphen (-) when dividing a word of two or more syllables when they are at the end of a line of writing.**

Remember: Words are divided into units of sound called *syllables*.

Important: **You must have at least 2 letters on the first line.**

_____ **ab-**

sent_____

You must have at least 3 letters on the second line

_____ dangerous-

Wrong: **ly**_____

_____ danger-

Right: **ously**_____

Use a dictionary to determine where words will be divided into syllables.

🙢🙢🙢🙢🙢🙢🙢🙢🙢🙢🙢🙢🙢🙢🙢🙢🙢🙢🙢🙢🙢🙢

Directions: Write your answer on the line.

ANSWERS MAY VARY/REPRESENTATIVE ANSWERS:

1. Write two words that use a hyphen: _____ **three-pronged** _____

2. Write a fraction in the first space and a two-digit number in the second:

_____ **one-fourth** _____   _____ **thirty-three** _____

3. Write a two-syllable word that uses the fourth rule: _____ **mus-**

tard_____

Hyphen:

Rule 1: Use a hyphen (-) to combine some closely related words.

    half-moon   top-notch

  Use a dictionary to determine if words should use a hyphen.

Rule 2: Use a hyphen (-) between fractions.

    one-third   three-fourths

Rule 3: Use a hyphen (-) between two-digit word numbers from 21 to 99.

    twenty-one   eighty-five

Rule 4: Use a hyphen (-) when dividing a word of two or more syllables when they are at the end of a line of writing.

    Remember: Words are divided into units of sound called *syllables*.

Important: You must have at least <u>2</u> letters on the first line.

                 ab-

sent_____

You must have at least <u>3</u> letters on the second line

               dangerous-

Wrong: **ly**_____

                danger-

Right: **ously**_____

  Use a dictionary to determine where words will be divided into syllables.

Directions: Write your answer on the line.

1. Write two words that use a hyphen: _____

2. Write a fraction in the first space and a two-digit number in the second:

  _____   _____

3. Write a two-syllable word that uses the fourth rule: _____

              _____

Hyphen:
Rule 1: Use a hyphen (-) to combine some closely related words.

three-cornered   triple-play

Use a dictionary to determine if words should use a hyphen.

Rule 2: Use a hyphen (-) between fractions.

one-eighth   three-sevenths

Rule 3: Use a hyphen (-) between two-digit word numbers from 21 to 99.

forty-two   fifty-five

Rule 4: Use a hyphen (-) when dividing a word of two or more syllables when they are at the end of a line of writing.
Remember: Words are divided into units of sound called *syllables*.

Important: You must have at least 2 letters on the first line.
_____ **tri-**
cycle_____

You must have at least 3 letters on the second line
_____ **yell-**
ing_____
Use a dictionary to determine where words will be divided into syllables.

ৰৡৰৡৰৡৰৡৰৡৰৡৰৡৰৡৰৡৰৡৰৡৰৡ

Directions: Place a hyphen where needed.

1.   My two-toned hair looks odd.

2.   Their aunt will be thirty-seven next month.

3.   She received twenty-four two-toned roses.

4.   Mix one-half cup of water with cornstarch.

5.   Our grandfather's tool set has a large, wooden ham-
     mer called a mallet.

Hyphen:
Rule 1: Use a hyphen (-) to combine some closely related words.

three-cornered   triple-play

Use a dictionary to determine if words should use a hyphen.

Rule 2: Use a hyphen (-) between fractions.

one-eighth   three-sevenths

Rule 3: Use a hyphen (-) between two-digit word numbers from 21 to 99.

forty-two   fifty-five

Rule 4: Use a hyphen (-) when dividing a word of two or more syllables when they are at the end of a line of writing.

Remember: Words are divided into units of sound called *syllables*.

Important: You must have at least 2 letters on the first line.

_____ tri-

cycle _____

You must have at least 3 letters on the second line

_____ yell-

ing _____

Use a dictionary to determine where words will be divided into syllables.

ॐॐॐॐॐॐॐॐॐॐॐॐॐॐॐॐॐ

Directions: Place a hyphen where needed.

1.   My two toned hair looks odd.

2.   Their aunt will be thirty seven next month.

3.   She received twenty four two toned roses.

4.   Mix one half cup of water with cornstarch.

5.   Our grandfather's tool set has a large, wooden ham
     mer called a mallet.

WORKBOOK PAGE 292

Underlining:

Rule 1:   Underline the name of an airplane, a ship, or a train.

ship, <u>Queen Mary</u>

~~If you are typing an underlined word, you may~~ *italicize* ~~it.~~   ship, *Queen Mary*

Rule 2:   Underline the letter(s), word(s), or number(s) out of context.

Your <u>2</u> in the address needs to be larger.
Make your <u>S</u> with a smaller loop.

~~If you are typing an underlined word, you may~~ *italicize* ~~it.~~

Your *2* in the address needs to be larger.
Make your *S* with a smaller loop.

Rule 3:   Underline the title of a book, magazine, movie, newspaper, play, television show, CD/tape/vinyl album, work of art, sculpture, opera, and long poem.

***Easy Grammar* Note: An item is usually underlined if you can receive it separately in the mail.**

book – <u>Slim and Miss Prim</u>   television show – <u>Zoom</u>
magazine – <u>Highlights</u>   movie – <u>Spirit</u>
newspaper – <u>London Times</u>   play – <u>Peter Pan</u>
CD/tape/vinyl album – <u>Arriving</u>   work of art – <u>Yakama Dancer</u>
sculpture – <u>Venus de Milo</u>   opera – <u>Aida</u>

In print, a title will be in *italics* rather than underlined.

Have you read *Slim and Miss Prim?*

ༀༀༀༀༀༀༀༀༀༀༀༀༀༀༀༀༀༀༀༀ

Directions: Write the following titles:

ANSWERS MAY VARY/REPRESENTATIVE ANSWERS:

1. Name of a book - _____**The Three Little Javalina**_____

2. Name of a movie - _____**Wilie Wonka and the Chocolate Factory**_____

3. Name of a television show - _____**High Five**_____

4. Name of a play or an album - _____**The Electric Sunshine Man**_____

624

Underlining:

Rule 1: Underline the name of an airplane, a ship, or a train.

ship, <u>Queen Mary</u>

If you are typing an underlined word, you may *italicize* it.   ship, *Queen Mary*

Rule 2: Underline the letter(s), word(s), or number(s) out of context.

Your <u>2</u> in the address needs to be larger.
Make your <u>S</u> with a smaller loop.

If you are typing an underlined word, you may *italicize* it.

Your *2* in the address needs to be larger.
Make your *S* with a smaller loop.

Rule 3: Underline the title of a book, magazine, movie, newspaper, play, television show, CD/tape/vinyl album, work of art, sculpture, opera, and long poem.

Easy Grammar **Note: An item is usually underlined if you can receive it separately in the mail.**

book – <u>Slim and Miss Prim</u>   television show - <u>Zoom</u>
magazine – <u>Highlights</u>   movie – <u>Spirit</u>
newspaper – <u>London Times</u>   play – <u>Peter Pan</u>
CD/tape/vinyl album - <u>Arriving</u>   work of art – <u>Yakama Dancer</u>
sculpture – <u>Venus de Milo</u>   opera – <u>Aida</u>

In print, a title will be in *italics* rather than underlined.

Have you read *Slim and Miss Prim*?

🦋🦋🦋🦋🦋🦋🦋🦋🦋🦋🦋🦋🦋🦋🦋🦋🦋🦋🦋🦋

Directions: Write the following titles:

1. Name of a book - _____

2. Name of a movie - _____

3. Name of a television show - _____

4. Name of a play or an album - _____

625

Underlining:

Rule 1:   Underline the name of an airplane, a ship, or a train.

train – <u>Thomas</u>

If you are typing an underlined word, you may *italicize* it.   *Thomas*

Rule 2:   Underline the letter(s), word(s), or number(s) out of context.

You forgot a <u>3</u> in your sum.

If you are typing an underlined word, you may *italicize* it.

You forgot a *3* in your sum.

Rule 3:   Underline the title of a book, magazine, movie, newspaper, play, television show, CD/tape/vinyl album, work of art, sculpture, opera, and long poem.

Easy Grammar Note: An item is usually underlined if you can receive it separately in the mail.

Her favorite book is <u>The Very Hungry Caterpillar</u>.

In print, a title will be in *italics* rather than underlined.

Her favorite book is *The Very Hungry Caterpillar*.

෨෨෨෨෨෨෨෨෨෨෨෨෨෨෨෨෨෨෨෨

Directions: Underline where needed.

1.   Is Dad reading <u>The Copywriter's Handbook</u>?

2.   Dot your <u>i</u> in your first word, Tomas.

3.   Their family likes to watch reruns of <u>Happy Days</u>.

4.   Do you know the color of the train, <u>Percy</u>?

5.   Have you listened to the CD, <u>Created in Your Love</u>?

6.   My favorite watercolor is Janet Fish's <u>Spring Party</u>.

7.   Your <u>Threa</u> in your title is misspelled; it should be spelled <u>Three</u>.

8.   My mother enjoys the magazine, <u>Arizona Foothills</u>.

Underlining:
Rule 1:   Underline the name of an airplane, a ship, or a train.

train – <u>Thomas</u>

If you are typing an underlined word, you may *italicize* it.   *Thomas*

Rule 2:   Underline the letter(s), word(s), or number(s) out of context.

You forgot a <u>3</u> in your sum.

If you are typing an underlined word, you may *italicize* it.

You forgot a *3* in your sum.

Rule 3:   Underline the title of a book, magazine, movie, newspaper, play, television show, CD/tape/vinyl album, work of art, sculpture, opera, and long poem.

***Easy Grammar* Note: An item is usually underlined if you can receive it separately in the mail.**

Her favorite book is <u>The Very Hungry Caterpillar</u>.

In print, a title will be in *italics* rather than underlined.

Her favorite book is *The Very Hungry Caterpillar*.

இஇஇஇஇஇஇஇஇஇஇஇஇஇஇஇஇஇஇஇஇ

Directions: Underline where needed.

1.   Is Dad reading The Copywriter's Handbook?

2.   Dot your i in your first word, Tomas.

3.   Their family likes to watch reruns of Happy Days.

4.   Do you know the color of the train, Percy?

5.   Have you listened to the CD, Created in Your Love?

6.   My favorite watercolor is Janet Fish's Spring Party.

7.   Your Threa in your title is misspelled; it should be spelled Three.

8.   My mother enjoys the magazine, Arizona Foothills.

Underlining:

Rule 1:   Use quotation marks (" ") to indicate someone's exact words.

"My pony's name is Trot," said Lizzy.

A. In a split quotation, place quotation marks around each part spoken.

"My answer," exclaimed Deca, "is right!"

B. In a split quotation, do not place the end quotation mark until the person has finished speaking.

"I'll phone Anna," said Lexi, "if you want. What is her number?"

🕉 *Periods and commas are placed inside quotation marks. Other punctuation is placed outside unless it is included in the actual quotation.*

Rule 2:   Use quotation marks (" ") to enclose the title of short poems, short stories, nursery rhymes, songs, chapters, articles, and essays.

poem ~ "Hot Line"   chapter ~ "Bears"
short story ~ "My Funny Cat"   article ~ "Get a Life"
nursery rhyme ~ "Three Men in a Tub" essay ~ "Mentoring"
song ~ "I've Been Working on the Railroad"

***Easy Grammar* Note: Any *item* that is contained within a larger one is usually placed in quotation marks.** For example:
A chapter is within a book.

🙧🙧🙧🙧🙧🙧🙧🙧🙧🙧🙧🙧🙧🙧🙧🙧🙧🙧🙧🙧

Directions: Write a short title.

1. poem - __**"Winter Clothes"**__   5. song - __**"America"**__

2. short story - __**"Gift of Gold"**__   6. article - __**"Melt Pounds Away"**__

3. essay - __**"Life in the Colonies"**__   7. chapter - __**"Plants"**__

4. nursery rhyme - __**"Hey, Diddle Diddle"**__

628

Underlining:

Rule 1:   Use quotation marks (" ") to indicate someone's exact words.

"My pony's name is Trot," said Lizzy.

A. In a split quotation, place quotation marks around each part spoken.

"My answer," exclaimed Deca, "is right!"

B. In a split quotation, do not place the end quotation mark until the person has finished speaking.

"I'll phone Anna," said Lexi, "if you want. What is her number?"

🕉 *Periods and commas are placed inside quotation marks. Other punctuation is placed outside unless it is included in the actual quotation.*

Rule 2:   Use quotation marks (" ") to enclose the title of short poems, short stories, nursery rhymes, songs, chapters, articles, and essays.

poem ~ "Hot Line"   chapter ~ "Bears"
short story ~ "My Funny Cat"   article ~ "Get a Life"
nursery rhyme ~ "Three Men in a Tub"   essay ~ "Mentoring"
song ~ "I've Been Working on the Railroad"

***Easy Grammar* Note: Any *item* that is contained within a larger one is usually placed in quotation marks.** For example:
A chapter is within a book.

🚲🚲🚲🚲🚲🚲🚲🚲🚲🚲🚲🚲🚲🚲🚲🚲🚲🚲🚲

Directions: Write a short title.

1. poem - _____   5. song - _____

2. short story - _____   6. article - _____

3. essay - _____   7. chapter - _____

4. nursery rhyme - _____

<u>**Note: In #2, be sure to point out that the comma is placed within the**</u>
<u>**quotation marks. The same is applicable to the period in #6.**</u>

Rule 1:   Use quotation marks (" ") to indicate someone's exact words.

"Where's Tessa?" asked Madison.

A. In a split quotation, place quotation marks around each part spoken.

"The little pinto," said Tom, "is my brother's horse."

B. In a split quotation, do not place the end quotation mark until the person has finished speaking.

"This hiking trail," said Parker, "looks good. Let's take it."

ॐ<u>**Periods and commas are placed inside quotation marks.**</u>
<u>**Other punctuation is placed outside unless it is included in the**</u>
<u>**actual quotation.**</u>

Rule 2:   Use quotation marks (" ") to enclose the title of short poems, short stories, nursery rhymes, songs, chapters, articles, and essays.

article ~ "Amelia Island"   poem ~ "Yawning"
chapter ~ "Bears"   short story ~ "Sammy Goes Fishing"
essay ~ "The Civil War"   song ~ "I Dream of Jeanie"
nursery rhyme ~ "Three Blind Mice"

Easy Grammar Note: <u>Any item that is contained within a larger one</u>
<u>is usually placed in quotation marks.</u> For example:
A newspaper (large) contains many articles (small).

🐎🐎🐎🐎🐎🐎🐎🐎🐎🐎🐎🐎🐎🐎🐎🐎🐎🐎🐎

Directions: Use quotation marks where needed.

1.   Hannah asked, "When will dinner be ready?"

2.   The song, "Created by Your Love," was written by his mother.

3.   "Momma, I need you to help me," said the little girl.

4.   Have you read the poem titled "The Sugar Lady" by Frank Asch?

5.   "Is Amelia Island," asked Peter, "off the coast of Florida?"

6.   I like the nursery rhyme, "Old King Cole."

Rule 1: **Use quotation marks (" ") to indicate someone's exact words.**

"Where's Tessa?" asked Madison.

A. In a split quotation, place quotation marks around each part spoken.

"The little pinto," said Tom, "is my brother's horse."

B. In a split quotation, do not place the end quotation mark until the person has finished speaking.

"This hiking trail," said Parker, "looks good. Let's take it."

🕉**Periods and commas are placed inside quotation marks. Other punctuation is placed outside unless it is included in the actual quotation.**

Rule 2: **Use quotation marks (" ") to enclose the title of short poems, short stories, nursery rhymes, songs, chapters, articles, and essays.**

article ~ "Amelia Island"   poem ~ "Yawning"
chapter ~ "Bears"   short story ~ "Sammy Goes Fishing"
essay ~ "The Civil War"   song ~ "I Dream of Jeanie"
nursery rhyme ~ "Three Blind Mice"

Easy Grammar Note: **Any item that is contained within a larger one is usually placed in quotation marks.** For example: A newspaper (large) contains many articles (small).

෴෴෴෴෴෴෴෴෴෴෴෴෴෴෴෴෴෴෴෴෴

Directions: Use quotation marks where needed.

1. Hannah asked, When will dinner be ready?

2. The song, Created by Your Love, was written by his mother.

3. Momma, I need you to help me, said the little girl.

4. Have you read the poem titled The Sugar Lady by Frank Asch?

5. Is Amelia Island, asked Peter, off the coast of Florida?

6. I like the nursery rhyme, Old King Cole.

Note: Encourage students to think in terms of the *item* being large or small to help determine underlining or using quotation marks. You are teaching for life-long application.

Directions: Place quotation marks or underline the following titles.

1.   a ship, <u>Lusitania</u>

2.   a book, <u>Daddy's Girl</u>

3.   a movie, <u>Free Willy</u>

4.   a poem, "Rhinos Purple, Hippos Green"

5.   an article, "How to Paint Your Room"

6.   a magazine, <u>Kids</u>

7.   a play, <u>American Spy</u>

8.   a short story, "Phoebe and the General"

9.   a song, "Getting to Know You"

10.   an album, <u>God Is Love</u>

11.   an airplane, <u>Air Force 1</u>

12.   a newspaper, <u>The Financial Times</u>

13.   a television show, <u>Jeopardy</u>

14.   a chapter, "Pronouns"

15.   a work of art, <u>Wagon Boss</u>

16.   an essay, "Comparing Plant Cells and Animal Cells"

17.   a train, <u>James</u>

18.   a nursery rhyme, "Baa, Baa, Black Sheep"

19.   a newspaper article, "The Stock Market"

632

Directions: Place quotation marks or underline the following titles.

1. a ship, Lusitania

2. a book, Daddy's Girl

3. a movie, Free Willy

4. a poem, Rhinos Purple, Hippos Green

5. an article, How to Paint Your Room

6. a magazine, Kids

7. a play, American Spy

8. a short story, Phoebe and the General

9. a song, Getting to Know You

10. an album, God Is Love

11. an airplane, Air Force 1

12. a newspaper, The Financial Times

13. a television show, Jeopardy

14. a chapter, Pronouns

15. a work of art, Wagon Boss

16. an essay, Comparing Plant Cells and Animal Cells

17. a train, James

18. a nursery rhyme, Baa, Baa, Black Sheep

19. a newspaper article, The Stock Market

WORKBOOK PAGE 297

A. Insert periods where needed.

1. I.   Mountains
       A.   Mt. Hood
       B.   Mt. Elden
   II. Hills

2. Mr. Contos now lives at 7252 N. Dee Ave.

3. On Mon., Aug. 26, they'll fly to Denmark.

ॐॐॐॐॐॐॐॐॐ

B. Insert commas where needed.

1. Emma, do you want to make a snowman?

2. Your dog may go with us, but your ferret needs to remain behind.

3. Her Victorian hat was decorated with three feathers, lace, and a large flower.

4. No, the church bells have not rung.

5. The company address is P. O. Box 30012, Gettysburg, PA 17325.

6. The United States declared its freedom on July 4, 1776.

7. Dakota said, "I need water for my hermit crab."

8. Kate and Becca, his granddaughters, went fishing with him.

9. Monday, October 10, 2005, was Canada's Thanksgiving Day.

10. Printz, Dave L.

11. During the morning, practice was held on the playground.

12. On January 1, 2016, she will be sixteen.

13. "We must measure the width of this room," said the carpet installer.

634

A.   Insert periods where needed.

1.   I   Mountains
         A   Mt Hood
         B   Mt Elden
     II   Hills

2.   Mr Contos now lives at 7252 N Dee Ave

3.   On Mon , Aug 26, they'll fly to Denmark

xxxxxxxxxx

B.   Insert commas where needed.

1.   Emma do you want to make a snowman?

2.   Your dog may go with us but your ferret needs to remain behind.

3.   Her Victorian hat was decorated with three feathers lace and a large flower.

4.   No the church bells have not rung.

5.   The company address is P. O. Box 30012 Gettysburg PA 17325.

6.   The United States declared its freedom on July 4 1776.

7.   Dakota said "I need water for my hermit crab."

8.   Kate and Becca his granddaughters went fishing with him.

9.   Monday October 10 2005 was Canada's Thanksgiving Day.

10.   Printz Dave L.

11.   During the morning practice was held on the playground.

12.   On January 1 2016 she will be sixteen.

13.   "We must measure the width of this room " said the carpet installer.

635

C. Directions: Use a question mark or an exclamation point where needed.

1. Where is my yoga outfit**?**

2. Ouch**!** I hurt my toe**!**

෨෨෨෨෨෨෨෨෨෨

D. Directions: Write the answer.

1. the contraction for **they are** - _____**they're**_____

2. the contraction for **I would** - _____**I'd**_____

3. the contraction for **will not** - _____**won't**_____

4. balloons belonging to one girl - _____**(one) girl's balloons**_____

5. balloons belonging to more than one girl - _____**girls' balloons**_____

6. balloons belonging to more than one child - _____**children's balloons**____

7. a barn for several horses - _____**horses' barn**_____

෨෨෨෨෨෨෨෨෨෨

E. Directions: Place a colon or a semicolon where needed.

1. Our bus leaves at 3:45 this afternoon**;** please be at the bus stop by then.

2. These items are missing from my drawer**:** a pen, an eraser, and a ruler.

3. Things that begin with <u>H</u>**:**
    -hamsters
    -habits
    -horses

4. Dear Ms. Listiack**:**

෨෨෨෨෨෨෨෨෨෨

F. Directions: Place a hyphen where needed.

1. Divide *partner* into syllables: _____**part-ner**_____

2. Seventy-four bubble-wrapped teapots were unboxed.

636

C. Directions: Use a question mark or an exclamation point where needed.

1. Where is my yoga outfit

2. Ouch I hurt my toe

ॐॐॐॐॐॐॐॐॐॐ

D. Directions: Write the answer.

1. the contraction for **they are** - _____

2. the contraction for **I would** - _____

3. the contraction for **will not** - _____

4. balloons belonging to one girl - _____

5. balloons belonging to more than one girl - _____

6. balloons belonging to more than one child - _____

7. a barn for several horses - _____

ॐॐॐॐॐॐॐॐॐॐ

E. Directions: Place a colon or a semicolon where needed.

1. Our bus leaves at 3 45 this afternoon please be at the bus stop by then.

2. These items are missing from my drawer a pen, an eraser, and a ruler.

3. Things that begin with <u>H</u>
    -hamsters
    -habits
    -horses

4. Dear Ms. Listiack

ॐॐॐॐॐॐॐॐॐॐ

F. Directions: Place a hyphen where needed.

1. Divide *partner* into syllables: _____

2. Seventy four bubble wrapped teapots were unboxed.

G. Directions: Use underlining where needed. ***WORKBOOK PAGE 299***

1. Have you seen the movie, <u>Mary Poppins</u>, starring Julie Andrews?

2. Do you know about the airplane, <u>Enola Gay</u>?

3. You'll like the cookbook titled <u>A Very Berry Cookbook</u>.

4. Your <u>p</u> needs to be capitalized in the word, <u>postmaster</u>.

5. His aunt went on a cruise to Alaska on the <u>Queen Star</u>.

ର୍ଭର୍ଭର୍ଭର୍ଭର୍ଭର୍ଭର୍ଭ

H. Directions: Use quotation marks where needed.

1. Joy asked, "Did you fill the birdbath?"

2. His favorite poem, "The Midnight Ride of Paul Revere," tells a story.

3. "Our friends have arrived," said Gretta.

4. Do you like the newspaper column titled "Theft Reports" each week?

ର୍ଭର୍ଭର୍ଭର୍ଭର୍ଭର୍ଭର୍ଭ

I. Directions: Write the following.

1. Write the abbreviations for the days of the week.

   a. Sunday – **Sun.**   e. Thursday – **Thurs.**

   b. Monday – **Mon.**   f. Friday – **Fri.**

   c. Tuesday – **Tues.**   g. Saturday – **Sat.**

   d. Wednesday – **Wed.**

2. Write the abbreviations for the months of the year.

   a. January – **Jan.**   f. September – **Sept.**

   b. February – **Feb.**   g. October – **Oct.**

   c. March – **Mar.**   h. November – **Nov.**

   d. April – **Apr.**   i. December – **Dec.**

   e. August – **Aug.**

638

G. Directions: Use underlining where needed.

1. Have you seen the movie, Mary Poppins, starring Julie Andrews?

2. Do you know about the airplane, Enola Gay?

3. You'll like the cookbook titled A Very Berry Cookbook.

4. Your p needs to be capitalized in the word, postmaster.

5. His aunt went on a cruise to Alaska on the Queen Star.

ᘓᘓᘓᘓᘓᘓᘓᘓᘓ

H. Directions: Use quotation marks where needed.

1. Joy asked, Did you fill the birdbath?

2. His favorite poem, The Midnight Ride of Paul Revere, tells a story.

3. Our friends have arrived, said Gretta.

4. Do you like the newspaper column titled Theft Reports each week?

ᘓᘓᘓᘓᘓᘓᘓᘓᘓ

I. Directions: Write the following.

1. Write the abbreviations for the days of the week.

   a. Sunday — _____   e. Thursday — _____

   b. Monday — _____   f. Friday — _____

   c. Tuesday — _____   g. Saturday — _____

   d. Wednesday — _____

2. Write the abbreviations for the months of the year.

   a. January — _____   f. September — _____

   b. February — _____   g. October — _____

   c. March — _____   h. November — _____

   d. April — _____   i. December — _____

   e. August — _____

PUNCTUATION

Review

Directions: Insert needed punctuation.

1. No, we haven't learned French.

2. Dear Sir:

3. Has Capt. Juan S. Ramos visited Dan's classroom?

4.
                                    43 Briar Lane

                                    Terre Haute, IN   47808

                                    July 4, 2005

Dear Liz,

    Yes, you're invited to our home at 12 W. Maple Street, Portland, Maine.

Bring the following: a sleeping bag, a backpack, and camping clothes. My

Dad will take us on an two-day camping trip.**(!)** Wow! I cant wait!

                                    Your friend,

                                    Tessa

5. Your <u>t</u> in <u>torn</u> isn't large enough, Parker.

6. I read the book titled <u>Full Moon</u>; you would enjoy reading it.

7. Austin said, "Many Japanese tourists visit the Grand Canyon."

8. The two boys' mother helped them to build a two-wheeled cart.

9. Mr. and Mrs. Fromm were married on Saturday, Oct. 8, 2005.

10. I should buy twenty-two bottles of water, but I don't have enough money.

11. Their flight will depart at 2:30 for San Antonio, Texas.

Name_____ **PUNCTUATION**

Date_____   **Review**

Directions: Insert needed punctuation.

1.   No we havent learned French

2.   Dear Sir

3.   Has Capt Juan S Ramos visited Dans classroom

4.
                                        43 Briar Lane

                                        Terre Haute, IN   47808

                                        July 4 2005

   Dear Liz

       Yes youre invited to our home at 12 W Maple Street Portland Maine

   Bring the following a sleeping bag a backpack and camping clothes My

   Dad will take us on an two day camping trip Wow I cant wait

                                        Your friend

                                        Tessa

5.   Your t in torn isnt large enough Parker

6.   I read the book titled Full Moon you would enjoy reading it

7.   Austin said Many Japanese tourists visit the Grand Canyon

8.   The two boys mother helped them to build a two wheeled cart

9.   Mr and Mrs Fromm were married on Saturday Oct 8 2005

10. I should buy twenty two bottles of water but I dont have enough money

11. Their flight will depart at 2 30 for San Antonio Texas

641

Name_____   **PUNCTUATION**

Date_____   **Test**

Directions: Insert needed punctuation.

1. We won't leave for Boise, Idaho, until 3:00.

2. That boy's father is a plumber; his mother is a lawyer.

3. Dot your i̲ above the letter, Anna.

4. Dr. Heard lives at 802 Robin Drive, Orlando, Fl 32087.

5. Who has read the poem titled "Egg Thoughts" by R. Hoban**?**

6. One woman from a ladies' club read the book titled <u>Jamberry</u> to us.

7. Jana said, "I couldn't reach the top shelf."

8. They became engaged on Mon., February 14, 2005.

9. Nanny used thirty-one shells to make a two-colored picture frame.

10. Dear Katie,

   Yeah! We have very exciting news! Mandy and Chan, our neigh-

   bors, want to take us to Niagara Falls next summer. **(!)** Do you want

   to come along**?**

                                      Your cousin,
                                      Kaylee

11.   Dear Judge Minz:

12.   Yes, we need the following: a carton of eggs, milk, and a loaf of bread.

13.   Mr. Wong stayed for a week, but he didn't have time to go to an art mu-
     seum.

14. "Matty's mother attended a meeting at the Roth Bldg. today," said Tate.
642

PUNCTUATION

Test

Directions: Insert needed punctuation.

1.   We wont leave for Boise Idaho until 3 00

2.   That boys father is a plumber his mother is a lawyer

3.   Dot your i above the letter Anna

4.   Dr Heard lives at 802 Robin Drive Orlando Fl 32087

5.   Who has read the poem titled Egg Thoughts by R Hoban

6.   One woman from a ladies club read the book titled Jamberry to us

7.   Jana said I couldnt reach the top shelf

8.   They became engaged on Mon February 14 2005

9.   Nanny used thirty one shells to make a two colored picture frame

10. Dear Katie

     Yeah We have very exciting news Mandy and Chan our neigh

     bors want to take us to Niagara Falls next summer Do you want

     to come along

                              Your cousin
                              Kaylee

11. Dear Judge Minz

12. Yes we need the following a carton of eggs milk and a loaf of bread

13. Mr Wong stayed for a week but he didnt have time to go to an art mu
     seum

14. Mattys mother attended a meeting at the Roth Bldg today said Tate

643

TO THE TEACHER:

Students will learn about writing appositives in the next few lessons. You may choose to spread these lessons over a period of many weeks or to teach them as a writing unit. I recommend doing all of these lessons <u>with</u> students. Be sure to teach lessons and to be enthusiastic in your discussions.

For more lessons and additional writing skills involving sentence structures, peruse the text, *Easy Writing*.

WRITING

An appositive is a word or phrase (group of words) that explains a noun.

Example: Spin**, their ferret,** is in a cage.

appositive

WITHOUT THE PHRASE, ***THEIR FERRET***, WE WOULDN'T KNOW WHO SPIN IS!

An appositive is placed next to the word it explains.

Example: We saw Lou, **our postman,** today.

appositive

WITHOUT THE PHRASE, ***OUR POSTMAN***, WE WOULDN'T KNOW WHO LOU IS!

An appositive is set off by commas.

Examples: Have you been to Denver, **the capital of Colorado**?

Miss Cook, **a nurse,** stopped to help.

🙰🙰🙰🙰🙰🙰🙰🙰🙰🙰🙰

Directions: Place the appositive by the word it explains. Be sure to insert a comma or commas where needed.

Example: He gave me a gowan. A gowan is a white field flower.

He gave me a gowan.

He gave me a gowan, *a white field flower*.

1. We asked Jana and Jo to go to the lake with us. Jana and Jo are our classmates.

We asked Jana and Jo, *our classmates,*

to go to the lake with us.

An appositive is a word or phrase (group of words) that explains a noun.

Example: Spin**, their ferret,** is in a cage.

appositive

WITHOUT THE PHRASE, ***THEIR FERRET***, WE WOULDN'T KNOW WHO SPIN IS!

An appositive is placed next to the word it explains.

Example: We saw Lou**, our postman,** today.

appositive

WITHOUT THE PHRASE, ***OUR POSTMAN***, WE WOULDN'T KNOW WHO LOU IS!

An appositive is set off by commas.

Examples: Have you been to Denver**, the capital of Colorado**?

Miss Cook**, a nurse,** stopped to help.

෴෴෴෴෴෴෴෴෴෴෴෴

Directions: Place the appositive by the word it explains. Be sure to insert a comma or commas where needed.

Example: He gave me a gowan. A gowan is a white field flower.

He gave me a gowan._____

He gave me a gowan, *a white field flower.*_____

1. We asked Jana and Jo to go to the lake with us. Jana and Jo are our classmates.
   We asked Jana and Jo_____

   to go to the lake with us._____

2. Grandma served watermelon. Watermelon is my favorite food.

____ **Grandma served watermelon,** *my favorite food.* ____

_____

3. They saw karos in New Zealand. Karos are small trees.

____ **They saw karos,** *small trees,* **in New Zealand.** ____

_____

4. Michael Jordan appeared on television. Michael is a basketball player.

____ **Michael Jordan,** *a basketball player,* ____

____ **appeared on televison.** ____

5. Are you attending the fiesta? It is Pablo's graduation party.

____ **Are you attending the fiesta,** *Pablo's graduation* ____

____ *party?* ____

6. We watched a movie. It was a scary one that frightened us.

____ **We watched a movie,** *a scary one that frightened* ____

____ *us.* ____

7. Tessa bought a kite. Tessa is Eddie's sister.

____ **Tessa,** *Eddie's sister,* **bought a kite.** ____

8. She sold the Bar S. The Bar S is a ranch in eastern Montana.

____ **She sold the Bar S,** *a ranch in eastern Montana.* ____

_____

2. Grandma served watermelon. Watermelon is my favorite food.

    Grandma served watermelon _____

_____

3. They saw karos in New Zealand. Karos are small trees.

    They saw karos _____ **in New** _____

    Zealand. _____

4. Michael Jordan appeared on television. Michael is a basketball player.

    Michael Jordan _____

    appeared on television. _____

5. Are you attending the fiesta? It is Pablo's graduation party.

    Are you attending the fiesta _____

_____

6. We watched a movie. It was a scary one that frightened us.

    We watched a movie _____

_____

7. Tessa bought a kite. Tessa is Eddie's sister.

    Tessa _____ **bought a kite.** _____

8. She sold the Bar S. The Bar S is a ranch in eastern Montana.

    She sold the Bar S _____

_____

An appositive is a word or phrase (group of words) that explains.

Example: Jacy, **their grandson,** is two months old.
                          appositive

WITHOUT THE PHRASE, *THEIR GRANDSON* , WE WOULDN'T KNOW WHO JACY IS!

An appositive is placed next to the word it explains.

Example: We studied amino acids, **building blocks of protein.**
                                                              appositive

BUILDING BLOCKS OF PROTEIN EXPLAINS AMINO ACIDS.

An appositive is set off by commas.

Examples: I like sushi, **a dish of rice and raw fish.**

This tine, **a prong on my fork,** is bent.

ৰ্চৰ্চৰ্চৰ্চৰ্চৰ্চৰ্চৰ্চৰ্চৰ্চৰ্চ

Directions: Place the appositive by the word it explains. Be sure to insert a comma or commas where needed.

Example: Gertrude Ederle was the first woman to swim the English Channel. She was only nineteen.

Gertrude Ederle, *the first woman to swim the*

English Channel, **was only nineteen.**

1.   Aren entered the hospital in a hurry. Aren is a doctor.

Aren, *a doctor,* **entered the**

hospital in a hurry.

An appositive is a word or phrase (group of words) that explains.

Example: Jacy**, their grandson,** is two months old.

appositive

WITHOUT THE PHRASE, *THEIR GRANDSON* , WE WOULDN'T KNOW WHO JACY IS!

An appositive is placed next to the word it explains.

Example: We studied amino acids**, building blocks of protein**.

appositive

BUILDING BLOCKS OF PROTEIN EXPLAINS AMINO ACIDS.

An appositive is set off by commas.

Examples: I like sushi**, a dish of rice and raw fish**.

This tine**, a prong on my fork,** is bent.

Directions: Place the appositive by the word it explains. Be sure to insert a comma or commas where needed.

Example: Gertrude Ederle was the first woman to swim the English Channel. She was only nineteen.

Gertrude Ederle, *the first woman to swim the*

English Channel, **was only nineteen.**

1.   Aren entered the hospital in a hurry. Aren is a doctor.

_____**Aren,**_____**, entered the**_____

_____**hospital in a hurry.**_____

2. His aunt and uncle made sorbet. Sorbet is an Eastern sherbet.

    His aunt and uncle made sorbet, *an Eastern sherbet.*

3. Martha Jane Canary was once a scout for General Custer. She was also known as "Calamity Jane."

    Martha Jane Canary, *also known as "Calamity Jane,"*

    was once a scout for General Custer.

4. Faith and Jenna are identical twins. They were born five minutes apart.

    Faith and Jenna, *identical twins,*

    were born five minutes apart.

5. A set of George Washington's teeth is kept at Mount Vernon. Mount Vernon is Washington's home.

    A set of George Washington's teeth is kept at Mount

    Vernon, *his home.*

6. Mr. London is a steel worker. Mr. London became our new mayor.

    Mr. London, *a steel worker,* **became**

    our new mayor.

7. Bill Robinson was a famous tap dancer in the 1930s. His nickname was "Bojangles."

    Bill Robinson, *a famous tap dancer in the 1930s,*

    was nicknamed "Bojangles."

652

2. His aunt and uncle made sorbet. Sorbet is an Eastern sherbet.

   __His aunt and uncle made sorbet,_____

   _____

3. Martha Jane Canary was once a scout for General Custer. She was also known as "Calamity Jane."

   __Martha Jane Canary,_____,___

   __was once a scout for General Custer._____

4. Faith and Jenna are identical twins. They were born five minutes apart.

   __Faith and Jenna,_____,_____

   __were born five minutes apart._____

5. A set of George Washington's teeth is kept at Mount Vernon. Mount Vernon is Washington's home.

   __A set of George Washington's teeth is kept at Mount__

   __Vernon,_____

6. Mr. London is a steel worker. Mr. London became our new mayor.

   __Mr. London,_____, became_____

   __our new mayor._____

7. Bill Robinson was a famous tap dancer in the 1930s. His nickname was "Bojangles."

   __Bill Robinson,_____,___

   __was nicknamed "Bojangles."_____

653

WORKBOOK PAGE 307

An appositive is a word or phrase (group of words) that explains a noun. An appositive is placed next to the word it explains.

        Example: Sara, **my cousin**, will arrive tomorrow.
                            appositive

An appositive is set off by a comma or commas.

        Example: That glass, **an old goblet,** was given to my mother.
                         appositive

                   🙵🙵🙵🙵🙵🙵🙵🙵🙵🙵🙵

Directions: Write a sentence using an appositive.

   Example: Emma talked with his mother. Emma is his karate instructor.

        Emma, his karate instructor, talked with his mother.

1.   Jack gave a speech. Jack is our class president.

        Jack, our class president, gave a speech.

2.   The artist painted a picture of a bobolink. A bobolink is a songbird.

        The artist painted a picture of a bobolink, a songbird.

3.   The winners were Mika and Rob. They received tickets to a concert.

        The winners, Mika and Rob, received tickets to a

        concert.

4.   Have you been to Sicily? Sicily is an island at the tip of Italy.

        Have you been to Sicily, an island at the tip of Italy?

5.   Flummery is good. Flummery is a dish made of boiled wheatmeal.

        Flummery, a dish made of boiled wheatmeal, is good.

Name_____

Date_____

An appositive is a word or phrase (group of words) that explains a noun. An appositive is placed next to the word it explains.

Example: Sara, **my cousin**, will arrive tomorrow.
                          appositive

An appositive is set off by a comma or commas.

Example: That glass, **an old goblet,** was given to my mother.
                          appositive

☙☙☙☙☙☙☙☙☙☙☙

Directions: Write a sentence using an appositive.

Example: Emma talked with his mother. Emma is his karate instructor.

    Emma, his karate instructor, talked with his mother.

1.   Jack gave a speech. Jack is our class president.

_____

2.   The artist painted a picture of a bobolink. A bobolink is a songbird.

_____

_____

3.   The winners were Mika and Rob. They received tickets to a concert.

_____

_____

4.   Have you been to Sicily? Sicily is an island at the tip of Italy.

_____

_____

5.   Flummery is good. Flummery is a dish made of boiled wheatmeal.

_____

_____

Name_____   **WRITING SENTENCES**

Date_____   **Appositives**

An appositive is a word or phrase (group of words) that explains a noun. An appositive is placed next to the word it explains.

Example: Lisa gave him a present, **a blue-striped shirt**.
                                                    appositive

An appositive is set off by a comma or commas.

Example: Kasha, **a fabric made from wool and hair**, is soft.
                          appositive

ఞఞఞఞఞఞఞఞఞఞఞ

Directions: Write a sentence using an appositive.

Example: Do you like gumbo? Gumbo is a spicy soup thickened with okra.

            Do you like gumbo, a spicy soup thickened with okra?

1. The new puppy fell over his dish and spilled his water. The new puppy is a white furry husky.

            The new puppy, a white furry husky, fell over his dish and

            spilled his water.

2. Paul is driving his new vehicle. His new vehicle is a red tractor-trailer.

            Paul is driving his new vehicle, a red tractor-trailer.

3. They used Masonite for their science project. Masonite is fiberboard made from wood fiber.

            They used Masonite, fiberboard made from wood fiber,

            for their science project.

4. We visited a kraal in Africa. A kraal is a village surrounded by a fence.

            We visited a kraal, a village surrounded by a fence,

            in Africa.

An appositive is a word or phrase (group of words) that explains a noun. An appositive is placed next to the word it explains.

Example: Lisa gave him a present, **a blue-striped shirt**.
appositive

An appositive is set off by a comma or commas.

Example: Kasha, **a fabric made from wool and hair,** is soft.
appositive

ৡৡৡৡৡৡৡৡৡৡৡৡ

Directions: Write a sentence using an appositive.

Example: Do you like gumbo? Gumbo is a spicy soup thickened with okra.

   Do you like gumbo, a spicy soup thickened with okra?

1. The new puppy fell over his dish and spilled his water. The new puppy is a white furry husky.

   _____

   _____

2. Paul is driving his new vehicle. His new vehicle is a red tractor-trailer.

   _____

   _____

3. They used Masonite for their science project. Masonite is fiberboard made from wood fiber.

   _____

   _____

4. We visited a kraal in Africa. A kraal is a village surrounded by a fence.

   _____

   _____

657

TO THE TEACHER:

The semicolon lessons first address determining if a group of words is a complete thought or an incomplete thought.

> Examples: I <u>fell</u> and <u>scratched</u> my knee.   (complete thought)
>
> Before <u>we</u> <u>went</u> to the movie. (incomplete thought)

If you choose to teach these as independent clauses and dependent clauses, do so. However, our **goal** is to help students to differentiate between a complete and incomplete thought in order to be able to use semicolons in writing. I suggest keeping the concept as simple as possible.

You will need to tell students that only one space is usually left after a semicolon.

NOTES

A **semicolon** is a comma with a period above it (;).

A semicolon may be used to join two complete thoughts. That means that each thought must be able to stand alone as a **complete sentence**.

It's important to know if the group of words expresses a complete thought.

Examples: Your hairbrush is on the floor. (**complete thought**)
                                                          (**sentence**)

Walked her dog. (**not a complete thought**)
Where's the subject? We don't know *who* walked her dog.

After we went to our game. (**not a complete thought**)

The sentence contains a **subject** (we) and a **verb** (went), but it does not express a complete thought. If you said to a friend, "After we went to our game," and walked away, your friend would have no idea what you are trying to tell him.

⤸⤸⤸⤸⤸⤸⤸⤸⤸⤸⤸

Directions: Write **S** in the blank if the group of words is a sentence (complete thought). Write **NS** in the blank if the group of words is not a sentence (not a complete thought).

1. _____**S**_____   Lucy rides her horse bareback.

2. _____**S**_____   A new pope had been chosen.

3. _____**NS**_____   Beginning to rain.

4. _____**NS**_____   When you are finished.

5. _____**S**_____   Mark was hired as a waiter.

6. _____**S**_____   Has a cat scratched your arm?

7. _____**NS**_____   Sent on an errand for ten minutes.

8. _____**NS**_____   After a roofer started a drill.

9. _____**NS**_____   Your idea funny.

10. _____**S**_____   Jan wants a purple coat.

Name_____

Date_____

A **semicolon** is a comma with a period above it **(;)**.

A semicolon may be used to join two complete thoughts. That means that each thought must be able to stand alone as a **complete sentence**.

It's important to know if the group of words expresses a complete thought.

Examples: <u>Your hairbrush is on the floor.</u>   (**complete thought**)
                                                                      (**sentence**)

<u>Walked her dog.</u>   (**not a complete thought**)
Where's the subject? We don't know *who* walked her dog.

<u>After we went to our game.</u> (**not a complete thought**)

The sentence contains a **subject** (<u>we</u>) and a **verb** (<u>went</u>), but it does not express a complete thought. If you said to a friend, "After we went to our game," and walked away, your friend would have no idea what you are trying to tell him.

ಈಶ್ಚಈಶ್ಚಈಶ್ಚಈಶ್ಚಈಶ್ಚಈಶ್ಚಈಶ್ಚಈಶ್ಚಈಶ್ಚಈಶ್ಚ

Directions: Write **S** in the blank if the group of words is a sentence (complete thought). Write **NS** in the blank if the group of words is not a sentence (not a complete thought).

1. _____   Lucy rides her horse bareback.

2. _____   A new pope had been chosen.

3. _____   Beginning to rain.

4. _____   When you are finished.

5. _____   Mark was hired as a waiter.

6. _____   Has a cat scratched your arm?

7. _____   Sent on an errand for ten minutes.

8. _____   After a roofer started a drill.

9. _____   Your idea funny.

10. _____   Jan wants a purple coat.

WRITING SENTENCES

Using Semicolons

A **semicolon** is a comma with a period above it **(;)**.

A semicolon may be used to join two complete thoughts. That means that each thought must be able to stand alone as a **complete sentence**.

It's important to know if the group of words expresses a complete thought.

> Examples: The car's fender is damaged.   **(complete thought)**
> **(sentence)**
>
> Susan in the pink sweater.   **(not a complete thought)**
> Where's the verb?
>
> If I earn a few dollars.   **(not a complete thought)**

The sentence contains a **subject** (I) and a **verb** (earn), but it does not express a complete thought.

ॐॐॐॐॐॐॐॐॐॐॐ

Directions: Write **S** in the blank if the group of words is a sentence (complete thought). Write **NS** in the blank if the group of words is not a sentence (not a complete thought).

1. __**NS**__   The landed in the bushes.

2. __**NS**__   Before she prepared food for a picnic.

3. __**NS**__   Breaking away and suddenly yelling.

4. __**S**__   She worked on a scrapbook.

5. __**NS**__   This limited to four people.

6. __**S**__   Many people have visited the Alamo.

7. __**NS**__   A fire in the fireplace.

8. __**S**__   That little girl speaks Spanish.

9. __**NS**__   They to a horse show last weekend.

10. __**NS**__   Having eaten at a local restaurant.

Name_____

Date_____

A **semicolon** is a comma with a period above it **(;)**.

A semicolon may be used to join two complete thoughts. That means that each thought must be able to stand alone as a **complete sentence**.

It's important to know if the group of words expresses a complete thought.

Examples: The car's fender is damaged. (**complete thought**)
(**sentence**)

Susan in the pink sweater. (**not a complete thought**)
Where's the verb?

If I earn a few dollars. (**not a complete thought**)

The sentence contains a **subject** (I) and a **verb** (earn), but it does not express a complete thought.

৯৯৯৯৯৯৯৯৯৯৯

Directions: Write **S** in the blank if the group of words is a sentence (complete thought). Write **NS** in the blank if the group of words is not a sentence (not a complete thought).

1. _____ The landed in the bushes.

2. _____ Before she prepared food for a picnic.

3. _____ Breaking away and suddenly yelling.

4. _____ She worked on a scrapbook.

5. _____ This limited to four people.

6. _____ Many people have visited the Alamo.

7. _____ A fire in the fireplace.

8. _____ That little girl speaks Spanish.

9. _____ They to a horse show last weekend.

10. _____ Having eaten at a local restaurant.

663

Name_____   **WRITING SENTENCES**

WORKBOOK PAGE 311

Date_____   **Using Semicolons**

A semicolon is a comma with a period above it (;). It joins two complete thoughts.

1st complete thought (sentence):   This lettuce has turned brown.
2nd complete thought (sentence):   I'll have to throw it away.

Example: This lettuce has turned brown**;** I'll have to throw it away.

The two thoughts must be about the same topic!

Wrong: My sister lives in Alaska**;** I'm having steak for dinner.

Right: My sister lives in Alaska**;** I'm visiting her this summer.

Sometimes, words such as *however* or *therefore* will follow the semicolon. Place a comma after *however* or *therefore.*

Example: I like fish**; *however*,** I don't like fish tacos.

ৡ৵ৡ৵ৡ৵ৡ৵ৡ৵ৡ৵ৡ৵ৡ৵ৡ৵ৡ৵ৡ৵

Directions: Use a semicolon where needed.

1.   Kim is in first grade**;** he is already reading.

2.   Stop the bus**;** I want to get off.

3.   Tessa has a sore throat**;** therefore, she didn't sing.

4.   Their car is old**;** however, it runs very well.

5.   She models for a designer**;** her picture appeared in *Fashion Q.*

6.   Mom didn't fish**;** however, she sat by the creek and read a book.

7.   Cody is taking college classes**;** he wants to be a history teacher.

8.   I like yams**;** they're one of my favorite foods.

9.   Tate entered church**;** therefore, he turned his cell phone off.

664

A semicolon is a comma with a period above it (;). It joins two complete thoughts.

1st complete thought (sentence):   This lettuce has turned brown.
2nd complete thought (sentence):   I'll have to throw it away.

Example: This lettuce has turned brown**;** I'll have to throw it away.

The two thoughts must be about the same topic!

Wrong: My sister lives in Alaska; I'm having steak for dinner.

Right: My sister lives in Alaska; I'm visiting her this summer.

Sometimes, words such as *however* or *therefore* will follow the semicolon. Place a comma after *however* or *therefore*.

Example: I like fish**; *however*,** I don't like fish tacos.

ॐॐॐॐॐॐॐॐॐॐॐ

Directions: Use a semicolon where needed.

1. Kim is in first grade he is already reading.

2. Stop the bus I want to get off.

3. Tessa has a sore throat therefore, she didn't sing.

4. Their car is old however, it runs very well.

5. She models for a designer her picture appeared in *Fashion Q*.

6. Mom didn't fish however, she sat by the creek and read a book.

7. Cody is taking college classes he wants to be a history teacher.

8. I like baked yams they're one of my favorite foods.

9. Tate entered church therefore, he turned his cell phone off.

WRITING SENTENCES

Date_____

Using Semicolons

A semicolon is a comma with a period above it (;). It joins two complete thoughts. The two thoughts must be about the <u>same</u> topic!

Sometimes, words such as *however* or *therefore* will follow the semicolon. Place a comma after *however* or *therefore*.

     Example: His arm is in a cast; ***however***, he climbed over the fence.

        ठ्ठ ठ्ठ ठ्ठ ठ्ठ ठ्ठ ठ्ठ ठ्ठ ठ्ठ ठ्ठ ठ्ठ

Directions: The first complete thought has been written for you. Place a semicolon and finish the sentence.

<u>Remember</u>: **You can use *however* or *therefore* if it makes sense. Don't forget the comma after these words.**

ANSWERS MAY VARY/REPRESENTATIVE ANSWERS:

1. <u>It has stopped raining</u>**; we can go to the park after all.**

2. <u>My friend twisted his ankle</u>**; however, he didn't fall.**

3. <u>Carla made blueberry tarts</u>**; however, she burned them.**

4. <u>The dusty road has many potholes</u>**; therefore, it will be repaired soon.**

5. <u>We have been assigned a social studies project</u>**; I'll do mine on the American Revolution.**

A semicolon is a comma with a period above it (;). It joins two complete thoughts. The two thoughts must be about the same topic!

Sometimes, words such as *however* or *therefore* will follow the semicolon. Place a comma after *however* or *therefore.*

      Example: His arm is in a cast; ***however,*** he climbed over the fence.

               🐾🐾🐾🐾🐾🐾🐾🐾🐾🐾🐾

Directions: The first complete thought has been written for you. Place a semicolon and finish the sentence.

Remember: **You can use *however* or *therefore* if it makes sense. Don't forget the comma after these words.**

1. It has stopped raining _____

    _____

2. My friend twisted his ankle _____

    _____

3. Carla made blueberry tarts _____

    _____

4. The dusty road has many potholes _____

    _____

5. We have been assigned a social studies project _____

    _____

A semicolon is a comma with a period above it (;). It joins two complete thoughts. The two thoughts must be about the same topic!

Sometimes, words such as *however* or *therefore* will follow the semicolon. Place a comma after *however* or *therefore*.

Example: His arm is in a cast; ***however,*** he climbed over the fence.

🐦🐦🐦🐦🐦🐦🐦🐦🐦🐦🐦

Directions: The first complete thought has been written for you. Place a semicolon and finish the sentence.

Remember: **You can use *however* or *therefore* if it makes sense. Don't forget the comma after these words.**

ANSWERS MAY VARY/REPRESENTATIVE ANSWERS:

1. Kim will be attending a job fair this week; **she wants a career as a store buyer.**

2. The car salesman showed the couple a car; **however, they didn't buy it.**

3. Patty has joined the band; **her first performance will be at tomorrow's parade.**

4. The child made a funny face; **her parents laughed and took her picture.**

5. The students like to write; **therefore, they are enjoying writing sentences using semicolons.**

A semicolon is a comma with a period above it (;). It joins two complete thoughts.   The two thoughts must be about the <u>same</u> topic!

Sometimes, words such as *however* or *therefore* will follow the semicolon. Place a comma after *however* or *therefore.*

Example: His arm is in a cast; ***however***, he climbed over the fence.

సᎾᎾᎾᎾᎾᎾᎾᎾᎾᎾᎾᎾ

Directions: The first complete thought has been written for you. Place a semicolon and finish the sentence.

<u>Remember:</u> **You can use *however* or *therefore* if it makes sense. Don't forget the comma after these words.**

1.   Kim will be attending a job fair this week_____

_____

2.   The car salesman showed the couple a car_____

_____

3.   Patty has joined the band_____

_____

4.   The child made a funny face_____

_____

5.   The students like to write_____

_____

TO THE TEACHER:

Teaching **compound sentences** should be easier in that students already have

had practice with the concept of complete thoughts. These will be reviewed

briefly. Then, students will learn how to write compound sentences.

NOTES

Name_____

WORKBOOK PAGE 314

Date_____

Writing Compound

Sentences

In order to understand compound sentences, we need to review *complete thoughts*.

Examples: Mary likes math.   (**complete thought**)

While Toya was on vacation. (**not a complete thought**)

The sentence contains a **subject** (Toya) and a **verb** (was), but it does not express a complete thought. More information is needed.

A compound sentence is formed by joining **two complete thoughts** with **and, but,** or **or**.

Their dad is a baker, **and** his mother is a teacher.

complete thought   **complete thought**

Granddad is an artist, **but** he doesn't sell his works.

complete thought   **complete thought**

అలాంత అలాంత అలాంత అలాంత అలాంత అలాంత

Directions: Write **S** in the blank if the group of words is a sentence (complete thought). Write **NS** in the blank if the group of words is not a sentence (not a complete thought).

1. ___**NS**___   When he signed his name.

2. ___**S**___   The company's president called a meeting.

3. ___**NS**___   Before he sat at his computer.

4. ___**S**___   The baby will be christened on Sunday.

5. ___**NS**___   Although we left for the party early.

6. ___**NS**___   Whenever the toddler becomes angry.

7. ___**S**___   Grandma won a 5k race.

8. ___**NS**___   After the last inning of the game.

9. ___**S**___   Mario's grades are always good.

672

Writing Compound

Sentences

In order to understand compound sentences, we need to review *complete thoughts*.

Examples: Mary likes math. (**complete thought**)

While Toya was on vacation. (**not a complete thought**)

The sentence contains a ***subject*** (Toya) and a ***verb*** (was), but it does not express a complete thought. More information is needed.

A compound sentence is formed by joining **two complete thoughts** with ***and***, ***but***, or ***or***.

Their dad is a baker, ***and*** his mother is a teacher.

complete thought   **complete thought**

Granddad is an artist, ***but*** he doesn't sell his works.

complete thought   **complete thought**

෪෪෪෪෪෪෪෪෪෪෪෪

Directions: Write **S** in the blank if the group of words is a sentence (complete thought). Write **NS** in the blank if the group of words is not a sentence (not a complete thought).

1. _____   When he signed his name.

2. _____   The company's president called a meeting.

3. _____   Before he sat at his computer.

4. _____   The baby will be christened on Sunday.

5. _____   Although we left for the party early.

6. _____   Whenever the toddler becomes angry.

7. _____   Grandma won a 5k race.

8. _____   After the last inning of the game.

9. _____   Mario's grades are always good.

673

Name_____   **Writing Compound**
WORKBOOK PAGE 315
Date_____   **Sentences**

A compound sentence is formed by joining **two complete thoughts** with **and**, **but**, or **or**.

They may board their dog, **or** they might have to take him along.

complete thought   **complete thought**

We placed strings of lights on our house, **but** they wouldn't blink.

complete thought   **complete thought**

Place a comma before a conjunction when it is joining two complete thoughts.

A pinto can be a type of horse, **but** it can also be a type of bean.

෴෴෴෴෴෴෴෴෴෴෴

COMPLETE THOUGHTS ARE ITALICIZED.
Directions: Circle each complete thought. Place a comma where needed.

1. *His sister is a gymnast,* but *she only practices once a week.*

2. *You may hand your paper to your friend,* or *you may place it in my basket.*

3. *They are going to Tulsa next year,* and *I'll meet them there.*

4. *Joan goes to bed early,* but *she doesn't like to get up in the morning.*

5. *The bus must be on time,* or *we will be late for school.*

6. *The Cherry Creek Arts Festival will be next week,* but *I can't attend.*

7. *An Airedale is a terrier,* and *it has a short, dense coat.*

8. *He has read several mysteries,* but *he hasn't read a biography.*

9. *Grandpa makes us breakfast on Mondays,* or *he takes us to a café.*

10. *Our family went to the zoo,* but *I didn't see any zebras.*
674

A compound sentence is formed by joining **two complete thoughts** with **and**, **but**, or **or**.

They may board their dog, **or** they might have to take him along.

> **complete thought**   **complete thought**

We placed strings of lights on our house, **but** they wouldn't blink.

> **complete thought**   **complete thought**

Place a comma before a conjunction when it is joining two complete thoughts.

A pinto can be a type of horse, **but** it can also be a type of bean.

ৰ্কৰ্কৰ্কৰ্কৰ্কৰ্কৰ্কৰ্কৰ্কৰ্কৰ্ক

Directions: Circle each complete thought. Place a comma where needed.

1.   His sister is a gymnast but she only practices once a week.

2.   You may hand your paper to your friend or you may place it in my basket.

3.   They are going to Tulsa next year and I'll meet them there.

4.   Joan goes to bed early but she doesn't like to get up in the morning.

5.   The bus must be on time or we will be late for school.

6.   The Cherry Creek Arts Festival will be next week but I can't attend.

7.   An Airedale is a terrier and it has a short, dense coat.

8.   He has read several mysteries but he hasn't read a biography.

9.   Grandpa makes us breakfast on Mondays or he takes us to a café.

10.   Our family went to the zoo, but I didn't see any zebras.

Name_____   **Writing Compound**

WORKBOOK PAGE 316

Date_____   **Sentences**

A compound sentence is formed by joining **two complete thoughts** with ***and, but***, or ***or***.

Place a **comma before a conjunction** when it is joining two complete thoughts.

   Example: Royce wrote a poem, but he didn't share it.
              complete thought   complete thought
              ৵৵৵৵৵৵৵৵৵৵৵৵

Directions: Write a conjunction and another complete thought to finish each compound sentence. Be sure to place a comma before the conjunction.

ANSWERS MAY VARY/REPRESENTATIVE ANSWERS:

1. My uncle was born in North Dakota, **but he moved to California at**

    the age of three._____

2. You may sit at this table, **or you may wait until another has been**

    cleared._____

3. Chessa painted her bedroom purple, **and she loves it**._____

    _____

4. Grandma bought stock last year, **and she made a nice profit.**____

    _____

5. Don wants to go to a dude ranch in Arizona, **but his wife wants to go**

    to a ranch in Montana._____

6. An usher asked Lala to sit down, **but Lalah asked for another seat**.___

    _____

Writing Compound

Sentences

A compound sentence is formed by joining **two complete thoughts** with *and, but,* or *or.*

Place a **comma before a conjunction** when it is joining two complete thoughts.

Example: Royce wrote a poem**,** but he didn't share it.
complete thought   **complete thought**

🌿🌿🌿🌿🌿🌿🌿🌿🌿🌿🌿

Directions: Write a conjunction and another complete thought to finish each compound sentence. Be sure to place a comma before the conjunction.

1. My uncle was born in North Dakota _____

_____

2. You may sit at this table _____

_____

3. Chessa painted her bedroom purple _____

_____

4. Grandma bought stock last year _____

_____

5. Don wants to go to a dude ranch in Arizona _____

_____

6. An usher asked Lalah to sit down _____

_____

Writing Compound

Sentences

A compound sentence is formed by joining **two complete thoughts** with **and**, **but**, or **or**. Place a **comma before the conjunction**.

Example: Our team scored the final goal, but we lost the game.

                   complete thought   **complete thought**

ฅ๛ฅ๛ฅ๛ฅ๛ฅ๛ฅ๛ฅ๛ฅ๛ฅ๛ฅ๛ฅ๛

Directions: Write a conjunction and another complete thought to finish each compound sentence.

ANSWERS MAY VARY/REPRESENTATIVE ANSWERS:

1.   The man demanded his money back**, but the manager refused to**

give it without a receipt.

2.   Their class visited a television station**, and they were able to walk**

onto several sets.

3.   Pedro may take his daughter horseback riding**, or they may go to a**

waterpark.

4.   An author signed books at a local bookstore**, and many had a chance to**

talk with him.

5.   They are having a cookout**, and all of their neighbors are invited**.

_____

6.   Snow drifted onto the road**, but motorists were able to drive**.

_____

7.   James is going to New York City on business**, but he still needs to**

purchase a ticket.

A compound sentence is formed by joining **two complete thoughts** with **and, but,** or **or.** Place a **comma before the conjunction.**

Example: Our team scored the final goal, but we lost the game.
          complete thought   **complete thought**

ॐ ॐ ॐ ॐ ॐ ॐ ॐ ॐ ॐ ॐ ॐ

Directions: Write a conjunction and another complete thought to finish each compound sentence.

1. The man demanded his money back _____

    _____

2. Their class visited a television station _____

    _____

3. Pedro may take his daughter horseback riding _____

    _____

4. An author signed books at a local bookstore _____

    _____

5. They are having a cookout _____

    _____

6. Snow drifted onto the road _____

    _____

7. James is going to New York City on business _____

    _____

TO THE TEACHER:

The first 10 lessons (days) of **DAILY GRAMS: Guided Review Aiding Mastery Skills - Grade 5** appear on the ensuing pages. These are placed here for you to experience the benefits of daily reviews.

Suggestions:

1. Make a copy for each student. Have students complete a *Daily Grams* review at the beginning of each English class. (This should take only a few minutes.) If you ask for volunteers to write the sentence combining on the board, it may take longer.

2. Ask students to read or write in journals until everyone is finished.

3. Using a transparency that you have made before class, go over the *Daily Grams* review. Be sure to solicit answers from students and discuss them. (The answer key is located after Day 10.)

4. Upon completion, move on to whatever you are doing in your regular lesson.

Daily Grams Workbooks are available for classroom use. They prove to be both time-saving and cost-effective.

680

CAPITALIZATION:

1. is jane's family going to anchorage, alaska, this year?

PUNCTUATION:

2. Tammys dad left at 1 30 in the afternoon

PARTS OF SPEECH: NOUNS
    A noun names a person, a place, a thing, or an idea.

   Circle any nouns:

3. Sharon bought an old sofa for her apartment.

PARTS OF SPEECH: ADVERBS

   Circle any adverbs that tell when:

4. We are going today or tomorrow.

ANALOGIES:
   Analogies show relationships. First, determine how the first two words are related. Then look at the third word and the possible answers. Choose the answer that has the same relationship to the third word.
   The first two words (set) may be synonyms (have similar meanings).

       Example: Mad is to angry as frequent is to _____.
                (a) always   (b) furious   **(c) often**   (d) infrequent

   Analogies may also be written in this manner:
                Mad : angry :: frequent : _____
                (a) always   (b) furious   **(c) often**   (d) infrequent

   Circle the correct answer:

5. large : enormous :: calm : _____
    (a) stormy   (b) upset   (c) peaceful   (d) preoccupied

SENTENCE COMBINING:

6. The pot is made of clay.
    The pot is filled with tulips.
    The tulips are yellow.

_____

_____ 681

DAY 2

CAPITALIZATION:

1. in september, mr. and mrs. pino will visit the grand canyon.

PUNCTUATION:

2. That plant is tall leafy and healthy

SUBJECT/VERB:
   The subject of a sentence tells *who* or *what* the sentence is about. The verb tells *what is (was)* or what *happens (happened)*.

Note: **Prepositional phrases usually aren't the subject or the verb. Deleting them makes finding the subject and verb easier.**

   Example: <u>Cal</u> <u><u>was</u></u> ~~on the phone~~ ~~with his best friend~~.

   Underline the subject once and the verb twice:

3. We laughed about the scar on my toe.

SENTENCE TYPES:
   A declarative sentence makes a statement.

   Write a declarative sentence about your shoe:

4. _____

ANALOGIES:
   Circle the correct answer:

5. smart : intelligent :: lives : _____
   (a) dwellings   (b) resides   (c) rural   (d) packs

SENTENCE COMBINING:

6. Kim's aunt is a dentist.
   Kim's aunt lives in Virginia Beach.

   _____

_____

CAPITALIZATION:

1. last saturday we went to riverside park on cherry lane.

PUNCTUATION:

2. No we cant follow you

PARTS OF SPEECH: **PREPOSITIONS**

Prepositional phrases begin with a preposition and end with a noun or a pronoun (such as *me, him, her, us*, or *them*). Commonly used prepositions are *to, for, from, in, into, on*, and *with.*

Circle any prepositional phrases:

3. Come with us.

PARTS OF SPEECH: **ADVERBS**

Circle any adverbs that tell *how:*

4. They skate fast.

ANALOGIES:
Circle the correct answer:

5. tasty : delicious :: tardy : _____
     (a) late   (b) naughty   (c) bell   (d) tired

SENTENCE COMBINING:

6. Their father is a salesman.
    Their grandfather is a salesman.

    _____

    _____

DAY 4

CAPITALIZATION:

1. is thomas jefferson's home located in virginia?

PUNCTUATION:

2. Their new address is 9 N Offenhauser Drive Flagstaff Arizona 86004

SUBJECT/VERB:
Underline the subject; circle the verb that agrees with the subject:

3. Dorita (has, have) a new baby brother.

PARTS OF SPEECH: NOUNS
A concrete noun names a real thing.   Example: milk
An abstract noun names an idea.   Example: truth

Write C if the noun is concrete; write A if the noun is abstract:

4. A. _____ magnet   B. _____ tower   C. _____ trust

SPELLING:
A word may end with a single consonant + e. A word ending with consonant + e usually drops that final e when adding a suffix (ending) that begins with a VOWEL. The e is not dropped if the suffix begins with a consonant.

Examples: time + ing = tim**ing**   time + less = time**less**

Write the correct spelling of these words:

5. A. frame + ed - _____

B. price + ing - _____

C. price + less - _____

SENTENCE COMBINING:

6. His cousin is on a baseball team.
His cousin plays third base.

_____

684 _____

CAPITALIZATION:

1.   my grandfather's favorite place is wood's canyon lake.

PUNCTUATION:

2.   I need the following raisins peanuts and coconut

PARTS OF SPEECH: VERBS

   Write the contraction:

3.   A.   who is - _____   D. did not - _____

   B.   have not - _____   E. I am - _____

   C.   we are - _____   F. I have - _____

PARTS OF SPEECH: PRONOUNS

   Circle the correct answer:

4.   (Jim and I, Me and Jim, Jim and me) found several deer paths.

SPELLING:

   Write the correct spelling of these words:

5.   A. use + ing - _____

   B.   use + ful - _____

   C.   lease + ed - _____

SENTENCE COMBINING:

6.   Maria called to her puppy.
   She held out her arms.

   _____

   _____

DAY 6

CAPITALIZATION:

1. on washington's birthday, I went to newport beach in california.

PUNCTUATION:

2. Dear Anna
           I ll meet you by the fountain
                    Pedro

PARTS OF SPEECH: ADVERBS

   Circle any adverbs that tell *where:*

3. The mouse scampered here and there.

DICTIONARY SKILLS: ALPHABETIZING

   Write these words in alphabetical order:

4. offer   pioneer   noodle   manner   onion   nerve

ANALOGIES:
   The first two words of an analogy may be antonyms (opposites). Again, look at your third word; your answer must have an opposite meaning of the third word.

      Example: Stay : leave :: quiet : _____
            (a) quite   **(b) noisy**   (c) peaceful   (d) dreams
   Circle the correct answer:

5. laugh : cry :: deep : _____
   (a) river   (b) depend   (c) shallow   (d) dry

SENTENCE COMBINING:

6. Allie's hair is brown.
    Allie's hair has blonde streaks in it.
    Allie's hair is curly.

_____

CAPITALIZATION:

1. is pike's peak part of the rocky mountains of the united states.

PUNCTUATION:

2. Taras wedding shower was held on December 31 2000

SYNONYMS/ANTONYMS/HOMONYMS:
Homonyms are words that sound alike but are spelled differently.

Write a homonym for the following words:

3. A. pale - _____   B. seen - _____

PARTS OF SPEECH: NOUNS
A common noun does not name a specific person, place, or thing. *bay*
A proper noun names a specific person, place, or thing. *Hudson Bay*

A *type* is a common noun. A pagoda is a <u>type</u> of building; it is a common noun.

Write <u>C</u> if the noun is common; write <u>P</u> if the noun is proper:

4. A. _____ horse   B. _____ palomino   C. _____ Breeze (name of a horse)

SPELLING:
A word ending with vowel + consonant +consonant (VCC) usually just adds a suffix. Examples: risk + ed = risk**ed**   bash + ful = bash**ful**

Write the correct spelling of these words:

5. A. post + ed - _____

   B. harm + less - _____

   C. board + ing - _____

SENTENCE COMBINING:

6. Aren is taking his mother to a restaurant.
   It is her favorite restaurant.
   It is her birthday.

   _____

   _____ 687

DAY 8

CAPITALIZATION:

1.   does mr. ernesto lopez work for the eagle express corporation?

PUNCTUATION:

   Punctuate this outline:

2.   I   Snakes
         A   Rattlesnakes
         B   Cobras
      II   Lizard

PARTS OF SPEECH: NOUNS
   A common noun does not name a specific person, place, or thing. *dog*
   A *type* **of a person, place, or thing is still a common noun.** *bulldog*
   A proper noun names a specific person, place, or thing.

      Examples: common noun - person   common noun - boy
                  proper noun - Marco

   Write C if the noun is common; write P if the noun is proper:

3.   A. ___   MONTH   B. ___   APRIL   C. ___   DAY   D. ___   TUESDAY

PARTS OF SPEECH: VERBS
   Circle the correct answer:

4.   She (don't, doesn't) know how to do that.

ANALOGIES:
   Circle the correct answer:

5.   sort : arrange :: block : _____
      (a) build   (b) obstruct   (c) allow   (d) wooden

SENTENCE COMBINING:

6.   Magma is molten rock.
      It forms below the earth's surface.

      _____

688 _____

CAPITALIZATION:

1. during the first week of september, matt attended park meadows school.

PUNCTUATION:

2. Capt C L Linski lives in a two story townhouse in Hollywood California

SENTENCE TYPES:

An interrogative sentence asks a question. It expresses a complete thought and ends with a question mark.

Write an interrogative sentence:

3. _____

PARTS OF SPEECH: CONJUNCTIONS

Conjunctions are joining words.

Unscramble these commonly used conjunctions:

4. A. ro - _____   B. nda - _____   C. btu - _____

ANALOGIES:

The first two words of an analogy may be antonyms (opposites). Then, the third word and the answer must also be opposites.

Example: enter : exit :: punish : _____
                (a) cry   **(b) reward**   (c) discipline   (d) scold

Enter is the opposite of *exit*; the opposite of *punish* is *reward.*

Circle the correct answer:

5. bold : timid :: narrow : _____
    (a) stingy   (b) decrease   (c) limited   (d) broad

SENTENCE COMBINING:

6. Sponges have no tissue.
    Sponges have no organs.

    _____

    _____

DAY 10

CAPITALIZATION:

1.   the rossen house at heritage square is a famous historical building.

PUNCTUATION:
A noun of direct address is used to speak to someone.
If the noun of direct address is the first word, place a comma after it.
   Example: *Marlo*, may I help you?
If the noun of direct address is the last word, place a comma before it.
   Example: May I help you, *Marlo*?
If the noun of direct address is anywhere within the sentence, place a comma before it and a comma after it.
   Example: May I, *Marlo*, go with you?

2.   Brian will you make strawberry filled pancakes for breakfast

SENTENCE TYPES:
Write an interrogative sentence:

3.   _____

PARTS OF SPEECH: VERBS
A verb may be one word: Example: Tate <u>kicked</u> the ball.
A verb phrase consists of more than one word.
   Verb phrase = helping verb(s) + main verb
   Example: Jonah <u>had planned</u> a party for his parents.

Underline the subject once and the verb phrase twice:

4.   Several speakers have presented their ideas.

ANALOGIES:
Circle the correct answer:

5.   always : never :: partially : _____
   (a) closely   (b) recently   (c) completely   (d) practically

SENTENCE COMBINING:

6.   Leeches are worms.
   They have suckers on both ends.

   _____

690 _____

MV/RA: Answers May Vary/Representative Answer(s)
ther sentence combinings are acceptable.

ay 1: 1. Is, Jane's, Anchorage, Alaska **2.** Tammy's dad left at 1:30 in the afternoon. **3.** Sharon, fa, apartment **4.** today, tomorrow **5.** (c) peaceful **6.** AMV/RA: The clay pot is filled with yellow lips.

ay 2: 1. In, September, Mr., Mrs., Pino, Grand, Canyon **2.** That plant is tall, leafy, and healthy. We laughed ~~about the scar~~ ~~on my toe~~. **4.** AMV/RA: My shoe is white with black stripes. **5. (b)** sides **6.** AMV/RA: Kim's aunt who is a dentist lives in Virginia Beach. Kim's aunt, a dentist, lives in rginia Beach. Kim's aunt is a dentist who lives in Virginia Beach.

ay 3: 1. Last, Saturday, Riverside, Park, Cherry, Lane **2.** No, we can't follow you. **3.** with us fast **5. (a)** late **6.** AMV/RA: Their father and grandfather are salesmen. Both their father and andfather are salesmen.

ay 4: 1. Is, Thomas, Jefferson's, Virginia **2.** Their new address is 9 N. Offenhauser Drive, Flagstaff, izona 86004. **3.** Dorita has **4.** A. **C** B. **C** C. **A** **5.** A. framed B. pricing C. priceless **6.** AMV/RA: s cousin plays third base on a baseball team. His cousin who is on a baseball team plays third base.

ay 5: 1. My, Wood's, Canyon, Lake **2.** I need the following: raisins, peanuts, and coconuts. . A. who's B. haven't C. we're D. didn't E. I'm F. I've **4.** Jim and I **5.** A. using B. useful leased **6.** AMV/RA: Maria called to her puppy and held out her arms. Calling to her puppy, Maria eld out her arms.

ay 6: 1. On, Washington's, Birthday, I, Newport, Beach, California **2.** Dear Anna, I'll meet you by ie fountain. Pedro **3.** here, there **4.** manner, nerve, noodle, offer, onion, pioneer **5. (c)** shallow . AMV/RA: Allie's brown curly hair has blonde streaks in it. Allie's curly hair is brown with blonde streaks.

ay 7: 1. Is, Pike's, Peak, Rocky, Mountains, United, States **2.** Tara's wedding shower was held on ecember 31, 2000. **3.** A. pail B. scene **4.** A. **C** B. **C** C. **P** **5.** A. posted B. harmless . boarding **6.** AMV/RA: Aren is taking his mother to her favorite restaurant for her birthday.

ay 8: 1. Does, Mr., Ernesto, Lopez, Eagle, Express, Corporation
. I. Snakes
  A. Rattlesnakes
  B. Cobras
 II. Lizards
. A. **C** B. **P** C. **C** D. **P** **4.** doesn't **5. (b)** obstruct **6.** AMV/RA: Magma is molten rock that irms below the earth's surface.

ay 9: 1. During, September, Matt, Park, Meadows, School **2.** Capt. C.L. Linski lives in a two-story iwnhouse in Hollywood, California. **3.** AMV/RA: Do you have any chewing gum? **4.** A. or B. and . but **5. (d)** broad **6.** AMV/RA: Sponges have neither tissue nor organs. Sponges have no tissue r organs.

ay 10: 1. The, Rossen, House, Heritage, Square **2.** Brian, will you make strawberry-filled pancakes ir breakfast? **3.** AMV/RA: Where are you going? **4.** speakers have presented **5. (c)** completely . AMV/RA: Leeches are worms that have suckers on both ends.

Assessment Test Answers   (TOTAL: 200 points)

You may use your own point system. See page iv for an explanation.

A. SENTENCE TYPES: (4 points)
1. **exclamatory**
2. **declarative**
3. **imperative**
4. **interrogative**

B. SENTENCES, FRAGMENTS, and RUN-ONS: (4 points)
1. **R-O**
2. **F**
3. **F**
4. **S**

C.   FRIENDLY LETTER: (5 points)

<u>   **heading**   </u>

5 North Drive
South Beach, OR   97366
June 22, 20—

Dear Terri,   <u>**salutation or greeting**</u>

     What are you doing this summer? Did you join a basketball
team? Have you gone hiking in the hills near your ranch? Are you
and your family coming to Oregon again this summer? <u>**body**</u>

Always, <u>**closing**</u>
Bo   <u>**signature**</u>

D.   CAPITALIZATION: (20 points ~ ½ point for each)
NOTE: If students capitalize any words that should not be capitalized, deduct a point.

1. **B**o travels on **I**nterstate 65 to **D**iamond **C**averns near **N**olin **L**ake **S**tate **P**ark.

2. "**O**ur women's club visited **T**emple **S**inai on **D**ole **S**treet," said **D**r. **J**o **M**ing.

3. **W**ill **M**om and **I** need to buy **G**erman chocolate at **M**ayday **F**oods?

4. **D**ear **J**ane,
    Did your **A**unt **J**enny study **E**nglish or history at **P**hoenix **C**ollege
during the summer she spent in the **W**est?
                      Your friend,
                      Jose

5. **H**ave you visited **C**liff **H**ouse at **P**oint **L**obos near the **G**olden **G**ate **B**ridge?
692

E. Punctuation: (20 points ~ ½ point each)
NOTE: If students insert additional punctuation, deduct a point.
Count quotation marks as 1 point per _set_.

1. "Hannah, was the meeting held on Mon., Sept. 12, 2005?" asked Ty.

2. Tate said quietly, "I don't want John's two-toned, rusted bike."

3. Has Mr. Dee, your neighbor, moved to 2 N. Dale Ln., Culver City, CA 90232?

4. Yikes! We have to leave at 4:00 and take the following: straws, ice, and twenty-two cups!

5. Yes, he read the book titled <u>Call of the Wild</u>, but he hasn't had the opportunity to read "The Raven," a poem by E. A. Poe.

F. Subjects and Verbs: (8 points)

NOTE: Deleting prepositional phrases helps students to identify subject and verb.
However, this was not part of the instructions.
Count 1 point for each correct subject and 1 for each correct verb.
Both parts of a compound must be identified in order to earn a point!

1. ~~After the snowstorm,~~ many small <u>children</u> <u>began</u> **(**to play**)** ~~in the snow~~.

2. <u>One</u> ~~of the pilots~~ <u>stood</u> and <u>greeted</u> passengers ~~at the airport~~.

3. The <u>doctor</u> and his <u>patient</u> <u>will talk</u> ~~about a pimple under his arm~~.

4. (<u>You</u>) <u>Stand</u> ~~by the man with the briefcase for a quick snapshot~~.

G. Contractions: (9 points)

1. she is - ____**she's**____   4. I shall - ____**I'll**____   7. who is - ____**who's**____

2. has not - ____**hasn't**____   5. cannot - ____**can't**____   8. is not - ____**isn't**____

3. I would - ____**I'd**____   6. will not - ____**won't**____   9. I have - ____**I've**____

H. You're/Your, It's/Its, and They're/Their/There: (4 points)

1. (There, Their, **They're**) playing soccer this afternoon.

2. (**You're**, Your) usually on time.

3. When (its, **it's**) sunny, they eat (there, **their**, they're) lunch outside.

I. Subject-Verb Agreement: (12 points)

NOTE: Deleting prepositional phrases helps students to make subject and verb agree.
    However, this was not part of the instructions.
    Count 2 points for each correct subject and 2 for each correct verb.
    Both parts of a compound must be identified!

1. <u>Chan</u> and his <u>brother</u> (<u>listen</u>, listens) ~~to country music~~.
2. Her <u>job</u> ~~for social services~~ (seem, <u>seems</u>) ~~like a good one~~.
3. <u>One</u> ~~of the girls~~ (sleep, <u>sleeps</u>) late.

J. Irregular Verbs: (12 points)

NOTE: Deleting prepositional phrases helps students to determine that there is no direct
    object in # 4. Therefore, the past participle must be *lain*.
    However, this was not part of the instructions.
    Count 1 point for the correct helping verb(s), and 1 point for each correct past
    participle. (The subject was only required to help students determine verb phrase.)

1. <u>Peter</u> **should have** (ran, **run**) ~~in the first race~~.

2. **Was** <u>ice</u> (froze, **frozen**) ~~on the park's pond~~?

3. <u>She</u> **must have** (came, **come**) alone.

4. Two <u>ladies</u> **have** (laid, **lain**) ~~by the pool for an hour~~.

5. <u>They</u> **may have** (went, **gone**) earlier.

6. Some <u>horses</u> **had** (**drunk**, drank) their water.

K. Tenses: (6 points)

NOTE: Deleting prepositional phrases helps students to determine subject and verb.
    However, this was not part of the instructions.
    Count 1 point for each correct subject *and* verb, and 1 point for each correct
    tense.

1. _____**FUTURE**_____   **Will** <u>**you**</u> **join** our team?
2. _____**PAST**_____   <u>**Water**</u> **lapped** ~~into the canoe~~.
3. _____**PRESENT**_____   My <u>**brothers**</u> **like** (to drive) ~~to Tulsa~~.

L. Common and Proper Nouns: (3 points)

1. _✓_   DOG   2. _✓_   POODLE   3. _____   FIFI

694

M. Singular and Plural Nouns: (8 points)

1. wax - **waxes**
2. miss - **misses**
3. goose - **geese**
4. puff - **puffs**
5. bluejay - **bluejays**
6. torch - **torches**
7. fun - **fun**
8. knife - **knives**

N. Possessive Nouns: (6 points)

1. dogs owned by his neighbor - **neighbor's dogs**
2. a closet used by guests - **guests' closet**
3. tools shared by more than one craftsman - **craftsmen's tools**

O. Identifying Nouns: (5 points)
NOTE: If students circle any words that are not nouns, deduct a point.
1. My **idea** is to take this **shovel**, a sleeping **bag**, two **tents**, and some strong **rope**.

P. Usage and Knowledge: (26 points)

1. Write a conjunction: **but** (**and** or **or**) (Accept correlative conjunctions, also.)
2. Write the antecedent: A crow flapped its wings. **crow**
3. Write an interjection: **Wow!** ANSWER MAY VARY!
4. Write a regular verb: **to bark** ANSWER MAY VARY!
   (Accept any form of *to bark* or other regular verb.)
5. Write a linking verb: **to seem** (*See page 122 for other linking verbs.*)
6. Name the predicate adjective of the following sentence: After the first washing, my new blue sweater became fuzzy. **fuzzy**
7. Write an abstract noun: **hope** ANSWER MAY VARY!
8. Is the verb action, linking, or neither? The soup <u>tastes</u> spicy. **linking**
9. Circle the correct answer: I can't see (nobody, **anybody**) from here.
10. Circle the correct answer: Jacob painted the shed (hisself, **himself**).
11. Circle the correct answer: Don't walk so (slow, **slowly**).
12. Circle the correct answer: You played (good, **well**).
13. Circle the correct answer: I don't feel (good, **well**).

Q. Identifying Adjectives: (7 points)
NOTE: If students circle any words that are not adjectives, deduct a point.
1. **Several** tourists visited **two old German** hotels near **a steep, forested** region.

R. Degrees of Adjectives: (6 points)

1. That city is (larger, **largest**) in the state.

2. Jacy becomes (**more energetic**, most energetic) after exercising.

3. Of the triplets, Faith is (more sensitive, **most sensitive**).

S. Adverbs: (7 points)
NOTE: If students circle any words that are not adverbs, deduct a point.
1. Bo is **not usually very late**, but he was delayed **today**.

2. We are going **downtown afterwards**.

T. Degrees of Adverbs: (6 points)

1. Marco climbed (higher, **highest**) on his fifth try.

2. Of the two birds, the ostrich runs (**more swiftly**, most swiftly).

3. She hit the ball (farther, **farthest**) of the entire team.

U. Pronouns: (14 points)

1. (Me and Roy, **Roy and I**, Roy and me) looked at a magazine.

2. Do you want to go with Emma and (I, **me**)?

3. We should send (they, **them**) some maps.

4. The winner was (**she**, her).

5. Our friends and (**we**, us) will visit Austin next year.

6. From (who, **whom**) did you receive your package?

7. Each ~~of the students~~ must take (**his**, their) turn. (*Deletion not required.*)

V. Nouns and Pronouns Used as Subjects, Direct Objects, Objects of the Preposition, and Predicate Nominatives: (8 points)

1. __D.O.__ Joe sliced an **apple**.   3. __S.__ After swimming, **we** eat a snack.

2. __O.P.__ One of the **boys** laughed. 4. __P.N.__ She in the black dress is my **sister**.
696

INDEX

699

CORRELATION of

Easy Grammar Student Workbook 5 with

Easy Grammar: Grade 5 teacher edition

workbook page 1   - teacher ed. p. 1
workbook page 2   - teacher ed. p. 3
workbook page 3   - teacher ed. p. 5
workbook page 4   - teacher ed. p. 7
workbook page 5   - teacher ed. p. 9
workbook page 6   - teacher ed. p. 13
workbook page 7   - teacher ed. p. 15
workbook page 8   - teacher ed. p. 17
workbook page 9   - teacher ed. p. 19
workbook page 10 - teacher ed. p. 21
workbook page 11 - teacher ed. p. 23
workbook page 12 - teacher ed. p. 25
workbook page 13 - teacher ed. p. 27
workbook page 14 - teacher ed. p. 29
workbook page 15 - teacher ed. p. 33
workbook page 16 - teacher ed. p. 35
workbook page 17 - teacher ed. p. 37
workbook page 18 - teacher ed. p. 39
workbook page 19 - teacher ed. p. 41
workbook page 20 - teacher ed. p. 43
workbook page 21 - teacher ed. p. 45
workbook page 22 - teacher ed. p. 49
workbook page 23 - teacher ed. p. 51
workbook page 24 - teacher ed. p. 57
workbook page 25 - teacher ed. p. 59
workbook page 26 - teacher ed. p. 61
workbook page 27 - teacher ed. p. 63
workbook page 28 - teacher ed. p. 65
workbook page 29 - teacher ed. p. 67
workbook page 30 - teacher ed. p. 69
workbook page 31 - teacher ed. p. 71
workbook page 32 - teacher ed. p. 73
workbook page 33 - teacher ed. p. 75
workbook page 34 - teacher ed. p. 78
workbook page 35 - teacher ed. p. 79
workbook page 36 - teacher ed. p. 81
workbook page 37 - teacher ed. p. 83
workbook page 38 - teacher ed. p. 85
workbook page 39 - teacher ed. p. 87

workbook page 40 - teacher ed. p. 90
workbook page 41 - teacher ed. p. 91
workbook page 42 - teacher ed. p. 92
workbook page 43 - teacher ed. p. 93
workbook page 44 - teacher ed. p. 95
workbook page 45 - teacher ed. p. 97
workbook page 46 - teacher ed. p. 101
workbook page 47 - teacher ed. p. 103
workbook page 48 - teacher ed. p. 104
workbook page 49 - teacher ed. p. 105
workbook page 50 - teacher ed. p. 107
workbook page 51 - teacher ed. p. 109
workbook page 52 - teacher ed. p. 111
workbook page 53 - teacher ed. p. 113
workbook page 54 - teacher ed. p. 115
workbook page 55 - teacher ed. p. 117
workbook page 56 - teacher ed. p. 119
workbook page 57 - teacher ed. p. 121
workbook page 58 - teacher ed. p. 124
workbook page 59 - teacher ed. p. 125
workbook page 60 - teacher ed. p. 127
workbook page 61 - teacher ed. p. 129
workbook page 62 - teacher ed. p. 131
workbook page 63 - teacher ed. p. 132
workbook page 64 - teacher ed. p. 133
workbook page 65 - teacher ed. p. 135
workbook page 66 - teacher ed. p. 137
workbook page 67 - teacher ed. p. 139
workbook page 68 - teacher ed. p. 141
workbook page 69 - teacher ed. p. 143
workbook page 70 - teacher ed. p. 145
workbook page 71 - teacher ed. p. 147
workbook page 72 - teacher ed. p. 149
workbook page 73 - teacher ed. p. 151
workbook page 74 - teacher ed. p. 153
workbook page 75 - teacher ed. p. 155
workbook page 76 - teacher ed. p. 157
workbook page 77 - teacher ed. p. 159
workbook page 78 - teacher ed. p. 161

*workbook page 302 - lined